NEW YORK FIELD CODES SERIES

VOLUME II

NEW YORK FIELD CODES SERIES

Volume I. The Code of Civil Procedure of the State of New-York (1850)

Volume II. The Code of Criminal Procedure of the State of New York (1850)

Volume III. The Civil Code of the State of New York (1865)

Volume IV. The Penal Code of the State of New York (1865)

Volume V. The Political Code of the State of New York (1860)

NEW YORK FIELD CODES SERIES

VOLUME II

THE CODE

OF

CRIMINAL PROCEDURE

OF THE

STATE OF NEW-YORK.

REPORTED COMPLETE

BY THE

COMMISSIONERS ON PRACTICE AND PLEADINGS.

General Introduction to the Series
by Michael Weber

THE LAWBOOK EXCHANGE, LTD.
Clark, New Jersey

New York Field Codes Series
ISBN 978-1-886363-40-3

Vol. I. The Code of Civil Procedure of the State of New-York
ISBN 978-1-886363-34-2

Vol. II. The Code of Criminal Procedure of the State of New York
ISBN 978-1-886363-35-9

Vol. III. The Civil Code of the State of New York
ISBN 978-1-886363-38-0

Vol. IV. The Penal Code of the State of New York
ISBN 978-1-886363-36-6

Vol. V. The Political Code of the State of New York
ISBN 978-1-886363-37-3

Lawbook Exchange edition 2011

The quality of this reprint is equivalent to the quality of the original work.

THE LAWBOOK EXCHANGE, LTD.
33 Terminal Avenue
Clark, New Jersey 07066-1321

Please see our website for a selection of our other publications and fine facsimile reprints of classic works of legal history:
www.lawbookexchange.com

Library of Congress Cataloging-in-Publication Data

New York (State). Commissioners on Practice and Pleadings.
The code of criminal procedure of the State of New-York / reported complete by the Commissioners on Practice and Pleadings.
p. cm. (New York Field codes, 1850-1865)
Originally published: Albany : Weed, Parsons, public printers. 1850.
ISBN 1-886363-35-8 (alk. paper)
1. Criminal procedure—New York (State) I. Title. II. Series.
KFN6155.A3 1997
345.747'05—dc21

97-42136
CIP

Printed in the United States of America on acid-free paper

GENERAL INTRODUCTION
TO THE SERIES

These five volumes (of which this is Volume II) contain the complete texts of the law codes drafted for New York State by David Dudley Field, and his colleagues during the years 1847 to 1865. They include Field's two procedural codes—Civil Procedure and Criminal Procedure—and three substantive codes—Political, Penal, and Civil. The two procedural codes were drafted first, pursuant to Article VI, Section 24, of the 1846 New York State Constitution, which stated:

> The Legislature at its first session after the adoption of the Constitution, shall provide for the appointment of three commissioners, whose duty it shall be to revise, reform, simplify, and abridge the rules and practice, pleadings, forms, and proceedings of the courts of record of this State, and to report thereon to the Legislature, subject to their adoption and modification from time to time.[1]

A separate provision of the Constitution called for commissioners "to reduce into a written and systematic code the whole body of the law of this state, or so much and such parts thereof as to the said commissioners shall seem practicable and expedient." This provision eventually resulted in the substantive political, penal, and civil codes.[2]

Field was perhaps the leading American proponent of codification. He served with both groups of commissioners.

---

[1] Quoted in Mildred V. Coe and Lewis W. Morse, "Chronology of the Development of the David Dudley Field Code," *Cornell Law Quarterly* 27 (1942): 238.

[2] Alison Reppy, "The Field Codification Concept," in *David Dudley Field: Centenary Essays Celebrating One Hundred Years of Legal Reform,* ed. Alison Reppy (New York: New York University School of Law, 1949), 37. Reppy's chapter is very useful for untangling the convoluted history of the commissions, the writing of the codes, and the fates of the codes in the New York legislature.

More than any other individual, Field was responsible for the drafting of all the codes. (He has been called "an inexhaustible one man codifying machine."[3])

New York, however, enacted only three: the Code of Civil Procedure—which is often referred to simply as "the Field Code"—and, after many years, the Code of Criminal Procedure and the Penal Code. But the significance of Field's work extended far beyond New York State. As one legal scholar has observed, Field's efforts changed how lawyers and judges do their work and led to "new ways of understanding the law itself."[4]

The Codification Movement

Field's codes were part of a wider codification movement in the United States in the first half of the nineteenth century.[5] In the 1830s, for example, a few years before Field's work began in New York, U.S. Supreme Court Justice Joseph Story was active in attempting to codify the Massachusetts law. The codification movement was an attempt to clarify the law and remove obsolete rules so that the law could be intelligible to ordinary citizens. Its proponents considered the existing body of law, based as it was on English common law, "inaccessible and uncertain . . . unnecessarily mysterious, complex, and overly technical."[6] Field remarked:

> The common law of New York, like the common law of England, from which it is in great part derived, consists of a vast number of rules of property and of conduct, which have been applied by the judicial tribunals, and which had their origin either in legislative enactments, now forgotten, or in

---

[3] Robert W. Gordon, review of *The American Codification Movement: A Study of Antebellum Legal Reform,* by Charles C. Cook, *Vanderbilt Law Review* 36 (1983): 435.

[4] William P. LaPiana, "Just the Facts: The Field Code and the Case Method," *New York Law School Law Review* 36 (1991): 304.

[5] See Charles C. Cook, *The American Codification Movement: A Study of Antebellum Legal Reform* (Westport, Conn.: Greenwood, 1981).

[6] Ibid., 5.

> traditions from ancient times, or in the consciences of the judges, as the cases came before them.[7]

Proponents of codification took to heart the critical observation of the great English reformer Jeremy Bentham that common law judges made law "as a man makes laws for his dog. When your dog does anything you want to break him of, you wait till he does it, and then you beat him for it."[8] They wanted more system, more precision, and more simplicity in the law. Many were impressed by France's Civil Code, established by Napoleon in 1804, which Edward Livingston had applied to Louisiana in the 1820s.

For some American codifiers, flushed by post-Revolutionary War patriotism, the great weight of the English common law was seen as an alien, un-American presence. A few wanted to go so far as to abolish the common law entirely. Most of the reformers, however, including Field, were not so radical. Their goal was to reduce the common law power of judges and give state legislators the chance to shape the law by reducing to statutory form those parts of the common law that could be plainly stated in a concise book of statutes.

Field's Range of Influence

David Dudley Field (1805–1894) was born in Haddam, Connecticut, into a family of high achievers.[9] Both his father, a minister, and mother were the children of Revolutionary War officers. Among his siblings were Stephen Johnson Field (1816–1899), who was appointed by President Lincoln to the United

---

[7] Introduction to *The Civil Code of the State of New York* (1865), in vol. III of this series, xiv.

[8] Quoted in Lawrence M. Friedman, *American Law* (New York: Norton, 1984), 92.

[9] Useful biographical sources are Helen K. Hoy, "David Dudley Field," in *Great American Lawyers,* ed. William Draper Lewis, vol. 5 (Philadelphia: Winston, 1908; reprint, South Hackensack, N.J.: Rothman, 1971); and the biography written by Field's younger brother, Henry M. Field, *The Life of David Dudley Field* (New York: Scribner's, 1898).

States Supreme Court in 1863, and Cyrus West Field, who laid the first transatlantic cable in 1866. While Field had extra ordinary intelligence, ability, and diligence, he was also competitive, cantankerous, and stubborn. He outlived three wives. (His childhood nurse called him "a most determined fellow."[10]) Not everyone felt affection for him, but very few questioned his legal skill. A colleague, subsequently dean of New York University's Law School, said, "For at least a third of a century, David Dudley Field was the most commanding figure at the American bar."[11]

After attending Williams College, Field studied law in Albany and New York City and was admitted to the New York Bar in 1828. He was active in politics as a Democrat but broke with the party over the Mexican War and slavery and in the 1850s became one of the founders of the Republican Party. Field played an important role in securing Abraham Lincoln's nomination as the Republican candidate for president in 1860. After the Civil War, however, he returned to the Democratic fold and was a close associate of Samuel J. Tilden.

Field was active as a lawyer for 60 years and participated in many notable cases heard by the Supreme Court, including *Ex parte Milligan* (1866), *Cummings* v. *Missouri* (1867), *Ex parte McArdle* (1868), and *United States* v. *Cruikshank* (1876). He provoked considerable controversy in the late 1860s and 1870s by serving as counsel to Jay Gould and James Fisk during the scandal involving the Erie Railroad and by defending New York's notorious William Marcy "Boss" Tweed.

The Origin of the Codes

Field valued precision and clarity. He greatly admired the sciences and mathematics, saying of the latter, "Its superiority over every other department of learning . . . is to be ascribed, I fancy, to the precision of its language."[12] No doubt this penchant

---

[10] Quoted in Stephen N. Subrin, "David Dudley Field and the Field Code: A Historical Analysis of an Earlier Procedural Vision," *Law and History Review* 6 (Fall 1988): 314.

[11] Austin Abbot, quoted in Field, *Life,* vii.

[12] Subrin, "David Dudley Field and the Field Code," 315.

contributed to Field's interest in the movement for codification of the law. He began working for codification in the late 1830s and was instrumental in having the provisions mandating commissions to reform the law of the state written into the 1846 New York Constitution.

Field's goal was to put all of New York's law into written form and to combine in one set of procedures the whole of actions in both law and equity. He wanted to reform the procedural law so that a legal dispute could be started with pleadings that clearly related what happened and settled in one court in one action. In his 1847 essay "What Shall Be Done with the Practice of the Courts?" Field wrote:

> What I propose, then, in respect to cases of legal cognizance, is this: that the present forms of action be abolished, and in their stead a complaint and answer required, each setting forth the real claim and defense of the parties. Such pleadings would be precisely similar to those proposed for equity cases, and we should thus have a uniform course of pleading for all cases, legal and equitable.
>
> . . .
>
> Let the plaintiff set forth his cause of action in his complaint briefly, in ordinary language, and without repetition; and let the defendant make his answer in the same way. Let each party verify his allegation by making oath that he believes it to be true. The complaint will then acquaint the defendant with the real charge, while the answer will inform the plaintiff of the real defense. The disputed facts will be sifted from the undisputed, and the parties will go to trial knowing what they have to answer. The plaintiff will state his case as he believes it, and as he expects to prove it. The defendant, for his part, will set forth what he believes and expects to establish . . . He will not be perplexed with questions of double pleading, nor shackled by ancient technical rules.[13]

---

[13] Quoted in Kermit L. Hall, William M. Wiecek, and Paul Finkelman, eds., *American Legal History: Cases and Materials,* 2nd ed. (New York: Oxford University Press, 1996), 323.

In September 1847 Field became one of the three commissioners—the other two were Arphaxad Loomis and David Graham—appointed by the New York legislature to reform legal procedures as mandated by the Constitution.[14] He replaced Nicholas Hill, who resigned because he was appalled that his colleagues were contemplating changes "so purely experimental, so sudden and general, and so perilous."[15] Field dominated the commission's work, which proceeded swiftly. The commission presented a draft of a Code of Civil Procedure to the legislature on February 29, 1848. The draft was enacted into law on April 12 of that year and has become known as the "Field Code." Subsequently the commission presented additional reports, proposing amendments to the code, some of which the legislature enacted. On December 31, 1849, the commission completed its work by presenting two complete codes: Civil Procedure and Criminal Procedure. Published in 1850, these codes are reprinted as volumes I and II of the present series. Years later, on July 1, 1881, an amended version of the Code of Criminal Procedure was enacted.[16]

Meanwhile, a separate commission also created in 1847 and charged with codifying the substantive law had made little progress, and it was abolished in 1850. But after intense effort Field in 1857 persuaded the legislature to set up a new commission empowered to fulfill the Constitution's mandate "to reduce into a written and systematic code the whole body of the law of the state of New York." Field, William Curtis Noyes, and Alexander W. Bradford were selected as the commissioners.[17] Over the next eight years they labored on three codes: a Political Code, embracing "the laws respecting the government of the state, its civil polity, the functions of its public officers, and the political rights and duties of its citizens"; a Civil Code, covering "the laws of personal rights and relations of property, and of obligations"; and a Penal Code, defining "all the crimes for which persons can be punished and the punishment for the

---

[14] Coe and Morse, "Chronology," 238.

[15] Lawrence M. Friedman, *A History of American Law,* 2nd ed. (New York: Simon & Schuster, 1986), 391.

[16] Reppy, "The Field Codification Concept," 33–8.

[17] Ibid., 38.

crime."[18] Field himself personally prepared the civil code. The entire scheme roughly paralleled the France's Code Napoleon. The Political Code was submitted to the legislature and published in 1860, the final version of the Penal Code was submitted in 1864 and published in 1865, and the final version of the Civil Code was submitted and published in 1865.[19] We reprint them in volumes III-V of the present series.

Field remained devoted to the cause of codification for the rest of his life. His interest even extended to the codification to international law, and in the 1870s he prepared a draft outline for a code of international law. He traveled to both Europe and Asia and was gratified to see the influence his New York codification work was having in Great Britain as well as in India and other British colonies.

When Field died in 1894 at the age of 89, a member of the New York Bar paid him this tribute:

> The magnitude of the results of his labors can scarcely be overestimated. . . . That he exerted a greater influence in modifying and simplifying the judicial systems of the United States and England than any other man of his time will hardly be denied. The world over, wherever the prevailing jurisprudence has had its origin in the English common law, the form and manner of conducting litigations and transacting the business of the courts are due to the influence of David Dudley Field.[20]

The Reception and Significance of the Field Codes

As we have seen, the New York legislature quickly passed Field's Code of Civil Procedure. The legislature later amended the code several times, however, and considerably diluted its concision and weakened the force of Field's reforms.

The other codes encountered much more difficulty in New York. Only two were enacted and both not until 1881: the Code of Criminal Procedure, which had been submitted initially in late

---

[18] Coe and Morse, "Chronology," 244–5.
[19] Ibid., 245.
[20] Quoted in Hoy, "David Dudley Field," 128.

1849, and the Penal Code of 1865. The New York Assembly passed the Civil Code four times, and the entire legislature did so twice—only to have it vetoed each time by the governor.[21] The Civil Code, which the commissioners claimed made important changes in "the rights of married women, the adoption of children, and the assimilation of the laws of real and personal by politicians. James C. Carter, a prominent property,"[22] sparked particularly intense debate. Opposition within the legal profession was intense, and the New York City Bar Association in 1883 unanimously passed a resolution against it.[23]

Opposition to the Civil Code—and to the codification movement in general—centered around two general points. The first was that no code, however skillfully prepared, could encompass all the wealth of experience embodied in the common law. The second was that codification would take control of the law away from the courts, where it belonged, and give it to legislatures run by politicians. James C. Carter. A prominent New York lawyer and a leading opponent of codification—he termed Field's work "grossly defective"[24]—wrote in essays in the 1880s:

> The question is [whether the] growth, development and improvement of the law [should] remain under the guidance of men selected by the people on account of their special qualifications for the work [or] be transferred to a numerous legislative body, disqualified by the nature of their duties for the discharge of this supreme function . . . [Courts apply] "a social standard of justice[,] . . . the product of the combined operation of the thought, the morality, the intellectual and moral culture of the time."[25]

These arguments carried the day in New York.

---

[21] Reppy, "The Field Codification Concept," 46.
[22] *Civil Code,* vol. III of this series, xxxi.
[23] Morton J. Horwitz, *The Transformation of American Law: 1870-1960* (Cambridge: Harvard University Press, 1977), 118.
[24] Quoted in Hoy, "David Dudley Field," 165.
[25] Quoted in Friedman, *A History of American Law,* 404.

But outside New York, especially in the newer western states and territories that did not have an inherited body of law, Field's codes enjoyed considerably more success. The Code of Civil Procedure—the "Field Code"—was adopted in Missouri as early as 1849. California, newly admitted to the Union, followed in 1851 with the help of Field's brother Stephen, who had been elected to the California legislature in 1850 after moving from New York the previous year. By 1862 ten more states and territories had adopted the Code of Civil Procedure, and by 1900 another 12 had done so.[26] In addition several states adopted a procedural criminal code and substantive penal, political, and civil codes based on Field's work. Indeed California enacted adaptations of all five of Field's codes. Portions of these codes are still in effect today.[27]

Ironically Field's attempts through codification to limit the role in America of English-derived common law had consequences for legal reform in Great Britain itself. The authors and proponents of the English Judicature Acts of 1873 and 1875, many of whom knew Field personally, were influenced by his work. Field's codes inspired lawmakers in the British colonies of India, Singapore, and Hong Kong as well.[28]

Field's codes, then, had great impact both in the United States and internationally and clearly are worthy of study today. Scholars agree, however, that Field's outstanding achievement remains the New York Code of Civil Procedure, the "Field Code." That code and the 1938 Federal Rules of Civil Procedure, which it influenced, remain the two most fundamental sets of

---

[26] The states and territories that adopted the Code of Civil Procedure by 1862 were, in addition to Missouri, California, Iowa, Indiana, Kansas, Minnesota, Nebraska, Nevada, Ohio, and Washington. By 1900 they had been joined by Arizona, Colorado, Idaho, Montana, New Mexico, North Carolina, North and South Dakota, Oklahoma, South Carolina, Utah, and Wyoming. Ibid., 394.

[27] See E. Allan Farnsworth, *An Introduction to the Legal System of the United States,* 2nd ed. (New York: Oceana, 1983); Friedman, *A History of American Law,* 405; and Horwitz, *The Transformation of American Law,* 117–8.

[28] Reppy, "The Field Codification Concept," 48.

rules in American civil procedure."[29] Section 554 of the Code of Civil Procedure contained the following revolutionary declaration:

> The distinction between actions at law and suits in equity, and for the forms of all such actions and suits heretofore existing, are abolished; and, there shall be in this state, hereafter, but one form of action, for the enforcement or protection of private rights and the redress or prevention of private wrongs, which shall be denominated a civil action.[30]

As Field intended, the code simplified the pleadings of plaintiff and defendant, limiting the former to a concise factual complaint, demurrer, and reply and the latter to a concise factual answer and demurrer. It adopted the rules of equity for the application of relief.[31] In the words of the great legal scholar Roscoe Pound:

> No treatises on the theory of legislation and no polemical tracts on law reform have led to such far-reaching concrete results. It [the Code of Civil Procedure] stands toward procedure in the world of the common law where Beccaria's treatise on Crimes and Punishments stood toward the nineteenth-century criminal law. It showed the way.[32]

Michael Weber

---

[29] Roscoe Pound, "David Dudley Field: An Appraisal," in *David Dudley Field: Centenary Essays Celebrating One Hundred Years of Legal Reform,* ed. Alison Reppy (New York: New York University School of Law, 1949), 11; Suprin, "David Dudley Field and the Field Code," 312.

[30] See page 225 of volume I of this series.

[31] Reppy, "The Field Codification Concept," 49–51.

[32] Roscoe Pound, "David Dudley Field: An Appraisal," 8.

THE CODE

OF

CRIMINAL PROCEDURE

OF THE

STATE OF NEW-YORK.

REPORTED COMPLETE

BY THE

COMMISSIONERS ON PRACTICE AND PLEADINGS.

ALBANY:

WEED, PARSONS & CO., PUBLIC PRINTERS.

1850.

REPORT.

TO THE LEGISLATURE OF THE STATE OF NEW-YORK.

The Commissioners on Practice and Pleadings have the honor to submit herewith, their complete Report of a Code of Criminal Procedure.

In presenting the result of this portion of their labors, the Commissioners deem it not inappropriate to refer to an objection, which has been taken to their consideration of the subject embraced in this report. It seems to have been supposed by some, that the regulation of the modes of procedure in the civil courts, was alone within the scope of their duties. A recurrence to the constitutional provision under which they were appointed, furnishes, however, an abundant answer to this objection. That instrument declares, that it shall be the duty of the Commissioners "to revise, reform, simplify and abridge the rules and practice, pleadings, forms and proceedings of the courts of record of this state, and to report thereon to the legislature, subject to their adoption and modification, from time to time." The same language is also used in the act under which they were originally appointed, as well as in that passed at the last session, extending the Commission. The term, "courts of record," clearly embraces the tribunals in which criminal, as well as civil justice is administered. Used, as it is, in the constitution, as a term of description, it comprehends the courts of oyer and terminer and sessions, and the mayor's and recorders' courts possessing criminal jurisdiction, and plainly imposes upon the Commissioners the duty of revising, simplifying and abridging the pleadings and practice in those courts; and as a necessary consequence, that of adapting the proceedings of other judicial and administrative officers, to such reforms in the practice as fall more literally within their expressly prescribed powers.

In their report of a code of criminal procedure, presented at the last session, the Commissioners took occasion to say, that they had weighed with great caution every view which had suggested itself to their minds, as well in respect to the principles upon which they should proceed, as to the details, even the minutest, by which those principles could be successfully carried into practice. It was, however, with them, a matter of regret, that owing to the pressure of time, by reason of the approaching expiration of the Commission, they were unable to present all the subjects which that code should have included, or to accompany their report with such explanations as might lighten the labors of the legislature in considering it.

In the code which accompanies this report, they have obviated these difficulties, and while they have in no respect departed from the principles of that formerly reported, they have comprehended the subjects which were then omitted, and have embodied in the code now presented, ample explanations of the principles and details which it contains. It is now, so far as the Commissioners have been able to make it, an entire body of criminal procedure, and in their judgment, will prove, if it should be adopted, a convenient substitute for the present regulations, whether existing at common law or by statute, in respect to the subjects to which it relates. It is unnecessary in this report, to make particular reference, either to the principles or to the details embraced in the proposed code. Those will be found explained in the provisions themselves, and in the notes by which they are accompanied. A brief reference, however, to the general plan of the code, is perhaps not improper.

It is divided into seven parts; the first of which relates to courts having original jurisdiction of criminal actions. In this part, are embraced the same provisions which are included in the code of civil procedure, respecting the organization and jurisdiction of the courts of original criminal jurisdiction. That code, being designed, among other things, to embrace the functions of all the judicial tribunals of the State, necessarily includes those which relate to the criminal courts. Their repetition in this code is required, in order to make it a complete guide to criminal procedure, and to dispense with an unnecessary reference from the one to the other; while, by the brevity of the provisions themselves, the code is not inconveniently extended.

The second part relates to the prevention of public offences;—a subject which, with but few exceptions, has been left unregulated by statute, and in regard to which, the Commissioners deem a system of practical regulation of the rights and duties of the private citizen, as well as of the public officer, both convenient and necessary.

The third part relates to judicial proceedings, for the removal of public officers by impeachment or otherwise. In this respect, also, the code supplies, what the Commissioners deem, an important defect in the existing statutory regulations. This part is confined to the removal of judicial officers and their clerks, and provides a uniform practice in this respect, for the want of which great embarrassmeuts have been experienced, especially in the proceedings for the removal of justices of inferior courts.

The fourth part relates to the proceedings in criminal actions prosecuted by indictment, and comprehends the local jurisdiction of public offences—the time of commencing criminal actions—the information and the proceedings thereon to the commitment, inclusive—

the proceedings after commitment and before indictment,—the indictment,—the proceedings on the indictment before trial,—the trial,—the proceedings after trial, and before judgment,—the judgment and execution, and appeals; and embraces also, under the head of miscellaneous proceedings,—bail,—compelling the attendance of witnesses,—examination of witnesses, conditionally,—examination of witnesses on commission,—inquiry into the insanity of the defendant, before trial, or after conviction,—compromising certain public offences, by leave of the court,—dismissal of the action, before or after indictment, for want of prosecution, or otherwise,—remitting the punishment in certain cases—proceedings against corporations,—entitling affidavits,—errors and mistakes, in pleadings and other proceedings,—disposal of property stolen or embezzled,—and reprieves, commutations and pardons.

The fifth part relates to proceedings in the police courts, which are substituted in place of the present courts of special sessions.

The sixth part relates to special proceedings of a criminal nature, and embraces coroners inquests, and the duties of coroners,—search warrants,—the outlawry of persons convicted of treason,—proceedings against fugitives from justice,—proceedings respecting persons held to labor or service, in a state or territory of the United States, and escaping into this state,—proceedings respecting bastards,—proceedings respecting vagrants,—proceedings respecting disorderly persons,—proceedings respecting the support of poor persons,—proceedings respecting masters, apprentices and servants,—criminal statistics,—and miscellaneous provisions.

The seventh part relates to costs in criminal actions, and in proceedings of a criminal nature.

To these are added an appendix, containing brief forms of indictments, in conformity with the provisions of this code.

From this enumeration of the subjects embraced in the code, it will be perceived that it is co-extensive with the whole range of, criminal practice. There is no branch of judicial procedure, which by the common concession of the people of this state, demands at the hands of the legislature, a more searching and thorough examination, or a more complete and effectual reform, than the principles and details of criminal practice. Depending, as society does, for its safety, on the one hand, upon the most rigorous enforcement of the law for the prevention and punishment of crime, and on the other, for a just protection to the life and liberty of the citizen, it will readily be perceived, that the task of adjusting the legislation of the state so as to effectuate the one object without undue prejudice to the other, is one of no easy accomplishment. It will therefore not be attributed to a false profession of diffidence on the part of the Commissioners, to say, that while they have approached the performance of this duty, with a determination, so far as they were able, to attain both these objects, they have at the same time realized the delicacy and difficulty of the work. In the discharge of that duty they have not been unmindful, on the one hand, that the rights of the citizen, in proceedings of a criminal nature, should be most thoroughly protected, while on the other they have not forgotten, that the interests of public justice should be paramount to the observance of the useless forms and unmeaning technicalities, by which it has been so often eluded.

In this code, the Commissioners have departed from the plan of the execution of their duties, as contained in their report of a code of civil procedure. In that report, they do not deem it necessary to go further into the details of the practical steps required in the conduct of a cause, than is essential to the successful carrying out of the principles which they propose. The rules there prescribed, are mainly designed for the government of courts of civil jurisdiction, embracing a body of intelligence and learning upon which the Commissioners feel a safe reliance may be placed, not merely for a faithful execution of the law, but for an intelligent and discriminating application of its provisions. They are designed also for that class of the profession, whose practice in those courts and whose experience of the rules governing legal procedure, afford, as the Commissioners believe, a just assurance that minuteness of detail would rather tend to confuse than to aid them in the application of principles, which they hope are expressed with sufficient clearness, and which, if that hope be well founded, can be readily and beneficially reduced to practice. Upon that confidence they are willing to rely, so far as the code of civil procedure is concerned; not doubting that when its provisions have become more familiar by practice, and its defects, not peculiar to this more than to any other human undertaking, shall have been remedied either by legislation or by benign judicial construction, it will be found to result in great benefit to the people, and in a still higher degree of moral elevation to the legal profession.

In the code of criminal procedure, however, a more detailed systeu of regulation is indispensable. In the rules which it prescribes, should be found a guide to the citizen, in the performance of the duties which are cast upon him for the preservation of public order,—to the unprofessional magistrate, in the exercise of a difficult and delicate discretion,—and to the executive officers of the law, in the performonce of duties designed for its due enforcement without an unnecessary or oppressive encroachment upon the rights of the citizen. This guide, in which the existing statutes are greatly deficient, and much of which is now furnished by subtle and almost inaccessible rules of the common law, the Commissioners have felt bound to supply, by provisions which, though minute are not unnecessary, and which shall distinctly and plainly place before all, not merely the duties they may be called upon to perform, but the manner in which they are to be performed. The provisions referred to, constitute no inconsiderable portion of the code; and in their arrangement as well as their style, the study has been to make them as plain and simple as possible. Where warrants have been prescribed or undertakings of bail required or allowed, their form has in every instance been given. In short the object has been to make the code a body of practical directions, intelligible in their character, with the addition of the proper means effectually to carry them out.

In submitting the result of their labors to the legislature, the Commissioners will not pretend to assert, that it is free from omissions and defects; for no human work can be without them. They have spared no effort to render it perfect, and in return, they ask for it the candid consideration of the legislature and the people.

All which is respectfully submitted.

ARPHAXED LOOMIS,
DAVID GRAHAM,
DAVID DUDLEY FIELD.

Albany, December 31, 1849.

TABLE OF CONTENTS

PART I.

TITLE I.

TITLE II.

TITLE III.

TITLE IV.

CHAPTER I.

CHAPTER II.

CHAPTER III.

TITLE V.

TITLE VI.

PART II.

TITLE I.

CHAPTER I.

CHAPTER II.

CHAPTER III.

TITLE II.

CHAPTER I.

CHAPTER II.

CHAPTER III.

CHAPTER IV.

PART III.

TITLE I.

TITLE II.

PART IV.

TITLE I

TITLE II.

TITLE III.

CHAPTER I.

CHAPTER II.

CHAPTER III.

CHAPTER IV.

CHAPTER V.

CHAPTER VI.

CHAPTER VII.

Examination of the case, and discharge of the defendant, or holding him to answer,........................83 – 103

TITLE IV.

Of proceedings after commitment, and before indictment,.... 104–136

CHAPTER I.

CHAPTER II.

CHAPTER III.

CHAPTER IV.

TITLE V.

CHAPTER I.

CHAPTER II.

CHAPTER III.

CHAPTER IV.

CHAPTER V.

CHAPTER VI.

CHAPTER VII.

TITLE VI.

CHAPTER I.

CHAPTER II.

CHAPTER III.

CHAPTER IV.

CHAPTER V.

TITLE VII.

CHAPTER I.

CHAPTER II.

CHAPTER III.

TITLE VIII.

CHAPTER I.

CHAPTER II.

CHAPTER III.

TITLE IX.

CHAPTER I.

CHAPTER II.

TITLE X.

CHAPTER I.

CHAPTER II.

CHAPTER III.

CHAPTER IV.

TITLE XI.

CHAPTER I.

ARTICLE I.

ARTICLE II.

ARTICLE III.

ARTICLE IV.

ARTICLE V.

ARTICLE VI.

ARTICLE VII.

ARTICLE VIII.

CHAPTER II.

CHAPTER III.

CHAPTER IV.

Evamination of witnesses, on commission,............... 326-334

CHAPTER V.

Inquiry into the insanity of the defendant, before trial, or after conviction, ...-.....,................................ 335-338

CHAPTER VI.

CHAPTER VII.

CHAPTER VIII.

CHAPTER IX.

CHAPTER X.

CHAPTER XI.

CHAPTER XII.

CHAPTER XIII.

PART V.

TITLE I.

TITLE II.

TITLE III.

PART IV.

OF SPECIAL PROCEEDINGS OF A CRIMINAL NATURE, 383-466

TITLE I.

TITLE II.

TITLE III.

TITLE IV.

CHAPTER I.

CHAPTER II.

TITLE V.

TITLE VI.

CHAPTER I.

CHAPTER II.

Appeals from the orders of magistrates, respecting bastards, 427–434

CHAPTER III.

TITLE VII.

TITLE VIII.

TITLE IX.

TITLE X.

TITLE XI.

TITLE XII.

PART VII.

OF THE COSTS IN CRIMINAL ACTIONS AND PROCEEDINGS, ... 467–469

GENERAL PROVISIONS AND DEFINITIONS APPLICABLE TO THIS CODE, ... 470–472

APPENDIX.

THE CODE

OF

CRIMINAL PROCEDURE.

THE CODE

OF

CRIMINAL PROCEDURE.

AN ACT

To Establish a Code of Criminal Procedure.

The People of the State of New-York, represented in Senate and Assembly, do enact as follows:

PRELIMINARY PROVISIONS.

§ 1. This act shall be known as THE CODE OF CRIMINAL PROCEDURE OF THE STATE OF NEW-YORK.

§ 2. This code is divided into seven parts.

The first relates to the courts having original jurisdiction of criminal actions.

The second relates to the prevention of public offences.

The third relates to judicial proceedings, for the removal of public officers by impeachment or otherwise.

The fourth relates to the proceedings in criminal actions prosecuted by indictment.

The fifth relates to proceedings in the police courts.

The sixth relates to special proceedings of a criminal nature.

The seventh relates to costs in criminal actions, and in proceedings of a criminal nature.

§ 3. A crime or public offence is an act or omission forbidden by law, and to which is annexed, upon conviction, either of the following punishments:

1. Death:

2. Imprisonment:

3. Fine:

4. Removal from office: or,

5. Disqualification to hold and enjoy any office of honor, trust or profit under this state.

This section embraces the definition of a public offence, in accordance with that given by Mr. Livingston, *Crim. Code, p.* 375, *art.* 75, except that it is adapted to the punishments prescribed by the statutes of this state. It includes also, under the head of crimes or public offences, all violations of public law, whether punishable by death, imprisonment or fine, or by removal from office, coupled with a disqualification to hold or enjoy any office of honor, trust or profit, under this state.

§ 4. Public offences are divided into,

1. Felonies: and,

2. Misdemeanors.

This is in conformity with the existing law.

§ 5. A felony is a public offence, punishable with death, or which is, or in the discretion of the court may be, punishable by imprisonment in a state prison.

The definition here given is more comprehensive than that given by the Revised Statutes. The provision there is: "The term 'felony,' when used in this act, or in any other statute, shall be construed to mean an offence for which the offender, on conviction, shall be liable by law to be punished by death or by imprisonment in a state prison." 2 *R. S.* *3d ed.*, 789, *sec.* 33.

It was held by the supreme court, in *Ward v. The People*, 3 *Hill*, 295, and by the court of errors, in the same case, 6 *Hill*, 144, that under this provision, *statute felonies* alone were defined, and that offences which were felonies at common law, (as for example, petit larceny,) still remained so, though not punishable by imprisonment in a state prison; though it was admitted that the legislature did not intend such a distinction. The proposed provision obviates the distinction, and establishes a rule applicable to all crimes, whether at common law or by statute.

§ 6. Every other public offence is a misdemeanor.

This section carries out the rule prescribed in the last.

§ 7. No person can be punished for a public offence, except upon legal conviction in a court having jurisdiction thereof.

Declaratory of the common law, and conformable in substance, to chap. 2, sec. 1, of the penal code reported for Massachusetts, in 1844.

§ 8. Every public offence must be prosecuted by indictment, except,

1. Where proceedings are had for the removal of a civil officer of the state, on an impeachment by the assembly, for wilful or corrupt misconduct in office:

2. Where proceedings are had for the removal of justices of the peace, police justices, and justices of justices' courts, and their clerks:

3. Offences arising in the militia, when in actual service; and in the land and naval forces in time of war, or which this state may keep with the consent of congress, in time of peace:

4. Petit larceny, not charged as a second offence:

5. Assault and battery, not charged to have been committed riotously, or upon a public officer in the execution of his duties:

6. Poisoning, killing, maiming, wounding, or cruelly beating an animal:

7. Racing animals, within one mile of the place where a court is held:

8. Committing a wilful trespass, or severing any produce or article from the freehold, not amounting to grand larceny:

9. Selling poisonous substances, not labelled as required by statute:

10. Maliciously removing, altering, defacing, or cutting down monuments or marked trees:

11. Maliciously breaking, destroying or removing mile stones, mile-boards or guide-boards, or altering an inscription thereon:

The constitution, *art.* 1, *sec.* 6, provides that "no person shall be held to answer for a capital or otherwise infamous crime (except in cases of impeachment, and in cases of the militia, when in actual service; and the land and naval forces in time of war, or which this state may keep, with the consent of congress, in time of peace; and in cases of petit larceny, under the regulation of the legislature,) unless on presentment or indictment, of a grand jury."

Under a similar provision in the constitution of 1821, *art.* 7, *sec.* 7, the legislature gave jurisdiction to the courts of special sessions, which proceeded without indictment, of the cases mentioned in this section from subdivision 4 to subdivision 11, both inclusive. 2 *R. S.*, 3*d ed.* 798, *sec.* 1.

The cases excepted in the first subdivision are those which, by the constitution, *art.* 6, *sec.* 1, are punishable by impeachment. Those in the second subdivision, are included in that part of the constitution which provides that justices of the peace and judges or justices of inferior courts not of record, and their clerks, may be removed after due notice, and an opportunity of being heard in their defence, by such county, city or state courts, as may be prescribed by law, for causes to be assigned in the order of removal." *Art.* 6, *sec.* 17. In this subdivision, the terms used are "justices of the peace, police justices and justices of justices' courts." This difference in phraseology is in accordance with section 12 of the code of civil procedure, by which all the courts of justice of this state, are declared to be "courts of record, except that justices' and police courts are deemed inferior courts not of record, within the section of the constitution," just referred to; and with section 16, of this code, by which, in reference to the enumeration of the courts of original criminal jurisdiction, the same declaration is made respecting the police courts. *See p.* 11.

The cases in the third subdivision, are excepted in the provision of the constitution first quoted.

§ 9. The proceeding, by which a party charged with a public offence is accused and brought to trial and punishment, is known as a criminal action.

§ 10. A criminal action is prosecuted in the name of the people of the state of New-York as a party, against the party charged with the offence.

§ 11. The party prosecuted in a criminal action, is designated in this code, as the defendant.

The last three sections treat the proceedings for the trial and punishment of public offences, as a *criminal action*. In doing so they follow the definition in the Code of Civil Procedure : "§ 5. An action is an ordinary proceeding in a court of justice, by which one party prosecutes another for the enforcement or protection of a right, the redress or prevention of a wrong, or the punishment of a public offence." "§ 7. Actions are of two kinds : 1. Civil, and 2. Criminal." "§ 9. A criminal action is prosecuted by the state as a party, against a person charged with a public offence, for the punishment thereof."

These definitions are in accordance with the authority of the most approved elementary writers.

§ 12. In a criminal action, the defendant is entitled,

1. To a speedy and public trial:

2. To be allowed counsel, as in civil actions; or he may appear and defend in person and with counsel; and,

3. To produce witnesses in his behalf, and to be confronted with the witnesses against him in the pre-

sence of the court; except that where the charge has been preliminarily examined before a magistrate, and the testimony reduced by him to the form of a deposition, in the presence of the defendant, who has, either in person or by counsel, cross-examined, or had an opportunity to cross-examine the witness; or where the testimony of a witness on the part of the people, who is unable to give security for his appearance, has been taken conditionally, according to sections 218 and 219, the deposition of the witness may be read, upon its being satisfactorily shown to the court that he is dead or insane, or cannot, with due diligence be found in the state.

The first subdivision of this section is taken from the bill of rights. 1 *R. S.*, *2d ed.* 95. *sec.* 14.

The second subdivision is taken from the constitution, *art.* 1. *sec.* 6.

In respect to the third subdivision, the Commissioners have found in the existing practice, some regulations, resulting from considerations of public policy, which have conflicted with the full and absolute enjoyment of the privileges guaranteed to the defendant by the bill of rights. They refer especially to the legislation applicable to the city of New-York, permitting the examination of a witness out of court, where, by reason of his being a non-resident of the state, his absence at the time of the trial might lead to the impunity of the defendant. *Laws of* 1844, *p.* 476, *sec.* 11. The provision in question was adopted, mainly with reference to a class of cases, where persons from other states were the victims of fraud or inpositions in that city, indictable as public offences; and provided for the examination of a witness upon notice to the defendant, and an opportunity to cross-examine, and for the introduction of the testimony thus taken, as evidence upon the trial. This, at present, constitutes the only exception to the rule as prescribed by the bill of rights, that the defendant must be confronted with the witnesses against him;—a a rule, which, before the local enactment just referred to, was understood to mean, that the testimony of all the witnesses on the part of the prosecution should be given in open court.

The Commissisoners are not insensible of the danger of multiplying the exceptions to this rule ; and while they fully appreciate the importance to the defendant, of being tried upon testimony, of the credibility of which the jury are enabled to judge, not merely from the facts stated by the witness, but from his manner of testifying, (which constitutes so important an element in the right of trial by jury,) they are at the same time well convinced that the interests of public justice should be guarded against a contingency, calculated to protect the guilty from the merited punishment of crime. For this purpose, they deem a relaxation of the rule that the defendant should in all cases be confronted with the witnesses against him, in the presence of the court, proper and necessary in two classes of case.

The first is, where a witness,—who has been examined before a committing magistrate, and whose testimony has been taken in the presence of the defendant, and upon an opportunity afforded him, of cross-examining the witness,—is, at the time of the trial, dead or insane, or cannot be found within the state. The second is, where a witness on the part of the prosecution, who is unable to give security for his appearance, to testify, has been conditionally examined in the presence of, or upon notice to the defendant, with an opportunity to cross-examine him.

The justice of these exceptions to the general rule, the Commissioners, after a careful consideration, have not felt at liberty to doubt. In both cases, the opportunity for a cross examination is afforded to the defendant;—an opportunity of which he will not fail to avail himself, when the law informs him that he fails to do so at the peril of losing the benefit of a cross-examination on the trial ; and in both, he is protected against the use of such testimony, except where a contingency has happened, by which, according to every principle of justice, the rights of the public should not be prejudiced.

These remarks are more especially applicable, to the case of a witness who is unable to give security for his appearance at the trial. It is one of the first principles of the law, that no man should be imprisoned but for a crime. This principle has been carried out by the legislature, in reference to the unfortunate debtor; and the only case to be found upon the statute book, in which it has been deemed proper to modify, if not entirely to contravene it, is that of a witness who is unable to give such security as a magistrate may prescribe, for his appearance upon the trial of a criminal action. Of the hardship to which this provision has given rise, it is perhaps unnecessary for the Commissioners to speak. Practical illustrations of that hardship might be multiplied, almost without number. Cases might be cited, where an individual, who has accidentally become the witness or the victim of a crime, has been incarcerated for months together, while the defendant was at large on bail; and if it were necessary, instances could be referred to, where the witness was thus incarcerated, while the defendant was virtually entirely discharged, by means of the system of giving worthless bail, of which such frequent and well founded complaints have been made. An abuse like this,—subversive as it is, of the first right of the citizen,—to be protected in the enjoyment of his liberty, where he has not by his own act, forfeited it to the law,—is in the judgment of the Commissioners, one which ought to be no longer permitted to exist, and which demands from the legislature the application of a prompt and speedy corrective. That it can be so applied, without prejudice to the just rights of the defendant, would seem hardly to admit of doubt; and guarded as it is, by the provisions of sections 218 and 219, by affording to the defendant an opportunity for a cross-examination, the Commissioners feel clear in recommending its adoption.

§ 13. No person can be subjected to a second prosecution for a public offence, for which he has once been prosecuted and duly convicted or acquitted.

This section is founded upon the provision of the constitution, which declares, that "no person shall be subject to be twice put in jeopardy for the same offence." *Art.* 1, *sec.* 6. It is declaratory of the principle, about which a difference of judicial opinion has existed in several of the states, but which was set at rest in this state in the case of *The People v. Goodwin*, 18 Johns. 200 — 203, that neither the discharge of a jury without a verdict, nor any thing but a legal acquittal, or conviction, is a bar to a second prosecution, or to another trial for the same offence, nor is in any sense within the constitutional protection.

§ 14. No person can be compelled, in a criminal action, to be a witness against himself; nor can a person charged with a public offence, be subjected before conviction, to any more restraint than is necessary for his detention to answer the charge,

The first clause is conformable to the constitution, *art.* 1, *sec.* 6.

The second is declaratory of the common law, which recognizes the detention of a prisoner as only justifiable to enforce his attendance at the trial, and not as a punishment.

§ 15. No person can be convicted of a public offence, where he is entitled to a trial by jury, unless by the verdict of a jury accepted and recorded by the court, or upon a plea of guilty, or upon judgment against him on a demurrer to the indictment in the case mentioned in section 349.

This section is in accordance with the existing law, and with the practice prescribed by the code, defining the only modes in which the defendant can be legally convicted. The phraseology of the section is substantially taken from the report of the Massachusetts Commisssoners, *ch.* 2, *sec.* 4.

PART I.

OF THE COURTS HAVING ORIGINAL JURISDICTION IN CRIMINAL ACTIONS.

TITLE I.

OF THE COURTS OF ORIGINAL CRIMINAL JURISDICTION, IN GENERAL.

§ 16. The following are the courts of justice in this state, having original jurisdiction of criminal actions:

1. The court for the trial of impeachments:

2. The courts of oyer and terminer:

3. The courts of sessions:

4. The city courts:

5. The police courts.

They are courts of record; except that the police courts are deemed inferior courts not of record, within the section of the constitution providing for the removal of justices of the peace, and judges or justices of inferior courts not of record, and their clerks, by such county, city, or state courts as may be prescribed by law; but for no other purpose.

This section contains an enumeration of the existing courts of criminal jurisdiction, except that the police courts are substituted for the courts of special sessions with substantially the same powers. The distinction between courts of record, and not of record, is abrogated, for the reasons stated in the note to section 20 of the Code of Civil Procedure.

TITLE II.

OF THE COURT FOR THE TRIAL OF IMPEACHMENTS.

§ 17. The court for the trial of impeachments has power to try impeachments, when presented by the assembly, of all civil officers of the state, except justices of the peace, justices of justices' courts, police justices, and their clerks, for wilful and corrupt misconduct in office.

The new constitution, *art.* 6, *sec.* 1, is silent as to the cases in which the assembly may impeach, conferring the power of impeachment upon that body in general terms. The constitution of 1821, *art.* 5, *sec.* 2, defined this power by applying it to " mal and corrupt conduct in office," which is substantially the same as in the constitution of 1777, *sec.* 33. As the power referred to in the present constitution is the same as that formerly existing, it seems useful to embody it in the above provision. The words " wilful and corrupt misconduct in office," convey the same idea, in what the Commissioners deem a preferable form of expression.

§ 18. The court is composed of the president of the senate, the senators or a majority of them, and the judges of the court of appeals or a majority of them. But on the trial of an impeachment against the governor, the lieutenant-governor cannot act as a member of the court.

Taken from the constitution, *art.* 6, *sec.* 1.

§ 19. The president of the senate, or in case of his impeachment, death or absence, the chief judge of the court of appeals, or in the absence of both, such other member as the court may elect, is the presiding judge of the court.

§ 20. The clerk and officers of the senate are the clerk and officers of the court for the trial of impeachments.

§ 21. There are no stated terms of this court; but upon the delivery of an impeachment from the assembly, the president of the senate must cause the court to be summoned to meet at the capitol in the city of Albany, on a day not less than thirty nor more than sixty days from the day of the delivery of the articles of impeachment.

Same as the judiciary act, *Laws of* 1847, *p.* 319, *sec.* 1.

§ 22. At the time and place appointed, and before the court proceeds to act on the impeachment, the clerk must administer to the presiding judge, and the presiding judge to each of the members of the court then present, an oath or affirmation truly and impartially to hear, try and determine the impeachment; and no member of the court can act or vote upon the impeachment, or any question arising thereon, without having taken this oath or affirmation.

Substantially the same as 2 *R. S.*, 3*d ed.* 224; except that the word "impeachment" on the 6th line, has been substituted instead of the words "the charge in question," in conformity with the difference of phraseology in this respect, between the constitution of 1821, *art.* 5, *sec.* 2, and the present, *art.* 6, *sec.* 1.

§ 23. When the court is held during the recess of the legislature, the president of the senate, the senators, and the clerk and officers, of the court, are entitled to the same compensation for their attendance thereon, and for travelling to and from the place where it is held, as is allowed them at a meeting of the senate.

Taken from 2 *R. S.*, 3*d ed.* 224, *sec.* 13, except that it includes the president of the senate and senators.

TITLE III.

OF THE COURTS OF OYER AND TERMINER.

SECTION 24. Court of oyer and terminer in each county.
25-27. Its jurisdiction.
28, 29. By whom held.
30. When and where held, and duration thereof.

§ 24. There is in each of the counties of this state, (except, that for this purpose, Fulton and Hamilton are deemed one county,) a court, denominated the court of oyer and terminer, with the jurisdiction conferred by the next three sections, and no other. But nothing contained in this section affects its jurisdiction in actions or proceedings now pending therein.

§ 25. The court of oyer and terminer has jurisdiction,

1. To inquire, by the intervention of a grand jury, of all public offences committed or triable in the county:

2. To try and determine any indictment found therein, or which may have been found at the court of sessions of the county, or at a city court therein, for an offence punishable with death:

3. To try and determine any indictment which may have been found at any of the courts mentioned in the second sub-division of this section, for an offence not punishable with death, and which may be sent or removed to the court of oyer and terminer, if in the opinion of that court it be proper to be tried therein:

4. To send any indictment found therein for an offence not punishable with death, or to send back any indictment which may have been sent or removed to that court, to the court of sessions of the county, or a city court therein, when in the opinion of the court of oyer and terminer, the same should not be tried in that court:

5. To inquire into the cause of the detention of persons imprisoned in the jail of the county, and make an order for their re-commitment or discharge, or otherwise, according to law:

6. To exercise the powers conferred upon it by other provisions of this code.

Substantially the same as 2 *R. S.*, 3*d ed.*, 270, 271, *sec.* 35, 36, 37.

§ 26. In addition to the jurisdiction conferred by the last section, jurisdiction was transferred to the courts of oyer and terminer in their respective counties, on the first Monday of July, 1847, of all indictments and proceedings then pending in the late courts of oyer and terminer; and also of all indictments and proceedings then pending in the late courts of general sessions of the peace, except in the city of New-York, and except in cases of which the courts of sessions may take cognizance, as provided in section 32.

Conformable to the Constitution, *art.* 14, *sec.* 5.

§ 27. Jurisdiction was likewise transferred to this court in the county of Monroe, on the thirtieth day of April, 1849, of all criminal actions and proceedings then pending in the late mayor's court of the city of Rochester, and of all proceedings incident to judgments rendered in that court in those actions and proceedings, on or before that day.

Taken from the act to abolish the mayor's court of the city of Rochester; *Laws of* 1849, *p.* 435, *sec.* 6.

§ 28. This court, (except in the city and county of New-York,) must be held by a judge of the supreme court as the presiding judge, together with the county judge, and two justices of the sessions, designated as prescribed by other statutes. If the justices of the sessions, or eit[illegible] [illegible]f them, be absent at a term of the court of oyer and [illegible]iner, or the office of those justices or either of th[illegible] [illegible] vacant, the county judge may supply the vacancy or deficiency, for the term, by designating the requisite number to form the court, from the justices of the peace of the county.

The first part of this section is taken from the section of the constitution, which provides that any one of the judges of the snpreme court may preside in courts of oyer and termimer in any county. *Const. art.* 6, *sec.* 6. That part of it which relates to the county judge and two justices of the sessions, is substantially the same as the provision of the judiciary act. *Laws of* 1847, *p.* 331, *sec.* 40.

§ 29. In the city and county of New-York, the court of oyer and terminer must be held by a judge of the the supreme court as the presiding judge, together with two of the aldermen of the city of New-York, designated as the common council may by ordinance prescribe.

By the existing statutes, as they have been construed by the court of errors, the court of oyer and terminer in the city and county of New-York may be held by one or more of the judges of the supreme court, or by either of the three judges of the court of common pleas of that city and county, together with the mayor, recorder and aldermen of that city, or with any two ot them. 2 *R. S.*, 3*d ed.*, 270, *sec.* 34, *subd.* 1; *The People v. White,* 24 *Wend.* 543–545. Upon this provision, a very embarrassing question arose in the case just cited. One of the judges of the court of common pleas had sat conjointly with a circuit judge and with two of the aldermen, and upon this state of facts, the chancellor expressed his opinion that the court was illegally constituted, and voted for the reversal of a judgment of conviction in a capital case. "The effect of this last provision," says, he, "was to authorise one or more of the justices of the supreme court, or one or more of the circuit judges, to sit in the court of oyer and terminer, with the mayor, recorder and aldermen, or any two of them; but excluding from the court when thus organized, the first judge of the court of common pleas, who is only authorised to preside in or be present in the court of oyer and terminer as a judge thereof, when a justice of the supreme court or a circuit judge does not constitute one of the members of the court. This is the only intelligible construction which I have been able to put upon the language of the statute; and as the second associate judge of the common pleas has no other powers in relation to the court of oyer and terminer, than such as were vested in the first judge, it follows of course, that the court which commenced the trial in this case was not legally organized; as it appears by the record that it was held before two persons who were not authorised to hold it *conjointly*. This is unquestionally an objection more of form than of substance, as it is not probable that the rights of the prisoner were really prejudiced thereby; though the decision of the court upon any question of law that arose, might have been been left undecided, if the court were equally divided in opinion. In a case involving the life of a fellow being, I do not feel myself authorised to disregard the legal objection to the organization of the court before which he was tried. I must, therefore, vote for a reversal of the judgment, so that the prisoner may have another trial for his life before a tribunal properly constituted for that purpose."

No distinct resolution having been adopted by the court upon this question, it is of course uncertain whether or not the views taken by the chancellor were sustained by the majority of the court. To obviate a similar embarrassment, it seems proper to declare, by what officers, in conjunction with a judge of the supreme court, the court of oyer and terminer may be held in the city and county of New-York. In practice, it was invariably held, under the old constitution, by a circuit judge with two of the aldermen; and under the present constitution, it is uniformly held by a judge of the supreme court with two of those officers. The judges of the common pleas are also omitted as presding judges of the court, in conformity with what appears to be the meaning of the constitutional provision that any one of the judges of the supreme court may preside in the courts of oyer and terminer in any county. *Const. art.* 6, *sec.* 6.

§ 30. The court of oyer and terminer must be held at the same place and commenced on the same day with the circuit in the county; and must be continued as long as the public interests require, whether the circuit remain in session or not.

TITLE IV.

OF THE COURTS OF SESSIONS.

CHAPTER I.

THE COURTS OF SESSIONS, IN GENERAL.

§ 31. There is in each of the counties of this state, a court, denominated a court of sessions, with the jurisdiction conferred by the next two chapters, and no other; but nothing contained in this section affects its jurisdiction in actions or proceedings now pending therein.

CHAPTER II.

THE COURTS OF SESSIONS, OTHER THAN IN THE CITY AND COUNTY OF NEW-YORK.

§ 32. The courts of sessions embraced in this chapter have jurisdiction,

1. To inquire, by the intervention of a grand jury, of all public offences committed or triable in the county:

2. To try and determine indictments found therein, or sent thereto by the court of oyer and terminer of the county, for public offences not punishable with death:

3. To remove justices of the peace, police justices, and justices of justices' courts, in their respective counties, and their clerks, after due notice and an opportunity of being heard in their defence, for causes to be stated in the order of removal:

4. To hear and determine appeals from orders of justices of the peace, under the provisions of this code, respecting the support of bastards:

5. To examine into the circumstances of persons committed to prison as parents of bastards, and to discharge them in the cases provided by this code:

6. To hear and determine complaints under the provisions of this code, respecting masters, apprentices, and servants:

7. To review the convictions of disorderly persons actually imprisoned, and to execute the powers conferred and duties imposed by this code, in relation to those persons:

8. To continue or discharge the recognizances, undertakings and bonds of persons bound to keep the

peace or to be of good behavior, or both; and to inquire into and determine the complaints on which they were founded:

9. To compel relatives of poor persons and committees of the estates of lunatics, to support such persons and lunatics, in the cases and manner prescribed by this code:

10. To exercise the powers conferred by this code, in relation to the estates of persons absconding and leaving their families chargeable to the public:

11. To exercise the powers conferred upon them by other provisions of this code.

The courts which have been heretofore known as *courts of general session*, (but which are denominated in the code, *courts of sessions*, in conformity with the constitution, which uniformly designates them by that name,) are retained with substantially the same powers as at present, except in one important particular. As they at present exist, the jurisdiction of these courts is confined to cases not punishable with death or imprisonment in a state prison for life; or in other words, where the utmost punishment prescribed by law is imprisonment for ten years; 2 *R. S. 3d ed.* 374, *sec.* 5, *subd.* 2; except that in the city of New-York, the jurisdiction of the court of sessions extends to all except capital cases. The reason of this difference is, that when it had its origin, the only one of these courts, in which the presiding judge was required to be a member of the legal profession, was that in the city of New-York; while in the other counties, he need not, and very frequently did not, possess this qualification. It was, therefore, deemed wise by the legislature, to provide that in cases requiring a high degree of punishment, the defendant should not be subjected to a trial, except where the presiding judge was a judge of the supreme court or a circuit judge. It is unnecessary to discuss the soundness of the ground on which this distinction rested; but assuming it to have been just, a sufficient reason is found against its further continuance, in the fact that the responsibility of the selection of competent judges has been, under our present constitution, assumed by the people. If we may judge by the past, there is but little ground of apprehension for the future, that this high responsibility will be lightly regarded, or carelessly or indiscreetly exercised. The selection of the present county judges has resulted in placing upon the bench of the court of sessions, in every county, men of ability and integrity, amply fitting them for the discharge of the duty which will be thrown upon them by the change referred to; and it is not to be doubted, that when their powers are increased, at least an equal degree of discrimination will be exercised in their selection.

Secondary to this argument,—for the Commissioners admit that it is not of primary importance,—is the necessity which exists, for relieving the judges of the supreme court from duties which can be as conveniently and safely performed by the county judges as by them. The legislature need not be informed, that this necessity has arisen from the great pressure of business in the supreme court in some of the judicial districts. As a consequence of its existence, the duty seems to be imperative, to devolve, at least in those districts, the portion of their duties connected with the courts of oyer and terminer, upon the courts of sessions; and thus leave the judges of the supreme court to the performance of that portion which demands their whole time and efforts, and which cannot constitutionally be performed by others.

An additional consideration, not without its weight in this connection, is that the jurisdiction of the courts of sessions will thus be rendered uniform throughout the state. In the city of New-York, the jurisdiction proposed, now exists in the court of sessions; and while it is not to be denied that some exceptions to the structure of the courts throughout the state, as well as in the modes of procedure, must exist in reference to that city, the Commissioners submit that it is not proper to multiply those exceptions beyond the peculiar exigencies by which they are demanded.

The jurisdiction of this court is also extended by the third subdivision, to the removal of justices of the peace, &c. Under the constitution of 1821, justices of the peace, and the special justices and assistant justices in the city of New-York, and their clerks, were removeable by the county courts, for causes particularly assigned, after notice of the charges against them, and an opportunity of being heard in their defence. *Const. of* 1821, *art.* 4, *sec.* 7—14. At that time the county courts were composed of a multiplicity of judges; but upon their abrogation by the new constitution, new county courts were created with but a single judge, called a county judge; except that in the city of New-York, the county court is still composed of the judges of the court of common pleas, and of the mayor, recorder and aldermen, as *ex officio* judgest of that court, and of the court of sessions. The framers of the present constitution, (no doubt from an unwillingness to vest this delicate power in a single judge,) introduced the provision now in force, authorizing the removal of justices of the peace, and judges or justices of inferior courts, not of record, and their clerks, after due notice, and an opportunity of being heard in their defence, *by such county, city or state courts, as may be prescribed by law,* for causes to be assigned in the order of removal. In the execution of this power, thus conferred upon the legislature, it was provided by section 25 of the judiciary act, that these officers may be removed by the supreme court, at any general term thereof. The inconvenience attendant upon the trial of any of these officers in the supreme court, as well to the parties themselves and their witnesses, as to the court, in burdening it with unnecessary business, has led the Commissioners to believe that it had better be transferred to the court of sessions, in accordance with the provision to that effect already referred to.

§ 33. In addition to the jurisdiction conferred by the last section, jurisdiction was transferred to and vested in these courts, in their respective counties, on the first Monday of July, 1847, of all indictments and proceedings similar to those mentioned in the last section, which were then pending in the late courts of general sessions of the peace.

Conformable to the constitution, *art.* 14, *sec.* 5.

§ 34. When an indictment is found in one of these courts for an offence punishable with death, the court must send it to the court of oyer and terminer of the county.

Same as 2 *R. S.*, *3d ed.* 274, *sec.* 6.

§ 35. These courts may also send an indictment, found therein and remaining undetermined, for an offence not punishable with death, to the next court of oyer and terminer of the same county, to be determined according to law; but that court, if in its opinion the same is not proper to be tried therein, may remit it back to the court by which it was sent, which must proceed thereon as if it had remained there.

Same as 2 *R. S*, *3d ed.* 275, *sec.* 7.

§ 36. These courts must be held by the county judge together with two justices of the sessions, designated as provided by other statutes. If the justices of the sessions, or either of them, be absent at a term of a court of sessions, or their office, or that of either of them, be vacant, the county judge may supply the vacancy or deficiency, for the term, by designating the requisite number to form the court, from the justices of the peace of the county.

Conformable to the constitution, *art.* 6, *sec.* 14; and to the judiciary act, *Laws of* 1847, *p.* 331, *sec.* 40.

§ 37. These courts must be held at the same place, and commence on the same day, as the terms of the county courts in their respective counties, and must be continued as long as the public interests require.

This section is introduced to obviate a doubt, (which the Commissioners, however, do not believe to be well founded,) as to the right of the courts of sessions to sit at the same time with the general terms of the county courts. See judiciary act, 1 *Laws of* 1847, *p.* 332, *sec.* 45 ; and amended Code of Procedure, *sec.* 31.

CHAPTER III.

THE COURT OF SESSIONS OF THE CITY OF NEW-YORK.

§ 38. The court known as the court of general sessions in and for the city and county of New-York, is continued, with the jurisdiction conferred by the next two sections, and no other, and is denominated the court of sessions of the city of New-York. But nothing contained in this section affects its jurisdiction of actions or proceedings now pending therein.

This section is designed to render the name of the court uniform with that of the other courts of sessions, in conformity with the constitution, which uniformly designates them by that name.

§ 39. This court has jurisdiction,

1. To inquire, by the intervention of a grand jury, of all public offences committed or triable in the city and county of New-York:

2. To try and determine any indictment found therein, or sent thereto by the court of oyer and terminer of the city and county of New-York, for a public offence not punishable with death:

3. To remove police justices and justices of the justices' courts in the city of New-York, and their clerks, after due notice and an opportunity of being heard in their defence, for causes to be stated in the order of removal:

4. In cases arising in the city and county of New-York, such as are enumerated in subdivisions 4 to 11, both inclusive, of section 32.

Substantially the same as 2 *R. S. 3d ed.*, 288, *sec.* 50, except as to the third subdivision which is introduced for the reasons stated in the note to sec. 32, p. 21, 22.

§ 40. When an indictment is found in this court for an offence punishable with death, it must be sent to the next court of oyer and terminer of the city and county of New-York.

Same 2 *R. S., 3d ed.*, 274 *sec.* 6.

§ 41. This court must be held, except as provided in the next section, by the recorder or city judge of the city of New-York, or by one of the judges of the court of common pleas of that city, as the presiding judge, together with two of the aldermen of the city, designated as the common council, may by ordinance, prescribe. But it is the especial duty of the recorder or city judges to hold the court and preside therein.

The existing statutory provisions on this subject are as follows:

"The first judge of the county courts of the city and county of New-York, and the mayor, recorder, and aldermen of the said city, or any three of them, of whom the said first judge, mayor or recorder shall always be one, shall have power to hold courts of general sessions in and for the city and county of New-York. It shall be the special duty of the recorder of the city of New-York, to hold the said court of general sessions." 2 *R. S*, *3d ed.*, 288, *sec.* 48, 49.

The section as proposed, is in conformity with the practice, as to the holding of this court, except that it gives the city judge concurrent powers with the recorder, and requires the aldermen who are to sit, to be designated by ordinance of the common council. This seems necessary to prevent many inconveniences and delays to which the court is now subjected, from the fact that no express regulation of the duty of the aldermen in this respect exists.

§ 42. When the court is convened for the purpose of exercising the jurisdiction conferred by the third subdivision of section 32, it must be held by the recorder or city judge of the city of New-York, and at least one of the judges of the court of common pleas of that city, together with the mayor and aldermen thereof, or a majority of those officers then in office.

The court, as constituted by this section, is precisely the same as the county court under the old constitution, by which these officers were triable.

§ 43. The court must be held on the first Monday of each month, and may be continued until the fourth Saturday thereafter, inclusive. Concurrent terms may also be held, as often as the recorder and city judge may from time to time, prescribe, by an order filed with the clerk.

The first part of this section is the same as 2 *R. S.*, *3d ed.*, 288, *sec.* 52, except that power is given to the court to sit until the *fourth* instead of the *third* Saturday, after its commencement. This is necessary, in consequence of the great amount of business in this court. The same reason has induced the Commissioners to recommend that power be given to hold concurrent terms.

§ 44. If the trial of a cause be commenced before the expiration of the term, the court may be continued beyond the term, till the completion of the trial, and the rendering of judgment on the verdict.

Same as *Laws of* 1846, *p.* 4, *ch.* 2; to prevent a failure of justice, owing to the legal expiration of the term. This power has often been necessary in practice.

§ 45. This court must be held at such place in the city of New-York, as now is or hereafter may be prescribed, by ordinance, by the common council of that city.

This is in conformity with the existing statute; *Laws of* 1838, *p.* 297, *ch.* 297; except that it omits the provision that the "alteration of the place of holding such courts shall, before the same takes effect, be notified in one or more of the public newspapers printed in the said city, for the period of not less than four weeks." There appears to be no necessity for such a provision.

TITLE V.

OF THE CITY COURTS.

§ 46. The courts known as the mayors' courts of the cities of Albany, Hudson and Troy, the recorders' courts of the cities of Buffalo, Utica and Oswego, and the city court of Brooklyn, are continued, with the criminal jurisdiction conferred upon them by the next four sections and no other: and shall be hereafter known as the city courts of those cities respectively. But nothing contained in this section affects their jurisdiction of actions or proceedings now pending therein.

A leading feature of the plan of the Commissioners, in respect to the organization and jurisdiction of the courts, has from the first been to render them, where they were alike in their general principles, uniform in all their details. The courts which are enumerated in this section, as they now exist, are of this character. Their jurisdiction, in the main, is analogous, within their particular localities, to that formerly exercised by the courts of common pleas. And yet even a superficial examination of the statutes by which they were from time to time created, will show that in the details of their jurisdiction, the greatest conceivable dissimilarity exists. For the purpose of this examination the legislature is referred to the following statutes:

Mayor's court of Albany, 2 *R. S.*, 3*d ed.* 294, 295, *sec.* 5, 6.
Recorder's court of Buffalo, 2 *R. S.*, 3*d ed.* 302, *sec.* 63.
Recorder's court of Utica, 2 *R. S.*, 3*d ed.* 307, *sec.* 89.
Recorder's court of Oswego, *Laws of* 1848, *p.* 490, *sec.* 3.
City court of Brooklyn, *Laws of* 1849, *p.* 170.

The name of city court is also substituted, as being uniform, while at the same time it conveys a general idea of the object and character of these courts.

§ 47. When organized as provided in section 51, for the purpose of exercising criminal jurisdiction, these courts have jurisdiction,

1. To inquire by the intervention of a grand jury, of all public offences committed in the city in which the court is established:

2. To try and determine an indictment found therein, or sent thereto by the court of oyer and terminer of the county, for a public offence not punishable with death, committed in that city.

The jurisdiction conferred by this section, is the same in the ci'y in which the court is established, as that of the court of sessions, in the county, as provided by the second and third subdivisions of section 32. It is extended to all cases less than capital, for the reasons mentioned in the note to that section, *p.* 20, 21.

§ 48. When an indictment is found at a city court, for an offence punishable with death, the court must send it to the next court of oyer and terminer of the county.

Taken from 2 *R S.*, 3*d ed* 274, *sec.* 6, as applicable to to the courts of sessions.

§ 49. These courts may also send an indictment, found therein and remaining undetermined, for an offence not punishable with death, to the next court of oyer and terminer of the same county, to be determined according to law; but that court, if in its opinion the same is not proper to be tried therein, may remit it back to the court by which it was sent, which must proceed thereon, as if it had remained there.

Taken from 2 *R. S.*, *3d ed.* 275, *sec.* 7.

§ 50. When an indictment is found at a court of oyer and terminer or of sessions, in a county embracing any of the cities in which a city court is established, for an offence not punishable with death, committed in that city, the court in which it was found may send it to the next city court in which it is triable; which must proceed to try and determine the indictment, as if it had been found therein.

Same as the powers conferred, and duties imposed upon the mayors' and recorders' courts, by the statutes referred to in the note to sec. 46, *p.* 29, 30.

§ 51. These courts must be held, for the exercise of their criminal jurisdiction, by the following judges:

1. The city courts of the cities of Albany, Buffalo, Hudson, Oswego, Troy and Utica, by the recorders of those cities,

2. The city court of the city of Brooklyn, by the city judge of that city,

Together with two of the aldermen of the city, designated as the common council may, by ordinance, prescribe.

This section is substantially the same as the corresponding sections in the statutes referred to in the note to section 46, *p.* 30.

§ 52. If the judge authorised to hold or preside at a city court for the exercise of its criminal jurisdiction, be disqualified from holding the court, as provided in the code of civil procedure, he must, upon the request of either party, file with the county clerk a certificate, stating the fact constituting the disqualification, and directing that the action or proceeding be transferred to the court of oyer and terminer of the county; and it must be transferred accordingly. If he refuse to do so, the supreme court, at a special term in the district, or a judge thereof, may, upon motion, after due notice, order the transfer to be made.

The provision requiring the transfer of the action in respect to which the disqualification exists, is the same in principle as sections 31 and 32 of the amended judiciary act, *Laws of* 1847, *p.* 643, 644, in respect to county and surrogates' courts. The power, however, is given to the supreme court to make the transfer, when the judge who is disqualified refuses to do so. This is necessary, in order to carry the rule creating the disqualification into complete effect.

§ 53. The times and places of holding the city courts are continued as at present prescribed, until the thirty-first day of December, 1850, inclusive, and no longer.

§ 54. After that time, a term of each of these courts, for the trial of issues and for the hearing and determination of all matters appertaining to its criminal jurisdiction, must be held, at such times and places in their respective cities as the common council thereof may by ordinance prescribe, and must be continued as long as the public interests require. The court is always open for the transaction of any other business.

TITLE VI.

OF THE POLICE COURTS.

SECTION 55. Courts of special sessions abolished, and police courts substituted.
56, 57. Their jurisdiction.
58. When, and by whom held, in the city and county of New-York.
59. In the other counties.

The police courts are substituted in place of the present courts of special sessions, with the jurisdiction formerly possessed by those courts. The name of "police courts" is given to them, by reason of the fact already referred to, that the contra-distinction between courts of general and special sessions, as known before the constitution, is removed by the designation of the former in that instrument as "courts of sessions." The term "police courts" also conveys more clearly the character of their jurisdiction. The organization of these courts remains unchanged, from that now belonging to the courts of special sessions, except in the city of New-York. In that city, they have heretofore been held on every Tuesday and Friday throughout the year, by the recorder and two aldermen. From the great accumulation of crime, especially of the smaller crimes, in that city, the prisons have become over-crowded, and the business of the court of general sessions has been greatly impeded by the vast number of cases to be disposed of by the special sessions. The latter court being required to be held during the term of the general sessions, as well as in vacation, it not unfrequently happens, that the business of the general sessions is interrupted during a great portion of the day, by the necessity imposed upon the same officers, in their character of a court of special sessions, to dispose of petty offences, solely cognizable in that court. To obviate the inconvenience of this interruption, a degree of haste is required, which is incompatible with a becoming administration of justice, even in the case of the lowest crime or the most abject criminal.

For the purpose of removing these evils—of confining the judges of the courts of sessions to their more appropriate duties—of enabling a more thorough investigation of the lower class of crimes—and of relieving the prisons from the great and unnecessary accumulation of prisoners—the Commissioners propose, that in the city of New-York, police courts be held at the several police offices, on Tuesday and Friday, of each week, by two of the police justices of that city, and by no other officer. (*Sec.* 58.) There will thus be held, three police courts on each of those days, at which the class of cases referred to can be conveniently as well as carefully disposed of.

§ 55. The courts of special sessions now existing, or which may be organized in pursuance of any statutory provision now in force, are abolished; and courts to be known as the police courts, as organized by this code, are substituted in their stead.

§ 56. The police courts have jurisdiction in the cases prescribed in the next section, of the following public offences committed in their respective counties:

1. Petit larceny, not charged as a second offence:

2. Assault and battery, not charged to have been committed riotously, or upon a public officer in the execution of his duties:

3. Poisoning, killing, maiming, wounding or cruelly beating an animal:

4. Racing animals, within one mile of the place where a court is held:

5. Committing a wilful trespass, or severing any produce or article from the freehold, not amounting to grand larceny:

6. Selling poisonous substances, not labelled as required by statute:

7. Maliciously removing, altering, defacing or cutting down monuments or marked trees:

8. Maliciously breaking, destroying or removing mile-stones, mile-boards or guide-boards, or altering an inscription thereon.

The same in substance, as 2 *R. S., 3d ed.* 798, 799, *sec.* 1.

§ 57. The jurisdiction conferred upon the police courts, by the last section, can, however, be exercised only in the following cases:

1. When the party charged, upon his being brought before a magistrate, requests to be tried by a police court: or,

2. When, not having made such request, and after having been required by the magistrate to give bail for his appearance at the next court of sessions in the county, he omits to do so for twenty-four hours.

Taken substantially from 2 *R. S., 3d ed.* 799, *sec.* 2, 3.

§ 58. In the city and county of New-York, these courts must be held at each of the police offices now or hereafter designated by the common council, on Tuesday and Friday of each week, by two of the police justices of that city, and by no other officer.

§ 59. In the other counties, the police court must be held by the magistrate issuing the warrant of arrest, or before whom the defendant is brought to answer the charge.

Substantially the same as 2 *R. S., 3d ed.* 801, *sec.* 23.

PART II.

OF THE PREVENTION OF PUBLIC OFFENCES.

TITLE I. Of lawful resistance.
II. Of the intervention of officers of justice.

This part embraces a variety of practical rules, which have not heretofore been made the subject of statutory enactment. With the exception of provisions in former statutes, for holding parties to keep the peace, and for the suppression of riots by the power of the county, or of the executive authority of the state,—the duties of both officers and citizens, in the prevention of offences, have been left entirely to the regulation of the common law. The consequence has been, that those, who, in a sudden emergency, are required to aid in the preservation of public order, have been left wholly uninformed as to their duty, unless as they may, (which has not often been the case,) have obtained it from the almost inaccessible sources to which they must resort.

The hardship of the necessity, which is thus cast upon the citizen, of either neglecting the performance of a duty which he owes to society, or of doing so at the peril of a transgression of the law, of which he is wholly uninformed, is well expressed by Mr. *Livingston*, in his report of a Criminal Code for Louisiana, *p.* 201. "The first dictates of common sense," says he, "inform an individual that he has a right to defend himself. The laws of society impose the obligation upon him of defending others, and of enforcing the execution of the laws. Magistrates and executive officers are required by official duty, to prevent or arrest violence and depredation; and the military force is told that it must assist the civil power, when legally called on. All this, the general language of the law gives the citizen to understand. But in our state it has never deigned to make such a record of its will as may enable any one, desirous of obeying, to discover boundaries between legal acts and transgression, in the performance of this duty. A correct moral sense, a determination to injure no one, may, with respect to a man's own actions, render a knowledge of positive law less necessary; but no prudence can foresee or prevent the necessity of self-defence; and every man may be called on in some capacity to protect others, or to defend the peace of the state; and yet, with every inclination to perform the duties of a good citizen on these occasions, he is continually arrested by the unavoidable doubts which must arise as to the propriety of personal exertion in the particular case, or the extent to which he may carry it."

Fully concurring in these views, the Commissioners have felt called upon to propose, at least a land mark, by which the right and the duty referred to, are distinctly defined. In doing so, they have deemed it proper to declare the cases in which, according to the common law, lawful resistance to the commission of a public offence may be made, either by the party about to be injured, or by other parties, or by the inintervention of public officers; and have accordingly introduced into the code, a variety of provisions of a practical nature, embracing these important subjects. These provisions include, in additiou to the matters above enumerated, security to keep the peace,—police in cities and villages, and their attendance at exposed places,—and the suppression of riots.

TITLE I.

OF LAWFUL RESISTANCE.

CHAPTER I.

GENERAL PROVISIONS, RESPECTING LAWFUL RESISTANCE.

§60. Lawful resistance to the commission of a public offence may be made,

1. By the party about to be injured:

2. By other parties.

CHAPTER II.

RESISTANCE BY THE PARTY ABOUT TO BE INJURED.

SECTION 61. In what cases, and to what extent.

§ 61. Resistance sufficient to prevent the offence, may be made by the party about to be injured,

1. To prevent an offence against his person:

2. To prevent an illegal attempt, by force, to take or injure property in his lawful possession.

CHAPTER III.

RESISTANCE BY OTHER PARTIES.

SECTION 62. In what cases.

§ 62. Any other person, in aid or defence of the person about to be injured, may make resistance, sufficient to prevent the offence.

TITLE II.

OF THE INTERVENTION OF THE OFFICERS OF JUSTICE.

CHAPTER. I.

INTERVENTION OF PUBLIC OFFICERS, IN GENERAL.

§ 63. Public offences may be prevented by the intervention of the officers of justice,

1. By requiring security to keep the peace:

2. By forming a police in cities and villages, and by requiring their attendance in exposed places:

3. By suppressing riots.

§ 64. When the officers of justice are authorised to act in the prevention of public offences, other persons, who by their command act in their aid, are justified in so doing.

CHAPTER II.

SECURITY TO KEEP THE PEACE.

The provisions of this chapter are condensed and simplified from, and are the same in substance as those contained in 2 *R. S.*, 3*d ed.* 781, 782, *sec.* 2–14.

§ 65. An information may be laid before any of the magistrates mentioned in section 147, that a person has threatened to commit an offence against the person or property of another.

§ 66. When the information is laid before the magistrate, he must examine on oath the complainant and any witnesses he may produce, and must take their depositions in writing, and cause them to be subscribed by the parties making them.

§ 67. If it appear from the depositions, that there is just reason to fear the commission of the offence threatened, by the person complained of, the magistrate must issue a warrant, directed generally to the sheriff of the county, or any constable, marshal or policeman of the city or town, reciting the substance of the information, and commanding the officer forthwith to arrest the person complained of, and bring him before the magistrate.

§ 68. When the person complained of is brought before the magistrate, if the charge be controverted, the magistrate must take testimony in relation thereto. The evidence must be reduced to writing, and subscribed by the witnesses.

§ 69. If it appear that there is no just reason to fear the commission of the offence alleged to have been threatened, the person complained of must be discharged.

§ 70. If, however, there be just reason to fear the commission of the offence, the person complained of may be required to enter into an undertaking, in such sum, not exceeding one thousand dollars, as the magistrate may direct, with one or more sufficient sureties, to abide the order of the next court of sessions of the county, and in the mean time to keep the peace towards the people of this state, and particularly towards the complainant.

§ 71. If the undertaking required by the last section be given, the party complained of must be discharged. If he do not give it, the magistrate must commit him to prison, specifying in the warrant, the requirement to give security, the amount thereof, and the omission to give the same.

§ 72. If the person complained of be committed for not giving security, he may be discharged by any two justices of the peace of the county, or police or special justices of the city, upon giving the same.

§ 73. An undertaking given as provided in section 70, must be transmitted by the magistrate to the next court of sessions of the county.

§ 74. A person, who, in the presence of a court or magistrate, assaults or threatens to assault another, or to commit an offence against his person or property, or who contends with another with angry words, may be ordered by the court or magistrate, to give security as provided in section 70, or if he refuse to do so, may be committed as provided in section 71.

§ 75. A person who has entered into an undertaking to keep the peace, must appear on the first day of the next term of the court of sessions of the county. If he do not, the court may forfeit his undertaking, and order it to be prosecuted, unless his default be excused.

§ 76. If the complainant do not appear, the person complained of may be discharged, unless good cause to the contrary be shown.

§ 77. If both parties appear, the court may hear their proofs and allegations, and may either discharge the undertaking, or require a new one, for a time not exceeding one year.

§ 78. An undertaking to keep the peace is broken, on the failure of the person complained of to appear at the court of sessions, as provided in section 75, or upon his being convicted of a breach of the peace.

§ 79. Upon the district attorney producing evidence of such conviction to the court of sessions to which the undertaking is returned, that court must order the undertaking to be prosecuted; and the district attorney must thereupon commence an action upon it in the name of the people of this state.

§ 80. In the action, the offence stated in the record of conviction, must be alleged as the breach of the undertaking, and is conclusive evidence thereof.

§ 81. Security to keep the peace or be of good behavior, cannot be required, except as prescribed in this chapter.

CHAPTER III.

POLICE IN CITIES AND VILLAGES, AND THEIR ATTENDANCE AT EXPOSED PLACES.

The provisions of this chapter sufficiently explain themselves. Section 82 refers to the special local laws now in force;

and section 83 declares a duty now existing at common law, but which the Commissioners think should be clearly enjoined by statute, for the more effectual preservation of the public peace.

§ 82. The organization and regulation of the police in the cities and villages in this state, are governed by special statutes.

§ 83. The mayor or other officer having the direction of the police in a city or village, must order a force, sufficient to preserve the peace, to attend any public meeting, when he is satisfied that a breach of the peace is to be apprehended.

CHAPTER IV.

SUPPRESSION OF RIOTS.

The provisions of this chapter contained in sections 84 to 87, inclusive, are the same in substance as 2 *R. S. 3d ed.*, 537, *sec.* 101–104. Those contained in sections 88 to 99, inclusive, (except section 96, as to which see the note thereto, *p.* 49, 50,) are in accordance with the spirit of the act to enforce the laws and preserve order; *Laws of* 1845, *p.* 53–56.

§ 84. When a sheriff or other public officer, authorised to execute process, finds or has reason to apprehend that resistance will be made to the execution of the process, he may command as many male inhabitants of his county as he may think proper, and any military company or companies in the county, armed and equipped, to assist him in overcoming the resistance, and if necessary, in seizing, arresting and confining the resisters and their aiders and abettors, to be punished according to law.

§ 85. The officer must certify to the court from which the process issued, the names of the resisters and their aiders and abettors, to the end that they may be proceeded against for contempt.

§ 86. Every person commanded by a public officer to assist him in the execution of process, as provided in section 84, who, without lawful cause, refuses or neglects to obey the command, is guilty of a misdemeanor.

§ 87. If it appear to the governor, that the power of the county is not sufficient to enable the sheriff to execute process delivered to him, he must, on the application of the sheriff, order such a military force from any other county or counties, as is necessary.

§ 88. When persons, to the number of twelve or more, armed with dangerous weapons, or to the number of thirty or more, whether armed or not, are unlawfully or riotously assembled in a city, village or town, the sheriff of the county and his under sheriff and deputies, the mayor and aldermen of the city, or the supervisor of the town, or president or chief executive officer of the village, and the justices of the peace or the police justices of the city, village or town, must go among the persons assembled, or as near to them as possible, and command them, in the name of the people of this state, immediately to disperse.

§ 89. If the persons assembled do not immediately disperse, the magistrates and officers must arrest them, or cause them to be arrested, that they may be punished according to law; and for that purpose, may command the aid of all persons present or within the county.

§ 90. If a person so commanded to aid the magistrates or officers, neglect to do so, he is deemed one of the rioters, and is punishable accordingly.

§ 91. If a magistrate or officer having notice of an unlawful or riotous assembly, mentioned in section 88 neglect to proceed to the place of the assembly, or as near thereto as he can with safety, and to exercise the authority with which he is invested for suppressing the same and arresting the offenders, he is guilty of a misdemeanor.

§ 92. If the persons assembled, and commanded to disperse, do not immediately disperse, any two of the magistrates or officers mentioned in section 88, may command the aid of a sufficient number of persons, and may proceed in such manner as in their judgment is necessary, to disperse the assembly and arrest the offenders.

§ 93. When there is an unlawful or riotous assembly, with intent to commit a felony, or to offer violence to person or property, or to resist by force the laws of the state, and the fact is made to appear to the governor, or to a judge of the supreme court, or to a county judge, or to the sheriff of the county, or to the mayor, recorder or city judge of a city, either of those officers may issue an order directed to the commanding officer of a division, brigade, regiment, battalion or company, to order his command, or any part of it, (describing the kind and number of troops,) to appear at a specified time and place to aid the civil authorities in suppressing violence and enforcing the law.

§ 94. The commanding officer, to whom the order is given, must forthwith obey it; and the troops required must appear at the time and place appointed, armed and equipped with ammunition as for inspection.

§ 95. When an armed force is called out for the purpose of suppressing an unlawful or riotous assembly, it must obey the orders in relation thereto, of either of the officers mentioned in section 93.

§ 96. The commanding officer must act entirely on the defensive, not suffering his men to fire, and permitting them to use their edged or pointed weapons only, to repel actual violence, except in one of the following cases:

1. If an attack be made on any one of the troops, by which his life is in danger, or if an attempt be made to disarm him, which he cannot otherwise avoid, he may defend himself by discharging his fire-arms:

2. If a general attack be made by the rioters upon the troops with fire-arms, missiles or other weapons, by which their lives are indiscriminately put in danger, the commanding officer may order the troops to fire; but not until an endeavor has been made to disperse the rioters, by means less dangerous to persons who may not be engaged in the riot:

3. If the troops cannot be placed between the rioters and the persons or property which they apparently intend to attack, and the illegal purpose of the riot be persevered in by means evidently dangerous to the lives or property of others, although no attack be made on the troops themselves, the magistrates or officers mentioned in section 93, or any two of them, may direct the commanding officer to disperse the rioters; which he is authorised to do by ordering the troops, first to use the bayonet or sword, and if they prove ineffectual to disperse the assembly, but not otherwise, then to discharge their fire-arms against them:

4. The troops must not be brought up to the place, until after the magistrate or other officer has proclaimed the office which he holds, and ordered the assembly to disperse; nor can they make a discharge of fire-arms against the rioters, until after a signal given by three discharges in rapid succession, with blank cartridges, and the lapse of a reasonable time thereafter.

5. Every endeavor must be used, both by the magistrates and civil officers, and by the officer commanding the troops, which can be made consistently with the preservation of life, to induce or force the rioters to disperse, before an attack is made upon them by which their lives may be endangered.

This section is *taken almost literally from Livingston's Criminal Code, p.* 499, 500, *art.* 130. The Commissioners cannot more aptly illustrate the propriety of its introduction, than by quoting the language of that learned jurist, in his report, *p.* 209, 210. "In all riots or insurrections," says he, "the immediate, sometimes the ultimate object is violence to some obnoxious person, or the plunder or destruction of property. To protect these, without the useless sacrifice of human life, is the object of the laws on this subject; therefore, all the provisions of this chapter are intended, if possible, to stop the violence by the fear of an armed force, without having recourse to its dreadful execution. The militia are only to be employed, where the ordinary civil power has been tried and found insufficient. It is, when practicable, to be stationed between the rioters and the object of their intended violence; to act strictly on the defensive, and under the direction of the magistrate. When the use of weapons becomes necessary, to use only those, such as the bayonet and sword, which may be directed solely against the assailants, without endangering the lives of others; leaving the more dangerous and uncontrollable effect of fire-arms, (which may injure the innocent as well as the guilty,) for the last resort. In no case can the armed force be brought up, before the magistrate has displayed a white flag, and ordered the rioters to disperse; and, unless to repel an attack endangering life, no order is to be given for the use of offensive arms, until half an hour has elapsed after the order to disperse without its being obeyed. The remarks on this chapter cannot be closed, without observing the essential difference between the nature of the armed force, the use of which is contemplated by the code, and that employed on similar occasions in England and other countries in Europe. There, it is composed of men entirely under the control of the executive branch of the government, upon which they depend entirely for subsistence. Here, except in the circumstances of their being organized and armed, they differ in nothing, from the power which is at the daily call of the civil officer. Without arms or military array, they are the common *posse comitatus*, as it is called, or the civil power of the county; the same ties of property, of family, of love of country and of liberty, to make them effective instruments for the suppression of disorder, and the most unfit, even when disciplined and armed, that could be chosen to promote any scheme of usurpation. The people can apprehend no danger to their liberties from such a force, even when it is actively employed against themselves, when, deceived by the factious, agitated by party, or indignant against real or imagined injury, they are led to oppose the operation of the laws. Yet with all these safeguards, the legislator would be unfaithful to his trust, who should neglect other precautions, against the necessary evil of employing the weapons of war in the work of peace."

In this Code, the Commissioners have substituted three rapid discharges of blank cartridge, as a signal more likely to arrest attention. The white flag may not readily be seen, by reason of darkness, or it may be found impracticable to display it. Instead of the lapse of half an hour, they propose that a *reasonable time* should be given for the rioters to disperse.

§ 97. When the governor is satisfied that the execution of civil or criminal process has been forcibly resisted in any county, by bodies of men, or that combinations to resist the execution of process by force, exist in any county, and that the power of the county has been exerted, and has not been sufficient to enable the officer having the process, to execute it, he may, on the application of the officer, or of the district attorney or county judge of the county, by proclamation to be published in the state paper, and in such papers in the county as he may direct, declare the county to be in a state of insurrection, and may order into the service of the state such number and description of volunteer or uniform companies, or other militia of the state, as he may deem necessary, to serve for such term, and under the command of such officer or officers as he may direct.

§ 98. The governor may, when he thinks proper, revoke the proclamation authorised by the last section, or declare that it shall cease, at the time and in the manner directed by him.

§ 99. A person who, after the publication of the proclamation authorised by section 97, resists or aids in resisting, the execution of process in a county declared to be in a state of insurrection, or who aids or attempts the rescue or escape of another from lawful custody or confinement, or who resists or aids in resisting, a force ordered out by the governor to quell or suppress an insurrection, is guilty of a felony, and is punishable by imprisonment in a state prison for not less than two years.

PART III.

OF JUDICIAL PROCEEDINGS FOR THE REMOVAL OF PUBLIC OFFICERS, BY IMPEACHMENT OR OTHERWISE.

TITLE I.

OF IMPEACHMENTS.

§ 100. When a civil officer of the state is impeached by the assembly, for wilful or corrupt misconduct in office, the articles of impeachment must be delivered to the president of the senate.

Substantially the same as 2 *R. S.*, 224, 3*d ed.*, *sec.* 14.

§ 101. The president of the senate must thereupon cause the court to be summoned to meet at the capitol in the city of Albany, on a day not less than thirty nor more than sixty days from the day of the delivery of the articles of impeachment. He must also cause a copy of the articles of impeachment, with a notice to appear and answer the same, at the time and place appointed for the meeting of the court, to be served on the defendant, not less than twenty days before the day fixed for the meeting of the court.

No provision is made in the existing statutes, as to the delivery of the articles of impeachment to the defendant. This seems necessary and proper.

As to the place of meeting of the court, this section is in conformity with section 21, *p.* 13.

102. The service must be upon the defendant personally, or if he cannot, upon diligent inquiry, be found in the state, the court, upon due proof of that fact, may order that publication be made in such manner as it deems proper, of a notice requiring him to appear at a specified time and place, and answer the articles of impeachment.

§ 103. If the defendant do not appear, the court, upon proof of service or publication as provided in the last two sections, may of their own motion, or for cause shown, assign another day for hearing the impeachment; or may then, or at any other time which it may appoint, proceed, in the absence of the defendant, to trial and judgment.

§ 104. When the defendant appears, he must answer the articles of impeachment; which he may do, either by objecting to their sufficiency, or of any article therein, or by denying the truth of the same.

§ 105. If the defendant object to the sufficiency of the impeachment, the objection must be in writing, but need not be in any specific form; it being sufficient, if it present intelligibly the grounds of the objection. If he deny the truth of the impeachment, the denial may be oral, and without oath, and must be entered upon the minutes.

§ 106. If an objection to the sufficiency of the impeachment be not sustained by a majority of the members of the court who heard the argument, the defendant must forthwith answer the articles of impeachment. If he plead guilty, or refuse to plead, the court must render judgment of conviction against him. If he deny the matters charged, the court must, at such time as they may appoint, proceed to try the impeachment.

The last five sections are new, but in conformity to the practice in criminal actions, to which this proceeding is analogous. The last sentence in section 98, is the same in substance as 2 *R. S., 3d ed.*, 224, *sec.* 17.

§ 107. The oath or affirmation prescribed by section 22, having been administered, the court must proceed to try and determine the impeachment, and may adjourn the trial from time to time.

The same as 2 *R. S., 3d ed.*, 224, *sec.* 19; except that the words "*or place,*" at the end of the section therein, are omitted in conformity with the judiciary act, *Laws of* 1847, *p.* 319, *sec.* 1; by which the court is required to meet at the capitol in the city of Albany.

§ 108. The defendant cannot be convicted on an impeachment, without the concurrence of two-thirds of the members present; and if two-thirds of the members present do not concur in a conviction, he must be declared acquitted.

The first clause of this section is take from the constitution; *art.* 6, *sec.* 1. The second is taken from 2 *R. S.*, 3*d ed.*, 224, *sec.* 21.

§ 109. After conviction, the court must immediately, or at such other time as it may appoint, pronounce judgment, in the form of a resolution, entered upon the minutes of the court. The vote upon the passage thereof must be taken by yeas and nays, and must also be entered upon the minutes.

§ 110. On the adoption of the resolution, by a majority of the members present, who voted on the question of acquittal or conviction, it becomes the judgment of the court.

§ 111. The judgment may be, that the defendant be suspended and removed from office, or that he be removed from office and disqualified to hold and enjoy a particular office or class of offices, or any office of honor, trust or profit under this state.

§ 112. If judgment of suspension be given, the defendant during the continuance thereof, is disqualified from receiving the salary, fees or emoluments of his office.

The provisions of the last four sections are, in the main, new, but are believed to be in accordance with the powers conferred upon this court by the constitution. By *art.* 6, *sec.* 1, of that instrument, it is provided that "judgment in case of impeachment *shall not extend further* than removal from office, or removal from office and disqualification to hold and enjoy any office of honor, trust or profit under this state," &c. The constitution does not undertake to define the different subordinate degrees, but only the utmost extent, of the punishment. Every thing but the latter, therefore, is in the discretion of the court as limited or defined by legislation. The object of an impeachment, and the effect of a conviction thereon, are to reach the party in his official character only; and he is, by the constitution, still subject to indictment and punishment, in his individual capacity. The only official punishment, therefore, to which he can possibly be subjected, short of removal and disqualification to hold any other office, is that provided for in section 112, of suspension and deprivation of the emoluments of office.

§ 113. A judicial officer cannot exercise his office, after being impeached, until he is acquitted.

Taken from the constitution, *art.* 6, *sec.* 1. The provision of the revised statutes on the subject of suspension was: "Every officer impeached shall be suspended from the exercise of his office until his acquittal." 2 *R. S*, 3*d ed.*, 225, *sec.* 23. It has been thought better to pursue literally the language of the constitution, leaving the question as to the effect of the impeachment, in cases of other than judicial officers, should it arise, open for judicial construction.

§ 114. If the president of the senate be impeached, notice of the impeachment must be immediately given to the senate by the assembly, that another president may be chosen.

Same as 2 *R. S.*, *3d ed.*, 225, *sec.* 24.

§ 115. If the offence for which the defendant is impeached be the subject of an indictment, the indictment is not barred by the impeachment.

This provision is founded upon the concluding clause of *art.* 6, *sec.* 1, of the constitution, which differs in an important particular from the constitution of 1821. By *art.* 5, *sec.* 2, of that instrument, after prescribing the punishment upon a conviction on an impeachment, it was declared that "the party *convicted* shall be liable to indictment and punishment, according to law." The term "*convicted*" was also used in the report of the judiciary committee of the convention which framed the present constitution; *Convention Journal*, *p.* 618; but in the constitution as adopted, the word "*impeached*" was substituted. Neither the journals nor the debates of the convention contain any mention of, or allusion to, the mode in which the change was effected.

TITLE II.

OF THE REMOVAL OF JUSTICES OF THE PEACE, POLICE JUSTICES, AND JUSTICES OF JUSTICES' COURTS, AND THEIR CLERKS.

The power to remove these officers is, as been observed in the note to section 32, *p.* 22, 23, conferred upon the courts of sessions, for the reasons there stated.

The practice, as prescribed in this title, is new, but is deemed convenient and proper. Heretofore, in cases of this kind, no uniform system of practice has existed. The constitution requires, (as did that of 1821,) nothing more than that an opportunity should be given to the accused party to be heard in his defence, and that the cause of removing him should be assigned in the order. In order to establish an uniformity of practice on this subject, the code provides, that an accusation in writing shall be presented to the presiding judge of the court of sessions, stating the offence charged, in ordinary and concise language, without repetition, and in such a manner as to enable a person of common understanding to know what is intended, and verified by the oath of the person making it, to the effect that he believes the charges to be true. The accusation is to be transmitted to the district attorney, who is to serve a copy of it on the defendant, and give him notice of at least twenty days, to appear and answer the accusation, either at a term of the court, or at any other time appointed by the presiding judge. The defendant must appear and answer the accusation, at the time appointed, or at another time to be assigned by the court. If he do not appear, the court may proceed to the trial in his absence. The answer may be, either an objection to the sufficiency of the accusation or a denial of its truth. If the former, the objection must be in writing, but without regard to form, so that it present intelligibly the grounds of the objection; if the latter, it may be oral and without oath. If the objection to the sufficiency of the accusation be not sustained, the defendant is required to answer it forthwith. If he plead guilty or refuse to answer, judgment of conviction is to be rendered. If he deny the accusation, he is to be tried immediately, or at a time to be appointed. He is not to be convicted, without the concurrence of a majority of the members who heard the trial; and if a majority do not convict him, he is to be acquitted. On conviction, judgment of removal is to be given, and entered upon the minutes, assigning therein the causes of the removal.

§ 116. An accusation in writing against a justice of the peace, a police justice or a justice of a justice's court, or any of their clerks, for wilful or corrupt misconduct in office, may be presented to the presiding judge of the court of sessions of the county, in or for which the officer accused is elected or appointed.

§ 117. The accusation must state the offence charged, in ordinary and concise language, without repetition, and in such a manner as to enable a person of common understanding to know what is intended; and must be verified by the oath of the person making it, to the effect that he believes the charges therein contained to be true.

§ 118. After receiving the accusation, the judge to whom it is delivered must forthwith cause it to be transmitted to the district attorney of the county, who must cause a copy thereof to be served upon the defendant, and require by written notice, of not less than twenty days, that he appear before the court of sessions of the county and answer the accusation, at a specified time, which must be either at a term of the court, or at any other time appointed by the presiding judge, by a written order filed with the clerk.

§ 119. The defendant must appear at the time appointed in the notice, and answer the accusation, unless, for sufficient cause, the court assign another day for that purpose. If he do not appear, the court may proceed to hear and determine the accusation in his absence.

§ 120. The defendant may answer the accusation either by objecting to the sufficiency thereof, or of any article therein, or by denying the truth of the same.

§ 121. If he object to the legal sufficiency of the accusation, the objection must be in writing, but need not be in any specific form; it being sufficient, if it present intelligibly the grounds of the objection.

§ 122. If he deny the truth of the accusation, the denial may be oral and without oath, and must be entered upon the minutes.

§ 123. If an objection to the sufficiency of the accusation be not sustained, the defendant must answer the accusation forthwith.

§ 124. If the defendant plead guilty, or refuse to answer the accusation, the court must render judgment of conviction against him. If he deny the matters charged, the court must immediately, or at such time as they may appoint, proceed to try the accusation.

§ 125. The defendant cannot be convicted, without the concurrence of a majority of the members of the court who heard the trial; if a majority do not concur in a conviction, he must be declared acquitted.

§ 126. Upon a conviction, the court must immediately, or at such other time as they may appoint, pronounce judgment that the defendant be removed from office. But to warrant a removal, the judgment must be given by a majority of the members of the court, who heard the trial, and must be entered upon the minutes, assigning therein the causes of removal.

PART IV.

OF THE PROCEEDINGS IN CRIMINAL ACTIONS PROSECUTED BY INDICTMENT.

TITLE I.

OF THE LOCAL JURISDICTION OF PUBLIC OFFENCES.

§ 127. Every person, whether an inhabitant of this or any other state or country, or of a territory or district of the United States, is liable to punishment, by the laws of this state, for a public offence committed by him therein, except where it is by law cognizable exclusively in the courts of the United States.

Declaratory of the existing law. Substantially in the language used by the Massachusetts Commissioners, *ch.* 3, *sec.* 1.

§ 128. When the commission of a public offence commenced without this state, is consummated within its boundaries, the defendant is liable to punishment therefor in this state, though he were out of the state at the time of the commission of the offence charged, if he consummated it in this state, through the intervention of an innocent or guilty agent, or by any other means proceeding directly from himself; and in such case, the jurisdiction is in the county in which the offence is consummated.

Declaratory of a principle much discussed, and in respect to which great doubts have existed, but which has at length been established by the case of *The People* v. *Adams*, 3 *Denio*, 190, which was affirmed by the court of appeals, *Adams* v. *The People*, 1 *Comst.* 173.

§ 129. When an inhabitant or resident of this state, by previous appointment or engagement, fights a duel, or is concerned as second therein, out of the jurisdiction of this state, and in the duel a wound is inflicted upon a person, whereof he dies in this state, the jurisdiction of the offence is in the county where the death happened.

Same as 2 *R. S.*, 3*d ed.* 746, *sec* 6.

§ 130. When an inhabitant of this state shall have left the same, for the purpose of eluding the operation of the provisions of the statutes relating to duelling and challenges to fight, with the intent or for the purpose of doing any of the acts prohibited therein, the jurisdiction is in the county of which the offender was an inhabitant when the offence was committed, or in any county in which, in the opinion of the governor, the evidence can be most conveniently obtained and produced, to be designated by him by a written appointment, filed in the office of the clerk of that county.

Same as 2 *R. S.*, 3*d ed.* 772, *sec.* 1 – 6.

§ 131. When a public offence is committed, partly in one county and partly in another, or the acts or effects thereof, constituting or requisite to the consummation of the offence, occur in two or more counties, the jurisdiction is in either county.

Taken from the report of the Massachusetts Commissioners, *ch.* 3, *sec.* 4 See also 2 *R. S.*, 3*d ed.* 813, *sec.* 47.

§ 132. When a public offence is committed on the boundary of two or more counties, or within five hundred yards thereof, the jurisdiction is in either county.

Same as 2 *R. S.*, *3d ed.*, 813, *sec.* 45.

§ 133 When an offence is committed in this state, on board a vessel navigating a river, lake or canal, or lying therein in the prosecution of her voyage, the jurisdiction is in any county through which the vessel is navigated in the course of her voyage, or in the county where the voyage terminates.

Same as 2 *R. S.*, *3d ed.*, 813, *sec.* 44. The words "or lying therein, in the prosecution of her voyage," are in conformity with the construction given to this section, by the supreme court, in *The People* v. *Hulse*, 3 *Hill*, 309.

§ 134. The jurisdiction of an indictment,

1. For forcibly and without lawful authority seizing and confining another, or inveigling or kidnapping him, with intent, against his will, to cause him to be secretly confined or imprisoned in this state, or to be sent out of the state, or to be sold as a slave, or in any way held to service, or of selling or i any manner transferring for a term the services or labor of a black, mulatto, or other person of color, forcibly taken, inveigled or kidnapped from this state, to any other state, place or country; or,

2. For decoying, or taking, or enticing away a child under the age of twelve years, with intent to detain and conceal it from its parent, guardian, or other person having the lawful charge of the child; or,

3. For inveigling, enticing or taking away an unmarried female of previous chaste character, under the age of twenty-one years, for the purpose of prostitution:

Is in any county in which the offence is committed, or into or out of which the person, upon whom the offence was committed, may in the commission of the offence, have been brought, or in which an act was done by the defendant in instigating, procuring, promoting, aiding in or being an accessary to the commission of the offence, or in abetting the parties concerned therein.

This section is in conformity with the existing statutes, so far as relates to kidnapping. 2 *R. S. 3d ed*, 753, *sec.* 28, 29, 32, 33.

The same principle is applicable to decoying away children, and abduction. In the first of these cases, it has been recommended by the Massachusetts Commissioners. *Ch.* 3, *sec.* 11.

§ 135. When the offence either of bigamy or of incest is committed in one county, and the defendant is apprehended in another, the jurisdiction is in either county.

Same as 2 *R. S. 3d ed.*, 773, *sec.* 10.

§ 136. When property feloniously taken in one county, by burglary, robbery, larceny or embezzlement, has been brought into another, the jurisdiction of the offence is in either county. But if, before the conviction of the defendant in the latter, he be indicted in the former county, the sheriff of the latter must upon demand, deliver him to the sheriff of the former county, upon being served with a copy of the indictment, and upon a receipt endorsed thereon by the sheriff of the former county, of the body of the defendant; and is, on filing the copy of the indictment and the receipt, exonerated from all liability in respect to the custody of the defendant.

The first sentence of this section is in conformity with 2 *R. S. 3d ed.*, 813, *sec.* 50. The second sentence is in accordance with the decision of the supreme court, in *The People v. Mason*, 9 *Wend.* 505.

§ 137. In the case of an accessary after the fact in the commission of a public offence, the jurisdiction is in the county where the offence of the accessary was committed, notwithstanding the principal offence was committed in another county.

Same as 2 *R. S. 3d ed.*, 813, *sec.* 48; except that it is confined to accessaries *after* the fact; the distinction between an accessary *before* the fact and a *principal* being abolished by this code.

§ 138. When an act charged as a public offence, is within the jurisdiction of another state, country or territory, as well as of this state, a conviction or acquittal thereof in the former, is a bar to a prosecution or indictment therefor in this state.

Same as 2 *R. S. 3d ed.*, 746, *sec.* 7.

§ 139. When an offence is within the jurisdiction of two or more counties, a conviction or acquittal thereof in one county, is a bar to a prosecution or indictment therefor in another.

Necessary to prevent two convictions for the same offence in different counties.

TITLE II.

OF THE TIME OF COMMENCING CRIMINAL ACTIONS.

§ 140. There is no limitation of time, within which a prosecution for murder must be commenced. It may be commenced at any time after the death of the person killed.

Same as 2 *R. S.*, *3d ed*, 812, *sec.* 37.

§ 141. An indictment for a public offence must be found within two years after its commission, in the following cases:

1. Falsely representing or personating any person, and in such assumed character marrying another:

2. Inveigling, enticing or taking away an unmarried female of previous chaste character, under the age of twenty-five years, for the purpose of prostitution:

3. Seducing and having illicit connection with an unmarried female of previous chaste character, under promise of marriage.

The limitation of a prosecution for falsely representing or personating any person, and in such assumed character marrying another, is, by the existing statutes, the same as prescribed in this section. 2 *R. S.*, 3*d ed.*, 763, *sec.* 49. So also, in the case of abduction. *Laws of* 1848, *p.* 118, *ch.* 105. Seduction has been included, as being within the principle of the other cases. *See Laws of* 1848, *p.* 148, *ch.* 111.

§ 142. In all other cases, an indictment for a public offence must be found withing three years after its commission.

Same as 2 *R. S.*. 3*d ed.*, 812, *sec.* 37.

§ 143. If, when the offence is committed, the defendant be out of the state, the indictment may be found within the term herein limited after his coming within the state; and no time, during which the defendant is not an inhabitant of or usually resident within the state, is part of the limitation.

Substantially the same as 2 *R. S.*, 3*d ed.*, 812, *sec.* 37.

§ 144 An indictment is found, within the meaning of the last three sections, when it is duly presented by the grand jury in open court, and there received and filed.

Intended to render the rule as to the period of computation, definite and certain.

TITLE III.

OF THE INFORMATION, AND PROCEEDINGS THEREON TO THE COMMITMENT INCLUSIVE.

CHAPTER I.

THE INFORMATION.

§ 145. The information is the allegation made to a magistrate, that a person has been guilty of some designated public offence.

§ 146. A magistrate is an officer, having power to issue a warrant for the arrest of a person charged with a public offence.

The definition of the term "magistrate," as used throughout the code, is here given, to save the unnecessary repetition of the official names of the officers who come within this description.

§ 147. The following persons are magistrates:

1. The judges of the supreme court:

2. The county judges, and special county judges:

3. The judges of the superior court of the city of New-York:

4. The judges of the court of common pleas of the city of New-York:

5. City judges:

6. Justices of the peace:

7. Police and other special justices, appointed or elected in a city, village, or town:

8. The mayors and recorders of cities.

The same as 2 *R. S.*, 3*d ed.*, 792, *sec.* 1; except in the omission of aldermen, who, in the opinion of the Commissioners, need not possess the powers of magistrates, and the addition of the city judges.

CHAPTER II.

THE WARRANT OF ARREST.

§ 148. When an information is laid before a magistrate, of the commission of a public offence, he must examine on oath the informant or prosecutor, and any witnesses he may produce, and take their depositions in writing, and cause them to be subscribed by the parties making them.

Substantially the same as 2 *R. S., 3d ed.* 793, *sec.* 2.

§ 149. The depositions must set forth the facts stated by the prosecutor and his witnesses, tending to establish the commission of the offence and the guilt of the defendant.

This section is intended to obviate the loose practice in use in the taking of depositions, by which, instead of stating the particular facts, conclusions of law are stated. It is very common, for example, to state in cases of larceny, nothing more, than that the property was feloniously stolen, taken and carried away, and that the complainant suspects that it was so stolen, &c., by the person charged. To sustain an indictment for perjury on the affidavit, if false, the particular matters of fact should be stated; leaving the conclusion of law to the magistrate.

§ 150. If the magistrate be satisfied therefrom, that the offence complained of has been committed, and that there is reasonable ground to believe that the defendant has committed it, he must issue a warrant of arrest.

Substantially the same as 2 *R. S., 3d ed.* 793, *sec.* 3.

§ 151. A warrant of arrest is an order in writing in the name of the people, signed by a magistrate, commanding the arrest of the defendant, and may be substantially in the following form:

"County of *Albany*, [or as the case may be.]

"In the name of the people of the state of New-York: To any sheriff, constable, marshal or policeman in this state, [or in the county of *Albany*, or as the case may be, as provided in sections 155 and 156.]

"Information upon oath having been this day laid before me, that the crime of, [designating it,' has been committed, and accusing C. D., thereof,

"You are therefore commanded, forthwith to arrest the above named C. D., and bring him before me, at— [naming the place,] or in case of my absence or inability to act, before the nearest or most accessible magistrate in this county.

"Dated at the *City of Albany*, [or'as the case may be,] this day of , 1850."

E. F. *Justice of the peace*,
[or as the case may be.]

§ 152. The warrant must specify the name of the defendant, or if it be unknown to the magistrate, the defendant may be designated therein by any name. It must also state an offence in respect to which the magistrate has authority to issue the warrant, and the time of issuing it, and the city, town or village where it is issued, and be signed by the magistrate with his name of office.

§ 153. The warrant must be directed to, and executed by, a peace officer.

§ 154. A peace officer is a sheriff of a county, or a constable, marshal or policeman of a city, town or village.

§ 155. If the warrant be issued by a judge of the supreme court, or of the superior court or court of common pleas, in the city and county of New-York, or by a county judge, or by the presiding judge of a city court, it may be directed generally to any sheriff, constable, marshal or policeman in the state, and may be executed by any of those officers to whom it may be delivered.

§ 156. If it be issued by any other magistrate, it may be directed generally to any sheriff, constable, marshal or policeman in the county in which it is issued, and may be executed in that county; or if the defendant be in another county, it may be executed therein, upon the written direction of a magistrate of that county endorsed upon the warrant, signed by him, with his name of office, and dated at the city, town or village where it is made, to the following effect: "This warrant may be executed in the county of *Monroe*," [or as the case may be.]

§ 157. The endorsement mentioned in the last section, cannot, however, be made, unless upon the oath of a credible witness, in writing, endorsed on or annexed to the warrant, proving the hand writing of the magistrate by whom it was issued. Upon this proof, the magistrate endorsing the warrant is exempted from liability to a civil or criminal action, though it afterwards appear that the warrant was illegally or improperly issued.

The last three sections are in substantial conformity with 2 *R. S*, *3d ed.*, 793. *sec.* 4—6.

§ 158. If the offence charged in the warrant be a felony, the officer making the arrest must take the defendant before the magistrate, who issued the warrant, or some other magistrate in the same county, as provided in section 162.

Substantially the same as 2 *R. S.*, *3d ed.*, 794, *sec.* 11.

§ 159. If the offence charged in the warrant be a misdemeanor, and the defendant be arrested in another county, the officer must, upon being required by the defendant, take him before a magistrate in that county who must admit the defendant to bail, and take bail from him accordingly.

Substantially the same as 2 *R. S.* 3d *ed.* 793, *sec.* 8.

§ 160. On taking bail, the magistrate must certify that fact on the warrant, and deliver the warrant and undertaking of bail to the officer having charge of the defendant. The officer must then discharge the defendant from arrest, and must without delay, deliver the warrant and undertaking to the clerk of the court at which the defendant is required to appear.

Substantially the same as 2 *R. S.*, *3d ed.*, 794, *sec.* 9.

§ 161. If, on the admission of the defendant to bail, as provided in section 159, bail be not forthwith given, the officer must take the defendant before the magistrate who issued the warrant, or some other magistrate in the same county, as provided in the next section.

Substantially the same as *2 R. S., 3d ed.*, 794, *sec.* 10.

§ 162. When, by the preceding sections of this chapter, the defendant is required to be taken before the magistrate who issued the warrant, he may, if the magistrate be absent or unable to act, be taken before the nearest or most accessible magistrate in the same county. The officer must, at the same time, deliver to the magistrate, the warrant with his return endorsed and subscribed by him.

Founded upon and the same in principle as 2 *R. S., 3d ed.*, 794, *sec.* 12.

§ 163. The defendant must, in all cases, be taken before the magistrate without unnecessary delay.

§ 164. If the defendant be taken before a magistrate other than the one who issued the warrant, the depositions on which the warrant was granted must be sent to that magistrate, or if they cannot be procured, the prosecutor and his witnesses must be summoned to give their testimony anew.

The last two sections are new, but necessary to carry out the spirit of the previous secti ns.

CHAPTER III.

ARREST BY AN OFFICER, UNDER A WARRANT.

The provisions of this chapter, and of chapters 4, 5 and 6, which follow, are intended to define the rights and duties, as well of public officers as of private citizens, in the arrest with or without a warrant, of persons charged with crime. In respect to this it may be remarked, as has been already done in reference to the right of lawful resistance to the commission of an offence, *p.* 36, 37, that they have been hitherto left wholly unregulated by positive or written law. If, in the one case, a system of appropriate regulation might have been excusably omitted, the Commissioners do not well see, with what propriety they could have overlooked its introduction, in respect to this branch of duty. The good order of society requires, in order that crime may be detected and punished, that the arrest of criminals should in all cases be justified, where, but for the existence of a well defined right, it would elude both detection and punishment. It is upon this great principle, that the rules of the common law, by which the extent of this right have been defined, are established. If it could be reasonably supposed, that in the thousand emergencies which arise, the public officer or the citizen was so well versed in those principles, as to be able safely to apply them, there would be no necessity for legislation. But when it is remembered, that in all these cases he acts at the peril of a lawful resistance, even to the extent of taking his life by the party arrested, or of the consequences of a civil action, where he has transcended his powers, the duty of the legislature, clearly to define them, would seem to be beyond dispute. It is a case of no unfrequent occurrence, that in the attempted arrest of a public offender, the citizen, who incurs great risk for the vindication of the law, is subjected to consequences like these; and the books are not barren of cases where the sacrifice of the life of an innocent person, acting under a mistaken but honest view of his duty, has been successfully defended, on the ground that he had transcended his authority. It may be true, that the common law sufficiently defines it; but it is equally true, that the sources of that law are hidden from the view of those who are most frequently called upon to exercise the power in question; and it is for the legislature to determine, whether it should be left in uncertainty and doubt, when by a few well timed enactments, the evil can be so easily remedied. The importance of this subject was not overlooked by Mr. Livingston, in his report of a criminal code, already referred to; and the Commissioners cannot forbear quoting the forcible and eloquent remarks with which he urges upon the legislature, the important and solemn duty of clear and distinct legislation upon this subject. "Officers of justice," says he, "often uneducated and overbearing men, either do not know, or designedly exceed the bounds of their authority. The accused sometimes submits to illegal acts; at others, resists those to which he ought to submit. The citizen, when legally called on to enforce the execution of the law, refuses to obey, or makes himself liable to a prosecution, for aiding in an illegal arrest; and it is believed that of all the cases of murder, manslaughter, violent assault and false imprisonment, reported in the books, no inconsiderable proportion will be found to have arisen from ignorance of rights and duties in granting warrants, in making arrests or resisting them—ignorance inevitable, from the state of our laws; for where, (it is asked on this, as it has been on former occasions,) where is the necessary information to be obtained? The written law is silent; the oracles who pronounce that which is unwritten, only speak when the case has already happened; and the unfortunate citizen, called on to act or suffer at a moment's warning, is forced to do it at his own risk; for those to whom he has confided the care of framing rules for his government, have hitherto obstinately refused, or negligently omitted to dictate them. It is time that this duty should be done: it is more than time that this reproach should be taken away from our legislation. You declare that every man who kills an officer in the legal discharge of his duty, is guilty of murder, and shall suffer death. You say that resistance to an unlawful arrest is justifiable; and you cruelly and wantonly refuse to explain what is a lawful and which an unlawful arrest. You refer to the contradictory and confused decisions of courts in a foreign country, for information on this all-important point. Do you understand those laws? Are they clear?—Deign then to clothe them in the words of legislative authority: publish them to your constituents. Are the cases contradictory?—Tell us which of them is the law. Are they confused and uncertain?—Explain them. Do you not understand them yourselves?—Then how should we your constituents be guided by them, in matters too on which depend life or death? If the rules now offerered are not approved, frame others. When obedience is exacted, under such a sanction, the least the people can require, is to be clearly and explicitely told what it is they are to obey. I feel that I am repeating here, ideas that have been more than once expressed, and that I am urging former arguments with a zeal that may be deemed indiscreet, and, I hope, is unnecessary; but I have a great, a holy duty to perform, and I dare not leave any part of it undone, from the fear of giving offence, or the hope of conciliating favor, much less that of gaining applause." *Liv. Crim. Code, p.* 211, 212.

The importance of this subject has been felt, and the necessity of legislation upon it admitted, by high legal authority in England. In the eighth report of the Commissioners on Criminal Law, (p. 43–48,) no less than thirty-one articles have been devoted to detailed provisions on the subject of arrests by constables and private persons without a warrant; and in their notes to the provisions recommended by them, they have collected a body of common law authority, the extent of which, of itself, by showing the utter impossibility of its being brought within the reach of the officer and the citizen, proves the necessity of its being compressed into a few plain and intelligible directions.

§ 165. Arrest is the taking of a person into custody, that he may be held to answer for a public offence.

§ 166. An arrest may be either,

1. By a peace officer, under a warrant;

2. By a peace officer, without a warrant: or

3. By a private person.

§ 167. Every person must aid an officer in the execution of a warrant, if the officer require his aid and be present and acting in its execution.

§ 168. If the offence charged be a felony, the arrest may be made on any day, and at any time of the day or night. If it be a misdemeanor, the arrest cannot be made on Sunday, or at night, unless upon the direction of the magistrate endorsed upon the warrant.

§ 169. An arrest is made by an actual restraint of the person of the defendant, or by his submission to the custody of the officer.

§ 170. The defendant is not to be subjected to any more restraint, than is necessary for his arrest and detention.

§ 171. The officer must inform the defendant that he acts under the authority of the warrant, and must also show the warrant, if required.

§ 172. If, after notice of intention to arrest the defendant, he either flee or forcibly resist, the officer may use all necessary means to effect the arrest.

§ 173. The officer may break open an outer or inner door or window of a dwelling-house, to execute the warrant, if, after notice of his authority and purpose, he be refused admittance.

§ 174. An officer may break open an outer or inner door or window of a dwelling house, for the purpose of liberating a person, who, having entered for the purpose of making an arrest, is detained therein, or when necessary for his own liberation.

CHAPTER IV.

ARREST BY AN OFFICER, WITHOUT A WARRANT.

175. A peace officer may, without a warrant, arrest a person,

1. For a public offence, committed or attempted in his presence:

2. When the person arrested has committed a felony, although not in his presence:

3. When a felony has in fact been committed, and he has reasonable cause for believing the person arrested to have committed it:

4. On a charge, made upon reasonable cause, of the commission of a felony by the party arrested.

§ 176. To make an arrest, as provided in the last section, the officer may break open an outer or inner door or window of a dwelling-house, if, after notice of his office and purpose, he be refused admittance.

§ 177. He may also, at night, without a warrant, arrest any person whom he has reasonable cause for believing to have committed a felony, and is justified in making the arrest, though it afterwards appear that a felony had not been committed.

§ 178. When arresting a person without a warrant' the officer must inform him of his authority and the cause of the arrest, except when he is in the actual commission of a public offence, or is pursued immediately after an escape.

§ 179. He may take before a magistrate, a person, who, being engaged in a breach of the peace, is arrested by a by-stander and delivered to him.

§ 180. When a public offence is committed in the presence of a magistrate, he may, by a verbal or written order, command any person to arrest the offender, and may thereupon proceed as if the offender had been brought before him on a warrant of arrest.

CHAPTER V.

ARREST BY A PRIVATE PERSON.

§ 181. A private person may arrest another,

1. For a public offence, committed or attempted in his presence:

2. When the person arrested has committed a felony, although not in his presence:

3. When a felony has been in fact committed, and he has reasonable cause for believing the person arrested to have committed it.

§ 182. He must, before making the arrest, inform the person to be arrested of the cause thereof, and require him to submit, except when he is in the actual commission of the offence, or when he is arrested on pursuit immediately after its commission.

§ 183. If the person to be arrested have committed a felony, and a private person, after notice of his intention to make the arrest, be refused admittance, he may break open an outer or inner door or window of a dwelling house, for the purpose of making the arrest.

§ 184. A private person, who has arrested another for the commission of a public offence, must, without unnecessary delay, take him before a magistrate, or deliver him to a peace officer.

CHAPTER VI.

RE-TAKING, AFTER AN ESCAPE OR RESCUE.

§ 185. If a person arrested, escape or be rescued, the person from whose custody he escaped or was rescued, may immediately pursue and retake him, at any time, and in any place in the state.

§ 186. To retake the person escaping or rescued, the person pursuing may, after notice of his intention and refusal of admittance, break open an outer or inner door or window of a dwelling house.

CAAPTER VII.

EXAMINATION OF THE CASE, AND DISCHARGE OF THE DEFENDANT OR HOLDING HIM TO ANSWER.

The subject embraced in this chapter has engaged the most anxious attention of the Commissioners. The existing practice in relation to it admits of great and essential improvement, not merely in its details, but in its principles. By that practice, the magistrate is required, upon the defendant being brought before him, to summon the witnesses on whose oath the warrant is founded, and to proceed to examine them in the presence of the defendant. He is then to take the examination of the defendant, after cautioning him that he is not bound to answer; and after the examination, he is to take the testimony of any witnesses whom the defendant may produce. Upon the completion of this proceeding, he is to decide whether there is sufficient cause to hold the defendant to answer, and to commit or discharge accordingly. 2 *R. S.* 793-795, *Sec.* 2-22.

An examination of the statutory provisions upon this subject, now in force, and a close observation of the course of practice under them, have convinced the commissioners of the necessity of some safeguards, which the law has not yet provided, being thrown around the rights of the defendant. While they are aware that many undue means have been afforded by the technicalities of the law, and in some instances by the laxness with which it has been administered,—evils for which they have endeavored to provide an adequate remedy,—they have resolved in this, as in other respects, to recommend the adoption of such proivsions as will protect the substantial rights of a party accused of crime. It is one of the proudest attributes of the system under which we live, and of the constitution by which the blessings of life, liberty and property are guaranteed, that no matter what may be the enormity of his crime,—no matter how great the intensity of public excitement against him,—no matter how abject or degraded he may be,—the life and liberty of the citizen are protected until they are forfeited by due process of law. It is no less true, that punishment derives its moral force, not so much from its severity, as from the certainty that it has been inflicted in compliance with the spirit of those institutions, and after every opportunity has been afforded to the accused, of defending himself by those means which the law has given for the protection of the innocent. The theory of our law is, that every man is presumed innocent until the contrary is established; and any portion of our system which assumes a contrary principle, demands prompt and immediate correction.

To no portion of the subjects referred to in this report, do these remarks apply with greater force, than to the initiatory proceedings for the ascertainment of the defendant's guilt. In the proceedings after his commitment, and upon his trial, his instincts teach him to seek the aid of those whose profession and experience may ensure the protection of his rights. But in the early stages of the accusation,—when he is hurried before a magistrate upon a charge of which he may be innocent, and of which, even if it be otherwise, the law has not yet adjudged him guilty,—the first dictate of duty seems to be, to inform him of his rights, and to afford him every opportunity to throw around himself the protection of the law. And yet, according to the existing system of practice, upon the idle fiction that every man is presumed to know the law, he is supposed to be informed of the first right secured to him by the constitution,—that of appearing and defending himself by counsel. If he happen to be ignorant of this, the examination of the case proceeds, and testimony is taken against him, which may be illegal in its character, or which, without the substantial opportunity for a cross examination, may in some contingencies be used against him on his trial.

Against this prejudice the Commissioners propose to guard, by requiring the magistrate to inform the defendant of his right to the aid of counsel in every stage of the proceedings, and before any further proceedings are had,—to allow the defendant a reasonable time to procure counsel, — and to send for such counsel in the city or town, as the defendant may name. *Sec.* 187, 188.

By the existing practice, when the defendant is brought before a magistrate, no time is limited, within which the case must be examined, preliminarily to the discharge or commitment of the defendant. This state of things leads to an abuse which the Commissioners have reason to believe has not unfrequently existed,—namely, the arrest of a person upon testimony which would be insufficient to hold him, and his detention until evidence can be hunted up, upon which the magistrate might be warranted in committing him. If the Commissioners had had power to collect the facts, in support of this and other statements which they will have occasion to submit, they do not doubt that they would have been able to lay before the legislature, the most conclusive evidence of the existence of this abuse. Nor has it stopped here. Cases have existed, where the defendant, after a long detention, in what is termed the *discretion* of the magistrate, has been discharged, for want of proof sufficient to hold him; or when he could be no longer held, has been committed as a vagrant, as the only device by which time could be obtained for procuring testimony against him.

The Commisssoners do not, in these remarks, intend to undervalue the importance of great vigilance, on the part of public officers, in the detection and prosecution of crime; but they are entirely at a loss to perceive the justice of a system, by the practical operation of which, the liberty of a citizen, be he who he may, is to be placed entirely at the discretion of the magistrate. When a man is charged with an offence, no one will deny that he should not be deprived of his liberty, for a moment, unless upon such proof as furnishes reasonable cause to believe him guilty of the crime. Or if he may be arrested without such proof, it will hardly be contended that he should, for any purpose, be unlimitedly held in custody as discretion or caprice may dictate. Yet such is the operation of the present system. "As soon as may be," is the uncertain limit now fixed for the examination of the defendant:—a limit too indefinite, where the liberty of a citizen is involved, unless he is to be presumed guilty of an offence, upon the charge of which there is not evidence sufficient even to warrant his examination.

To obviate this injustice, the Commissioners propose that the examination must be completed at one sitting, unless the magistrate, for good cause shown by affidavit, adjourn it; the adjournment to be for not more than two days at each time, nor more than six days in all, unless by consent or on motion of the defendant. *Sec.* 190.

§ 187. When the defendant is brought before a magistrate upon an arrest either with or without warrant on a charge of having committed a public offence, the magistrate must immediately inform him of the charge against him, and of his right to the aid of counsel in every stage of the proceedings, and before any further proceedings are had.

§ 188. He must also allow the defendant a reasonable time to send for counsel, and adjourn the examination for that purpose; and must, upon the request of the defendant, require a peace officer to take a message to such counsel in the town or city, as the defendant may name. The officer must without delay and without fee, perform that duty.

§ 189. The magistrate must, immediately after the appearance of counsel, or if none appear and the defendant require the aid of counsel, after waiting a reasonable time therefor, proceed to examine the case.

§ 190. The examination must be completed at one session, unless the magistrate, for good cause shown by affidavit, adjourn it. The adjournment cannot be for more than two days at each time, nor more than six days in all, unless by consent or on motion of the defendant.

§ 191. If an adjournment be had for any cause, the magistrate must commit the defendant for examination, or discharge him from custody, upon the deposite of money as provided in this code, as security for his appearance at the time to which the examination is adjourned.

If the examination be for any cause adjourned, the magistrate has now no power to admit the defendant to bail Some power should exist, to relieve the defendant from actual custody, during the progress of the examination. The Commissioners propose that this may be done upon the deposite of a sum to be fixed by the magistrate. Bail could not well be taken, according to the system prescribed on that subject, which requires a full opportunity for examination into the sufficiency of the proposed bail; a proceeding which would occupy nearly all the time fixed by section 190, for the examination of the charge.

§ 192. The commitment for examination is by an endorsement signed by the magistrate, on the warrant of arrest, to the following effect: "The within named A. B., having been brought before me under this warrant, is committed for examination, to the sheriff of the county of ," or, in the city and county of New-York, "to the keeper of the city prison of the city ef New-York."

§ 193. At the examination, the magistrate must, in the first place, read to the defendant the depositions of the witnesses examined on the taking of the information, and if the defendant request it, must summon the witnesses so examined, if they be in the county. He must also issue subpœnas for additional witnesses required by the prosecutor or the defendant.

More full and explicit than the existing provision, 2 *R. S*, 3*d. ed.*, 794, *sec.* 14, but not variant in principle.

§ 194. The witnesses must be examined in the presence of the defendant, and may be cross-examined in his behalf.

Same as provided in 2 *R. S.*, 3*d. ed.*, 794, *sec.* 15.

§ 195. When the examination of the witnesses on the part of the people is closed, the magistrate must distinctly inform the defendant, that it is his right to make a statement in relation to the charge against him, (stating to him the nature thereof;) that the statement is designed to enable him, if he see fit, to answer the charge and to explain the facts alleged against him, that he is at liberty to waive making a statement, and that his waiver cannot be used against him on the trial.

§ 196. If the defendant waive his right to make a statement, the magistrate must make a note thereof, immediately following the depositions of the witnesses against the defendant; but the fact of his waiver cannot be used against the defendant on the trial.

§ 197. If the defendant choose to make a statement, the magistrate must proceed to take it in writing, without oath, and must put to the defendant the following questions only :

What is your name and age?

Where were you born?

Where do you reside, and how long have you resided there?

What is your business or profession?

Give any explanation you may think proper, of the circumstances appearing in the testimony against you, and state any facts which you think will tend to your exculpation.

§ 198. The answer of the defendant to each of the questions must be distinctly read to him, as it is taken down. He may thereupon correct or add to his answer, and it must be corrected until it is made conformable to what he declares is the truth.

According to the present practice, after the examination of the witnesses for the people is closed before the magistrate, the next stage of the proceedings is what is called the "examination" of the defendant. This examination must be taken in all cases of felony, and in cases of misdemeanor, if the defendant require it, or the magistrate think it necessary. Before taking it, the defendant is to be informed of the charge against him, and is to be allowed a reasonable time to send for counsel, who may examine and cross-examine the witnesses. This, however, it is to be observed, is not to be done until the witnesses on the part of the prosecution are examined. 2 *R. S.*, *3d ed.* 794, *sec.* 14, 15. At the commencement of the examination, the defendant is to be informed by the magistrate that he is at liberty to refuse to answer any question which may be put to him; but no restriction is placed upon the magistrate, in regard to the questions which may be put. The answers of the defendant are to be reduced to writing and read to him, with the right on his part to correct them; and when made conformable to what he declares to be the truth, are to be authenticated by the magistrate.

In this proceeding, the Commissioners have discovered principles which they deem at war with the rights of the accused. The very term "examination," which is used in the statute, and the proceedings pointed out as the mode of taking it, all seem to be a departure from the spirit of the constitutional declaration, which provides that "no person shall be compelled, in any criminal case, to be a witness against himself." The object of the examination, as it was originally instituted, was, not to place the defendant in the hands of a cross-examining magistrate, who might, according to the principles of the French practice, by the exercise of ingenuity, extract from him evidence of his guilt. But it was designed, in the humane and benign spirit of the common law, to give the defendant an opportunity, by a voluntary explanation, to exculpate himself from the charge. In this light it has uniformly been regarded by the courts. The very provision of the existing statutes, requiring that the defendant shall be cautioned by the magistrate that he is not bound to answer, clearly shows that this was the design of the legislature.

The same view of the subject was taken by Mr. Livingston, in restricting the examining magistrate, as is substantially proposed by the Commissioners, *sec.* 197, "to give any explanation he may think proper of the circumstances appearing in the testimony against him, and to state any facts that he thinks will tend to his exculpation." *Liv. Crim. Code*, 507, *art.* 173.

In the same spirit, also, the English Commissioners, in their eighth report, already referred to, *p.* 55, *art.* 32, proposed a provision that "if any case be made out against the accused, he must be asked what he has to say against the charge, and his answer or defence is to be taken down in writing."

Notwithstanding, however, the obvious policy of the law, in providing for the defendant this mode of exculpation, it has been, not unfrequently, and it might almost be said without exaggeration, uniformly, supposed in practice, that the examination of the defendant was designed for wholly different purposes. Instead of his being informed, as the fact is, that it is furnished to him as a shield and is not to be used against him as a sword, he is by a loose course of practice, if no other motive be imputable, led to believe that it is one of the ordinary proceedings against him, having in view the establishment of his guilt. He is accordingly examined by a series of searching questions,—oftentimes proceeding upon the assumption of his guilt,—and is driven to the alternative of equivocating as to facts, or of denying circumstances plainly true, or of what is occasionally his resort, declining to answer. Those who are in the slightest degree conversant with criminal trials, can well attest how successfully the adoption of either of these alternatives, can be used against the defendant on his trial. If he equivocate, or if he deny a circumstance the existence of which is certain, the most conclusive inference of guilt is drawn against him. And if, as his only refuge from the torture of a cross-examination, he decline to answer the question, he learns, when it is too late, the fatal character of his error, in supposing that his legal privilege will protect him from the inference of guilt uniformly urged against him from the mere fact of his silence.

To counteract, by appropriate legislation, consequences like these, seems to be a plain and palpable duty. It is but carrying out the spirit of the rule familiar to every lawyer, and having its foundation in the plainest reason, that the exercise of a right shall not prejudice the party by whom it is exerted. It was well said by an eminent English judge, when a counsel was commenting on the refusal of a witness to answer a question, the answer to which tended to criminate him, that the comment was unfair, because the law gave the witness the right to decline, and that it would cease to be a right, the moment it could be used to his prejudice.

Deeply impressed with the correctness of these views, the Commissioners have proposed to dispense entirely with this examination, and to substitute in its place, what the law designed should alone be furnished, an opportunity to the defendant to make a statement in his exculpation. They accordingly provide, that when the examination of the witnesses on the part of the people is closed, the magistrate shall inform the defendant that it is his right to make a statement in relation to the charge against him; that the statement is designed to enable him, if he see fit, to answer the charge, and to explain the facts alleged against him;—that he is at liberty to waive it;—and that his waiver cannot be used against him on the trial. *Sec.* 19[illegible]. If he elect to make the statement, it is then to be taken by the magistrate, who, instead of being left at liberty to put every form of question which his ingenuity may suggest, is restricted to asking the defendant general questions as to his age and residence, and the like, and to asking him to give any explanation he may think proper, of the circumstances appearing against him, and to state any facts which he thinks will tend to his exculpation. *Sec.* 197.

§ 199. The statement must be reduced to writing by the magistrate, or under his direction, and authenticated in the following form:

1. It must set forth in detail, that the defendant was informed of his rights as provided in section 195, and that after being so informed, he made the statement.

2. It must contain the questions put to him, and his answers thereto, as provided in sections 197 and 198.

3. It may be signed by the defendant, or he may refuse to sign it: but if he refuse to sign it, his reason therefor must be stated as he gives it:

4. It must be signed and certified by the magistrate.

This section carries out fully the principle of those just referred to, and is substantially in accordance with the views of Mr. Livingston, as embodied in his Code of Criminal Procedure. *Liv. Crim. Code*, 507, *art.* 173, *subd.* 2.

§ 200. After the waiver of the defendant to make a statement, or after he has made it, his witnesses, if he produce any, must be sworn and examined.

Same as 2 *R. S.*, 3*d ed.* 794, *sec.* 14, modified to adapt it to the waiver of a statement by the defendant, as provided in the code, *sec.* 188, 189. See also, *Liv. Crim Code*, 507, *art.* 174.

§ 201. The witnesses produced on the part either of the people or of the defendant, can not be present at the examination of the defendant; and while a witness is under examination, the magistrate may exclude all witnesses who have not been examined. He may also cause the witnesses to be kept separate, and to be prevented from conversing with each other, until they are all examined.

Same as 2 *R. S.*, *3d ed.* 795, *sec.* 19.

§ 202. The magistrate must also, upon the request of the defendant, exclude from the examination, every person, except the clerk of the magistrate, the prosecutor and his counsel, the attorney-general, the district-attorney of the county, the defendant and his counsel, and the officer having the defendant in custody.

The object of this section is to carry out more fully the spirit of the last. The policy of the statutes has always been, to prevent the concocting of a charge against a defendant, upon collusive or false testimony. The law excludes the witnesses, while another witness or the prisoner is under examination, with this view. The object of the rule may be wholly defeated, if, though not present, one witness may be informed of the testimony of another, by persons who are present.

Another advantage will result from the adoption of this section. If the examination must necessarily be public, the consequence may be that the testimony upon the mere preliminary examination will be spread before the community, and a state of opinion created, which, in cases of great public interest, will render it difficult to obtain an unprejudiced jury. The interests of justice require that the case of the defendant should not be prejudged, if it can be avoided; and no one can justly complain, that until he is put upon his trial, the dangers of this pre-judgment are obviated.

To guard the rights of the defendant against a secret examination, the section provides that it shall not be conducted in private, unless at his request.

§ 203. The testimony given by each witness must be reduced to writing, as a deposition, by the magistrate or under his direction, and authenticated in the following form:

1. It must state the name of the witness, his place of residence, and his business or profession:

2. It must contain the questions put to the witness, and his answers thereto; each answer being distinctly read to him as it is taken down, and being corrected or added to, until it is made conformable to what he declares is the truth:

3. If a question put be objected to on either side, and overruled, or the witness decline answering it, that fact, with the ground on which the question was overruled, or the answer declined, must be stated:

4. The deposition must be signed by the witness, or if he refuse to sign it, his reason for refusing must be stated in writing, as he gives it:

5. It must be signed and certified by the magistrate.

A portion of the examination of the case by the magistrate, which has been conducted with extreme looseness, prejudicial alike to the people and the defendant, is the examination of the witnesses for and against the charge. The existing statutes 2 *R. S.* 3*d ed*, 795, *sec.* 2), require nothing more than that the magistrate shall examine the witnesses and reduce their testimony to writing, and require their signatures thereto. In taking down the testimony, the practice has been very common, to take such portions of the statements of the witness, as the magistrate deems material; omitting entirely the questions put, and professing to give nothing more than the substance of the evidence. When it is remembered how essential it is, in testing the credibility of witnesses who have been previously examined, to point with certainty to their former statements on oath, relating to the same subject, and how important this right may become to the people as well as to the defendant, it will be readily admitted that the testimony in the precise form in which it was given, leaving no room for doubt or misconstruction as to its meaning, should be carefully preserved. Daily experience shows, that in the mode in which depositions are taken by the examining magistrate, when the attempt is made to impeach a witness by the production of his deposition, nothing is more common than his escape from the force of the contradiction, by his own statement and that of the magistrate, that the substance of the testimony only, and not the language of the witness, had been taken.

It is proposed to correct this evil, by requiring that the deposition of the witness contain the questions put and the answers given; each answer being distinctly read to the witness, as it is taken down, and being corrected or added to until it is made conformable with what he declares is the truth; and that if a question put be objected to and overruled, or the witness decline answering it, that fact, with the ground on which the question was overruled or the answer declined, must be stated.

§ 204. The magistrate or his clerk must keep the depositions taken on the information or on the examination, and the statement of the defendant, if any, until they are returned to the proper court; and must not permit them to be inspected by any person, except a judge of a court having jurisdiction of the offence, the attorney-general, the district attorney of the county, and the defendant and his counsel.

§ 205. A violation of the provisions of the last section is punishable as a misdemeanor.

The last two sections have in view the same objects as are stated in the *note to sec.* 202, *p.* 94, and enforce them by the same penalty as is now applied by statute, to the disclosure of the fact that an indictment for a felony has been found against a party not arrested. 2 *R. S., 3d ed.* 812, *sec.* 39. The principle in both cases is the same, namely, to prevent the defeat or prejudice of justice, and the penalty should be the same.

§ 206. If the defendant be held to answer the charge, the magistrate or his clerk having the custody of the depositions taken on the information or examination, and of the statement of the defendant, must, on payment of his fees at the rate of five cents for every hundred words, and within two days after demand, furnish to the defendant, or his counsel, a copy of the depositions and statement, or of either of them, or permit him to take a copy.

A practice, which has been extensively pursued, and which, in the view of the Commissioners, is incompatible with the due administration of justice, is the refusal to permit the defendant to have copies of the depositions taken against him. It has been customary in some portions of the state, when the depositions are returned to the court, to deliver them over to the district attorney, by whom they are retained with as much secrecy as a counsel in a civil action would use in concealing from his adversary, the testimony by which success was to be attained. The right of the defendant to the inspection of the depositions, has been frequently resisted by public prosecutors, as incompatible with the interests of the prosecution.

It has been said in justification of this practice, that if the opportunity were afforded to the defendant of inspecting these depositions, he might thereby be permitted to escape under cover of a false defence; and even courts, when applied to, to enforce what the Commissioners believe to be the right of the defendant, have refused to lend their aid in its enforcement. It is a rule of the common law, that the defendant shall have every reasonable opportunity to meet and answer the charges and proofs against him; and the Commissioners are not disposed to treat with seriousness, the answer that the right should not exist, because by possibility it may be abused. The theory of a prosecution is, that the defendant is called upon to explain circumstances appearing against him, which, if unexplained, tend to establish his guilt; and to deny him this right, is to convert a criminal prosecution into the means of destroying the defendant, by springing upon him on the trial, when wholly unprepared to explain them, a state of facts, which, if the opportunity had been allowed, would have admitted of abundant explanation.

In accordance with views similar to those here expressed, the British parliament have within a few years enacted, "that all persons who shall be held to bail or committed to prison for any offence against the laws, shall be entitled to require and have, on demand, (from the person who shall have the lawful custody thereof, and who is thereby required to deliver the same,) copies of the examinations of the witnesses respectively upon whose depositions they have been so held to bail or committed, on payment of a reasonable sum for the same, not exceeding 1½*d.* for each folio of 90 words: provided, that if such demand shall not be made before the day appointed for the commencement of the assizes or sessions, at which the trial is to take place, such person shall not be entitled to have any copy of such examination of witnesses, unless the judge or other person to preside at such trial shall be of opinion, that such copy may be made and delivered without delay or inconvenience to such trial; but it shall nevertheless be competent for such judge, &c, if he shall think fit, to postpone such trial, on account of such copy of the examination of witnesses not having been previously had by the party charged. And all persons under trial, are entitled, at the time of their trial, to inspect, without fee or reward, all depositions (or copies thereof,) which have been taken against them, and returned into the court before which such trial shall be had. 6 & 7 *W.* 4 *ch.* 114, *sec.* 3, 4.

§ 207. After hearing the proofs, and the statement of the defendant, if he have made one, if it appear, either that a public offence has not been committed, or that there is no sufficient cause to believe the defendant guilty thereof, the magistrate must order the defendant to be discharged, by an endorsement on the depositions and statement, signed by him, to the following effect: "There being no sufficient cause to believe the within named A. B. guilty of the offence within mentioned, I order him to be discharged."

§ 208. If, however, it appear from the examination, that a public offence has been committed and that there is sufficient cause to believe the defendant guilty thereof, the magistrate must, in like manner, endorse on the depositions and statement, an order, signed by him, to the following effect: "It appearing to me by the within depositions (and statement, if any,) that the offence therein mentioned, [or any other offence, according to the fact, stating generally the nature thereof,] has been committed, and that there is sufficient cause to believe the within named A. B. guilty thereof, I order that he be held to answer the same."

§ 209. If the offence be not bailable, the following words, or words to the same effect, must be added to the endorsement: "and that he be committed to the sheriff of the county of ," [or in the city and county of New-York, "to the keeper of the city prison of the city of New-York."]

§ 210. If the offence be bailable, and bail be taken by the magistrate, the following words, or words to the same effect, must be added to the endorsement mentioned in section 208; "and I have admitted him to bail, to answer, by the undertaking hereto annexed."

§ 211. If the offence be bailable and the defendant be admitted to bail, but bail have not been taken, the following words, or words to the same effect, must be added to the endorsement mentioned in section 208: "and that he be admitted to bail in the sum of dollars, and be committed to the sheriff of the county of ," [or in the city and county of New-York, "to the keeper of the city prison of the city of New-York,"] until he give such bail."

§ 212. If the magistrate order the defendant to be committed as provided in sections 209 and 211, he must make out a commitment, signed by him, with his name of office, and deliver it, with the defendant, to the officer to whom he is committed, or if that officer be not present, to a peace officer, who must immediately deliver the defendant into the proper custody, together with the commitment.

§ 213. The commitment must be to the following effect:

"County of *Albany*, [or as the case may be.]
"In the name of the people of the State of New-York:
"To the sheriff of the county of *Albany*," [or in the city

and county of New-York, "to the keeper of the city prison of the city of New-York:"]

"An order having been this day made by me, that A. B. be held to answer, upon a charge of [stating briefly the nature of the offence,] you are commanded to receive him into your custody and detain him, until he be legally discharged."

Dated at *the city of Albany*, [or as the case may be,] this day of , 1850."

C. D., *Justice of the peace*."
[or as the case may be.]

The last seven sections are more full than the existing statutory provisions, 2 *R. S.*, 3*d ed.* 795, *sec.* 21, 22, and contain practical forms as well as directions, which can be conveniently carried out.

§ 214. On holding the defendant to answer, the magistrate may take from each of the material witnesses examined before him on the part of the people, a written undertaking, to the effect that he will appear and testify at the court to which the depositions and statement are to be sent, or that he will forfeit the sum of one hundred dollars.

§ 215. When the magistrate is satisfied, by proof on oath, that there is reason to believe that any such witness will not appear and testify, unless securitybe required, he may order the witness to enter into a written undertaking, with such sureties, and in such sum as he may deem proper, for his appearance as specified in the last section.

§ 216. Infants and married women, who are material witnesses against the defendant, may in like manner be required to procure sureties for their appearance, as provided in the last section.

§ 217. If a witness, required to enter into an undertaking to appear and testify, either with or without sureties, refuse compliance with the order for that purpose, the magistrate must commit him to prison until he comply or be legally discharged.

The last four sections are the same in substance, as 2 *R. S., 3d ed.* 795, *sec.* 22, 24, 25, 26.

§ 218. When, however, it satisfactorily appears, by the examination on oath of the witness or any other person, that the witness is unable to procure sureties, he may be forthwith conditionally examined, on behalf of the people, in the manner and with the effect provided in this code, and must thereupon be discharged.

§ 219. The last section does not apply to the prosecutor, or to an accomplice in the commission of the offence charged.

The reasons for the introduction of section 218, are stated in the note to *sec.* 12, *p.* 7–9. The exception in *sec.* 219, as to the prosecutor or an accomplice, is obviously just. In neither of these cases, should the defendant be deprived of the benefit of a cross-examination before the trial jury.

§ 220. When a magistrate has discharged a defendant, or has held him to answer, as provided in sections

207 and 208, he must return to the next court of oyer and terminer of the county, or city court having power to inquire into the offence, by the intervention of a grand jury, (or in the city and county of New-York, to the next court of sessions,) at or before its opening on the first day, the warrant, if any, the depositions, the statement of the defendant, if he have made one, and all undertakings of bail, or for the appearance of witnesses, taken by him.

This section is the same as 2 *R. S.*, 3*d ed.* 796, *sec.* 28, 29, except in requiring the return of the papers, when the defendant is discharged, as well as when he is held to answer. A due regard for the interests of the public, seems to render it proper, that an examination of the case by the court, should be had, notwithstanding the discharge of the defendant by the magistrate; to the end that it may be submitted to the grand jury, if in the opinion of the court, the magistrate has erred in discharging the defendant. It is, moreover, proper that these proceedings should be preserved as public records, instead of being left, as they may be, under the present system, exposed to loss or to uses prejudicial to an innocent party.

TITLE IV.

OF PROCEEDINGS AFTER COMMITMENT, AND BEFORE INDICTMENT.

CHAPTER I.

PRELIMINARY PROVISIONS.

SECTION 221, 222. Public offences, how prosecuted.

The provisions contained in this chapter, are properly introductory to the subject, and in conformity with the rule declared in *sec.* 8, *p.* 4 — 6.

§ 221. All public offences prosecuted in a court of oyer and terminer, or in a court of sessions, or in a city court, must be prosecuted by indictment, except as provided in the next section.

§ 222. When, however, the proceedings are had for the removal of justices of the peace, police justices or justices of justices' courts, or their clerks, before a court of general sessions, they may be commenced by an accusation in writing, as provided in sections 116 and 117.

CHAPTER II.

FORMATION OF THE GRAND JURY.

§ 223. A grand jury is a body of men, not less than sixteen nor more than twenty-three in number, returned at stated periods from the citizens of the county, before a court of competent jurisdiction, and chosen by lot, and sworn to inquire of public offences committed or triable in the county.

§ 224. A grand jury must be drawn for every term of the following courts:

1. The court of oyer and terminer, except in the city and county of New-York:

2. The court of sessions of the city of New-York, and the city courts.

§ 225. A grand jury may also be drawn,

1. For every other court of sessions, when specially ordered by the court, or by the board of supervisors:

2. For the court of oyer and terminer in the city and county of New-York, upon the order of a judge of the supreme court elected in the first judicial district.

These sections are designed to save the necessity of the summoning of a grand jury for all the criminal courts. They direct that it be summoned for the oyer and terminer only, (except in the city of New-York,) and for the city courts. For the oyer and terminer in New-York, and for the sessions in other counties, a grand jury may be summoned upon a special order.

It is believed that under this provision, as many grand juries will be summoned as the public interests require, while the harmony of the system, in reference to the return of complaints by magistrates to certain prescribed courts, as provided in section 220, *p.* 102, will be promoted by it.

§ 226. If made by the court, the order must be entered upon its minutes, and a copy thereof filed with the county clerk, at least thirty days before the term for which the jury is ordered. If made by the board of supervisors, a copy thereof, certified by the clerk of the board, must be filed with the county clerk, at least thirty days before the term; and when so filed, is conclusive evidence of the authority for drawing the jury.

§ 227. A misdescription, however, of the title of the court, does not affect the validity of the order, if it can be plainly understood therefrom, what court is intended.

§ 228. If at least sixteen persons, qualified to serve as grand jurors, and who have been summoned, do not appear, or if the number of grand jurors attending be reduced below sixteen, the court may order the sheriff to summon a sufficient number, (specifying it,) to complete the grand jury.

Taken from 2 *R. S.*, 3*d ed.*, 810, *sec.* 23.

§ 229. In the city and county of New-York, the names of persons so required to complete the grand jury, must be drawn by the county clerk, in the presence of the sheriff or under sheriff, and of one or more members of the court, from the grand jury box of undrawn ballots, in the manner in which the grand jury was drawn.

§ 230. In any other county, the names of the persons required to complete the grand jury may, in the discretion of the court, be drawn as provided in the last section, or may be publicly designated by the court, from the by-standers or the body of the county.

It frequently happens that the requisite number do not attend; and in that case, the sheriff is directed by the court to summon a sufficient number to complete the panel. In the performance of this duty, he is placed under no restriction, but is at liberty to summon such persons as he may choose. Without intending to impute to any public officer, the wilful neglect or corrupt performance of his duties, it cannot fail to strike the common sense of every man, as somewhat unaccountable, that the law, after having made the most full provision for drawing the jury by lot from the county box, in the presence of three sworn public officers, and after imposing upon them every restraint adapted to the prevention of unfairness, should in the last resort, have left the selection of sometimes a large portion of the grand jury, to the mere will of the officer, whose caprice in the selection of the jury originally it was the very object of the law to prevent. The provisions of the existing statutes on this subject, to which allusion has just been made, imposing checks upon the possibility of abuse in this particular, were introduced from no idle jealousy of the integrity of the officer, but because, in the excitements, political and otherwise, which not unfrequently arise, it was deemed wise to protect it from suspicion ; and no sound reason can be given, why that principle should not be fully carried out, especially where it can be done without inconvenience.

§ 231. The sheriff must accordingly, in the manner required in respect to the grand jurors originally drawn, forthwith summon the persons whose names are drawn or designated, as provided in the last two sections, who must attend and serve as if they had been originally summoned as grand jurors, and subject to the same penalties, unless excused or discharged by the court.

Same as 2 *R. S.*, 3*d ed.*, 810, *sec.* 24.

§ 232. If an offence be committed during the sitting of the court, after the discharge of the grand jury, the court may, in its discretion, direct an order to be entered, that the sheriff summon another grand jury.

Same as 2 *R. S.*, 3*d ed.*, 811, *sec.* 34.

§ 233. The names of the persons to be summoned, if in the city and county or New-York, must be drawn in the same manner as the original grand jurors. If in in any other county, they may be drawn or designated as prescribed in section 230.

§ 234. The sheriff must accordingly, in the manner required in respect to the grand jurors originally drawn, forthwith summon the persons whose names are so drawn or designated, who must attend and serve, as if they had been originally summoned as grand jurors, and subject to the same penalties, unless excused or discharged by the court.

The remarks in the note to sections 229 and 230, are applicable to the last two sections.

§ 235. No more than twenty-three, nor less than sixteen persons can be sworn on a grand jury; nor can a grand jury proceed to any business, unless sixteen members at least are present.

Taken from 2 *R. S. 3d ed* 810, *sec.* 26.

§ 236. When more than twenty-three persons summoned as grand jurors attend to serve, the clerk must prepare separate ballots containing their names, folded as nearly alike as possible, and so that the names cannot be seen, and must deposit them in a box. He must then openly draw out of the box twenty-three ballots; and the persons whose names are drawn, constitute the grand jury. The names remaining in the box, as well as those drawn, must be returned to the box of drawn grand jurors.

This section is new, but designed to provide for a case of frequent occurrence, and which is omitted in the existing statutes.

§ 237. A person held to answer a charge fcr a public offence, may challenge the panel of the grand jury, or an individual grand juror.

§ 238. A challenge to the panel may be interposed, for one or more of the following causes only:

1. That the requisite number of ballots was not drawn from the grand jury box of the county:

2. That notice of the drawing of the grand jury was not given:

3. That the drawing was not had, in the presence of the officers designated by the code of civil procedure: and

4. That the drawing was not had, at least fourteen days before the court.

§ 239. A challenge to an individual grand juror may be interposed, for one or more of the following causes only:

1. That he is a minor:

2. That he is an alien:

3. That he is insane:

4. That he is the prosecutor upon a charge against the defendant:

5. That he is a witness on the part of the prosecution, and has been served with process or bound by an undertaking, as such:

6. That a state of mind exists on his part, in reference to the case or to either party, which satisfies the court, in the exercise of a sound discretion, that he

cannot act impartially and without prejudice to the substantial rights of the party challenging.

§ 240. The challenges mentioned in the last three sections may be oral, and must be entered upon the minutes, and tried by the court, in the same manner as challenges in the case of a trial jury which are triable by the court.

§ 241. The court must allow or disallow the challenge, and the clerk mnst enter its decision upon the minutes.

§ 242. If a challenge to the panel be allowed, the grand jury are prohibited from inquiring into the charge against the defendant by whom the challenge was interposed. If they should, notwithstanding, do so, and find an indictment against him, the court must direct it to be set aside.

§ 243. If a challenge to an individual grand juror be allowed, he can not be present at, or take part in the consideration of the charge against the defendant who interposed the challenge, or the deliberations of the grand jury thereon.

§ 244. The grand jury must inform the court of a violation of the last section, and it is punishable by the court as a contempt.

By 2 *R. S.*, *3d. ed.*, 810, *sec.* 27, 28, it is provided, that " a person held to answer to any criminal charge, may object to the competency of any one summoned to serve as a grand juror, before he is sworn, on the ground that he is the prosecutor or complainant upon any charge against such person, or that he is a witness on the part of the prosecution, and has been subpœnaed or been bound in a recognizance as such; and if such objection be established, the person so summoned shall be set aside; and that no challenge to the array of grand jurors, or to any person summoned to serve as a grand juror, shall be allowed in any other cases than such as are above specified."

The sections proposed are intended as a substitute for these provisions. They are much more full, and the principles which they embody seem just and reasonable. They are, that the panel may be set aside, where such irregularities have occurred in drawing the grand jury, as depart from the substantial requirements of the law, and as, in their own nature, tend to the prejudice of the defendant; and that the challenges to individual grand jurors extend to cases of personal disqualification, and to the case of the prosecutor, or of one on whose part, such a state of mind exists, as satisfies the court, in the exercise of a sound discretion, that he cannot act impartially, and without prejudice to the substantial rights of the party challenging.

§ 245. From the persons summoned to serve as grand jurors, and appearing, the court must appoint a foreman. The court must also appoint a foreman, when a person already appointed is discharged or excused, before the grand jury are dismissed.

The first part of this section is taken from 2 *R. S.*, 810, 3*d. ed.*, *sec.* 26; the remaining portion is intended to provide for a case of frequent occurrence, but for which no provision is now made.

§ 246. The following oath must be administered to the foreman of the grand jury: "You, as foreman of this grand jury, shall diligently inquire and true presentment make, of all public offences against the people of this state, committed or triable within this county, [or in a city court, "within this city,"] of which you shall have or can obtain legal evidence: you shall present no person through malice, hatred or ill will, nor leave any unpresented through fear, favor, or affection, or for any reward, or the promise or hope thereof; but in all your presentments or indictments, you shall present the truth, the whole truth, and nothing but the truth, according to the best of your skill and understanding. So help you God!"

§ 247. The following oath must be immediately thereupon administered to the other grand jurors present: "The same oath which your foreman has now taken before you on his part, you and each of you shall well and truly observe on your part. So help you God!"

§ 248. If, after the foreman is sworn, any grand juror appear, and be admitted as such, the oath, as prescribed in section 246, must be administered to him, commencing, "You, as one of this grand jury," and so on, to the end.

The oath prescribed in the last three sections, is substantially the same as at present It puts, however, in plainer language, the precise duties of the grand jury.

§ 249. The grand jury being impanelled and sworn, must be charged by the court. In doing so, the court must read to them the provisions of this code, from section 253 to section 269, both inclusive, and must give them such information. as it may deem proper, as to the nature of their duties, and any charges for public offences returned to the court, or likely to come before the grand jury. The court need not, however, charge them respecting violations of a particular statute.

This section makes it the duty of the court to charge the grand jury as to their duties, as those duties are defined in the code. It also dispenses with the necessity of charging them as to the violation of particular statutes; a portion of the charge which is uniformly regarded as a mere formality, and which scarcely ever in practice leads to an indictment for the offences referred to, although they are daily and openly committed.

§ 250. The grand jury must then retire to a private room, and inquire into the offences cognizable by them.

Declaratory of the existing practice.

§ 251. The grand jury must appoint one of their number as clerk, who must preserve minutes of their proceedings, (except of the votes of the individual members on a presentment or indictment,) and of the evidence given before them.

Taken from 2 *R. S.*, *3d. ed*, 811, *sec.* 30.

§ 252. The grand jury, on the completion of the business before them, must be discharged by the court; but whether the business be completed or not, they are discharged by the final adjournment of the court.

CHAPTER III.

POWERS AND DUTIES OF THE GRAND JURY.

In approaching the subject of the powers and duties of the grand jury, the Commissioners have felt much embarrassment, and have, therefore, devoted to it, the patient and laborious consideration which it demanded. The value of this institution is at the present day variously regarded. By some, it is deemed of the highest importance, as furnishing, by reason of its secrecy, a most valuable aid in the efficient detection and punishment of crime; while, by others, it has been regarded, by reason of that very secrecy, as subversive of the rights, and destructive of the liberty of the citizen. Upon which side the balance of the argument preponderates, it is not for the Commissioners to say, or even to suggest. One thing, however, is certain; that the preservation of its usefulness, like that of every other department in the administration of the laws, depends upon a clear and well understood definition of its powers. To leave these vague and unlimited, is to make the institution itself an object of jealousy and alarm. It is retained and perpetuated by the constitution, and it is not the design of the Commissioners to abridge any of its just attributes, or to propose anything which can in the slightest degree impair its usefulness or efficiency. But they at the same time, regard it as their duty, to propose in respect to it, such provisions as will carry into effect its objects, accordcording to the spirit of the institution itself, and in harmony alike with the interests of the public and of the citizen. It had its origin in England, at a time when the conflicts between the power of the government on the one hand, and the rights of the subject on the other, were fierce and unremitting; and it was wrung from the hands of the crown, as the only means by which the subject, appealing to the judgment of his peers, under the immunity of secrecy, and of irresponsibility for their acts, could be rendered secure against oppression. Happily, in our country, no illustration of its value in this respect, has been furnished. But it was nevertheless, introduced among us in the same spirit in which it took its rise in the mother country, and as the very language of the constitution shows, was designed to be a means of protection to the citizen against the dangers of a false accusation, or the still greater peril of a sacrifice to public clamor. That language is, that "no person shall be held to answer for a capital or otherwise infamous crime, (except in cases which are enumerated,) unless on presentment or indictment of a grand jury."

Acting within this sphere, the institution of a grand jury may be justly regarded, not merely as a safeguard to private right, but as an indispensable auxiliary to public justice; and within these limits, it is the duty alike of the legislature and of the people, to sustain it in the performance of its duties. But when it transcends them,—when it can be used for the gratification of private malignity,—or when, wrapping itself in the secresy and immunity with which the law invests it, its high prerogatives are prostituted to purposes frowned upon by every principle of law and of human justice,—it may become an instrument dangerous alike to public and to private liberty.

That it has been so used, is a fact which admits of no disguise. Cases are not unfrequent, where parties stimulated by avarice or revenge, have found their way into the secrecy of a grand jury room, and upon a state of facts which would not warrant the commitment of the defendant in any other form, have succeeded in obtaining an indictment against him.

It is well known, among the legal profession at least, that the just legislation, which has abolished the imprisonment of the debtor in a civil action, has led to an unexampled number of complaints, against many whose greatest crime was their misfortune, upon the allegation of the fraudulent procurement of property; and the experience of every lawyer will attest the fact, that there are few cases in which the disappointed creditor would not, if he could, invoke the aid of the criminal law, as the means, not so much of punishment, as of coercion. In cases of this kind, as well as in others rather of a private than of a public nature, it will be readily perceived, there is some danger that the grand jury may be used for purposes not only unnecessary, but absolutely hostile to the interests of the public. This is but one class of cases illustrating the danger of allowing the grand jury, under their general power to inquire into all offences triable within their county, to hear complaints in the first instance and to originate accusations. But a still more striking example of the danger of this unrestricted power, is to be found in the fact, that cases have existed, where prosecutors who have been defeated before the examining magistrate, have availed themselves of the privilege of the subpœna of the district attorney, to present themselves before the grand jury, and upon a one sided statement obtain an indictment. The powers and duties of the grand jury being in this respect wholly undefined, the practical result has been, that private information conveyed to a grand juror, or the permission of the district attorney, (who may literally be said to keep the keys of the grand jury room,) has led to numberless prosecutions prompted by private interest, and to speculations npon the fears of the unfortunate, which would have been defeated by a public scrutiny, or by an opportunity afforded to the accused of explaining or defending himself against the charge.

If the grand jury is to be preserved in its purity,—if the confidence of the people is to be enlisted in its behalf, without which its usefulness must cease,—these things must be corrected by wholesome legislation. The grand jury was designed to be, and the Commissioners are willing to admit, in most cases is, a body of discreet and thinking men, called together to protect the public interests, and not to be converted into instruments of private cupidity or vengeance. Instead of being an accusing party, it is and ought to be a judicial tribunal. Instead of acting hastily and unadvisedly, upon an accusation against the citizen, and placing him upon trial for the gratification of private feeling, it should be made to stand upon the higher ground of vindicating the dignity of the public law. To do this, limits must be set to the extent of its powers, and restrictions must be placed upon their exercise. Without these,—rendered necessary by the secrecy by which the grand jury is surrounded,—the full assurance cannot exist, that public and private interests are safe in its hands.

Under the present system, these safeguards cannot be found. Within the sphere of what they choose to consider their duties, the grand jury is omnipotent. Accusations in which the public are deeply concerned, may be dismissed without a question. Indictments may be preferred upon slight evidence or upon no evidence; and the action of the grand jury is beyond the reach of the law. And in short, acting, as it does, without responsibility, there is no slight reason to fear, that from being conservative in its aims, it may ultimately degenerate into an object of private aversion. From the abuses of which it is susceptible, and which have been too often practised under its unconscious sanction, it is not to be disguised, that even now its moral power is waning, and unless preserved by legislation, may eventually cease.

These remarks are made in no unfriendly spirit to the existence of this institution, but from a firm conviction, that to preserve its usefulness, and indeed its very existence, the restraints, as well as the safeguards of the law, must be thrown around its action. To effect this object, the first principle which the Commissioners assume is, that the functions of the grand jury as an accuser and as a judge should be separated. It is not proposed to abridge their powers, in respect to the inquiry into the commission of crime. Those seem to be an inherent element in their composition; but the proceedings which are taken upon them should be essentially different. When the accused is arrested and brought before a magistrate, an opportunity is afforded him of answering the charge, and of explaining the circumstances tending to establish his guilt. A responsible accuser is also presented, to whom he may look for redress, if the accusation be malicious or unfounded; but when he is accused by the grand jury, this protection is denied him, and he is dragged before the bar of justice, to answer a charge possibly as false in its substance, as it may be malicious in the motive by which it is prompted. A course of practice which results in this injustice, is not to be defended upon any principle sanctioned by the wisdom of the common law. Its theory is, that every man shall have a full opportunity to meet an accusation against him; and it is a violation of that theory, that he should be subjected to any stage of condemnation, without the privilege of being heard in his own defence. The Commissioners have accordingly proposed two modes of proceeding, upon the action of the grand jury; first, that where the defendant has been held to answer the charge, and in no other case, the grand jury may, if they believe him guilty, find an indictment against him; second, that if, upon an investigation of a charge against him, whether originated by themselves or presented by another, they believe he is guilty of a public offence, they must proceed by presentment. The indictment is defined to be an accusation, presented by the grand jury to a competent court, charging the defendant with a public offence. The presentment is an informal statement by the grand jury, representing that a public offence has been committed which is triable within the county and that there is reasonable ground for believing that the defendant has committed it. *Sec.* 256, 257. Upon the former, he is of course to be held for trial; but upon the latter, he is only to be held for examination before a magistrate, in the same manner as if an information had been given to the magistrate in the first instance, and with the same opportunity for explanation or defence.

These provisions, though new in practice, are in principle no innovations. In the criminal code recently adopted in Virginia, a similar provision is contained. *Laws of Virginia*, 1848, *page* 145, *sec.* 16. And it may be safely asserted, that the principle contained in them is in consonance with the common law itself. In a late case in Pennsylvania, the office of a grand jury was stated by judge King, to be confined to the examination of such cases as were presented by the attorney general, after previous binding over by a committing magistrate. This doctrine was held, in a case where a communication had been received from the grand jury, stating that charges had been made by one of their number, to the effect, that one or more members of a public trust had been guilty of converting to their own use public money, and asking that witnesses should be furnished them to enable them to examine the charge.

The remarks of the learned judge are so clear and forcible, that the Commissioners cannot forbear giving them :

" The third and last of the extraordinary modes of criminal procedure," says he, " known to our penal code, is that which is originated by the presentment of a grand jury. A presentment, properly speaking, is the notice taken by a grand jury, of any offence, from their own knowlege or observation, without any bill of indictment being laid before them at the suit of the commonwealth. Like an indictment, however, it must be the act of the whole jury, not less than twelve concurring in it. It is, in fact, as much a criminal accusation, as an indictment, except that it emanates from their own knowledge, and not from the public accuser, and except that it wants technical form. It is regarded as instructions for an indictment. That a grand jury may adopt such a course of procedure, without a previous preliminary hearing of the accused, is not to be questioned by this court. And it is equally true, that in making such a presentment, the grand jury are entirely irresponsible either to the public or to individuals aggrieved ; the law giving them the most absolute and unqualified indemnity, for such an official act. Had the grand jury, on the present occasion, made a legal presentment of the parties named in their communication, the court would, without hesitation, have ordered bills of indictment against them, and would have furnished the grand jury with all the testimony, oral and written, which the authority we are clothed with would have enabled us to obtain. While the power of presentment is conceded, we think no reflecting man would desire to see it extended, a particle beyond the limit fixed to it by precedent and authority. It is a proceeding which denies the accused the benefit of a preliminary hearing ; which prevents him from demanding the endorsement of the name of the prosecutor on the indictment before he pleads,—a right he possesses in every other case,—and which takes away all his remedies for malicious prosecution, no matter how unfounded the accusation, on final hearing, may prove to be : a system which certainly has in it nothing to recommend its extension.

" Grand juries are high public functionaries, standing between the accuser and accused. They are the great security to the citizens against vindictive prosecution, either by government, or political partizans, or by private enemies. In their independent action, the persecuted have found the most fearless protectors; and in the records of their doings, are to be discovered the noblest stands against the oppression of power, the virulence of malice, and the intemperance of prejudice. These elevated functions do not comport with the position of receiving individual accusations from any source, not preferred before them by the responsible public authorities, and not resting in their own cognizance, sufficient to authorize a presentment. Nor should courts give, unadvisedly, aid or countenance to any such innovations. For if we are bound to send for persons and papers, to sustain one charge, by a grand juror, before the body, against one citizen, we are bound to do so upon every charge which every other grand juror, present and future, following the precedent now sanctioned, may think proper hereafter to prefer. It is true, that in the existing state of our social organization, but partial and occasional evils might flow from grand juries receiving, entertaining, and acting on criminal charges against citizens, not given them by the public authorities, nor within their own cognizance. But we connot rationally claim exemption from the agitations and excitements, which have at some period of its history convulsed every nation. Those communities which have ranked among the wisest and the best, have become, on occasions, subject to temporary political and other phrensies, too vehement to be resisted by the ordinary safeguards provided by law for the security of the innocent. Under such irregular influences, the right of every member of a body like a grand jury, taken immediately from the excited mass, to charge what crime he pleases on whom he pleases, in the secret conclave of the grand jury room, might produce the worst results. It is important, also, in the consideration of this question, to be borne in mind, that the body so to be clothed with these extraordinary functions, is perhaps the only one of our public agents that is totally irresponsible for official acts. When the official existence of a grand jury terminates, they mingle again with the general mass of the citizens, intangible for any of their official acts, either by private action, public prosecution, or legislative impeachment. That the action of such a body should be kept within the powers clearly pertaining to it, is a proposition self-evident; particularly where a doubtful authority is claimed, the exercise of which has a direct tendency to deprive a citizen of any of the guarantees of his personal rights, secured by the constitution. Our system of criminal administration is not subject to the reproach that there exists in it, an irresponsible body, with unlimited jurisdiction. On the contrary, the duties of a grand jury, in direct criminal accusations, are confined to the investigation of matters given them in charge by the court, of those preferred before them by the attorney general, and of those which are sufficiently within their own knowledge and observation, to authorise an official presentment. And they cannot, on the application of any one, originate proceedings against citizens, which is a duty imposed by law on other public agents. This limitation of authority we regard as alike fortunate for the citizen and the grand jury. It protects the citizen from the persecution and annoyance which private malice or personal animosity, introduced into the grand jury room, might subject him to. And it conserves the dignity of the grand jury, and the veneration with which they ought always be regarded by the people, by making them an umpire between the accurer and the accused, instead of assuming the office of the former.

"We have less difficulty in coming to these conclusions, from the consciousness that they have no tendency to give immunity to the parties named in the communication of the grand jury, if they have violated any public law. The charge preferred by the grand juror, alluded to in the communuiuation, is clear and distinct. It is one, over which every committing magistrate of the city and county of Philadelphia has jurisdiction. Any one of this numerous body may issue his warrant of arrest against the accused, his subpœna for the persons and papers named, and may compel their appearance and production. And if sufficient probable cause is shown, that the accused have been guilty of the crimes charged against them, he may bail or commit them to answer to this court. The differences to the accused, between this procedure and that proposed, are, that before a primary magistrate, the defendants have a responsible accuser, to whom they may look, if their personal and official characters have beem wantonly and maliciously and falsely assailed. They have the opportunity of hearing the witnesses, face to face. They may be assisted by counsel, in cross-examining those witnesses and sifting from them the whole truth. And not the least, they by this means know, what crime is precisely charged against them; and when, where and how it is said to have been perpetrated :—rights which we admit and feel the value of, and of which we would most reluctantly deprive them, even if we had the legal authority to do so.

"On the whole, we are of opinion that we act most in accordance with the rights of the citizen, most in conformity with a wise and equal administration of the public law, by declining to give our aid to facilitate the extraordinary proceedings, proposed against the parties named in the communication of the grand jury; and by referring any one, who desires to prosecute them for the offences charged, to the ordinary tribunals of the commonwealth, which possess all the jurisdiction necessary for that purpose, and can exercise it, more in unison with the rights of the accused, than could be accomplished by the mode proposed in the communication of the grand jury." *Wharton's Criminal Law*, 117, 118, *note.*

The spirit of the rule so well expressed in this extract, is embodied and carried out in the provisions proposed by the Commissioners, continuing in the grand jury, all their powers in respect to the investigation of charges of crime. It is proposed to guard against hasty and ill advised accusations, by giving to the defendant, upon presentment by the grand jury, (where he has not been already held to answer,) the same opportunity of answering or explaining the charge, as if he had been proceeded against by an information before a magistrate; while, on the other hand, he is to be committed or bailed, upon the presentment, in precisely the same manner as upon an indictment. In this manner, the rights of the defendant are protected, and the demands of public justice are abundantly answered.

By other provisions, the duties of the grand jury, in relation to the kind and degree of evidence upon which they may legitimately act, are defined. In practice, there is no established rule upon the subject; and grand jurors are left wholly uninformed, except as they are occasionally instructed upon it by the court, as to the precise line of duty marked out for them by the law. The consequence has been, that acting very honestly under a mistaken view of their powers, indictments are frequently presented by them, upon evidence wholly inadmissible, and which, even if admissible, was legally inconclusive. In one case, an indictment for false pretences was found, upon a one-sided and extra judicial affidavit taken in another state. In another, a witness was conducted into the grand jury room, with a long written narative prepared by another, and was sworn by the grand jury, generally, as to the truth of the statement; and without further examination or a single question as to the particular facts constituting the accusation, the witness was dismissed and an indictment found. In both these instances, too, the cases originated before the grand jury ; no previous complaint having been made. Nor was any remedy within the reach of the defendants. Indicted, as they were, upon palpably illegal evidence, there was no way of bringing the facts before the court, so as to justify an application to quash the indictments. The Commissioners have reason to believe that innumerable cases of a similar and even of a more flagrant character have existed, and could, if necessary, be furnished. These, however, are deemed sufficient, to illustrate the necessity of legislation, to guard against the continuance of the abuse—arising, too, from no dishonesty of motive, on the part of the grand jury, but from the fact that the delicate and difficult duties of the grand jury in this respect are entirely undefined by law.

The remedy proposed by the Commissioners, is to be found in the provisions which declare, that in the investigation of a charge for the purpose of either presentment or indictment, the grand jury can receive no other evidence than such as is given by witnesses produced and sworn before them, or furnished by legal documentary evidence, or by the depositions of witnesses, taken under such circumstances as to make them legally admissible; and further, that they shall receive none but legal evidence, and the best evidence in degree, to the exclusion of hearsay, or secondary evidence. *Sec.* 259, 260. These are elementary and simple rules of evidence. They are the rules applicable to every judicial investigation, in accordance with which the examination before the magistrate must be conducted, and by which the final examination of the case before the trial jury is governed. They are rules, too, of plain and familiar meaning, and can be easily applied; or in case of doubt in respect to them, that doubt can be readily removed, by the resort of the grand jury to the advice of the court or any member of it, or of the district attorney, who are in this as in every other stage of their proceedings, their legal advisers.

Another question of considerable practical difficulty has presented itself to the Commissioners. How far is the grand jury bound or authorised to hear evidence in exculpation of the defendant? Regarding it as a mere accusing body, the answer would be plain, that they are confined to the evidence offered in support of the accusation. But viewing them as a judicial tribunal, it might be said with much propriety, that their powers and duties in this respect are more comprehensive. The Commissioners do not, however, adopt either extreme. The object of a public prosecution is to place the defendant on trial, when there is such reasonable evidence of his guilt as to afford a fair ground to charge him with the offence. His defence or explanation is, then properly the subject of inquiry, and in such case should be submitted to the trial jury. It should, nevertheless, be made their duty, and so the Commissioners propose to make it, to weigh all the evidence submitted to them, and when they have reason to believe that other evidence, within their reach, will explain away the charge, to order it to be produced; and for that purpose, they should be authorised to require the district attorney to issue process for the witnesses. *Sec* 261. And as the concluding rule on this subject, the grand jury should be distinctly informed by the law, that they ought to find an in dictment, when all the evidence, taken together, is such, as in their judgment would warrant a conviction by the trial jury. *Sec.* 262.

In some of the views of the Commisioners, as well as in the conclusion at which they have arrived on the subject, they find, themselves fully sustained by an article published in the *London Law Magazine, No.* 64, on the subject of *defects of criminal procedure.* This article is extracted by the British Commissioners in their *Eighth Report, p.* 357—369, as being expressly written in answer to the questions propounded in the form of a circular by the Commissioners. In addition to the commendation of the Commissioners upon it, it bears the signature of *J. Pitt Taylor*, Esq., a distinguished modern writer upon legal subjects.

In this note, the Commissioners have extracted that part of the article only which relates to grand juries. It will be observed, that its reasoning goes to the extent of abolishing the grand jury altogether. This, as the Commissioners have remarked, cannot, in this state, constitutionally be done. The reasoning referred to, and the facts adduced in this article are not however the less valuable, as demonstrating the necessity of circumscribing and more clearly defining, the powers and duties of the grand jury.

"According to the existing practice, prosecutions by indictment may commence, either by bringing against the defendant a public accusation before a magistrate, or a private accusation before the grand jury. Let us imagine that the first course is adopted. Complaint having been made to a magistrate, and the accused having been summoned or apprehended, the prosecutor and his witnesses are called upon, in a public court, and in the presence of the defendant, to state on oath the circumstances on which the charge is founded. The accused or his legal adviser, has then an opportunity of cross-examining the witnesses, of calling others to contradict them, and of making any statement, with the view of explaining, justifying or disproving the charge. If the facts be intricate, if important witnesses be absent, or if time be required for a more careful scrutiny, the inquiry may be postponed to some future day; till, at length, the case having been fully and openly heard on both sides, and the testimony having been reduced into writing, the magistrate decides whether or not the circumstances are sufficiently suspicious to warrant their submission to a jury. If this decision be in the negative, the accused is discharged; if in the affirmative, he is committed or bailed.

"Such being the nature of the preliminary investigation before a magistrate, it would seem that, for the purposes of justice, no further inquiry would be requisite previous, to the trial. But this is not the law; before the case can be presented for the consideration of the jury, the prosecutor and his witnesses, who may either be the parties previously examined, or different persons, must go, one by one, before a secret tribunal, composed of twenty-three gentlemen unacquainted with the law, and repeat the substance of their accusation, in the absence of the accused. No means are provided for testing the accuracy of their statements; the depositions taken before the committing magistrate, excepting at the Old Bailey, are not before them; neither, with a similar exception, is any person present, beyond the grand jurors themselves, to marshal the evidence, or in any way to conduct the proceedings. If, after this inquiry, twelve out of the twenty-three jurors consider that a prima facie case of guilt is established, a true bill is found and the indictment is tried; if a like number entertain a contrary opinion, the bill is rejected, and the prosecutor must then either abandon the charge, or try his fortune before another grand jury on some future occasion.

"Now, if we contrast the different modes in which these two examinations are conducted, is it not obvious that, even supposing no collusive practices to exist, and assuming the committing magistrate to have no more legal experience than the members of the grand jury, his decision is more likely to be correct than theirs; that where they agree with him, they do not corroborate him, where they differ from him, they are probably wrong; thus, they can seldom do good, and may often do evil. But, if this be the case, when the committing magistrate is a mere justice of the peace, with how much greater force does the argument apply, when, as in London, Liverpool and Manchester, he is a professional man, well acquainted with the rules of evidence, and admirably fitted, from long experience, to unravel the tangled thread of human testimony.

"Besides, it is idle to suppose, that frauds are not daily practised on the grand jury. At the preliminary inquiry before the magistrate, the defendant has an opportunity of ascertaining who are the witnesses who depose against him, and what is the nature of their evidence. If, then, he be admitted to bail, what is to prevent *him*—if he be committed to custody, what is to prevent his friends from tampering with the witnesses? It would be useless, or at least highly dangerous, to attempt to do so if they were only to be examined at the trial; because, on that occasion, the evidence being given in a public court would be publicly known, and the depositions being returned to that court, any material variance in the testimony would be immediately detected, and would render the witnesses liable to an indictment for perjury. But the case is far different before the grand jury. There the jurors being sworn to secrecy, and each witness being examined alone, who is to discover any falsehood that one or more of them may be bribed to utter? Yet, if any unexplained inconsistency appear in the narrative, the grand jury can scarcely fail to doubt its truth, and the consequence is that the bill is ignored. The prosecutor has no means of avoiding this result. He knows that some of his witnesses have betrayed him; perhaps he has reason to suspect the individual who has done so; but he has no remedy. An indictment for perjury must specify the words spoken, and how can he discover what those words were?

The law, indeed, may say that a false witness before a grand jury is subject to prosecution ; but the law does not add how a conviction can be obtained; and we believe that, with one solitary exception, no trace can be discovered of such a proceeding.

"Again, if the witnesses are of such a character as to preclude the hope of their being successfully suborned, the accused may still escape, providing he can only bribe, (and this is no difficult matter,) some person to go to the prosecutor, and pretend that he is acquainted with facts corroborative ot the charge. These facts being narrated with the semblance of zeal, the confidence of the prosecutor is gained; the defendant's friend, with the witnesses previously examined, is sent before the grand jury, and there, by an artful statement, throws such doubt on the matter, that no bill is found. It is true, that both these last mentioned abuses might be partially avoided, either by making the grand jury perform their functions as in former days they frequently did, in open court, or by directing that the attorney for the crown should in all cases attend them with the depositions, and conduct the examination of the witnesses, and by distinctly empowering him, as also the grand jurors themselves, to repeat the evidence of any witness whom it might become necessary to indict for perjury. Still the inutility of the inquiry must remain as before ; and when we find, as we presently shall do, that this useless machinery is productive alike of a large expense to the country, and of serious inconvenience to witnesses, are we not justified in advocating its immediate abolition ?

"Next, let us suppose that the prosecutor, in the first instance, goes before the grand jury. In this case, the earliest intimation of the charge which the accused receives, is, that a bill is found against him. The particulars are kept secret; who his accusers are, or what they have testified against him, he has no means of discovering; indeed he cannot, except in some cases of high treason, so much as demand a copy of their names; nor in cases of felony, is he entitled, even to a copy of the indictment. The law, which now, in fairness, enables him, immediately after the investigation has closed before the magistrate, to obtain a copy of the depositions, at a small cost, and at the trial, to inspect these depositions, without any cost at all, refuses any such indulgence, in the case of a bill being found without a previous examination. That which the legislature admits to be just in the one case, it wholly disregards in the other; and thus, while a man, who has been publicly accused before a magistrate, has the amplest means of showing the character and motives of the witnesses, and of confuting the charge against him, a party, secretly attacked before the grand jury, is placed on his trial, under circumstances of cruel disadvantage, and must rely on chance, rather than the purity of his conduct, to establish his innocence. But this is not all. A prosecutor who prefers a bill before the grand jury, is not compelled to proceed to trial, in the event of its being found, neither are his witnesses bound over to appear and testify in court. A door is consequently opened to the most disgraceful practices. A bill found by perjury, becomes the instrument of extortion to the innocent but timid man; a bill found by true testimony, is employed with still greater power, to wring money from the guilty."

§ 253. The grand jury has power, and it is their duty, to inquire into all public offences committed or triable in the county, and to present them to the court, either by presentment or indictment, as provided in the next two sections.

§ 254. Upon such inquiry, they may, where the defendant has been held by a magistrate to answer the charge, and in no other case, if they believe him guilty thereof, find an indictment against him.

§ 255. In all other cases, if, upon investigation, the grand jury believe that a person is guilty of a public offence, they can proceed by presentment only.

§ 256. An indictment is an accusation in writing, presented by a grand jury to a competent court, charging a person with a public offence.

§ 257. A presentment is an informal statement in writing by the grand jury, representing to the court, that a public offence has been committed, which is triable in the county, and that there is reasonable ground for believing that a particular individual, named or described, has committed it.

§ 258. The foreman may administer an oath, to any witness appearing before the grand jury.

§ 259. In the investigation of a charge, for the purpose of either presentment or indictment, the grand jury can receive no other evidence than,

1. Such as is given by witnesses produced and sworn before them, or furnished by legal documentary evidence: or,

2. The deposition of a witness, in the cases mentioned in the third subdivision of section 12.

§ 260. The grand jury can receive none but legal evidence, and the best evidence in degree, to the exclusion of hearsay or secondary evidence.

§ 261. The grand jury is not bound to hear evidence for the defendant; but it is their duty to weigh all the evidence submitted to them, and when they have reason to believe that other evidence, within their reach, will explain away the charge, they should order such evidence to be produced; and for that purpose, may require the district attorney to issue process for the witnesses.

§ 262. The grand jury ought to find an indictment, when all the evidence before them, taken together, is such as in their judgment would, if unexplained or uncontradicted, warrant a conviction by the trial jury.

§ 263. If a member of the grand jury know, or have reason to believe, that a public offence has been committed, which is triable in the county, he must declare the same to his fellow jurors, who must thereupon investigate the same.

§ 264. The grand jury must inquire,

1. Into the case of every person imprisoned in the jail of the county, on a criminal charge, and not indicted:

2. Into the condition and management of the public prisons in the county; and

3. Into the wilful and corrupt misconduct in office, of public officers of every description, in the county.

§ 265. They are also entitled to free access, at all reasonable times, to the public prisons, and to the examination, without charge, of all public records in the county.

The last three sections are declaratory of the existing powers of the grand jury.

§ 266. The grand jury may, at all reasonable times, ask the advice of the court, or of any member thereof, or of the district attorney of the county; but unless such advice be asked, neither of those officers are permitted to be present during the sessions of the grand jury; nor is any other person permitted to be present during their sessions, except the members of the grand jury, and a witness actually under examination.

> This section is intended as a substitute for the provision of the Revised Statutes, that " the district attorney of the county shall be allowed at all times to appear before the grand jury, on his request, for the purpose of giving information relative to any matter cognizable by them; and may be permitted to interrogate witnesses before them, when they shall deem it necessary: but no district attorney, constable or other person, except the grand jurors, shall be permitted to be present during the expression of their opinions or the giving of their votes, upon any matter before them." *2 R. S. 3d ed.* 811, *sec.* 33.
>
> The object of the proposed section is, to afford the grand jury every proper advice from the court or the district attorney; but in all other respects to leave them to conduct the investigation according to their own judgment.

§ 267. Every member of the grand jury must keep secret, whatever he himself, or any other grand juror may have said, or in what manner he, or any other grand juror may have voted, on a matter before them.

§ 268. A member of the grand jury may, however, be required by any court, to disclose the testimony of a witness examined before the grand jury, for the purpose of ascertaining whether it is consistent with that given by the witness, before the court; or to disclose the testimony given before them by any person, upon a charge against him for perjury in giving his testimony, or upon his trial therefor.

§ 269. A grand juror cannot be questioned for anything he may say, or any vote he may give, in the grand jury, relative to a matter legally pending before the jury, except for a perjury of which he may have been guilty, in making an accusation, or giving testimony to his fellow jurors.

Declaratory of the existing privileges of the grand jury.

CHAPTER IV.

PRESENTMENT, AND PROCEEDINGS THEREON.

This chapter is designed to provide for the mode of finding a presentment, and of proceeding thereon, in accordance with the views stated in the note at the head of chapter 3, of this title, *p.* 115—129. In other respects, the provisions of this chapter sufficiently explain themselves.

§ 270. A presentment cannot be found, without the concurrence of at least twelve grand jurors. When so found, it must be signed by the foreman.

§ 271. The presentment, when found, must be presented by the foreman, in the presence of the grand jury, to the court, and must be file dwith the clerk.

§ 272. When the grand jury make a presentment, they must return to the court therewith, the depositions of the witnesses examined before them, or the minutes, or a copy thereof, of the testimony on which the presentment is made.

§ 273. When the depositions are returned, as provided in the last section, they must be filed with the clerk of the court, and can not be inspected by any person, except the court, the clerk and his deputies or assistants, and the district attorney, until after the arrest of the defendant.

§ 274. A violation of the provisions of the last section is punishable as a contempt, and as a misdemeanor.

§ 275. After the arrest of the defendant, the clerk must, on payment of his fees, at the rate of five cents for every hundred words, within two days after the demand, furnish a copy of the depositions to the defendant or his counsel.

§ 276. No grand juror, district attorney, clerk, judge or other officer, can disclose the fact of a presentment having been made for a felony, until the defendant has been arrested. But this prohibition does not extend to a disclosure, by the issuing or in the execution of a warrant to arrest the defendant.

§ 277. A violation of the provisions of the last section is punishable as a contempt, and as a misdemeanor.

§ 278. If the court deem that the facts stated in the presentment constitute a public offence, triable in the county, it must direct the clerk to issue a bench warrant for the arrest of the defendant.

§ 279. The clerk, on the application of the district attorney, may accordingly, at any time after the order, whether the court be sitting or not, issue a bench warrant, under his signature and the seal of the court, into one or more counties.

§ 280. The bench warrant, upon a presentment, must be substantially in the following form:

"County of *Albany*, [or as the case may be.]

"In the name of the people of the state of New-York—

"To any sheriff, constable, marshal or policeman in this state. A presentment having

[SEAL.] been made on the day of

1850, to the *court of sessions of the county of Albany*, [or as the case may be,] charging C. D. with the crime of, [designating it generally.]

"You are therefore commanded, forthwith to arrest the above named C. D., and take him before E. F., a magistrate of this county, or in case of his absence or inability to act, before the nearest or most accessible magistrate in this county.

"City [or "town"] of , the day of , 1850.

"By order of the court.

"G. H., clerk."

§ 281. The bench warrant may be served in any county; and the officer serving it must proceed thereon, in all respects, as upon a warrant of arrest on an information, as provided in sections 158 to 161, both inclusive, except that when served in another county, it need not be endorsed by a magistrate of that county.

§ 282. The magistrate, when the defendant is brought before him, must proceed upon the charge contained in the presentment, in the same manner in all respects as upon a warrant of arrest on an information, as provided in sections 187 to 220, both inclusive.

§ 283. Upon the arrest of the defendant, the clerk with whom the presentment and depositions are filed, must, without delay, furnish to the magistrate before whom the defendant is taken, a certified copy of the presentment and depositions.

TITLE V.

OF THE INDICTMENT.

CHAPTER I.

FINDING AND PRESENTATION OF THE INDICTMENT.

§ 284. An indictment cannot be found, without the concurrence of at least twelve grand jurors. When so found, it must be endorsed, "A true bill," and the endorsement must be signed by the foreman of the grand jury.

§ 285. If twelve grand jurors do not concur in finding an indictment, the depositions, (and statement, if any,) transmitted to them, must be returned to the court, with an endorsement thereon, signed by the foreman, to the effect that the charge is dismissed.

The last two sections are substantially the same as 2 *R. S.*, *3d. ed.* 812, *sec.* 36.

§ 286. The dismissal of the charge does not, however, prevent its being again submitted to a grand jury, as often as the court may so direct. But without such direction, it cannot be again submitted.

This section is designed to provide a convenient check upon the practice which now prevails, of repeated applications to the grand jury for an indictment, where it has been already dismissed. Cases have existed, where, after frequent dismissals of the indictment, the perseverance of the prosecutor has at length succeeded in procuring it to be found. The Commissioners are not prepared to say, that an indictment should not be found after one or more dismissals; for they are ready to admit, that by reason of the discovery of new testimony, or of other facts intimately connected with the due administration of justice, it may be both expedient and necessary, that the case should be submitted to another grand jury. To prevent, on the one hand, the abuse referred to, and to guard the interests of the public, on the other, they have proposed that the dismissal of the charge shall not prevent its being again submitted to the grand jury, as often as the court shall direct; but that without such direction, it shall not be again submitted.

§ 287. When an indictment is found, the names of the witnesses examined before the grand jury, or whose depositions may have been read before them, as provided in section 259, must, in all cases, be inserted at the foot of the indictment, or endorsed thereon, before it is presented to the court.

This provision is in accordance with the English practice, which, with all its supposed severity in the punishment of crime, proceeds upon the principle that no advantage shall be denied to the defendant, adapted to enable him to meet and defend the charge. And indeed, so far has it been carried in that country, that the judges are in the constant habit of requiring the prosecuting counsel to place upon the stand as witnesses, all who were examined before the grand jury. In a case recently reported, where the counsel for the prosecution had refused to do this, because the witness was adverse to the prosecution, the judge declared that unless the counsel called him, he himself would do so, that the defendant might have the privilege of across-examination; and gave as his reason, a sentiment alike honorable to the bench and to the law, that the object of a public prosecution was the attainment of truth and not the conviction of the defendant.

§ 288. An indictment, when found by the grand jury, as prescribed in section 284 must be presented by their foreman, in their presence, to the court, and must be filed with the clerk, and remain in his office as a public record.

Taken from 2 *R. S.*, 3*d. ed.*, 812, *sec.* 38.

CHAPTER II.

FORM OF THE INDICTMENT.

The Commissioners have bestowed upon the subject of the form of the indictment, most careful and anxious reflection; and after weighing every consideration connected with it, they can confidently say, that they have arrived at a result satisfactory to their own minds, and which they believe will be found to be in accordance with the wise and just demand of public opinion. They will not flatter themselves with the idea, that their labors in this respect will meet with the universal approbation of the legal profession; but placing themselves upon the immutable principles of common sense, and regardless of denunciation as visionary reformers, they will be content to rest their claims to having faithfully performed their duty, upon the wisdom and intelligence of the people. They are not ignorant of the fact, that their proposed reform will strike at the root of a system, artificial and absurd in itself, and which is only saved from the contempt it merits, by the frequent use of the names of venerable legal authorities, under whose sanction it has grown and ripened into maturity. For what are called the time honored institutions of the past, they entertain a high and becoming regard; but when they are told that the machinery of the law, invented and put in operation in an age of comparative darkness, and permitted to remain, for no other reason than that it was easier to continue its use than to reform it, constitutes an exception to the spirit of the age, whose distinguishing characteristic is advancement and reform, they are compelled to wonder at the blind devotion, which would deny in this respect, the clear and peremptory demand of the public voice. Nor will they allow themselves to believe that absurdities and fictions, so glaring and gross in themselves, as to provoke the laughter and contempt of the intelligent, will be permitted to continue longer than until a safe substitute for them can be found.

The object of pleading, whether in civil or criminal actions, is to inform the parties of the facts alleged by each against the other, with such clearness and distinctness as to enable them to prepare for the trial of disputed facts, or for the application of the law to those which are admitted. Refine as we may, upon the mode of effecting this object, the most devoted worshipper of the ancient forms will not deny that this is the only legitimate object of pleading. And in its application to criminal cases, in which no special pleading is required on the part of the defendant, by the code, (except where a former conviction is pleaded, which must be in a brief, prescribed form,) the elements of pleading may be still further condensed into this definition: that it is a statement of a crime imputed to the prisoner, with such a particularity of circumstances only, as will enable him to understand the charge and prepare for his defence, and as will authorise the court,—applying the law to the facts charged,—to give the appropriate judgment upon conviction. Indeed, adopting the definition given by the elementary writers, it will not be found to vary from that just stated. "In the statement of the indictment," says Mr. Archbold, "all the ingredients in the offence with which the defendant is charged, the facts, circumstances and intent constituting it, must be set forth with certainty and precision, without any repugnancy or inconsistency; and the defendant must be charged directly and positively with having committed it."

Yet, upon this simple definition has been built a superstructure of rules and illustrations, the utter ridiculousness of which is a reproach to legal science. In the first place, it is said, that the indictment must be certain as to the party indicted; by which is meant, that he must be described by his name, or as a person unknown to the grand jurors, in which case something must be stated to ascertain who is intended—He must also be designated by his "mystery," which, according to Mr. Archbold, means his trade, art or occupation. Again, it must be certain as to the person against whom the offence was committed, and as to the time and place of its commission; but according to Mr. Archbold, "although time and place must thus be laid with certainty, it never was necessary that it should be laid according to the truth." *Archb. Crim. Pl. 9th ed.*, 40. It must also be certain as to the fact, circumstances and intent, constituting the offence. So far as these rules require the facts to be stated with truth, and as they tend to inform the defendant with precision what charge he is called upon to answer, they are certainly unobjectionable. But when we come to see, that according to the existing practice, this certainty means everything but what it would seem to import, astonishment may well be expressed that its continuance should be deemed desirable. The uninitiated in the mysteries of pleading can scarcely conceive, how entirely futile these rules have become, by the mass of fiction in which they are imbedded. The terms "certainty as to the fact, circumstances and intent," would naturally convey to the mind that the information to be given to the defendant is precisely such as should be furnished to him. But instead of that, it is nothing more nor less than a legal creation, which, in its practical operation, is often made the means of defeating justice upon a mere quibble, or of artfully and adroitly concealing from the defendant the nature of the charge against him.

When we are asked, what is meant by certainty, in the sense in which it is used in these rules, we have but to recur to the author just referred to, for a brief and comprehensive, though it must be confessed not a very satisfactory or intelligible answer. "Certainty" says he, "is of three kinds: certainty to a certain intent in every particular; which is required only in pleas, &c., of estoppel and pleas in abatement; certainty to a common intent, which is required in ordinary pleas; and certainty to a certain intent in general, which is required in declarations and indictments. The latter is a medium between the other two; not so great a degree of certainty as the first, and a greater degree of certainty than the second. I shall endeavor further to define them. Where certainty to a certain intent in every particular is required, the court will presume the negative of every thing the pleader has not expressly affirmed, and the affirmative of every thing the pleader has not expressly negatived; or, in the words of Lord Coke, the pleader must exclude every conclusion against him. Where certainty to a common intent only is required, the court will presume, in favor of the pleader, every proposition which by reasonable intendment is impliedly included in the pleading, though not expressed; and where words are made use of, which admit of a natural sense, and also of an artificial one, or one to be made out by argument or inference, the natural sense shall prevail." (*Arch. Crim. Pl. 9th Ed.* 43)

In illustration of this rule, scores of cases, if it were necessary, might be presented, to show to what an absurd length quibbling upon it has been carried, and how often justice has been entirely defeated by its application. A few only will be referred to. Mr. Livingston, in his notes on the criminal code reported by him, gives the following example: "In an indictment for forgery, a stroke of the pen, which occurred in the instrument, had not been copied in the indictment. The prisoner being convicted, his counsel moved in arrest of judgment, and assigned the omission of this stroke for cause. The paper and the indictment were handed up to the bench, and the judge, not being able with the naked eye to discover any difference, had recourse to a glass, and by the aid of a strong magnifier, discovered something which he said was either a *tick*, (a word of which I do not profess to know the meaning,) or a letter,—which, he would not or could not determine;—but submitted it to the jury, with directions, if they found it to be the one, (I forget which,) to convict, if the other to acquit; and to aid in the determination of this important question, he handed them his glass—the microscopic powers of which determined them in favor of the acquitting alternative—and the prisoner was discharged; if the judge's glass had not been brought into court, or had been of a lower power, he would have been hanged." *Liv. Crim. Code.* 225, 226, *note.*

In a spirit of greater gravity, however, Mr. Archbold, in illustrating the rule respecting certainty, cites a great variety of cases, from the earliest down to the latest period. For example:—"An indictment on that part of the Black Act, (now repealed,) which made it felony *wilfully and maliciously* to shoot at a person in a dwelling house or other place, was holden bad, because it charged the offence to have been done *unlawfully and maliciously*, omitting the word *wilfully*. *R.* v. *Davis,* 1 *Leach,* 556. Some of the judges indeed thought that 'maliciously' included 'wilfully;' but the greater number held, that as 'wilfully' *and* 'maliciously' were both mentioned in the statute, as descriptive of the offence, both must be stated in the indictment. So, an indictment upon stat. 7 & 8 *G.* 4, *c.* 30, *s.* 2, for feloniously, voluntarily, and maliciously setting fire to a barn, was holden bad, because the words of the statute are '*unlawfully* and maliciously.' *R.* v. *Turner,* 1 *Mood. C. C.* 239. So, an indictment upon stat. 9 G. 4, *c.* 31, *s.* 12, charging the prisoner with 'feloniously, wilfully, and maliciously cutting,' &c., is not sufficient; the words of the statute being '*unlawfully* and maliciously.' *Reg.* v. *Ryan,* 2 *Mood. C. C.* 15. So where an indictment on the repealed stats. 15 *G,* 2, *c.* 34, and 14 *G.* 2, *c.* 6, which made it felony without benefit of clergy, to steal any cow, ox, heifer, &c., charged the defendant with stealing a cow, and in evidence it was proved to be a heifer, this was holden to be a fatal variance; for the statute having mentioned both cow and heifer, proved that the words were not considered by the legislature as synonymous. *R.* v. *Coke,* 2 *East, P. C.* 617; 1 *Leach,* 123. *See also R.* v. *Douglass,* 1 *Camp.* 212. So, where an indictment charged in one count that the defendant did break *to get* out, and in another, that he did break *and get* out, it was holden insufficient, because the words of the statute are 'break out.' *R.* v. *Compton,* 7 *C. & P.* 139.

"In like manner it was decided, that, as the repealed stat. 15 *G.* 2, *c.* 34, specified lambs as well as sheep, a defendant could not be convicted for stealing sheep, upon an indictment for stealing lambs; *R.* v. *Loom*, 1 *Mood. C. C.* 160; and a similar construction has been put upon the stat. 7 & 8 *G.* 4, *c.* 29 *s.* 25, *R.* v. *Puddifoot*, 1 *Mood. C. C.* 247. But in *Reg.* v. *M'Cully*, 2 *Mood. C. C.* 34, an indictment under that statute for killing a sheep, with intent to steal the carcase, was held to be supported by proof of killing a ram or ewe; the words of the statute being 'ram, ewe, sheep, or lamb;' a majority of the judges considering 'sheep' a generic term, including the former words. So also, an indictment upon the repealed stat. 2 *G.* 2, *c.* 25, (which made the stealing of 'bank notes' felony), charging the defendant with stealing 'a certain note *commonly called* a bank note,' was holden bad, because it did not follow the description of property in the statute. *R.* v. *Craven*, *R.* & *R.* 14; 2 *East*, *P. C.* 601, 602. So, under the repealed stat. 2 & 3 *Ed.* 6, c. 33, which contained only the words 'horse, gelding, or mare,' upon an indictment for stealing two colts, the judges were unanimously of opinion, that, as colts were not mentioned *eo nomine* in the statute, they could not take notice that they were of the horse species." *R.* v. *Beaney*, *R.* & *R.* 416; *Archb. Crim. Pl.* 9*th ed.*, 50, 51.

These illustrations are given, with no view of appealing to the mere prejudices of the unprofessional man, against the technicalities and subtleties which have been invented as the means of administering justice; but are presented to the candid and sober judgment of the legislature, as an argument too strong to be resisted, against the further continuance of what, it cannot but be admitted, is a perversion of the first principles of justice and a violence to common sense. No matter by what names or by how great antiquity its defence may be attempted, the intelligence of the age demands that the darkness and mysticism of past centuries should, in the science of law, as it has in every other, yield to the more advanced enlightenment of the present day.

Happily for the cause of legal reform, the attempt which the Commissioners have made, to substitute for these senseless technicalities, a system of pleading, founded upon the unerring principles of justice, and having for their end the attainment of right without regard to form, is no new or visionary experiment. More than twenty-five years ago, Mr. Livingston, under the authority of the legislature of Louisiana, engaged himself in the effort to reform the modes of criminal procedure; and among the subjects to which he directed his attention, the most prominent was the simplification of the rules of pleading. Instead of the unintelligible subtleties which he found to grow out of the common law rules on the subject, he reduced the art of pleading to a plain, comprehensive and practical system. In place of the mystical terms "certainty to a common extent, certainty to a certain intent in general, and certainty to a certain intent in particular," he saw no difficulty in substituting the clear and intelligible rule, that all that was necessary in an indictment, should be that "the act or omission charged be so clearly and distinctly set forth, as to enable a man of common understanding to know what is intended." *Liv. Crim. Code*, 520, *art.* 254, *subd.* 6.

In more recent times, and in the country from which our legal institutions have been borrowed, the sagacity of our great jurist has been justly appreciated; and as a proof that what has been deemed in the Commissioners, an act of reckless and visionary presumption, has been regarded in that country as practicable and just, the fact need only to be mentioned, that the British Commissioners, after the fullest consultation with the bench and the bar of that country, have recommended the adoption, almost in terms, of the provision just referto. In their eighth report, p. 76, is embraced the following provision:—"All acts, omissions and circumstances essential to the offence, must be so plainly, directly and distinctly stated, as to enable a man of ordinary understanding to know what is intended"

Resting upon this weight of authority, to say nothing of the principle involved in the proposition, the Commissioners had expected, though it seems without just reason, that the introduction of this rule into the code of civil procedure, would have met with more favor than it has been its fate to receive. They will, however, permit themselves to indulge the hope, that their attempt to translate into intelligible English, the phrase "certainty to a common intent" may be more favorably appreciated.

In accordance with the views already expressed, the Commissioners have resolved to recommend, that all the forms of pleading in criminal actions, heretofore existing, be abolished, and that hereafter the forms of pleading and the rules by which their sufficiency are to be determined, shall be those which are prescribed by the code. The rules to be substituted in their place, *sec.* 291—312, are few and simple, and in the main come recommended by the high authorities to which allusion has just been made. Referring the legislature to the sections themselves, for a more full explanation of them, the Commissioners will content themselves with a brief recapitulation of the principles which they embody.

First ;—The indictment must contain the title of the action, specifying the name of the court to which the indictment is presented, and the names of the parties, and a statement of the acts constituting the offence, in ordinary and concise language, without repetition, and in such a manner as to enable a person of common understanding to know what is intended.

Second ;—It must be direct and certain, as it regards the party, and the offence, and the particular circumstances of the offence charged, when they are necessary to constitute a complete offence.

Third ;—It must charge but one offence, and in one form only ; except that where the offence may be committed by the use of different means, the indictment may allege the means in the alternative.

Fourth ;—The words used must be construed in their usual acceptation in common language, except such words and phrases as are defined by the law, which are to be construed according to their legal meaning.

Fifth ;—Words used in a statute to define a public offence, need not be strictly pursued in the indictment ; but other words conveying the same meaning may be used.

Sixth ;—The indictment is sufficient, if it can be understood therefrom, 1. That it is entitled in a court having authority to receive it, though the name of the court be not accurately set forth ; 2. That it was found by a grand jury of the county in which the court was held ; 3. That the defendant is named, or if his name cannot be discovered, that he be described by a fictitious name, with the statement that he has refused to discover his real name; 4. That the offence was committed at some place within the jurisdiction of the court ; except where the act, though done without the local jurisdiction of the county, is triable therein ; 5. That the offence was committed at some time prior to the time of finding the indictment ; 6. That the act or omission, charged as the offence, is clearly and distinctly set forth, in ordinary and concise language, without repetition, and in such a manner as to enable a person of common understanding to know what is intended; 7. That the act or omission, charged as the offence, is stated with such a degree of certainty, as to enable the court to pronounce judgment upon a conviction, according to the right of the case.

Seventh;—The indictment is not deemed insufficient, nor are the trial, judgment or other proceedings thereon be affected, by reason of any defect or imperfection in matters of form, not tending to the prejudice of the defendant.

These constitute the elements of the system of pleading, recommended by the Commissioners; to which are added others of a subordinate character, designed to render them convenient in their practical operation. They have also incorporated in the code, the general form of an indictment; and have given in an appendix, several forms of indictments applicable to particular cases, proposing that in others, forms may be used as nearly similar as the nature of the case may permit. That the difference may be seen, between those now in use and those proposed by the Commissioners, they will submit the present form of an indictment for murder, and that substituted by the code.

The present form is as follows:

"County of Columbia, ss: The jurors of the people of the State of New-York, in and for the body of the county of Columbia, upon their oath present, that John Jones, late of the first ward of the city of Hudson, in the county of Columbia, laborer, not having the fear of God before his eyes, but being moved and seduced by the instigation of the devil, on the first day of January, in the year of our Lord one thousand eight hundred and fifty with force and arms, at the ward, city and county aforesaid, in and upon one William Green, in the peace of God and of the said people, then and there being, feloniously, wilfully and of his malice aforethought, did make an assault, and that the said John Jones, then and there riding upon a certain horse, of the value of fifty dollars, the said horse in and upon the said William Green, then and there feloniously, wilfully and of his malice aforethought, did ride and force, and him, the said William Green, with the horse aforesaid, then and there, by such riding and forcing, feloniously, wilfully and of his malice aforethought, did cast and throw to and upon the ground; by means whereof the said horse, with his hinder feet, him, the said William Green, so cast and thrown to and upon the ground, as aforesaid, in and upon the hinder part of the head of him, the said William Green, then and there did strike and kick, thereby, then and there giving to the said William Green, in and upon the said hinder part of the head of him, the said William Green, one mortal fracture and contusion, of which said mortal fracture and contusion, he, the said William Green, then and there instantly died. And so the jurors aforesaid, upon their oath aforesaid, do say, that the said John Jones, him, the said William Green, in manner and form aforesaid, feloniously, wilfully and of his malice aforethought, did kill and murder, against the peace of the people of the state of New-York, and their dignity."

This, it will be observed, is but one count. If there be the slightest possibility that any other mode of killing or means of death should appear upon the trial, a careful pleader will of course insert as many counts, in the same form, adapting them to the possible difference in proof, as will obviate the danger of a variance between the evidence and the indictment.

Under the code, the same case, which can only be set forth in a single count, would be stated as follows:

"Court of Oyer and terminer, of the county of Columbia.

The people of the state of New-York }
against }
John Jones. }

"John Jones is accused by the grand jury of the county of Columbia, by this indictment, of the crime of murder, committed as follows:

"The said John Jones, on the first day of January, 1849, at the city of Hudson, in this county, without the authority of law, and with malice aforethought, killed William Green, by riding over him with a horse."

§ 289. All the forms of pleading in criminal actions, heretofore existing, are abolished; and hereafter, the forms of pleading, and the rules by which the sufficiency of pleadings is to be determined, are those prescribed by this code.

§ 290. The first pleading on the part of the people, is the indictment.

§ 291. The indictment must contain,

1. The title of the action, specifying the name of the court to which the indictment is presented, and the names of the parties.

2. A statement of the acts constituting the offence, in ordinary and concise language, without repetition, and in such manner as to enable a person of common understanding to know what is intended.

§ 292. It may be substantially in the following form:

Court of oyer and terminer of the county of ; [stating the proper county.]

or,

Court of oyer and terminer of the city and county of New-York.

or,

Court of sessions of the county of , [stating the proper county.]

or,

Court of sessions of the city of New-York.

or,

City court of the city of ; [stating the proper city.]

The people of the state of New-York
against
A. B.

A. B. is accused by the grand jury of the [here insert the name of the county, or of the city, or of the city and county, in which the indictment is found,] by this indictment, of the crime of , [here insert the name of the offence, if it have one, such as treason, murder, arson, manslaughter, or the like, or if it be a misdemeanor, having no general name, such as libel, assault and battery, or the like, insert a brief description of it, as it is given by law;] committed as follows:

The said A. B., on the day of , 1850, at the town, [or city or village, as the case may be,] of , in this county, [here set forth the act charged as an offence, according to the form adapted to the case as provided in the next section].

§ 293. The manner of stating the act constituting the offence, as set forth in the appendix to this code, is sufficient, in all cases where the forms there given are applicable. In other cases, forms may be used, as nearly similar as the nature of the case will permit.

§ 294. The indictment must be direct and certain, as it regards,

1. The party charged:

2. The offence charged:

3. The particular circumstances of the offence charged, when they are necessary to constitute a complete offence.

§ 295. When a defendant is indicted by a fictitious or erroneous name, and in any stage of the proceedings his true name is discovered, it may be inserted in the subsequent proceedings, referring to the fact of his being indicted by the name mentioned in the indictment.

§ 296. The indictment must charge but one offence, and in one form only: except that where the offence may be committed by the use of different means, the indictment may allege the means in the alternative.

§ 297. The precise time at which the offence was committed, need not be stated in the indictment; but it may be alleged to have been committed at any time before the finding thereof, except where the time is a material ingredient in the offence.

§ 298. When an offence involves the commission of, or an attempt to commit a private injury, and is described with sufficient certainty in other respects to identify the act, an erroneous allegation as to the person injured or intended to be injured, is not material.

§ 299. The words used in an indictment must be construed in their usual acceptation, in common language, except words and phrases defined by law, which are to be construed according to their legal meaning.

§ 300. Words used in a statute to define a public offence, need not be strictly pursued in the indictment;

but other words, conveying the same meaning, may be used.

§ 301. The indictment is sufficient, if it can be understood therefrom.

1. That it is entitled in a court having authority to receive it, though the name of the court be not accurately stated:

2. That it was found by a grand jury of the county, or if in a city court, of the city in which the court was held:

3. That the defendant is named, or if his name cannot be discovered, that he is described by a fictitious name, with the statement that he has refused to discover his real name:

4. That the offence was committed at some place within the jurisdiction of the court; except where, as provided by sections 128 to 137, both inclusive, the act though done without the local jurisdiction of the county, is triable therein:

5. That the offence was committed at some time prior to the time of finding the indictment:

6. That the act or omission, charged as the offence, is clearly and distinctly set forth, in ordinary and concise language, without repetition, and in such a manner as to enable a person of common understanding to know what is intended:

7. That the act or omission, charged as the offence, is stated with such a degree of certainty, as to enable

the court to pronounce judgment, upon a conviction, according to the right of the case.

§ 302. No indictment is insufficient, nor can the trial, judgment, or other proceedings thereon be affected, by reason of a defect or imperfection in matter of form, which does not tend to the prejudice of the substantial rights of the defendant, upon the merits.

§ 303. Neither presumptions of law, nor matters of which judicial notice is taken, need be stated in an indictment.

This section is the same in substance, as *sec.* 134, *Code of* 1848.

§ 304. In pleading a judgment or other determination of, or proceeding before, a court or officer of special jurisdiction, it is not necessary to state the facts conferring jurisdiction; but the judgment or determination may be stated to have been duly given or made. The facts constituting jurisdiction, however, must be established on the trial.

Same in substance, as *sec.* 161, *Amended Code.*

§ 305. In pleading a private statute, or a right derived therefrom, it is sufficient to refer to the statute, by its title and the day of its passage, and the court must thereupon take judicial notice thereof.

Same in substance, as *sec.* 163, *Amended Code.*

§ 306. An indictment for libel need not set forth any extrinsic facts, for the purpose of shewing the application to the party libelled, of the defamatory matter on which the indictment is founded: but it is sufficient to state generally, that the same was published concerning him; and the fact that it was so published, must be established on trial.

Same in substance, as *sec.* 164, *Amended Code.*

§ 307. When an instrument, which is the subject of an indictment for forgery, has been destroyed or withheld by the act or procurement of the defendant, and the fact of the destruction or withholding is alleged in the indictment, and established on the trial, the misdescription of the instrument is immaterial.

Taken from *Livingston's Crim. Code*, 521, *art.* 270.

§ 308. In an indictment for perjury or subornation of perjury, it is sufficient to set forth the substance of the controversy or matter in respect to which the offence was committed, and in what court, or before whom, the oath alleged to be false was taken, and that the court or person before whom it was taken, had authority to administer it, with proper allegations of the falsity of the matter on which the perjury is assigned; but the indictment need not set forth the pleadings, record or proceedings with which the oath is connected, nor the commission or authority of the court or person before whom the perjury was committed.

This section is intended to carry out the principle contained in *sec.* 304, and will have the effect of dispensing with many technical recitals, leading to variances between the indictment and the proof, and calculated to defeat the ends of justice. The Virginia criminal code, *Laws of Va.*, 1848, *p.* 143, *sec.* 5, contains a similar provision.

§ 309. Upon an indictment against several defendants, any one or more may be convicted or acquitted.

Declaratory of the existing rule.

§ 310. The distinction between an accessary before the fact and a principal, and between principals in the first and second degree, in cases of felony, is abrogated; and all persons concerned in the commission of a felony, whether they directly commit the act constituting the offence, or aid and abet in its commission, though not present, must hereafter be indicted, tried aud punished as principals, as in the case of a midemeanor.

§ 311. An accessary after the fact to the commission of a felony, may be indicted, tried and punished, though the principal felon be neither indicted nor tried.

The last two sections abrogate the distinction between principals in the first and second degree, and between principals and accessaries, in cases of felony. There is no distinction in the punishment, in reference to these several degrees of crime. The only distinction between them is, in the form in which they shall be described, and in the order of their trial. By the common law, which in this respect is still in force in this state, the accessary cannot be tried until after the principal is convicted. The moral character of the guilt is the same in both cases, and the legal punishment of both is identical. But by the operation of the rule just referred to, the accessary, though he may be equally guilty with the principal,—nay, even more guilty, for he may have instigated the commission of the crime,—is enabled to escape, because, by accident or otherwise, the principal cannot be tried and punished. A case occurred many years ago in

Massachusetts, illustrating the practical absurdity of this distinction. The principal and accessary in the commission of a heinous murder, were both arrested and indicted for the crime; but before the trial of either, the principal committed suicide; and though the case was a strong one against the accessary, he was discharged, by the application of this rule, the principal not having been convicted. The distinction referred to does not exist in cases of misdemeanor, where all who commit the offence are deemed principals; and the Commissioners see no reason for its further continuance, in cases of felony.

§ 312. A person may be indicted, for having, with the knowledge of the commission of a public offence, taken money or property of another, or a gratuity or reward, or an engagement or promise therefor, upon an agreement or understanding, express or implied, to compound or conceal the offence, or to abstain from a prosecution therefor, or to withhold any evidence thereof, though the person guilty of the original offence have not been indicted or tried.

The reasons stated in the note to sections 310, and 311 are applicable to this section.

CHAPTER III.

ARRAIGNMENT OF THE DEFENDANT.

§ 313. When the indictment is filed, the defendant must be arraigned thereon, before the court in which it is found, if it be triable therein, or if not, before the court to which it is sent or removed.

§ 314. If the indictment be for a felony, the defendant must be personally present; but if for a misdemeanor only, his personal appearance is unnecessary, and he may appear upon the arraignment by counsel.

§ 315. When his personal appearance is necessary, if he be in custody, the court may direct the officer in whose custody he is, to bring him before it to be arraigned; and the officer must do so accordingly.

§ 316. If the defendant have been discharged on bail, or have deposited money instead thereof, and do not appear to be arraigned, when his personal attendance is necessary, the court, in addition to the forfeiture of the undertaking of bail or of the money deposited, may direct the clerk to issue a bench warrant for his arrest.

The provisions of the four preceding sections, are substantially the same as the existing practice, except in reference to the deposit of money, instead of bail.

§ 317. The clerk, on the application of the district attorney, may accordingly at any time after the order, whether the court be sitting or not, issue a bench warrant into one or more counties.

§ 318. The bench warrant upon the indictment must, if the offence be a felony, be substantially in the following form:

"County of *Albany*, [or as the case may be.]

"In the name of the people of the state of New-York:

To any sheriff, constable, marshal or policeman in this state. An indictment having been found on the day of , 1850, in the *court* [SEAL.] *of sessions of the county of Albany*, [or as the case may be,] charging C. D. with the crime of [designating it generally.]

"You are therefore commanded, forthwith to arrest the above named C. D., and bring him *before that court*, [or if the indictment have been sent or removed to another court, before the *court of oyer and terminer of that county*, [or as the case may be,] to answer the indictment; or if the court have adjourned for the term, that you deliver him into the custody of the sheriff of the county of *Albany*, [or as the case may be, or in the city and county of New-York "to the keeper of the city prison of the city of New-York."]

"City [or town] of , the day of , 1850.

"By order of the court,

E. F., clerk."

§ 319. If the offence be a misdemeanor, the bench warrant must be in a similar form, adding to the body thereof, a direction to the following effect: "or if he require it, that you take him before any magistrate in that county, or in the county in which you arrest him, that he may give bail to answer the indictment."

§ 320. If the offence charged be bailable, the court, upon directing the bench warrant to issue, must fix the amount of bail; and an endorsement must be made upon the bench warrant and signed by the clerk, to the following effect:—"The defendant is to be admitted to bail in the sum of—— dollars."

§ 321. The bench warrant may be served in any county, in the same manner as a warrant of arrest, except, that when served in another county, it need not be endorsed by a magistrate of that county.

§ 322. If the defendant be brought before a magistrate of another county for the purpose of giving bail, the magistrate must proceed in respect thereto, in the same manner as if the defendant had been brought before him upon a warrant of arrest, and the same proceedings may be had thereon, as provided in sections 158 to 161, both inclusive.

§ 323. When the indictment is for a felony, and the defendant, before the finding thereof, has given bail for his appearance to answer the charge, the court, to which the indictment is presented, or sent or removed for trial, may order the defendant to be committed to actual custody, either without bail, or unless he give bail in an increased amount, to be specified in the order.

§ 324. If the defendant be present when the order is made, he must be forthwith committed accordingly. If he be not present, a bench warrant must be issued and proceeded upon, in the manner provided in this chapter.

§ 325. If the defendant appear for arraignment, without counsel, he must be informed by the court that it is his right to have counsel before being arraigned, and must be asked if he desire the aid of counsel.

This section is designed to protect the rights of the defendant and to carry out the principle already referred to in the note to sections 187 to 189, *p.* 84–87.

§ 326. The arraignment must be made by the court, or by the clerk or district attorney, under its direction, and consists in reading the indictment to the defendant, and delivering to him a copy thereof, and of the endorsements thereon, including the list of witnesses endorsed on it, or appended thereto, as provided in section 287, and in asking him whether he pleads guilty or not guilty to the indictment.

The same as the existing practice, except in requiring a copy of the indictment with the list of witnesses, to be delivered to the defendant upon his arraignment. No good reason is perceived, why the right secured to a party in a civil action, to be served with a copy of the pleading he is called upon to answer, should not be extended to criminal cases.

§ 327. When the defendant is arraigned, he must be informed that if the name by which he is indicted be not his true name, he must then declare his true name, or be proceeded against by the name in the indictment.

§ 328. If he give no other name, the court may proceed accordingly.

§ 329. If he allege that another name is his true name, the court must direct an entry thereof in the minutes of the arraignment; and the subsequent proceedings on the indictment may be had against him, by that name, referring also to the name by which he is indicted.

The last three sections are designed to obviate the necessity of a plea of misnomer, and at the same time to protect the rights of the defendant. A provision, similar in principle, is contained in *Liv. Crim. Code*, 523, *art* 280.

§ 330. If, on the arraignment, the defendant require it, he must be allowed until the next day, or such further time may be allowed him, as the court may deem reasonable, to answer the indictment.

§ 331. If the defendant do not require time, as provided in the last section, or if he do, then on the next day, or at such further day as the court may have allowed him, he may, in answer to the arraignment, either move the court to set aside the indictment, or may demur or plead thereto.

The modes pointed out in this section are the only ones in which the defendant can, by the existing practice, answer the indictment.

CHAPTER IV.

SETTING ASIDE THE INDICTMENT.

§ 332. The indictment must be set aside, by the court in which the defendant is arraigned, and upon his motion, in either of the following cases:

1. When it is not found, endorsed and presented, as prescribed in sections 284 and 288.

2. When the names of the witnesses examined before the grand jury, or whose depositions may have been read before them, are not inserted at the foot of the indictment, or endorsed thereon, as prescribed in section 287.

3. When a person is permitted to be present during the session of the grand jury, while the charge em-

braced in the indictment is under consideration, except as provided in section 266.

The practice provided in this section, is a substitute for the motion to quash an indictment, and comprizes, as the grounds for the motion, such matters only as affect the substantial rights of the defendant.

§ 333. If the motion to set aside the indictment be not made, the defendant is precluded from afterwards taking the objections mentioned in the last section.

By the existing practice, the motion to quash an indictment may, in the discretion of the court, be made after plea or demurrer. The grounds upon which it may be made, being such as do not affect the merits of the cause, though they may touch a substantial right, it is deemed proper to provide that the motion be made before plea or demurrer.

§ 334. The motion must be heard at the time of the arraignment, unless, for good cause, the court postpone the hearing to another time.

§ 335. If the motion be denied, the defendant must immediately answer the indictment, either by demurring or pleading thereto.

§ 336. If the motion be granted, the court must order that the defendant, if in custody, be discharged therefrom, or if admitted to bail, that his bail be exonerated, or if he have deposited money instead of bail, that the money be refunded to him; unless it direct that the case be re-submitted to the same or another grand jury.

§ 337. If the court direct that the case be re-submitted, the defendant, if already in custody, must so remain, unless he be admitted to bail; or if already admitted to bail, or money have been deposited instead thereof, the bail or money is answerable for the appearance of the defendant to answer a new indictment.

The last two sections are intended to prevent the setting aside of an indictment being productive of a prejudice to public justice, by leaving it discretionary with the court, either to discharge the defendant or to re-submit the case to another grand jury.

§ 338. Unless a new indictment be found, before the next grand jury of the county or city is discharged, the court must on the discharge of such grand jury, make the order prescribed by section 336.

To prevent undue delay, it seems proper to provide that the new indictment should be found within a prescribed time.

§ 339. An order to set aside an indictment, as provided in this chapter, is no bar to a future prosecution for the same offence.

In accordance with the existing rule.

CHAPTER V.

DEMURRER.

§ 340. The only pleading on the part of the defendant, is either a demurrer or a plea.

§ 341. Both the demurrer and the plea must be put in in open court, either at the time of the arraignment, or at such other time as may be allowed to the defendant for that purpose.

The last two sections are in accordance with the present practice.

§ 342. The defendant may demur to the indictment, when it appears upon the face thereof, either,

1. That the grand jury, by which it was found, had no legal authority to inquire into the offence charged, by reason of its not being within the local jurisdiction of the county:

2. That it does not substantially conform to the requirements of sections 291 and 292:

3. That more than one offence is charged in the indictment:

4. That the facts stated do not constitute a public offence:

5. That the indictment contains any matter, which, if true, would constitute a legal justification or excuse of the offence charged, or other legal bar to the prosecution.

The grounds of demurrer here stated do not vary from the present practice, and are all of them substantial.

§ 343. The demurrer must be in writing, signed either by the defendant or his counsel, and filed. It must distinctly specify the grounds of objection to the indictment, or it may be disregarded.

§ 344. Upon the demurrer being filed, the objections presented thereby must be heard, either immediately, or at such time as the court may appoint.

§ 345. Upon considering the demurrer, the court must give judgment, either allowing or disallowing it; and an order to that effect must be entered upon the minutes.

§ 346. If the demurrer be allowed, the judgment is final upon the indictment demurred to, and is a bar to another prosecution for the same offence, unless the court, being of opinion that the objection on which the demurrer is allowed may be avoided in a new indictment, direct the case to be re-submitted to the same or another grand jury.

§ 347. If the court do not direct the case to be resubmitted, the defendant, if in custody, must be discharged, or if admitted to bail, his bail is exonerated, or if he have deposited money instead of bail, the money must be refunded to him.

§ 348. If the court direct that the case be submitted anew, the same proceedings must be had thereon, as are prescribed in sections 337 and 338.

§ 349. If the demurrer be disallowed, the court must permit the defendant, at his election, to plead; which he must do forthwith, or at such time as the court may allow. If he do not plead, judgment must be pronounced against him.

By the existing practice, a judgment against the defendant upon a demurrer, is final, if the offence charged be a misdemeanor, but otherwise, if it be a felony. See *The Queen v. Bowen*, 1 *C. & K.* 501. There seems to be no good reason why, in either case, the defendant should not be permitted to plead; and this section proposes to modify the rule accordingly.

§ 350. When the objections mentioned in section 342, appear upon the face of the indictment, they can only be taken by demurrer; except that the objection to the jurisdiction of the court over the subject of the indictment, or that the facts stated do not constitute a public offence, may be taken at the trial, under the plea of not guilty, and in arrest of judgment.

It is a well established principle, that consent cannot give jurisdiction, where the court does not already possess it, over the subject of the indictment : and the portion of this section, which provides that that objection may be taken at the trial or in arrest of judgment, is declaratory of the common law.

The other branch of this section, which allows the objection, that the facts stated do not constitute a public offence, to be taken at the trial or in arrest of judgment, is equally proper, but for a different reason. Nothing can be more idle, than to proceed to the conviction of a defendant, upon a state of facts appearing on the face of the indictment, which would not warrant a legal judgment against him.

CHAPTER VI.

PLEA.

§ 351. There are three kinds of pleas to an indictment. A plea of

1. Guilty:

2. Not guilty:

3. A former judgment of conviction or acquittal of the offence charged; which may be pleaded either with or without the plea of not guilty.

The only special plea allowed by the code, is that of a former judgment of conviction or acquittal. The reason for this is, that it is not fairly presumable that the prosecution will be required to be informed beforehand of any other matter of defence.

§ 352. Every plea must be oral, and must be entered upon the minutes of the court.

In conformity with the existing practice.

§ 353. The plea must be entered in substantially the following form:

1. If the defendant plead guilty:—"The defendant pleads, that he is guilty of the offence charged in this indictment:"

2. If he plead not guilty:—"The defendant pleads, that he is not guilty of the offence charged in this indictment:"

3. If he plead a former conviction or acquittal: "The defendant pleads, that he has already been convicted, (or acquitted, as the case may be,) of the offence charged in this indictment, by the judgment of the court of —— (naming it,) rendered at ——, (naming the place,) on the —— day of ——."

These forms are given, (and especially the last,) to obviate the necessity of a demurrer, if the plea, as it might be drawn under the existing rules, should not be substantially sufficient.

§ 354. A plea of guilty can in no case be put in, except by the defendant himself in open court, unless upon an indictment against a corporation; in which case, it may be put in by counsel.

Some doubt has existed as to whether the defendant may, in a case of misdemeanor, plead guilty by counsel. It is safer that this plea be invariably put in, in person, except in the case of a corporation, which cannot appear except by counsel.

§ 355. The court may, at any time before judgment upon a plea of guilty, permit it to be withdrawn, and a plea of not guilty substituted.

§ 356. The plea of not guilty is a denial of every material allegation in the indictment.

§ 357. All matters of fact, tending to establish a defence, other than that specified in the third sub-division of section 351, may be given in evidence under the plea of not guilty.

The last three sections are declaratory of the existing practice.

§ 358. If the defendant were formerly acquitted on the ground of a variance between the indictment and the proof, or the indictment were dismissed upon an objection to its form or substance, without a judgment of acquittal, it is not an acquittal of the same offence.

§ 359. When, however, he was acquitted on the merits, he is deemed acquitted of the same offence, notwithstanding a defect in form or substance, in the indictment on which he was acquitted.

The last two sections are substantially the same as *2 R. S., 3d ed.* 788, *sec.* 27, 28.

§ 360. When the defendant shall have been convicted or acquitted, upon an indictment for an offence consisting of different degrees, the conviction or acquittal is a bar to another indictment for the offence charged in the former, or for any inferior degree of that offence, or for an attempt to commit the same, or for an offence necessarily included therein, of which he might have been convicted under that indictment as provided in sections 501 and 502.

Declaratory of the existing rule.

§ 361. If the defendant refuse to answer the indictment, by demurrer or plea, a plea of not guilty must be entered.

Taken from 2 *R. S.*, 3*d ed.* 816, *sec.* 72.

CHAPTER VII.

REMOVAL OF THE ACTION, BEFORE TRIAL.

The existing practice, in respect to the removal of an indictment before trial, is proposed to be abolished. By the present statutes, an indictment may be removed from a court of sessions to the court of oyer and terminer of the same county, by the order of a judge of the supreme court; and an indictment may also be removed by a similar order, from a court of oyer and terminer, to the supreme court. In either case, sufficient reason reasons must be shown for the removal, and when removed, the court may remit the case to the court from which the removal was had.

It is proposed, instead of this inconvenent practice, to substitute, in all cases, a removal by the supreme court, where good cause is shown, into the court of oyer and terminer of the same or another county. The object usually sought by the removal of an indictment into the supreme court, is the change of the venue to another county, where a fair trial can not be had in the county in which the indictment was found; and a removal into the court of oyer and terminer of the same county was ordinarily asked, in consequence of the difficulty of the case. Both these objects are attained, by the uniform mode of procedure proposed in the code. The application is to be made to the supreme court for this purpose; and if sufficient cause be shown, the order of that court removing the cause into the oyer and terminer of the same or another county, is final.

§ 362. All writs and other proceedings heretofore existing, for the removal of criminal actions prosecuted by indictment, from one court to another before trial, are abolished; and the only mode of removing a criminal action, prosecuted by indictment, from one court to another, before trial, is that prescribed by this chapter.

§ 363. A criminal action, prosecuted by indictment, may, at any time before trial, on the application of the defendant, be removed from the court in which it is pending, as provided in this chapter, in the following cases:

1. From a court of sessions or a city court, to the court of oyer and terminer of the same county, for good cause shown:

2. From a court of oyer and terminer or sessions, or a city court, to the court of oyer and terminer of anoth-

er county, on the ground that a fair and impartial trial cannot be had in the county or city where the indictment is pending.

§ 364. If one or more trials be had, and a new trial is necessary, either by reason of the discharge of a jury without a verdict, or of the granting of a new trial, the removal may be allowed at any time before the new trial.

§ 365. The application for the order of removal must be made to the supreme court, at a special term in the district, upon notice of at least ten days to the district attorney of the county where the indictment is pending, with a copy of the affidavits or other papers on which the application is founded.

§ 366. To enable the defendant to make the application, a judge of the supreme court may, in his discretion, upon good cause shown by affidavit, make an order staying the trial of the indictment until the application can be made and decided.

§ 367. When an application for an order to stay the trial is made to a judge of the supreme court, he must endorse his decision on the affidavits or other papers presented to him, and cause them to be immediately filed with the clerk of the court in which the indictment is pending.

§ 368. If the application for an order to stay the trial be made to one judge and denied, a similar application cannot be made to another judge.

§ 869. A violation of the last section is punishable as a misdemeanor, and as a contempt of the court in which the indictment is pending; and that court must vacate an order of removal made in violation thereof.

§ 370. If the supreme court order the removal of the action, a certified copy of the order for that purpose must be delivered to and filed by the clerk of the court where the indictment is pending; who must thereupon transmit the same with a certified copy of the pleadings and proceedings in the action, including the undertakings for the appearance of the defendant or of the witnesses, to the court to which the action is removed.

§ 371. If the defendant be in custody, and the removal be to the court of oyer and terminer of anothe county than that where the indictment is pending, the order must provide for the removal of the defendant, by the sheriff of the county where he is imprisoned, to the custody of the proper officer of the county to which the action is removed; and he must be forthwith removed accordingly.

§ 372. An order for the removal of the action is of no effect, unless a certified copy thereof be filed, as required by section 370, before a juror is sworn to try the indictment. The court to which it is removed, must thereupon proceed to trial and judgment therein.

TITLE VI.

OF THE PROCEEDINGS ON THE INDICTMENT, BEFORE TRIAL.

CHAPTER I.

THE MODE OF TRIAL.

§ 373. An issue of fact arises,

1. Upon a plea of not guilty: or,

2. Upon a plea of a former conviction or acquittal of the same offence.

§ 374. An issue of fact must be tried by a jury of the county in which the indictment was found, unless the action be removed, by order of the supreme court, into the court of oyer and terminer of another county, as provided in the second subdivision of section 363.

This section is founded upon 2 *R. S.*, 3*d ed.* 819, *sec.* 1, as modified by section 363, of this code.

§ 375. If the indictment be for a misdemeanor, the trial may be had in the absence of the defendant, if he appear by counsel; but if for a felony, he must be personally present.

Declaratory of the existing practice. See also, *Liv. Crim. Code*, 527, *art.* 320.

CHAPTER II.

FORMATION OF THE TRIAL JURY.

§ 376. The jurors duly drawn and summoned for the trial of issues of fact, at a circuit court, are also the jurors for the trial of issues of fact upon indictments at the court of oyer and terminer held at the same time; and those summoned for the trial of issues of fact, in civil actions, at a city court, are in like manner, the jurors for the trial of issues of fact upon indictments, at that court.

Taken in part from 2 *R. S.*, 3*d. ed.* 819, *sec.* 2. The rest of the section carries out the same principle.

§ 377. A jury must be drawn for the courts of sessions, (except in the city and county of New-York,) only when ordered by the court, or by the supervisors of the county,

§ 378. The order may require, that a jury be drawn for all or any of the terms of the court, or for a particular term; and must specify the number of jurors to be drawn, not exceeding thirty-six, and the name of the court for which they are to be drawn.

§ 379. If made by the court, the order must be entered upon its minutes, at least thirty days before the term for which the jury is ordered. If made by the board of surpervisors, a copy thereof, certified by the clerk of the board, must be filed with the clerk of the county, at least thirty days before the term; and when so filed, is conclusive evidence of the authority for the drawing of the jury.

§ 380. A misdescription of the title of the court, does not affect the validity of the order, if it can be plainly understood therefrom what court is intended.

§ 381. A judge of the supreme court elected in the first judicial district, if he think it necessay, may, by an order in writing, to be filed, at least thirty days before the court, with the clerk of the city and county of New-York, direct an additional number of jurors to be summoned for a court of oyer and terminer in that city and county.

By the 8th section of the act in relation to jurors in the city of New-York, *Laws of* 1847, *p.* 736, the several courts in that city may order as many jurors to be summoned for their respective courts, as in their judgment may be necessary. Some doubt has been expressed as to whether this supersedes the former provisions, *2 R. S. 3d ed*, 509, *sec.* 24, which are substantially the same as those contained in the proposed sections. These sections are in no respect inconsistent with the provisions of the local act referred to, and should, in the opinion of the Commissioners, be adopted, as tending to obviate the inconvenience often arising from the insufficiency of the number of jurors summoned for the circuit.

§ 382. At the opening of the court, the clerk must prepare separate ballots, containing the names of the persons returned as jurors, with their places of residence, and occupations, which must be folded as nearly alike as possible, and so that the name cannot be seen, and must deposit them in a sufficient box.

This section is taken substantially from 2 *R. S.*, 3*d ed.*, 516, *sec.* 59.

§ 383. When the indictment is called for trial, and before drawing the jury, either party may require the names of all the jurors in the panel to be called, and that an attachment issue against those who are absent; but the court may, in its discretion, wait or not, for the return of the attachment.

Designed to enforce the performance of jury duty, and to insure, if practicable, a trial by the panel summoned for that purpose.

§ 384. Before the name of any juror is drawn, the box must be closed, and shaken, so as to intermingle the ballots therein. The clerk must then, without looking at the ballots, draw them from the box, through a hole in the lid, so large only as conveniently to admit the hand.

In substantial conformity with 2 *R. S.*, *3d. ed.*, 517, *sec.* 66.

§ 385. When the jury is completed, the ballots containing the names of the jurors sworn, must be laid aside, and kept apart from the ballots containing the names of the other jurors, until the jury so sworn is discharged.

Taken from 2 *R. S.*, *3d. ed.*, 516, *sec.* 62.

§ 386. After the jury are so discharged, the ballots, containing their names, must be again folded, and returned to the box; and so on, as often as a trial is had.

Taken from 2 *R. S.*, *3d ed.*, 516, *sec.* 63.

§ 387. If a juror be absent, when his name is drawn, or be set aside, or excused from serving on the trial, the ballot containing his name must be folded, and returned to the box, as soon as the jury is sworn.

Taken from 2 *R. S.*, *3d ed.*, 517, *sec.* 67.

§ 388. When a jury has been duly drawn and summoned, if, upon calling the indictment for trial, twenty-four of the jurors summoned do not appear, the court must order the sheriff to summon as many persons as it may think proper, at least sufficient to make twenty-four jurors, from whom a jury for the trial of the indictment must be selected.

The provision of the Revised Statutes on this subject is as follows:—"When twenty-four jurors, duly drawn and summoned do not appear, or when, by reason of there being one or more juries impanelled, or in consequence of jurors being set aside, or for any other reason, there shall not remain twenty-four ballots, containing the names of jurors then attending, the court shall order the sheriff to summon from the by-standers, or from the county at large, so many persons qualified to serve as jurors, *as shall be necessary to make at least twenty-four jurors*, from whom a jury for the trial of the indictment may be selected." 2 *R. S.*, 3*d ed.*, 819, *sec.* 3.

The proposed section is the same in substance as that quoted, except that the court is authorised to direct the summoning of "*as many persons as it may think proper, at least sufficient to make twenty-four jurors,*" instead of "*so many persons qualified to serve as jurors, as shall be necessary to make at least twenty-four jurors,*" in conformity with the construction given to the provision of the Revised Statutes, in *The People v. Colt*, 3 *Hill*, 435, 436.

§ 389. In the city and county of New-York, the names of the persons required to complete the jury, must be drawn by the county clerk, in the presence of the sheriff or under sheriff, and of one or more of the members of the court, from the trial jury box of that city and county. The drawing must be conducted, in all respects, as prescribed by the code of civil procedure, in relation to the drawing of a grand jury.

§ 390. In any other county, the names of the persons required to complete the jury, may, in the discretion of the court, be drawn as provided in the last section, or may be publicly designated by the court, from the by-standers, or the body of the county.

§ 391. The names of the persons summoned to complete the jury, must be written on distinct pieces of paper, folded each as nearly alike as possible, and so that the name can not be seen, and must be deposited in the box mentioned in section 382.

§ 392. The clerk must thereupon, under the direction of the court, publicly draw out of the box, so many of the ballots, one after another, as are sufficient to form the jury.

See notes to sections 229, 230, p. 107, 108.

§ 393. The jury consists of twelve men, chosen by lot as prescribed in this chapter, and sworn to try and determine the issue by an unanimous verdict.

§ 394. If a sufficient number cannot be obtained from the box to form a jury, the court may, as often as is necessary, order the sheriff to summon so many persons, qualified to serve as jurors, as it deems sufficient, to form a jury; and the provisions of sections 389 and 390 govern the execution of the order. The jurors so summoned must be called from the list returned by the sheriff, and so many of them, not excused or discharged, as may be necessary to complete the jury, must be impanelled and sworn.

CHAPTER III.

CALENDAR OF ISSUES FOR TRIAL.

§ 395. The district attorney must, at least four days before the term, furnish the clerk with a note of the several indictments then pending and to be tried at the next term, containing the title of each indictment, and the day when it was filed, and specifying whether it be for a felony or a misdemeanor, and whether the defendant be in custody or on bail.

§ 396. The clerk must, therefrom, prepare a calendar of the indictments to be tried at the term, enumerating them according to the date of the filing of the indictment, and specifying opposite the title of each action, whether it be for a felony or a misdemeanor, and whether the defendant be in custody or on bail; and must in like manner enter thereon all indictments found during the term, and on which issues of fact are joined.

§ 397. The issues on the calendar must be disposed of in the following order, unless, npon the application of either party, for good cause, the court direct an indictment to be tried out of its order:

1. Indictments for felony, where the defendant is in custody:

2. Indictments for misdemeanor, where the defendant is in custody:

3. Indictments for felony, where the defendant is on bail: and

4. Indictments for misdemeanor, where the defendant is on bail.

§ 398. An indictment pending before the term cannot be tried thereat, unless it be placed on the calendar, as provided in sections 395 and 396, except with the consent of the defendant.

The last four sections propose a course of proceeding, as to the order of the trial of causes, which the Commissioners believe will be conducive to great convenience both to the bench and bar, and at the same time promote the substantial rights of the people and of the defendant. Great complaints have existed, (especially in those parts of the state where there is a large amount of criminal business,) of the inconvenience resulting from a want of regulation on this subject. The order of the trial of criminal cases is, as the practice now stands, entirely under the control of the district attorney, who may bring them on in any order and at any time he may see fit. This has led to much embarrassment, not merely to the defendant, who is thus compelled to be ready for trial at any moment, but to the court, whose business is often delayed and thrown into confusion, by the necessity of the postponement of the trial, which arises from the fact that no rule as to the order of business is prescribed. The Commissioners propose as a remedy for this inconvenience, that a calendar shall be made of all the indictments ready for trial at each court, arranging them in the order in which the indictments were found, and distinguishing between felonies and misdemeanors, and between the cases in which the defendant is in custody or on bail. The cases are then to be tried in this order; first, those in which the defendant is in custody; and second, those in which he is on bail. Either party may apply, however, for a postponement of the trial; but if no sufficient cause be shown for the postponement, it must be tried or dismissed, subject to the right of the court, according to the justice of the case, to determine whether or not a dismissal of the indictment shall be a bar to another prosecution. See *p.* 186, 187.

§ 399. After his plea, the defendant is entitled to at least four days to prepare for his trial, if he require it.

The object of this provision is, to give the defendant a reasonable opportunity to prepare for trial, after plea. It may be objected, that unnecessary delay may be produced thereby; but the Commissioners cannot see any just ground for the objection. In civil actions, the cause cannot even be put upon the calendar for trial, unless upon ten days previous notice: and surely no good reason can be given why a case involving the life or liberty of the defendant, should be pressed on with undue haste.

§ 400. The clerk must keep a register of all the criminal actions in the court, in which he must enter,

1. All cases returned to the court by a magistrate whether the defendant be discharged or held to answer:

2. All indictments found in the court, or sent or removed thereto for trial, with the time of finding the indictment, or when it was sent or removed: and

3. The time of arraignment, of the demurrer or plea, and of the trial, conviction or acquittal of the defendant,; together with a brief note of all the other proceedings in the action.

§ 401. The register must be submitted to the court at its opening at every term.

The object of the last two sections, is to bring, at every term, to the notice of the court, the business pending before it. This will enable the court to exercise a supervision over the criminal business, which is required by a due regard for the public interests.

CHAPTER IV.

POSTPONEMENT OF THE TRIAL.

The practice in respect to the postponement of the trial in criminal cases, is now wholly unregulated, either by statute or rule. The district attorney may require the trial of the cause, at any time which may suit his convenience, and may, without giving any reason, postpone or delay the trial as long as he pleases, subject only to the power of the court to discharge the defendant, either on bail or on his own recognizance, if the cause be not brought to trial before the end of the second term. 2 *R. S.* 3*d. ed.* 821, *sec.* 28—30.

The defendant, on the other hand, must be always ready, and unless a sufficient legal cause for postponement be shown, the case may be brought to trial at any time. Even if he be discharged on bail or on his own recognizance, the indictment still remains, and he may, at any time, no matter how distant, be compelled in like manner to go to trial.

This is not so in civil actions. By the *Amended Code of Procedure, sec.* 258, it is provided that, "either party giving the notice, may bring the issue to trial, and in the absence of the adverse party, unless the court for good cause otherwise direct, may proceed with his case, and take a dismissal of the complaint, or a verdict or judgment, as the case may require."

Why should a different principle prevail in criminal cases? Why, if the defendant show no sufficient ground for postponement, should he be compelled to go to trial, while no such duty is imposed upon the prosecution?

This chapter embodies principles which abundantly explain themselves, protecting alike the interests of the public and the rights of the defendant.

§ 402. When an indictment is called for trial, or at any time previous thereto, the court may, upon sufficient cause shown by either party, direct the trial to be postponed to another day in the same term, or to another term. The affidavits read on both sides upon the application, must at the same time be filed with the clerk.

§ 403. If, when the indictment is called for trial, the defendant appear for trial, and no sufficient cause for postponing the same be shown by the district attorney, the court must order the indictment to be discharged; unless, being of opinion that the public interests require the indictment to be retained for trial, it direct it to be so retained.

§ 404. If the court order the indictment to be discharged, the order is not a bar to another prosecution for the same offence, unless the court so direct. If the court so direct, judgment of acquittal must be entered.

CHAPTER V.

CHALLENGING THE JURY.

§ 405. A challenge is an objection made to the trial jurors, and is of two kinds:

1. To the panel:

2. To an individual juror.

The same as the existing practice, except that instead of challenges to the array or to the polls, they are more plainly designated as challenges to the panel, or to an individual juror. See *Liv. Crim. Code*, 528, *art.* 321.

§ 406. When several defendants are tried together, they cannot sever their challenges, but must join therein.

In accordance with the existing rule.

§ 407. A challenge to the panel, is an objection made to all the trial jurors returned, and may be taken by either party, as well to the panel returned for the term, as to the additional panel ordered to complete the jury as prescribed by section 388.

In conformity with the present practice.

§ 408. A challenge to the panel can be founded only on a material departure from the forms prescribed by the code of civil procedure, in respect to the drawing and return of the jury, or on the intentional omission of the sheriff to summon one or more of the jurors drawn.

Taken from *Liv. Crim. Code*, 528, *art.* 324; and in accordance with the spirit of the existing statute. 2 *R. S.*, 3*d. ed.*, 515, 516, *sec.* 56, 57.

§ 409. A challenge to the panel must be taken, before a juror is sworn, and must be in writing, specifying plainly and distinctly the facts constituting the ground of challenge.

Declaratory of the existing practice. 1 *Gra. Prac.* 3d. *ed.*, 769.

§ 410. If the sufficiency of the facts alleged as a ground of challenge be denied, the adverse party may except to the challenge. The exception need not be in writing, but must be entered upon the minutes of the court; and thereupon the court must proceed to try the sufficiency of the challenge, assuming the facts alleged therein to be true.

§ 411. If, on the exception, the court deem the challenge sufficient, it may, if justice require it, permit the party excepting, to withdraw his exception, and to deny the facts alleged in the challenge. If the exception be allowed, the court may, in like manner, permit an amendment of the challenge.

The provisions of the last three sections are the same as the existing practice, except substituting "*exception*" for "*demurrer*" to the challenge.

§ 412. If the challenge be denied, the denial may, in like manner, be oral, and must be entered upon the minutes of the court; and the court must proceed to try the question of fact.

§ 413. Upon the trial of the challenge, the officers, whether judicial or ministerial, whose irregularity is complained of, as well as any other persons, may be examined to prove or disprove the facts alleged as the ground of the challenge.

§ 414. If, either upon an exception to the challenge, or a denial of the facts, the challenge be allowed, the court must discharge the jury, so far as the trial of the indictment in question is concerned; and no other jury for the trial thereof, can be summoned for the same term. If it be disallowed, the court must direct the jury to be impanelled.

§ 415. Before a juror is called, the defendant must be informed by the court, or under its direction, that if he intend to challenge an individual juror, he must do so when the juror appears, and before he is sworn.

§ 416. A challenge to an individual juror, is either,

1. Peremptory, or

2. For cause.

The last five sections are substantially in accordance with the existing practice.

§ 417. It must be taken when the juror appears, and before he is sworn; but the court may, for good cause, permit it to be taken after the juror is sworn, and before the jury is completed.

The general rule now is, that a challenge to an individual juror must be taken when the juror appears. It is proposed to qualify it, by giving to the court the discretion to allow it to be interposed after the particular juror is sworn, and before the jury is completed. This is in accordance with the case of *The People v Damon*, 13 *Wend*, 351, in which it was held that, a juror who, *after he is sworn in chief* and has taken his seat, is discovered to be incompetent to serve, may, in the exercise of a sound discretion, be set] aside by the court, at *any time before evidence is given;* and that this may be done even in a *capital case*, and as well for cause existing *before* as *after* the juror is sworn.

§ 418. A peremptory challenge can be taken by the defendant only, and may be oral. It is an objection to a juror, for which no reason need be given, but upon which the court must exclude him.

In conformity with the existing practice.

§ 419. If the offence charged be punishable with death or with imprisonment in a state prison for life, the defendant is entitled to twenty peremptory challenges. On a trial for any other offence, he is entitled to five peremptory challenges.

Taken from 2 *R. S. 3d. ed.*, 819, *sec.* 9; and from *Laws of* 1847, *p.* 130, *ch.* 134.

§ 420. A challenge for cause may be taken either by the people, or by the defendant.

§ 421. It is an objection to a particular juror, and is either,

1. General, that the juror is disqualified from serving in any case; or

2. Particular, that he is disqualified from serving in the case on trial.

§ 422. General causes of challenge are,

1. A conviction for a felony:

2. A want of any of the qualifications prescribed by the code of civil procedure, to render a person a competent juror:

3. Unsoundness of mind, or such defect in the faculties of the mind or organs of the body, as renders him incapable of performing the duties of a juror.

§ 423. Particular causes of challenge are of two kinds:

1. For such a bias, as, when the existence of the facts is ascertained, in judgment of law disqualifies the juror, and which is known in this code as implied bias:

2. For the existence of a state of mind on the part of the juror, in reference to the case, or to either party, which satisfies the triers, in the exercise of a sound discretion, that he cannot try the issue impartially and without prejudice to the substantial rights of the party challenging, and which is known in this code as actual bias.

§ 424. A challenge for implied bias may be taken for all or any of the following causes, and for no other:

1. Consanguinity or affinity within the ninth degree, to the person alleged to be injured by the offence

charged, or on whose complaint the prosecution was instituted, or to the defendant:

3 *Bl. Com.* 363.

2. Standing in the relation of guardian and ward, attorney and client, master and servant, or landlord and tenant, or being a member of the family of the defendant, or of the person alleged to be injured by the offence charged, or on whose complaint the prosecution was instituted, or in his employment on wages:

Liv. Crim. Code, p. 529, *art.* 330, *subd.* 2.

3. Being a party adverse to the defendant in a civil action or having complained against, or been accused by him in a criminal prosecution:

4. Having served on the grand jury which found the indictment, or on a coroner's jury which inquired into the death of a person whose death is the subject of the indictment:

The first part of this subdivision is taken from 2 *R. S.* 3*d ed.*, 819, *sec.* 9. That part which excludes a coroner's juror is founded on the same principle.

5. Having served on a trial jury, which has tried another person for the offence charged in the indictment:

Liv. Crim. Code, p. 529, *art.* 330, *subd.* 4.

6. Having been one of a jury formerly sworn to try the same indictment, and whose verdict was set aside,

or which was discharged without a verdict, after the cause was submitted to it:

Liv. Crim. Code, p. 529, *art.* 330, *subd.* 5.

7. Having served as a juror, in a civil action brought against the defendant, for the act charged as an offence:

Liv. Crim. Code, p. 529, *art.* 330, *subd.* 5.

8. If the offence charged be punishable with death, the entertaining of such conscientious opinions as would preclude his finding the defendant guilty: in which case he shall neither be permitted nor compelled to serve as a juror.

This subdivision is somewhat broader in its terms than the existing statute, but conformable to the construction which has been given it. The Revised Statutes provide that "persons of any religious denomination, whose opinions are such as to preclude them from finding any defendant guilty of an offence punishable with death, shall not be compelled or allowed to serve as jurors on the trial of an indictment for any offence punishable with death." 2 *R. S.* 3*d. ed,* 820, *sec.* 12. In *The People v. Damon,* 13 Wend. 351, it was held by the supreme court that "a person whose opinions are such as to preclude him from finding a defendant guilty of an offence punishable with death, is an incompetent juror on the trial of an indictment for an offence subjecting to that punishment; it is not the opinions on this subject of the *religious denomination* to which he belongs which exclude him, but his own opinions; and therefore, if he entertains them, though he does not belong to a religious denomination, he is incompetent to serve as a juror."

§ 425. A challenge for actual bias may be taken for the cause mentioned in the second subdivision of section 423, and for no other cause.

The last six sections are intended to establish a clear and intelligible, as well as just rule, in respect to the grounds of exclusion of jurors on challenge. No subject in the whole range of criminal practice, has been found more productive of delay, or of embarrassment in the trial of causes, than this, and there is none which, in the present understanding of the rules applicable to it, calls more loudly for legislative interposition. Whether the embarrassments referred to arise from the rules which exist at the common law, or from a loose or mistaken application of them, it is immaterial to enquire. It is enough to know that they exist, and that without the establishment of some uniform standard of decision, their existence must inevitably continue. The fundamental principle on which the right of challenge rests, is, that every citizen, whether in a civil or criminal action, is entitled to the determination of his cause by a fair and impartial jury, and although in early times, a different principle prevailed, and the jury were taken from the neighborhood for the very reason that they were supposed to know something of the controversy, the wisdom of a more modern age has established as a test of the fitness of a juror, his perfect and entire impartiality between the parties. As a means of ascertaining whether this impartiality exists, the common law has established two forms of challenge, the one for *principal cause*,—the other *for favor*. The difference between these two forms of challenge is that the former is based upon the allegation of a fact which carries with it evident marks, either of malice or favor, and is sufficient of itself to exclude the juror, without leaving anything to the discretion of the triers or of the court; while the latter, though of the same nature, is of inferior degree, and is to be resorted to only where, though the juror is not so palpably partial as to give cause for a principal challenge, yet there are grounds to suspect that he will act under some undue influence or bias, in which case the triers, in the exercise of a sound discretion, may reject him.

Under the former challenge, the sole enquiry is, whether the fact alleged as the ground of exclusion exists, or if it exist, whether it be sufficient. With a single exception, which will be presently alluded to, the grounds of this challenge are clearly defined and well understood—They embrace the case of relationship to either of the parties, interest in the event, and such other facts of a similar nature, and which are enumerated in section 424, as when once established, to render it manifest that the juror cannot act impartially. At an early day, however, the courts resolved to regard the formation or expression of opinion by a juror as to the right of the case, as a ground of principal challenge, instead of leaving it, where it more properly belonged as a ground of challenge for favor, and out of this has arisen all the confusion and embarrassment of which so much complaint is made—The question, what degree of opinion will exclude the juror on principal challenge, or is more properly referable to the challenge for favor, though much discussed in the courts of this state, has never yet been so far settled as to relieve trials of the delays and difficulties by which they have been beset in its application. The cases all agree in the abstract rule that the formation or expression of an opinion as to the guilt or innocence of the defendant is a ground of principal challenge; or in other words, that when it is ascertained that the juror has formed or expressed such an opinion, the law adjudges and the court is bound to declare him incompetent.

(*Ex parte*, *Vermilyea*, 6 Cowen, 564 ; *The People v. Vermilyea*, 7 Cowen, 108 ; *The People v. Mather*, 4 Wend. 231 ; *The People v. Rathbun*, 21 Wend. 542 ; *The People v. Bodine*, 1 Denis, 281 ; *The People v. Honeyman*, 3 Denio, 121 ; *Freeman v. The People* 4 Denio, 33.)

Beyond this, however, the boundary between a principal challenge and a challenge for favor, as well as the degree of opinion which is necessary to sustain either of them, has not been clearly defined, although a nearer approach has been made to a rule on the subject, than is to be found in the earlier cases. In *The People v. Bodine*, 1 Denio, 307, 308, the supreme court remarked:—

"A fixed and absolute opinion may be necessary to sustain a challenge for *principal* cause; but not so where the challenge is *for favor*. In the first species of challenge, the result is a conclusion of *law*, upon ascertained facts; but in the latter, the conclusion is a matter of *fact*, to be found by the triers. No certain rule can be laid down for their guidance. They are sworn to try whether the juror challenged *stands indifferent*; (*Gra. Prac. 2d. ed.*, 307; 1 *Trials per Pais*, 205; *Anonymous*, 1 *Salk.* 152, *pl.* 1; *Bac. Abr. Juries, E.* 12, *notes;*) and this must be determined upon their conscience and discretion, in view of the facts and circumstances in evidence before them. It is competent to prove that the juror challenged and the opposite party are in habits of great intimacy; that they are members of the same society, partners in business, or the like. The feelings of the juror may also be shown, and that whether they amonnt to positive partiality or ill will, or not; as his views and opinions also may be whether mature, absolute or hypothetical. Indeed, any and every fact or circumstance from which bias, partiality or prejudice may justly be inferred, although very weak in degree is admissable on this issue; and the inquiry should by no means be restricted to the isolated question of a fixed and absolute opinion as to the guilt or innocence of the prisoner." And in the more recent case of *The People v. Honeyman*, 3 Denio, 124, the court in referring to the case of *The People v. Bodine*, as establishing the principle that it is for the good sense of the triers to determine how far the opinion formed or expressed by a juror has affected his mind so as to render him competant, remarked:—If we have not been sufficiently explicit already, recent events render it proper to add, that although evidence which tends to show a bias on the mind of the juror must be received, it by no means follows that the juror should be set aside by the triers for slight causes. If, for example, the juror has heard, or has read in a newspaper, that the prisoner is guilty of the crime laid to his charge, and has given credit to the statement, the evidence of those facts must be received; and the triers must not be instructed, as matter of law, that they are not at liberty to reject the juror. Still it would not be a wise or judicious act on their part to set aside the juror, unless they found that he had such a settled opinion concerning the prisoner's guilt, that he could not disregard what he had read, or heard out of court, and render his verdict on the evidence alone." And again:— "Intelligent and right minded men, when they enter the jury box, know how to lay aside what they have heard and read out of doors, and pronounce their verdict upon the evidence, and upon that alone."

Notwithstanding these views, however, furnishing a guide to the discretion of triers upon a challenge to the favor, it will be perceived that no rule, which can be safely enforced, has been established in respect to the degree of opinion necessary to sustain a principal challenge. The rule remains, that the formation or expression of an opinion sustains that challenge, and in its practical application, courts have not felt themselves safe in going beyond that simple inquiry. In the case of *Mary Bodine*, the attempt at a second trial in

New-York failed, though eight thousand jurors were summoned, more than two thousand of whom were examined on principal challenge, and answered in the affirmative to the question, whether they had formed or expressed an opinion as to the guilt or innocence of the prisoner. Had those challenges been taken to the favor, the sensible test suggested by the supreme court in the cases just cited might have been safely applied, and the jury readily formed, if in the exercise of their sound discretion, upon sifting the degree or extent of opinion, the triers had been satisfied that it was not such as to endanger the substantial rights of the prisoner.

Another and not less striking inconvenience, not to say, absurdity, in allowing the formation or expression of an opinion as a ground of principal challenge, is, that after it has been overruled by the court, it may be again made a ground of challenge to the favor and re-submitted to triers. The practical result is, that after a solemn examination of the question by the court and its decision, the whole matter is again gone over, and triers are virtually called upon to overrule that decision, and to exclude a juror whom the court has already adjudged competent.

To remedy these evils, the sections under consideration propose,

1. To restrict the principal challenge, (or as it is termed in the Code, a challenge for implied bias,) to the cases mentioned in section 424, in which, when the fact is established, the partiality of the juror is manifest; and to confine within the challenge to the favor, (or as it is termed, actual bias,) an objection to the juror proceeding upon the formation or expression of an opinion, or any other ground showing him to be not impartial.

2. To define the kind of bias which will justify the triers in excluding the juror, to be the existence of a state of mind on the part of a juror in reference to the case or to either party, which satisfies the triers, in the exercise of a sound discretion, that he cannot try the issue impartially, and without prejudice to the substantial rights of the party challenging.

To carry out these views, a subsequent section, (*sec.* 435,) provides that, "on the trial of a challenge for actual bias, when the evidence is concluded, the court must instruct the triers, that it is their duty to find the challenge true, if the evidence establishes the existence of a state of mind on the part of the juror in reference to the case or to either party, which satisfies them, in the exercise of a sound discretion, that he cannot try the issue impartially and without prejudice to the substantial rights of the party challenging; otherwise they must find the challenge not true. The court can give them no other instruction."

§ 426. An exemption from service on a jury is not a cause of challenge, but the privilege of the person exempted.

Declaratory of the existing rule.

§ 427. In a challenge for implied bias, one or more of the causes stated in section 424 must be alleged. In a challenge for actual bias, the cause stated in the second subdivision of section 423 must be alleged. In either case, the challenge may be oral, but must be entered upon the minutes of the court.

The practice has been, to challenge generally *for principal cause* or *for favor.* The supreme court, however, in *Freeman v. The People*, 4 *Denio*, 31, 32, held that the distinct ground of the challenge must be stated. This section is in conformity with that decision.

§ 428. The adverse party may except to the challenge, in the same manner as to a challenge to the panel; and the same proceedings must be had thereon, as prescribed in section 410, except that if the exception be allowed, the juror must be excluded. The adverse party may also orally deny the facts alleged as the ground of challenge.

§ 429. If the facts be denied, the challenge must be tried as follows:

1. If it be for implied bias, by the court:

2. If it be for actual bias, by triers.

The last two sections are in substantial conformity with the present practice.

§ 430. The triers are three impartial persons, not on the jury panel, appointed by the court. All challenges for actual bias must be tried by the triers thus appointed, a majority of whom may decide.

A challenge of this kind is now tried as follows :—If two jurors have been already called, and take the box without challenge, it must be tried by them; if not, the court appoint two indifferent persons to try it, and who are thence named triers. If the triers try one juror and he be found indifferent, he and the two triers shall try the next. *Co Lit.* 158. And when two jurors shall be sworn upon the jury, they become triers, in the case of all subsequent challenges, and supersede the persons previously sworn as triers. 1 *Bl. Com.* 363. This is a very inconvenient practice, and one which for many reasons should be simplified. At one time you have two, then three, then two triers; and when there are three, questions have arisen as to whether their finding should be unanimous. This is put an end to by the proposed section. It seems to be objectionable also, to allow the jurors who are try the main issue, to be embarrassed by any collateral questions, and possibly to be in some degree prejudiced, by being compelled to determine on the admission of their fellow jurors. The decision of such questions is, and should be, kept distinct from the principal trial. The mode proposed seems to be both convenient and proper.

§ 431. The triers must be sworn, generally, to inquire whether or not the several persons who may be challenged, and in respect to whom the challenges shall be given to them in charge, are true, and to decide the same according to the evidence.

§ 432. Upon the trial of a challenge to an individual juror, the juror challenged may be examined as a witness, to prove or disprove the challenge; and is bound to answer every question pertinent to the inquiry therein.

§ 433. Other witnesses may also be examined on either side; and the rules of evidence applicable to the trial of other issues, govern the admission or exclusion of testimony, on the trial of the challenge.

§ 434. On the trial of a challenge for implied bias, the court must determine the law and the fact, and must either allow or disallow the challenge, and direct an entry accordingly upon the minutes.

The last four sections are declaratory of the existing rules.

§ 435. On the trial of a challenge for actual bias, when the evidence is concluded, the court must instruct the triers, that it is their duty to find the challenge true, if the evidence establishes the existence of a state of mind on the part of the juror, in reference to the case or to either party, which satisfies them, in the exercise of a sound discretion, that he cannot try the issue impartially and without prejudice to the substantial rights of the party challenging; and that if otherwise, they must find the challenge not true. The court can give them no other instruction.

Declaratory of the rule as laid down in *The People v. Bodine*, 1 *Denio*, 307, 308. See an extract from the opinion of the court in that case, in note to sec. 420 – 425, *p.* 197, 198.

§ 436. The triers must thereupon find the challenge either true or not true; and their decision is final. If they find it true, the juror must be excluded.

§ 437. All challenges to an individual juror, except peremptory, must be taken, first by the defendant, and then by the people: and each party must exhaust all his challenges, before the other begins.

§ 438. The challenges of either party need not all be taken at once; but they must be taken separately, in the following order, including in each challenge, all the causes of challenge belonging to the same class:

1. To the panel:

2. To an individual juror, for a general disqualification:

3. To an individual juror, for implied bias:

4. To an individual juror, for actual bias.

§ 439. If all the challenges on both sides be disallowed, the defendant may still take a peremptory challenge, unless the peremptory challenges be exhausted.

The last four sections are the same as the existing practice.

TITLE VII.

OF THE TRIAL.

CHAPTER I.

THE TRIAL.

§ 440. The jury having been impanelled and sworn, the trial must proceed in the following order:

1. If the indictment be for a felony, the clerk or district attorney must read it, and state the plea of the defendant to the jury. In all other cases, this formality may be dispensed with:

2. The district attorney, or other counsel for the people, must open the case, and offer the evidence in support of the indictment:

3. The defendant or his counsel may then open his defence, and offer his evidence in support thereof:

4. The parties may then, respectively, offer rebutting testimony only, unless the court, for good reason, in furtherance of justice, permit them to offer evidence upon their original case:

5. When the evidence is concluded, unless the case is submitted to the jury on either side, or on both sides,

without argument, the counsel for the people must commence, and the defendant, or his counsel, may conclude the argument to the jury.

6. The court must then charge the jury:

This section is in conformity with the existing practice, except the 5th sub-division, which gives to the defendant or his counsel the right to conclude the argument to the jury. This provision, independently of the high authority of Mr. Livingston, seems to the Commissioners to be well sustained, not merely by every consideration of humanity, but by every principle of justice. In defending its introduction, that learned jurist observes—"The order in which the case is opened to the jury, and the proof introduced, is the same as that now in use; but a material change is made, by giving the closing argument to the defendant. It was thought that this was proper and just, because it is an *advantage*, that is to say, a benefit to one party, that the other does not and cannot, from the nature of things, enjoy. To whom shall this be given,—to the accuser or the accused,—to him who asserts or him who denies? Humanity and justice seem to dictate the answer. Every address to a judge must be supposed to contain a new allegation of fact, a new argument, or a new answer to rebut those which have been offered on the other side. To close the debate, therefore, without suffering the accused to reply to such allegation or argument, would be, in so much as regards it, to decide on his case without hearing him. The same thing may be said of the prosecution. The remedy would be, to suffer the argument to go on, until both parties declared they had nothing further to say; but this would rarely happen, and never until the discussion had been protracted to a length so highly inconvenient as not to be permitted. It seems, then, as has been said, that the nature of the case imposes the necessity of giving this advantage to the one party or the other. To give it to the prosecution, sometimes defeats the ends of justice, by enlisting the feelings of humanity on the side of the accused. There is in human nature, when not perverted, a feeling repugnant to oppression, which generally supposes power to be wrong, and ascribes innocence to weakness, whenever they come in competition with each other; and few cases give such scope to the imagination to exert itself in this way, as that of a criminal on his trial. Squalid in his appearance, his body debilitated by confinement, his mind weakened by misery or conscious guilt, abandoned by all the world, he stands alone, to contend with the fearful odds that are arrayed against him. It is true, he has counsel assigned him; but here again the same feelings operate, to lead the judgment astray. This counsel is generally the youngest counsellor at the bar, who is thus made to enter the lists with one of the highest abilities and standing; —with a reputation so well established as to have made him the choicc of government, as the depository of its interests. If you add to all this, the decided advantage of the closing argument, given to a practised advocate, whom long habit has taught to avail himself of every weak argument or suspicious fact, and a zeal in the performance of his duty has taught to believe it proper to do so:—do this, and of two opposite effects, one must be produced, both injurious to the fair administration of justice: either the jury will be swayed by the sentiment I have endeavored to describe, and feel an undue bias in favor of the prisoner: or if this fails to act, the last inexpression given with the force of eloquence and professional skill, may, in doubtful cases, have injurious consequences to the innocent. But give the last word to the accused, and you will do little more than counterbalance the disadvantages inseparable from his situation; while, by this show of humanity and disdain of using the power in your hands, you neutralize the sentiment that would otherwise be felt in his favor. The provision here recommended makes part of the French code of criminal procedure, and it is said to have, in practice, the most beneficial effects." *Liv. Crim. Code*, 232, 233.

In addition to the high authority of Mr. Livingston in its support, the Commissioners have been informed that petitions, very numerously signed, from the county of Chenango, and other counties, were presented at a recent session of the legislature.

The petitioners among other things, well say: "Your petitioners deem it a matter of right to every person accused, to be allowed to *answer* the *arguments* urged, as well as the *proofs* given against him, which often, (and especially in cases of innocence,) affect him more injuriously than the evidence itself. Upon a trial lasting several days, or it may be weeks, where a mass of evidence is given, what man can *anticipate and answer* before hand, every mode of reasoning and all the arguments by which the guilt of the accused may be attempted to be proved and established? Or, all improper inferences which may be ably drawn from each portion of the evidence? Yet, the present law requires this *impossibility*, of one on trial upon a charge involving his liberty or life! Clearly he should have a full opportunity to *answer* every inference and argument, relied upon to prove his guilt. But the law closes his mouth, before these *arguments* are made or heard; and requires the jury to form no opinion until after the trial closes; the last thing before which, is, that one, two or more counsel are to reason the jury into a conviction of guilt, and to all that may be thus urged, to this most important, and often *decisive* part of the trial, no word of answer, of explanation or reply is permitted! A change in this respect would never prevent the conviction of the guilty, against whom sufficient evidence was produced to warrant a conviction, but would, in a great degree, protect the innocent from becoming the victims of the injustice and cruelty of the law, or of the prejudices or mistakes of the jury, a result to which this mode of conducting a trial has so often led."

The circumstances which, in all probability, gave rise to this petition from a large body of farmers and others in the counties above referred to, are within the knowledge of the Commissioners. A reputable citizen of Chenango county, was indicted in the city of New York, for the forgery of a draft for 30,000 dollars, which in a civil action tried in Otsego county, had been recovered upon by him, by the verdict of a jury affirming its genuineness. He was, notwithstanding, brought to trial in New-York for the forgery. The trial lasted three weeks. On the closing of the evidence, the presiding judge, (*Edmonds*,) declared himself convinced of the genuineness of the draft, and advised that the prosecution be abandoned. The counsel for the people, (one of whom was an eminent lawyer, retained by the private prosecutors,) refused to defer to the opinion of the court, and insisted on going to the jury. The cause was summed up at great length, the private counsel referred to closing the argument, and occupying a day and a half. The cause was submitted to the jury, with a renewed expression of the judge's opinion, and the result was, that after being out all night, the jury disagreed and were discharged.

Nor is this feature of private counsel closing the argument in public prosecutions, of unfrequent occurrence. In cases of great importance, it happens every day. The argument, therefore, that the representative of the public should have this privilege, in practice often fails. It frequently falls into the hands of distinguished lawyers, representing the feelings of private parties, who, though nominally disinterested, are impelled by the strongest feelings of revenge to obtain a conviction. While the practice continues, of permitting private counsel in criminal prosecutions, (a right which was seriously questioned in the *Commonwealth* v. *Knapp*, 9 *Pick.* 496,) it can hardly be contended that the fate of a person, whose life may perhaps be involved in the controversy, should be exposed to the danger of the closing remarks of able and eloquent counsel.

§ 441. When the state of the pleadings requires it, or in any other case, for good reasons and in the sound discretion of the court, the order prescribed in the last section may be departed from. But in every case, the defendant has the right to close the argument to the jury.

Designed to apply to cases where the affirmative is with the defendant, as where he pleads a former conviction or acquittal. In other respects, the same in principle as the last section.

§ 442. If the indictment be for an offence punishable with death, two counsel on each side may argue the cause to the jury; in which case, they must do so alternately. If it be for any other offence, the court may, in its discretion, restrict the argument to one counsel on each side.

Conformable with the existing practice.

§ 443. A defendant in a criminal action is presumed to be innocent, until the contrary be proved; and in case of a reasonable doubt whether his guilt is satisfactorily shown, he is entitled to be acquitted.

§ 444. When it appears that a defendant has committed a public offence, and there is reasonable ground of doubt, in which of two or more degrees he is guilty, he can be convicted of the lowest of those degrees only.

Declaratory of existing rules; and taken substantially from the Report of the Massachusetts Commissioners, ch. 2, sec. 7, 8.

§ 445. When two or more defendants are jointly indicted for a felony, any defendant requiring it, must be tried separately. In other cases, defendants, jointly indicted, may be tried separately or jointly, in the discretion of the court.

Same as 2 *R. S., 3d ed* 820, *sec.* 20.

§ 446. When two or more persons are included in the same indictment, the court may, at any time before the defendant has gone into his defence, on the application of the district attorney, direct any defendant to be discharged from the indictment, that he may be a witness for the people.

§ 447. When two or more persons are included in the same indictment, and the court is of opinion, that in regard to a particular defendant, there is not sufficient evidence to put him on his defence, it must order him to be discharged from the indictment, before the evidence is closed, that he may be a witness for his co-defendant. The order is an acquittal of the defendant discharged, and a bar to another prosecution for the same offence.

The last section is taken from 2 *R. S.*, 3*d ed.*, 820, *sec.* 19. The preceding section is intended to carry out the same principle for the benefit of the people.

The effect of the discharge would be nothing, unless it amounted to an acquittal.

§ 448. The rules of evidence in civil cases are applicable also to criminal cases, except as otherwise provided in this code.

§ 449. A confession of a defendant, whether in the course of judicial proceedings or to a private person, cannot be given in evidence against him, when made under the influence of fear produced by threats; nor is it sufficient to warrant his conviction, without additional proof that the offence charged has been committed.

There is perhaps no rule of evidence in criminal cases, which has given rise to more discussion in the courts, than that which relates to confessions in criminal cases It is proposed by this section to declare the rule, so that there may be no doubt hereafter, and at the same time to open the door to confessions in many cases where they are now excluded. The law has been too tender in this respect. It should be its policy, as the Commissioners conceive, to let in all the light possible, trusting to the discretion of juries to distinguish between the false and the true. Confessions, not excluded by this rule, may be given in evidence, with all the circumstances attending them; and the jury will give such credence to it, as its own character and those circumstances may justify.

§ 450. Upon a trial for treason the defendant cannot be convicted, unless upon the testimony of two witnesses to the same overt act, or of one witness to one overt act, and another witness to a different overt act of the same treason. But if two or more distinct treasons, of different kinds, be alleged in the indictment, two witnesses to prove different treasons, are not sufficient to warrant a conviction.

Taken from 2 *R. S.* 3*d ed.*, 820, *sec.* 15.

§ 451. Upon a trial for treason, evidence cannot be admitted, of an overt act not expressly charged in the indictment; nor can the defendant be convicted, unless one or more overt acts be expressly alleged therein.

Taken from 2 *R. S.*, 3*d ed.*, 820, *sec.* 16.

§ 452. Upon a trial for a conspiracy, in a case where an overt act is necessary to constitute the offence, the defendant cannot be convicted, unless one or more overt acts be expressly alleged in the indictment, nor unless one or more of the acts alleged be proved; but any other overt act, not alleged in the indictment, may be given in evidence.

Taken from 2 *R. S.*, 3*d ed.* 820, *sec* 17.

§ 453. Proof of actual penetration into the body, is sufficient to sustain an indictment for rape, or for the crime against nature.

The Commissioners have learned, with some surprise, that objections have been taken to this section, as presented in their fourth report, *sec.* 472: 1. That it is an innovation upon the existing rules of evidence; 2. That it is too vague and indefinite in its terms ; and, 3. That it is out of place in a code of procedure.

But for the fact that their attention has been specially called to these objections, and that some very learned lawyers have regarded this provision with marked ridicule, the Commissioners would have contented themselves, with a very brief note of the provision of the revised statutes from which it has been copied. The criticisms which have been made upon it, however, lead them, as an act of justice to themselves, to dwell for a few moments upon the objections above referred to.

First, then, it is said that this section is an innovation upon the rules of evidence. The following is the provision of the revised statutes, from which this section has been copied:—"Proof of actual penetration into the body, shall be sufficient to sustain an indictment for rape, or for the crime against nature." 2 *R. S*, *3d. ed*, 820, *sec.* 18. The only difference between the section as proposed in the code, and that contained in the revised statutes, it will be perceived, is the substitution in the code, of the present, for the future tense. This has been done in accordance with the custom, in acts declaratory of existing rules, and not prescribing new ones, to adopt that form of expression. In regard to the wisdom of the rule, as thus prescribed, the Commissioners need only to refer to the notes of the revisers of the statutes. 3 *R. S.*, *2d. ed.*, 848, *note to sec.* 17. From these it appears, that thes ection as reported by the revisers, contained the following addition :—"without evidence of the circumstances which usually terminates a sexual connexion." This addition, however, was stricken out by the legislature, and the section passed as above quoted. The reasons for its introduction are thus stated by the revisers, in the note above referred to. "By the common law, a most indelicate circumstance was required to consummate either of the offences specified; cases have occurred in this state, where such proof has been dispensed with; but in others, it has been required. By one of the late acts of the British parliament, the same provision with that above proposed, is adopted." The British act referred to by the revisers, 9 *G. IV.*, *c.* 31, *sec.* 18., provides as follows: "Whereas, upon the trials for the crimes of buggery and of rape, and of carnally abusing girls under the respective ages hereinbefore mentioned, offenders frequently escape by reason of the difficulty of the proof which has been required, of the completion of those several crimes; for remedy thereof, be it enacted, that it shall not be necessary, in any of those cases, to prove the actual emission of seed in order to constitute a carnal knowledge, but that the carnal knowledge shall be deemed complete upon proof of penetration only." The old rule on the subject, which is abrogated by the British act, as well as by the revised statutes, will be found in *Rex v. Harmwood,* 1 East, P. C., 440; *Rex v. Sheridan,* 1 East, P. C., 438; *Rex v. Burrows,* R. & R., 519.

The *second* objection,—that the proposed section is vague and indefinite, seems, after what has been stated, hardly to deserve a serious answer. This precise provision has been practised upon in this state for nearly twenty years; and neither the ingenuity of the bar nor the astuteness of the bench, has as yet discovered that it is either vague or obscure; and in presenting it for re-enactment in the same form, the Commissioners will allow themselves to hope that it will be found no less intelligible than before.

But *third,*—it is said that this section is not appropriate in a code of procedure merely. Here again, they will refer to the Revised Statutes as a safe precedent. This section, as well as the three which precede it, forms a portion of the chapter, entitled "*Of proceedings in criminal cases.*" *See* 2 *R. S.* 3*d ed.*, 790. By a reference to other provisions of the code, it will be seen that it is proposed to repeal the whole of this chapter. If, therefore, the Commissioners had omitted this and similar sections, they would have receded from the settled policy of the legislation of this state for the last twenty years, and in abolishing rules well established and founded in perfect justice, would have returned to the absurd and exploded rules of the common law.

§ 454. A conviction cannot be had upon the testimony of an accomplice, unless he be corroborated by such other evidence as tends to connect the defendant with the commission of the offence; and the corroboration is not sufficient, if it merely show the commission of the offence, or the circumstances thereof.

This section is declaratory of what juries are now invariably advised by the courts, both in England and in this state, to require, in order to warrant a conviction upon the testimony of an accomplice. It is true, that the jury may convict upon the testimony of an accomplice alone. But it is, nevertheless, always considered necessary, in order to induce the jury to credit his testimony, to give other evidence confirmatory of at least some of the leading circumstances of his story, from which the jury may be able to presume that he has told the truth as to the rest. *Arch. Cr. Pl. 9th ed.*, 148. As to the character of this confirmation, it was at one time said, that if an accomplice were confirmed as to the particulars of the story, he need not receive confirmation as to the person charged. *Rex v. Birkett, Russ. & Ry.*, 252. But this doctrine has been rejected in later cases; inasmuch as the confirmation as to the circumstances, proves only that the accomplice was participant in the felony, not that the particular party charged was his confederate. *Rex v. Webb.* 6 *C. & P.*, 595; *Rex v. Wilkes,* 7 *C. & P.*, 172; *Rex v. Farler;* 8 *C. & P.*, 107; *Regina v. Dyke,* 8 *C. & P.*, 261; *Regina v. Birkett,* 8 *C. & P.*, 732.

In one of the cases just cited, *Rex v. Webb,* 6 *C. & P.*, 595, *Williams, J.*, said,—that the prosecution "must show something that goes to bring the matter home to the prisoner. Proving by other witnesses, that the robbery was committed in the way described by the accomplice, is not such confirmation of him, as will entitle his evidence to credit so as to affect other persons. Indeed, I think it is really no confirmation of him at all; as every one will give give credit to a man who avows himself a principal felon, for at least knowing how the felony was committed. It has been always my opinion, that confirmation of this kind is of no use whatsoever." And in one of the cases above cited, *Rex v. Wilkes,* 7 *C. & P.*, 272, *Alderson, B.*, said—"The confirmation of the accomplice as to the commission of the felony, is really no confirmation at all; because it would be a confirmation as much if the accusation were against you and me, as it would be as to those prisoners who are now upon their trial. The confirmation which I always advise juries to require, is a confirmation of the accomplice in some fact which goes to fix the guilt on the particular person charged. You may legally convict on the evidence of an accomplice only, if you can safely rely on his testimony; but I advise juries never to act on the evidence of an accomplice, unless he is confirmed as to the particular person who is charged with the offence."

This practice has been recognized in this state, in *The People v. Davis*, 21 *Wend.* 313, 314, and in *The People v. Costello*, 1 *Denio*, 87, 88.

The Commissioners see no reason why the practice, thus sanctioned, should not have the force of a rule, and they have therefore proposed it in the terms expressed in this section.

§ 455. Upon a trial for having, with intent to cheat or defraud another, designedly, by any false pretence, obtained the signature of any person to a written instrument, or having obtained from any person any money, personal property or valuable thing, no evidence can be admitted of a false pretence expressed orally, and unaccompanied by a false token or writing, unless the pretence, or some note or memorandum thereof, be in writing, either subscribed by, or in the handwriting of the defendant. But this section does not apply to a prosecution for falsely representing or personating another, and in such assumed character receiving money or property.

Allusion has already been made, *p.* 117, to the frequency of this class of prosecutions, and to the danger of extending facilities for the use of it, (as there is much reason to believe it is too often used,) as a means of collecting or coercing the payment of a debt. As the law now stands, any oral false pretence, by which the property of the prosecutor is obtained, may be made the subject of an indictment; and a party, who would fail in a civil suit in recovering the value of the property sold, because the sale was not evidenced by a writing, may by this form of proceeding, prosecute his debtor for a crime and cause him to be imprisoned in the state prison. The principle embodied in this section is intended to obviate this injustice, by applying to mere verbal representations the rule, long since adopted by the legislature and sanctioned by public policy, in respect to civil contracts; a rule which has been recently extended to promises, given in evidence to revive a debt barred by the statute of limitations. *Amended Code, sec.* 110.

§ 456. Upon a trial for inveigling, enticing or taking away an unmarried female of previous chaste character, under the age of twenty-five years, for the purpose of prostitution, or aiding or assisting therein, or for having, under promise of marriage, seduced and had illicit connexion with an unmarried female of previous chaste character, the defendant cannot be convicted upon the testimony of the person injured, unless she is corroborated by other evidence, tending to connect the defendant with the commission of the offence.

The acts to punish abduction, *Laws of* 1848, *p.* 118, *ch.* 105, and seduction, *Laws of* 1848, *p.* 148, *ch.* 111, both provide, that a conviction shall not be had on the testimony of the female, "unsupported by other evidence." The spirit of the rule is, as the Commissioners believe, in accordance with the views expressed in the note to section 451; and they have therefore proposed that the corroboratory evidence should tend to connect the defendant with the commission of the offence.

§ 457. If it appear by the testimony, that the facts proved constitute an offence of a higher nature than that charged in the indictment, the court may direct the jury to be discharged, and all proceedings on the indictment to be suspended, and may order the defendant to be committed, or continued on or admitted to bail, to answer any new indictment which may be found against him for the higher offence.

§ 458. If an indictment for the higher offence be dismissed by the grand jury, or be not found at or before the next term, the court must again proceed to try the defendant on the original indictment.

The last two sections are taken from *Liv. Crim. Code*, 535, *Art.* 389.—It is proper that if the grand jury have indicted the defendant for an offence less in degree than that of which the evidence shows him guilty, the jury should be discharged, to the end that he may be indicted for the higher offence.

§ 459. The court may also direct the jury to be discharged, where it appears that it has not jurisdiction of the offence, or that the facts, as charged in the indictment, do not constitute an offence punishable by law.

The reason for this section is, that, in neither of the cases provided for, would a conviction be of any effect. Where the court has no jurisdiction of the offence, even consent cannot confer it; and where the facts, as charged in the indictment, do not constitute an offence punishable by law, the court must arrest the judgment.

§ 460. If the jury be discharged, because the court has not jurisdiction of the offence charged in the indictment, and it appear that it was committed out of the jurisdiction of this state, the court may order the defendant to be discharged, or to be detained for a reasonable time specified in the order, until a communication can be sent by the district attorney to the chief executive officer of the state, territory or district where the off ence was committed.

§ 461. If the offence were committed within the exclusive jurisdiction of another county of this state, the court must direct the defendant to be committed for such time as it deems reasonable, to await a warrant from the proper county for his arrest; or if the offence be a misdemeanor only, it may admit him to bail, in an undertaking, with sufficient sureties, that he will, within such time as the court may appoint, render himself amenable to a warrant for his arrest, from the proper county, and if not sooner arrested thereon, will attend at the office of the sheriff of the county where the trial was had, at a time particularly specified in the undertaking, to surrender himself upon the warrant, if issued, or that his bail will forfeit such sum as the court may fix, and to be mentioned in the undertaking.

§ 462. In the case provided for in the last section, the clerk must forthwith transmit a certified copy of the indictment and of all the papers in the action, filed with him, to the district attorney of the proper county; the expense of which transmission is chargeable to that county.

§ 463. If the defendant be not arrested, as provided in section 461, on a warrant from the proper county, he must be discharged from custody, or his bail in the action be exonerated, or money deposited instead of bail refunded, as the case may be; and the sureties in the undertaking mentioned in that section must be discharged.

§ 464. If he be arrested, the same proceedings must be had thereon, as upon the arrest of a defendant in another county, on a warrant of arrest issued by a magistrate.

§ 465. If the jury be discharged, because the facts as charged do not constitute an offence punishable by law, the court must order that the defendant, if in custody, be discharged therefrom, or if admitted to bail, that his bail be exonerated, or if he have deposited money instead of bail, that the money deposited be refunded to him, unless in its opinion a new indictment can be framed, upon which the defendant can be legally convicted; in which case, it may direct that the case be re-submitted to the same or another grand jury,

§ 466. If the court direct that the case be submitted anew, the same proceedings must be had thereon, as are prescribed in sections 337 to 339, both inclusive.

The last seven sections are intended to prevent the discharge of the defendant from working a defeat of public justice.

§ 467. If, at any time after the evidence on either side is closed, the court deem it insufficient to warrant a conviction, it may advise the jury to acquit the defendant. But the jury are not bound by the advice; nor can the court for any cause prevent the jury from giving a verdict, except as provided in sections 446, 447, 457 and 459.

Where the evidence is wholly insufficient to warrant a conviction, nothing is more common than for the court to advise an acquital; and in such cases, it has seldom occurred that the jury disregard the advice. Indeed, in practice, it almost amounts to a binding direction. Upon a full examination of the the authorities, however, in *The People v. Harris*, tried at the New-York circuit, in May, 1847, Judge *Edmonds* held that the prosecution might still insist upon going to the jury. See *note to sec.* 440, *p.* 208. To put an end to all doubt as to the extent of the rule, it is deemed advisable to declare it.

§ 468. When, in the opinion of the court, it is proper that the jury should view the place in which the offence is charged to have been committed, or in which any other material fact occurred, it may order the jury to be conducted, in a body, in the custody of proper officers, to the place, which must be shown to them by a judge of the court, or by a person appointed by the court for that purpose.

§ 469. The officers must be sworn to suffer no person to speak to or communicate with the jury, nor to do so themselves, on any subject connected with the trial, and to return them into court without unnecessary delay, or at a specified time.

It is usual in practice, where the parties consent, to allow the jury to view the premises where the crime was committed. It seems proper that the court should, without the necessity of resorting to a consent, have this power. It is also recommended in *Liv. Crim. Code*, 532, *art.* 357.

§ 470. If a juror have any personal knowledge, respecting a fact in controversy in a cause, he must declare it in open court, during the trial. If, during the retirement of the jury, a juror declare a fact, which could be evidence in the cause, as of his own knowledge, the jury must return into court. In either of these cases, the juror making the statement must be sworn as a witness, and examined in the presence of the parties.

This section is taken substantially from *Liv. Crim. Code*, 533, *art.* 366. A juror cannot legally present any fact to his colleagues, except on oath, as a witness; and it seems useful to declare his duty in this respect.

§ 471. The jurors sworn to try an indictment, may, at any time before the submission of the cause to the jury, in the discretion of the court, be permitted to separate, or be kept in charge of proper officers. The officers must be sworn to keep the jurors together until the next meeting of the court, to suffer no person to speak to or communicate with them, nor to do so themselves, on any subject connected with the trial, and to return them into court at the next meeting thereof.

The separation of the jury after they are sworn and before the cause is submitted to them, is, in practice, and especially in cases of felony, allowed by consent only. No good reason exists, why it should not be allowed by the court, under proper safeguards.

§ 472. The jury must also, at each adjournment of the court, whether permitted to separate or kept in charge of officers, be admonished by the court, that it is their duty not to converse among themselves, on any subject connected with the trial, or to form or express any opinion thereon, until the cause is finally submitted to them.

The admonition prescribed in this section is not unfrequently given, but the practice on the subject is not uniform. The purposes of justice require, that jurors should not commit their opinions upon a case, until it is finally submitted to them. It is not easy to prevent their doing so, to some extent, when they are kept together during the progress of the trial; for the merits of the cause will naturally be the subject of conversation among them. With the advice prescribed in this section, however, a conscientious juror will feel it to be his duty to keep his judgment uncommitted, at least by the expression of an opinion.

§ 473. If, before the conclusion of the trial, a juror become sick, so as to be unable to perform his duty, the court may order him to be discharged. In that case, a new juror may be sworn, and the trial begin anew, or the jury may be discharged, and a new jury then or afterwards impannelled.

Declaratory of the existing rule.

§ 474. The court must decide all questions of law, which arise in the course of the trial.

In conformity with the law as it now stands.

§ 475. On the trial of an indictment for libel, the jury have the right to determine the law and the fact.

Taken from the constitutson, *art.* 1, *sec.* 8.

§ 476. On the trial of an indictment for any other offence than libel, questions of law are to be decided by the court, saving the right of the defendant to except; questions of fact, by the jury. And although the jury have the power to find a general verdict, which includes questions of law as well as of fact, they are bound, nevertheless, to receive as law what is laid down as such by the court.

This section defines more clearly than it is understood at present, the line of demarcation between the duties of the court and of the jury. Nothing is more common, than for juries in criminal cases to be told that they are the judges of the law as well as of the fact ; and as a matter of authority merely, the weight of the highest judicial names in this country may be cited in support of and against this proposition. In this state, the balance of judicial authority is in favor of the principle, that the jury in criminal cases, are bound to take the law from the court, with the exception of the case of libel; in which, by the constitution, the right is expressly given to the jury to determine both the law and the fact.

To put an end, however, to all doubt on the subject, the Commissioners propose to declare the rule, in as clear and comprehensive terms as they have been able to devise, that on the trial of an indictment for any other offence than libel, questions of law are to be decided by the court, saving the right of the defendant to except ; questions of fact by the jury ; and that although the jury have the power to find a general verdict, which includes questions of law as well as of fact, they are bound nevertheless, to receive as law, what is laid down as such by the court.

The rule as to the relative duties of the court and jury, in respect to questions of law and fact, has been frequently misunderstood; and it has been very common to tell juries in criminal cases, that they are judges of the law and fact. This is not so. The rule in this state may now be considered settled, as laid down in this section. All the cases on the subject, as well as the principles applicable to it, have been reviewed, in the case of *the People v. Pine*, 2 Barb. Sup. Ct. Rep., 568—570, and the conclusion stated in this section, adopted as the true rule. The case of *libel* is of course an exception ; having been made so by the constitution. *See note to the last section, p.* 223.

§ 477. In charging the jury, the court must state to them, all matters of law which it thinks necessary for their information in giving their verdict; and if it present the facts of the case, must, in addtion to what it may deem its duty to say, infor.n the jury that they are the exclusive judges of all q stions of fact.

This section naturally arises out of the last, and is likewise in accordance with the existing rule.

§ 478. After hearing the charge, the jury may either decide in court, or may retire for deliberation. If they do not agree without retiring, one or more officers must be sworn, to keep them together in some private and convenient place, without food or drink, except bread and water, unless otherwise ordered by the court; and not to permit any person to speak to or communicate with them, nor do so themselves, unless it be by order of the court, or to ask them whether they have agreed upon a verdict and to return them into court when they have so agreed, or when ordered by the court.

In accordance with the existing practice.

§ 479. When a defendant, who has given bail, appears for trial, the court may, in its discretion, at any time after his appearance for trial, order him to be committed to the custody of the proper officer of the county, to abide the judgment or further order of the court; and he must be committed and held in custody accordingly.

This power is now exercised. It is, however, deemed proper, especially in connection with the provisions on the subject of bail, hereafter referred to, to make it a positive rule.

CHAPTER II.

CONDUCT OF THE JURY, AFTER THE CAUSE IS SUBMITTED TO THEM.

§ 480. A room must be provided by the supervisors of the county, (or if the trial be in a city court, by the corporate authorities of the city,) for the use of the jury, upon their retirement for deliberation, with suitable furniture, fuel, lights and stationery. If the supervisors or corporate authorities neglect, the court may order the sheriff to do so; and the expenses incurred by him in carrying the order into effect, when certified by the court, are a county charge.

Jurors often complain that suitable conveniences are withheld from them; and it is well known that they are seldom furnished with means, such as stationery, to facilitate their labors. This section seems just in itself, and is moreover introduced to obviate the grounds of complaint referred to.

§ 481. While the jury are kept together, either during the progress of the trial or after their retirement for deliberation, they must be provided by the sheriff, upon the order of the court, at the expense of the county, (or if the trial be in a city court, at the expense of the city,) with suitable and sufficient food and lodging.

This section is founded on the same principle as the last, but applies only to the case of a jury kept together during the trial, and before the cause is submitted to them.

§ 482. Upon retiring for deliberation, the jury may take with them all papers, (except depositions,) which have been received as evidence in the cause, or copies of such parts of public records or private documents, given in evidence, as ought not, in the opinion of the court, be taken from the person having them in possession.

The rule, as it exists at common law, is, that when the jury withdraw, they may take with them letters patent, deeds under seal, and exemplifications of depositions in equity, if the witnesses be dead; and with the assent of the parties they may take with them books, or writings under seal. *Vicary v. Farthing, Cro. El.* 411; *Rex v. Burdett,* 1 *L. Raym.* 148; *S. C.,* 3 *Salk.* 645. The indefiniteness of this rule often leads to controversy at the close of the trial, and renders it proper that the rights of the jury in this respect should be more distinctly prescribed. The provision contained in this section, seems just and reasonable. Depositions are excepted, because, like all the rest of the evidence, the facts they contain should be left to the recollection of the jury. To permit the jury to take these, without at the same time furnishing them with notes of the other testimony, (which cannot be done,) would be to give an undue advantage to the testimony furnished by deposition.

§ 483. The jury may also take with them notes of the testimony or other proceedings on the trial, taken by themselves or any of them, but none taken by any other person.

This provision, allowing the jury to take out their own notes, is introduced to obviate an objection which has been sometimes suggested, as to its propriety. No sound objection seems to exist to such a practice.

§ 484. After the jury have retired for deliberation, if there be a disagreement between them, as to any part of the testimony, or if they desire to be informed of a point of law arising in the cause, they must require the officer to conduct them into court. Upon their being brought into court, the information required must be given, in the presence of, or after notice to the district attorney and the defendant or his counsel.

Conformable to and declaratory of the existing rule. 2 *Hale, P. C.*, 296; 1 *Chit. Archb*, *8th Lond. ed.* 400. A similar provision is recommended in *Liv. Crim. Code*, 532, *art.* 358.

§ 485. If, after the retirement of the jury, one of them become so sick as to prevent the continuance of his duty, or any other accident or cause occur, to prevent their being kept together for deliberation, the jury may be discharged.

§ 486. Except as provided in the last section, the jury cannot be discharged, after the cause is submitted to them, until they have agreed upon their verdict, and rendered it in open court, unless by the consent of both parties entered upon the minutes, or unless, at the expiration of such time as the court deems proper, it satisfactorily appear, that there is no reasonable probability that the jury can agree.

§ 487. In all cases where a jury are discharged, or prevented from giving a verdict, by reason of an accident or other cause, except where the defendant is discharged from the indictment, during the progress of the trial, or after the cause is submitted to them, the cause may be again tried at the same or another term.

§ 488. While the jury are absent, the court may adjourn from time to time, as to other business: but it is nevertheless deemed open, for every purpose connected with the cause submitted to the jury, until a verdict is rendered or the jury discharged.

§ 489. A final adjournment of the court discharges the jury.

The last five sections are declaratory of the existing rules.

CHAPTER III.

THE VERDICT.

§ 490. When the jury have agreed upon their verdict, they must be conducted into court by the officer having them in charge. Their names must then be called, and if all do not appear, the rest must be discharged without giving a verdict. In that case, the cause may be again tried, at the same or another term.

Declaratory of the existing practice. A similar provision is contained in *Liv. Crim. Code,* 534, *art.* 370, 371.

§ 491. If the indictment be for a felony, the defendant must, before the verdict is received, appear in person. If it be for a misdemeanor, the verdict may be rendered in his absence.

§ 492. If the jury appear, they must be asked by the court or the clerk, whether they have agreed upon their verdict; and if the foreman answer in the affirmative, they must, on being required, declare the same.

The last two sections are declaratory of the existing practice.

§ 493. The jury may either render a general verdict, or where they are in doubt as to the legal effect of the facts proved, they may, except upon an indictment for libel, find a special verdict.

Substantially the same as 2 *R. S.*, 3*d. ed.*, 517, *sec.* 68, except as to libel, in which case they are judges of law and fact. *See sec.* 475, p. 223.

§ 494. A general verdict upon a plea of not guilty, is either "guilty" or "not guilty;" which imports a conviction or acquittal of the offence charged in the indictment. Upon a plea of a former conviction or acquittal of the same offence, it is either "for the people," or "for the defendant."

Conformable to the issues prescribed by sections 351 and 373, p. 169, 176.

§ 495. A special verdict is that by which the jury find the facts only, leaving the judgment to the court. It must present the conclusions of fact, as established by the evidence, and not the evidence to prove them; and these conclusions of fact must be so presented, as that nothing remains to the court, but to draw conclusions of law upon them.

Declaratory of the existing rule. *Fuller* v. *Van Geesen*, 4 *Hill*, 171, 174; *Birckhead* v. *Brown*, 5 *Hill*, 645, 646.

§ 496. The special verdict must be reduced to writing, by the jury or in their presence, entered upon the minutes of the court, read to the jury, and agreed to by them, before they are discharged.

§ 497. The special verdict need not be in any particular form, but is sufficient, if it present intelligibly the facts found by the jury.

By the present rul s of the supreme court, *Rule* 18, a special verdict may be either settled at the trial, or drawn up and settled afterwards. There being no form about it, as prescribed by this section, it seems to be more convenient to have it settled and entered at the trial. It can occupy but little time, and all possibility of error or mistake as to the facts found is thus avoided.

§ 498. The special verdict may be brought to argument by either party, upon five days notice to the other, at the same or another term of the court; and upon the hearing thereof, the counsel for the defendant may conclude the argument.

§ 499. The court must give judgment upon the special verdict, as follows:

1. If the plea be not guilty, and the facts prove the defendant guilty of the offence charged in the indictment, or of any other offence of which he could be con-

victed, under that indictment, as provided in sections 501 and 502, judgment must be given accordingly; but if otherwise, judgment of acquittal must be given:

2. If the plea be a former conviction or acquittal of the same offence, the court must give judgment of conviction or acquittal, according as the facts prove or fail to prove the former conviction or acquittal.

§ 500. If the jury do not, in a special verdict, pronounce affirmatively or negatively on the facts necessary to enable the court to give judgment, or if they find the evidence of facts merely, and not the conclusions of fact from the evidence, as established to their satisfaction, the court must order a new trial

This section is in conformity with the existing practice. See the cases cited in 1 *Gra. Prac., 3d ed.*, 775, *note* 1.

§ 501. Upon an indictment for an offence consisting of different degrees, the jury may find the defendant not guilty of the degree charged in the indictment, and guilty of any degree inferior thereto, or of an attempt to commit the offence.

Taken from 2 *R. S., 3d ed.*, 789, *sec.* 30.

§ 502. In all other cases, the defendant may be found guilty of any offence, the commission of which is necessarily included in that with which he is charged in the indictment.

This section is intended to provide for a class of cases not comprehended within the last section, but embraced within the common law rule. In *The People* v. *Jackson*, 3 *Hill*, 92. it was held, that under an indictment for producing an abortion of a quick child, which by statute is a felony, the defendant might be convicted though it turn out that the child was not quick, and the offence, therefore, a mere misdemeanor. It was admitted in that case, that the provision of the Revised Statutes, from which the last section is taken, did not authorize such a conviction, but that it had not affected the common law rule, by which the conviction was justified. This section is declaratory of the principle thus established, and of the rule of the common law referred to in the case cited.

§ 503. On an indictment against several, if the jury cannot agree upon a verdict as to all, they may render a verdict as to those in regard to whom they do agree, on which a judgment must be entered accordingly; and the case, as to the rest, may be tried by another jury.

The object of this section is sufficiently apparent. The practice which it prescribes is sometimes pursued, but it has no where the express authority of law. As every defendant, in a case of felony, has a right to a separate trial, and may, in the discretion of the court, have that privilege in a case of misdemeanor, there seems to be no reason why the jury should not be allowed to acquit one defendant, though unable to agree as to another.

§ 504. When there is a verdict of conviction, in which it appears to the court, that the jury have mistaken the law, the court may explain the reason for that opinion, and direct the jury to reconsider their verdict; and if, after the reconsideration, they return the same verdict, it must be entered. But when there is a verdict of acquittal, the court cannot require the jury to reconsider it.

§ 505. If the jury render a verdict which is neither a general nor a special verdict as defined in sections 494 and 495, the court may, with proper instructions as to the law, direct them to reconsider it; and it can not be recorded, until it be rendered in some form, from which it can be clearly understood what is the intent of the jury, whether to render a general verdict, or to find the facts specially, and to leave the judgment to the court.

§ 506. If the jury persist in finding an informal verdict, from which, however, it can be clearly understood that their intention is to find in favor of the defendant, upon the issue, it must be entered in the terms in which it is found, and the court must give judgment of acquittal. But no judgment of conviction can be given, unless the jury expressly find against the defendant, upon the issue, or judgment be given against him on a special verdict.

The last three sections sufficiently explain themselves, and the justice of the provisions they contain, seems manifest. Substantially similar provisions are recommended in *Liv. Crim. Code*, 536, *art*. 394-396.

§ 507. When a verdict is rendered, and before it is recorded, the jury may be polled, on the requirement of either party; in which case, they must be severally asked whether it is their verdict; and if any one answer in the negative, the jury must be sent out for further deliberation.

§ 508. When the verdict is given, and is such as the court may receive, the clerk must immediately record it in full upon the minutes, and must read it to the jury and inquire of them whether it is their verdict. If any juror disagree, the fact must be entered upon the minutes, and the jury again sent out; but if no disagreement be expressed, the verdict is complete, and the jury must be discharged from the case.

§ 509. If judgment of acquittal be given on a general verdict, and the defendant be not detained for any other legal cause, he must be discharged as soon as the judgment is given; except that when the acquittal is for a variance between the proof and the indictment, which may be obviated by a new indictment, the court may order his detention, to the end that a new indictment may be preferred, in the same manner and with the like effect, as provided in sections 465 and 466.

§ 510. If a general verdict be rendered against the defendant, or a special verdict be given, he must be remanded, if in custody, or if on bail he may be committed to the proper officer of the county, to await the judgment of the court upon the verdict. When committed, his bail is exonerated, or if money be deposited instead of bail, it must be refunded to the defendant.

The last four sections are in conformity with the existing practice, except the provision in sec. 510, as to refunding money deposited instead of bail, which grows out of the provisions of this Code, *sec.* 648–651, which will be hereafter referred to.

§ 511. If the defence be the insanity of the defendant, the jury must be instructed, if they acquit him on that ground, to state that fact with their verdict. The court may thereupon, if the defendant be in custody, and they deem his discharge dangerous to the public peace or safety, order him to be committed to the state lunatic asylum, until he become sane.

In conformity with the existing practice. *See* 1 *R. S. 3d ed.* 813, 814, *sec.* 44, 47.

TITLE VIII.

OF THE PROCEEDINGS AFTER TRIAL, AND BEFORE JUDGMENT.

CHAPTER I.

BILL OF EXCEPTIONS.

§ 512. On the trial of an indictment, exceptions may be taken by the defendant, to a decision of the court, upon a matter of law, by which his substantial rights are prejudiced and not otherwise, in any of the following cases:

1. In disallowing a challenge to the panel of the jury, or to an individual juror for implied bias:

2. In admitting or rejecting witnesses or testimony, or in charging the triers, on the trial of a challenge to a juror for actual bias:

3. In admitting or rejecting witnesses or testimony, or in deciding any question of law, not a matter of discretion, or in charging or instructing the jury upon the law, on the trial of the issue.

This section proposes to retain the right to a bill of exceptions, as it now exists, with this important restriction, however, that it is available only where the substantial rights of the defendant have been prejudiced. The rule on this subject, both in civil and criminal cases, now is, that upon a *case* which is made for the purpose of moving for a new trial, the court may enquire whether substantial justice has been done, even though a rule of law have been violated; but where the question comes up on a *bill of exceptions*, the law presumes the prejudice, and the party is entitled to a correction of the error. *The People v. Bodine*, 1 Denio, 296; *Herrick v. Stover*, 5 Wend 580–587; *Farmers' and Manufacturers' Bank v. Whinfield*, 24 Wend. 428; *Horton v Hendershot*, 1 Hill, 118; *Coles v Marquand*, 2 Hill, 447; *Myers v. Malcolm*, 6 Hill, 296, and note: *Haine v. Davey*, 4 Ad. & Ell. 892; *Cameron v. Erwin*, 5 Hill, 272; *Mansfield v. Wheeler*, 23 Wend. 79. It is true that the supreme court, in a later case, *The People v. Lohman*, 2 Barb. Sup. court. Rep. 221, 222, intimated, that they might disregard exceptions not having a direct reference to the merits of the cause. But such is not the rule, though the Commissioners, in proposing this section, deem it proper that it should be made so by legislation.

§ 513. A bill containing the exceptions must be settled and signed by the presiding judge, and filed with the clerk.

The same as the existing practice; except that the bill of exceptions is to be signed by the presiding judge, instead of being signed and sealed, as at present, by all the members of the court. The only object of the signature is to authenticate the bill of exceptions; which can be done as well by the presiding judge alone, as in conjunction with the other judges; while the latter course is productive, oftentimes, of great delay and inconvenience.

§ 514. The bill of exceptions must be settled at the trial, unless the court otherwise direct. If no such direction be given, the point of the exception must be particularly stated in writing, and delivered to the court, and must immediately be corrected or added to, until it is made conformable to the truth.

The present statute provides, that "on the trial of any indictment, exceptions to any decision of the court may be made by the defendant, in the same cases and manner provided by law in civil actions." 2 *R. S.*, *3d ed.* 820, *sec.* 21. By the rules of the supreme court, *Rule* 18, the party excepting, is not required to prepare, at the trial, his bill of exceptions, but shall merely reduce his exceptions to writing, and deliver them to the judge, or the judge shall himself note the points, as he may elect; and by other rules, the bill of exceptions shall be drawn up, amended and settled, within a prescribed time. In criminal cases, it is desirable to avoid the delay necessary to settle the bill of exceptions, in the manner prescribed in civil cases; and for this purpose, the present section proposes, that it be settled, at the trial, unless the court otherwise direct. This can always conveniently be done, except where it is necessary to set forth the evidence; and in those cases, as the section provides, the present practice can be adopted.

§ 515. If the bill of exceptions be not settled at the trial, it must be prepared and served, within five days thereafter, on the district attorney, who may, within five days, serve on the defendant or his counsel, amendments thereto. The defendant may then, within five days, serve the district attorney with a notice to appear before the presiding judge of the court, at a specified time, not less than five nor more than ten days thereafter, to have the bill of exceptions settled.

The same in substance, as the existing practice, except in substituting *five* days instead of *four.* See *rules* 15 *and* 18, *of the supreme court.*

§ 516. At the time appointed, the judge must settle and sign the bill of exceptions.

Same as the existing practice, except that the bill of exceptions is to be settled by the presiding judge. See *note to sec.* 514, p. 239.

§ 517. The time for preparing the bill of exceptions or the amendments thereto, or for settling the same, may be enlarged by the consent of the parties, or by the presiding judge, or by a judge of the supreme court, but by no other officer.

§ 518. If the bill of exceptions be not served within the time prescribed in section 515, or within the enlarged time therefor, as prescribed in the last section, the exceptions are deemed abandoned. If it be served, and the parties omit, within the time limited by section 515, the one to prepare amendments, and the other to give notice of appearance before the judge, they are respectively deemed, the one to have agreed to the bill of exceptions, and the other to the amendments.

The last two sections are in accordance with the existing practice.

§ 519. The bill of exceptions must contain so much of the evidence only, as is necessary to present the questions of law upon which the exceptions were taken, or as may shew that the decision excepted to has not prejudiced the substantial rights of the defendant; and the judge must, upon the settlement of the bill, whether agreed to by the parties or not, strike out all other matters contained therein.

Same as the existing rule. See *Rule* 27, *of the supreme court.*

§ 520. The bill of exceptions must be filed with the clerk of the court, at the time of or before taking the appeal.

CHAPTER II.

NEW TRIALS.

The power to grant a new trial in a criminal case, after conviction, was, until very recently, understood to belong to the courts of oyer and terminer, but to no other court of criminal jurisdiction. It had indeed been the subject of express adjudication, in early as well as in more modern cases; but it has been very lately held otherwise, by the supreme court, in the second district, in the case of *The People v. The Judges of the Dutchess oyer and terminer.* 2 Barb. Sup. Court Rep. 282. This result was arrived at, upon a very critical and elaborate examination of the structure of the criminal courts, and upon an inquiry into the question whether they were courts of general or inferior jurisdiction; and upon the determination of that question, the former decisions of the supreme court, and the practice of half a century were overruled

Assuming this decision to be authoritative, the necessity for legislation is obvious; and no reason presents itself, why it should not be exerted in favor of the continuance of a power long existing, and it is believed, safely exercised. It is true, that the learned judge, by whom the opinion of the court was delivered, argues strenuously against the existence of this jurisdiction; placing himself upon the ground that in cases calling for its exercise, the interposition of the pardoning power affords sufficient relief. In this conclusion, the Commissioners cannot agree. If the defendant have been improperly convicted, he should neither suffer the punishment nor the disgrace which attaches to his conviction. The law should supply the means of correcting the error; and if it fail to do so, it is remiss in its highest duty,—that of full protection to the rights of the citizen.

Nor do the Commissioners design to confine this power to the courts of oyer and terminer. They have already proposed to increase the jurisdiction of the courts of sessions, and the city courts, and have advanced in support of that proposition a reason which equally applies to the conferment upon them, of the power in question. See *p.* 21, 22.

The view of the subject of new trials in criminal cases here presented, has also been taken by the British Commissioners, in their eighth report, *p.* 18–24, and is enforced by them, by the most conclusive reasoning.

"The question," say they, " whether a motion for a new trial ought to be entertained, is one of high importance to the due administration of justice. It involves two main points: first, whether such a course is material for the purpose of distinguishing between guilt and innocence, and if so, whether any reason warrants the rejection of such a test. If any doubt should exist on the first question, it is one which would most properly be decided by experience. On this point, however, there is no room for doubt. Actual experience, not only in respect of civil, but even of criminal proceedings, where the test is allowed to operate, proves its importance. In truth, so long as human judgment is fallible, it must be necessary to use means for the correction of error and mistake. It may be said that this cannot be done without delay and expense. It cannot, however, be doubted that deliberate justice, although necessarily attended with more or less delay, is preferable to the injustice incident to improvident haste, and necessarily resulting from the neglect of reasonable means for the exclusion of error. The expenditure of labor and cost in criminal investigations, can scarcely be placed in competition with the evils which must inevitably result from want of due caution. The question resolves itself mainly into this, whether the cost of correction can fairly be placed in competition with the evils likely to result from the want of correction

"We apprehend that the right, even of the legislature, to inflict capital punishment, rests on the grounds of strict and cogent necessity, and that to go beyond that limit, involves a transgression in *foro cœli*, which is criminal in the legislator himself. The Divine prohibition plainly extends to every unwarranted destruction of human life. There is no authority to control or limit it beyond that which may be inferred from strict necessity; no hypothesis which can be framed as to the origin of civil society, and the duty of obedience to its laws, can warrant the conclusion that the legislator has, either expressly or impliedly, the power to direct capital punishment on any other ground.

"If this principle be applicable to the infliction of capital punishment, where, from the nature of the offence, the infliction of a less penalty would be equally beneficial to society, it is, *a fortiori*, applicable, if reasonable and practicable means be not provided for ascertaining, previously to the infliction of capital punishment, that the accused is really guilty of a crime to which such a penalty is annexed by the law. Errors of the former kind apply only to such as are actual delinquents; those of the latter involve the destruction of the innocent.

"The observations thus applicable to capital punishment, are obviously applicable also, although in an inferior degree, to the minor penalties of transportation, or loss of liberty, or even property; the right to inflict the latter as well as the former, rests upon the principle of necessity for the prevention of wrong.

"It appears to us, that the law of England is at present very defective, as regards the means afforded for the correction of errors in criminal proceedings; and especially such as are frequently, and indeed are almost necessarily, incident to the trial by jury. In this respect, indeed, the law is inconsistent, in entertaining the motion for a new trial in some instances, and denying it in others, without any adequate reason for the distinction; and is thus faulty, either in denying a new trial where it would be consistent with justice to grant one, or in granting a new trial where it ought properly to be withheld. The instances in which a new trial is grantable, are confined to those where the prosecution is for a misdemeanor only, and is pending in the Court of Queen's Bench. We cannot but observe that the distinction thus made in the first instance, between indictments for felony and those for misdemeanor pending in the Court of Queen's Bench, is one not warranted by any intelligent principle. It would indeed seem to be more reasonable that, as the penalties for felony are usually more severe than those which attach to a mere misdemeanor, larger means for the correction of error should be afforded in the former case than in the latter. The distinction between cases of misdemeanor, pending in the Court of Queen's Bench, and those pending in other criminal courts, seems also to be destitute of any sound principle. It may perhaps, as to prosecutions removed from inferior courts into the Court of Queen's Bench, be said, that it is presumed that they are of more difficult investigation, and therefore that more ample means ought to be allowed, for accurate inquiry and for the correction of errors. This may occasionally be so; but the presumption cannot possibly warrant so wide a distinction as that which is made in practice; the difficulties which give rise to the application for a new trial, are frequently of a nature not to be foreseen, and often depend on the conduct of witnesses, or of the jury, or of the direction of a judge or presiding magistrate, and not at all on the nature of the cause itself. Besides, as a defendant in a cause depending in the higher court, has always the benefit of being tried before one of the judges of the superior courts, the proceedings are less likely to stand in need of correction, than they are when the trial is had before an ordinary ma istrate.

"It is also to be observed, that the distinction has been some times received with jealousy, as operating in favor of such as can well afford to remove the indictment into the higher court, by writ of *certiorari*.

"A brief reference to the ancient law may not be unimportant, to show that the present distinction is not warranted by any principle recognized by that law, but is in truth the casual result of change in circumstances. Formerly, as appears from the ancient text writers and authorities, jurors were not persons who, like those of the present day, decided as judges of facts upon the testimony of others; they were themselves the very eye and ear witnesses of the facts, or were persons likely, from proximity to the place in question, to possess the best means of judging accurately; and they determined according to their own actual or presumed knowledge. There could therefore be no new trial, on the ground that the testimony on which the verdict was founded was false or insufficient to warrant the verdict. In doubtful cases, recourse was had to the trial by ordeal, or to a process of compurgation; and it was not until after the abandonment of the former superstitious modes of trial, that juries began to exercise the important duty of deciding upon evidence. The great intrinsic defects incident to such a tribunal, and the inconvenience and injustice experienced for want of due means of correction, at last occasioned a most important change in the law as regarded civil causes, in admitting motions for new trials—a great improvement, but which was not extended to criminal proceedings, beyond the narrow limits to which we have already alluded. It is notorious, that at the present day, the hearing of motions for new trials in civil causes is one of the most important and frequent occupations of the common law courts; and it cannot be doubted that without the means of correcting errors and mistakes thus afforded, the trial by jury would be regarded as unsatisfactory and unsafe.

"A new trial in civil proceedings, is now allowed on the plain and simple ground that the practice is essential to justice, for the purpose of correcting errors and miscarriages in its administration, which cannot be excluded, but which require remedy. These, however, are not peculiar to civil proceedings. Some of them are even more likely to occur in criminal than in civil proceedings. Questions of civil right are for the most part dependent on facts, the effect rather than the existence of which is disputed. Criminal questions, on the contrary, frequently depend on transactions of a hidden and secret nature, the truth of which is oftentimes difficult to unravel; and, in consequence, resort must often be had to a chain of presumptive or circumstantial evidence. Looking therefore to the nature of the inquiry, it is quite as likely that error or mistake should occur in the investigation on a criminal charge, as on that of a mere civil claim. As regards the consequences of error in the one case and the other, it cannot be denied that a failure of justice in a criminal case, where it may concern not only property, liberty, but even life itself, is of much more serious importance than in civil cases, where a mere question of property is concerned. These positions and their consequences are too obvious to be dwelt upon; yet, admitting them to be true, the conclusions must necessarily be, that the precautions necessary to exclude error in the one case are, *a fortiori*, necessary in the other. If, with a view to exclude the possibility of injustice, a man is to be allowed the benefit of a new trial, where property to the amount of 20*l*. is at stake, it is hard to deny him protection to the same extent, where his life is in jeopardy. If the question whether a pauper be legally settled in parish A., or parish B., is not to be determined without power of appeal to the Court of Queen's Bench, it is harsh to condemn him to be transported for life to a penal settlement, without power of appeal. The law in this respect is at variance with itself, and several evil consequences naturally result..

"Great injustice is often done to an innocent party, who, but for the technical rule, would entitle himself to a new trial; for it cannot be doubted that cases not unfrequently occur, when the convict is either altogether innocent, or not guilty of the aggravated affence charged.

"Although it is well known that instances in which innocent persons have unfortunately been convicted, are by no means rare, it may be proper to refer to a portion of the examination, which have been taken by us on this subject.

"Sir *F. Pollock*, (now lord chief baron of the exchequer,) in answer to the question:—'There is another great difference 'between felonies and misdemeanors, with respect to the granting of a new trial; it can be had where an indictment is 'before the court of king's bench, but none can be had in case 'of felony; do you conceive that that difference is one which 'requires any alteration?' said, 'The question that is now 'proposed to me recals some circumstances which occurred a 'few years ago, when Mr. Wilde, of College-hill, an attorney, was one of the sheriffs of London; and I will endeavor to give to the Commissioners, (I am afraid but imperfectly,) some of the circumstances which occurred during 'his shrievalty, and I wish that I had been at all aware 'that an opportunity would have occurred of adverting to 'these circumstances, as I would have taken care to have been 'provided with more distinct information; but I think the 'Commissioners will probably feel it their duty, when I have 'stated as far as I know the facts to which I advert, to endeavor to procure the attendance of Mr. Wilde himself, and 'to obtain from him more minutely the cases to which I refer. I think he was sheriff during part of a year only, having been elected upon the death of one of the sheriffs chosen 'in September, 1827. I am not quite certain I am correct 'as to the date, but am right within a year. During the 'seven months he was in office, by his exertions he saved 'several men from public execution, I think as many as seven, 'but I am certain as to five. I had frequent communications 'with him upon those cases, while they proceeded. My impression is, that several out of those cases were cases of 'perfect and entire innocence, and that the others were cases 'of innocence, with reference to the capital part of the charge. 'The then secretary of state, Sir Robert Peel, paid great attention to every application for mercy, and having satisfied 'himself in each case, that the prerogative of the crown ought 'to interfere, the lives of every one of the individuals were 'spared. It is impossible to speak in too high terms of the 'zeal, humanity, unsparing labour and expense, which Mr. 'Wilde bestowed upon these occasions, but the result satisfied me that the parties were in several instances guiltless of 'any crime, and in all cases, were such as did not justify capital punishment; and Sir Robert Peel, after much labor in 'the investigation, was of the same opinion. It has always, 'since this occurred, been impressed upon my mind as a very 'appalling fact, that in one year so many persons were saved 'from public execution, for which I believe most, if not all of 'them, had been actually ordered; and though, I believe, 'undoubtedly, the sheriffs of London are in general conspicuous for an active, humane and correct discharge of their 'duty, they have not all, and cannot have, the means of 'bringing to the investigation of such subjects, the same facility and the same unsparing exertion that Mr. Wilde afforded while he was sheriff; and I am persuaded, and have been, ever since I knew those facts, that unless the practical difficulties are insuperable, which I do not apprehend would be 'the case, some legal constitutional mode ought to be adopt- 'ed, by which errors and mistakes, from whatever source 'arising, should be corrected in criminal trials, as well as they 'may now be in civil cases.'

"In consequence of Sir F. Pollock's suggestion, Mr. Wilde was examined, and stated that in the space of nine months, during which he was one of the sheriffs of London, no less than six persons who had been capitally convicted at the Old Bailey, and left for execution, were saved from death, in consequence of investigations showing that they had been improperly convicted. Being asked, 'Is it your belief that many 'innocent persons do suffer from the want of a proper mode 'of inquiry?' he answered, 'I think many innocent persons 'have suffered—the term innocent, I use with reference to 'the offence with which they are charged.' In answer to the question, 'From your own personal experience on the subject, and your general observations and knowledge, do you 'think that it would be desirable to provide some more cer- 'tain means for inquiry, in cases of doubt, after conviction?' he said, 'I think it indispensably called for. From the want 'of it, the sheriffs and officers of the prison, who, of course, 'are the only persons in constant communication with the 'prisoners, are often placed in a most painful situation, in 'having to judge how far, consistently with the discharge of 'their own duties, they ought to interfere.'

* * * * * * *

"Where a party has been convicted, improper evidence having been received against him, or legal evidence for him having been rejected on the trial, injustice is done to him if the objection be disregarded, and injustice is done to society in allowing the objection to prevail to his actual and final discharge. To take a middle course in such a case, in mitigating the sentence on account of the doubt, is not only unjust, but highly absurd: he cannot have been guilty of a fraction of the offence, and therefore ought not to be subjected to a fraction of the punishment. A wrong is done, either to the accused, in punishing him at all, or to the public, in not punishing him according to his desert. Where the verdict of guilty is fairly warranted by proper evidence, but a doubt arises as to sanity, identity or other material fact from collateral sources, difficulties result which cannot well be removed but by a new trial. The execution of the sentence would, though legal, be barbarous; to exercise the royal prerogative, without a searching investigation, would be unadvisable and impolitic. The instituting a strict inquiry, would be in effect to grant a second trial; it would at least admit the necessity for one, and it would be made under circumstances the most disadvantageous to the discovery of the truth, without any of the powers and sanctions which in courts of justice are provided against fraud and imposition.

"We know, from long experience, that zealous exertions are frequently made on the part of the government, for correcting any suggested error or mistake in respect of criminal convictions, and also that those exertions have, in many instances, been highly beneficial, in rescuing convicted but innocent persons, from capital and other highly penal sentences. Still, as such inquiries must usually be conducted in secret, they are not unfrequently, however unjustly, the subject of popular jealousy or suspicion. It is also necessary to observe, that such an inquiry and statement as are necessary, in order to raise a sufficient case for further investigation by authority, are often beyond the reach of persons so unfortunately situated. The difficulties in the way of a prisoner obtaining a revision of his sentence, after an unjust conviction, are forcibly stated by Mr. Wilde in his evidence before your Majesty's Commissioners on Criminal Law. Being asked his opinion, whether a prisoner had any sufficient means of procuring a revision of his case, he says:—'I do 'not consider that at present there are any sufficient means. 'The prisoner convicted in London and Middlesex, may pre- 'sent a petition to the King in Council, through the Home 'Secretary, which may of course state all the grounds, either 'of fact or in law, upon which the conviction ought not to 'have taken place, and craving the mercy of the crown; or 'if tried at the assizes, may present a similar petition to the 'judge who tries him. This cannot be considered as in 'the nature of an appeal. From the state of destitu- 'tion and ignorance in which prisoners generally are, and 'from the want of a court and proper officers, the prisoners 'have not the means for bringing their cases in a proper 'state for reconsideration; and I think I may state, that 'the prisoners generally consider that the only benefit 'that they can derive from a petition so presented, is from 'the mercy of the Crown. Practically speaking, unless 'sheriffs, magistrates and governors of prisons, and their 'officers, or charitable individuals, exert themselves in col-

'lecting and authenticating the grounds upon which a pri-'soner seeks for the relief, and subsequently take the trouble 'of communicating with the Secretary of State, the prisoners 'have little or no chance of a successful result to their ap-'plication. This applies as well to those who are innocent, 'as to those who merely seek for a mitigation of the sen-'tence.'

"'From the experience you have personally had, do you 'think it just and proper, or even necessary that there should 'be some regular and settled mode by which prisoners, even 'after conviction, may obtain a revision of their case in par-'ticular instances?' 'I do; and I am perfectly satisfied 'that many persons have suffered punishments, where they 'have been positively innocent of the crime with which they 'are charged, and which, if there had been any court of 'appeal, with, of course, proper officers appointed, to whom 'the parties accused might have stated their grounds of ap-'peal, there would have been a reversal of their conviction 'or sentence.'

"'In your judgment, are the generality of prisoners 'aware of the means by which a revision may be occasion-'ally obtained, by an application to the secretary of state?' 'I have no doubt that it is known in prison conversation, 'that there is what is called a revision of the case, (that is, 'in capital felonies, but not otherwise;) but it is only done 'in the form of a petition, and is therefore rather an appeal 'to mercy, than the assertion of a right, and it is attended 'with considerable difficulties to the prisoners, from their 'poverty and destitution.'

"'Have you had opportunities, from filling the offices of 'sheriff and under sheriff, of knowing what the situation is, 'of persons who have been convicted, and the difficulty of 'obtaining a revision of their case?' 'I have had that op-'portunity; for, during the time I was in office, both as 'sheriff and under sheriff, I never failed attending in court, 'at the trial of prisoners at the sessions at the Old Bailey, 'and I was constantly through the prison of Newgate.'

"'Now, from the experience you have had, in your judg-'ment do you think it essential to justice, that revisions should 'occasionally take place after conviction?' 'Yes, I think so: in 'all important cases to the prisoners, where, if injustice is done, 'it would be more serious than in minor offences, although, 'upon principle, justice should of course be equal to all.'"

The views thus expressed in the report of the British Commissioners, have attracted much attention in that country. In an article in the *London Jurist, vol.* 2, *part* 2, *p.* 449, 450, several extracts from the report are given, and in concluding a review, highly commendatory of the principles contained in it, the reviewer observes: "After these extracts from the report, containing such sound and convincing reasons for the proposed change in the law, any observations of our own would be superfluous. To our minds they seem unanswerable; and we have inserted them in our pages, in the hope that it may be the means of making them known to some of our readers, who would not probably see them in the bulky volume of the report."

§ 521. A new trial is a re-examination of the issue, in the same court, before another jury, after a verdict has been given.

§ 522. A new trial can be granted by the court in which the former trial was had, only in the cases provided in section 524.

§ 523. The granting of a new trial places the parties in the same position, as if no trial had been had All the testimony must be produced anew; and the former verdict cannot be used or referred to, either in evidence or in argument.

§ 524. The court in which a new trial is had upon an issue of fact, has power to grant a new trial, when a verdict has been rendered against the defendant, by which his substantial rights have been prejudiced, upon his application, in the following cases:

1. When the trial has been had in his absence, if the indictment be for a felony;

2. When the jury has received any evidence out of court, other than that resulting from a view, as provided in section 468.

3. When the jury have separated without leave of the court, after retiring to deliberate upon their verdict, or been guilty of any misconduct by which a fair and due consideration of the case has been prevented:

4. When the verdict has been decided by lot, or by any means other than a fair expression of opinion on the part of all the jurors:

5. When the court has misdirected the jury in a matter of law, or has refused to instruct them as prescribed in section 477;

6. When the verdict is contrary to law or evidence. But no more than two new trials can be granted, for this cause alone.

§ 525. The application for a new trial must be made before judgment, and can be made only upon leave granted by the court.

§ 526. If leave be granted, the court must prescribe the time and manner of making the application.

CHAPTER III.

ARREST OF JUDGMENT.

§ 527. A motion in arrest of judgment is an application, on the part of the defendant, that no judgment be rendered on a plea or verdict of guilty, or on a verdict against the defendant on a plea of a former conviction or acquittal. It may be founded on any of the defects in the indictment, mentioned in section 342.

§ 528. The court may also, on its own view of any of these defects, arrest the judgment, without motion.

The last two sections are substantially conformable to the existing practice.

§ 529. The motion must be made, before or at the time when the defendant is called for judgment. If made before, it must be on notice to the district attorney, or in his presence.

When the defendant is called for judgment, he may now move in arrest. It seems reasonable to provide that if the motion be made before that time, it should be on notice to the district attorney.

§ 530. The effect of allowing a motion in arrest of judgment, is to place the defendant in the same situation in which he was before the indictment was found.

Declaratory of the existing rule.

§ 531. If, from the evidence on the trial, there is reasonable ground to believe the defendant guilty, and a new indictment can be framed upon which he may be convicted, the court may order him to be re-committed to the officer of the proper county, or admitted to bail anew, to answer the new indictment. If the evidence show him guilty of another offence, he must be committed or held thereon; and in neither case, is the verdict a bar to another prosecution or indictment for the same offence. But if no evidence appear, sufficient to charge him with any offence, he must, if in custody, be discharged, or if admitted to bail, his bail is exonerated, or if money have been deposited instead of bail, it must be refunded to the defendant; and the arrest of judgment operates as an acquittal of the charge upon which the indictment was founded.

TITLE IX.

OF THE JUDGMENT AND EXECUTION.

CHAPTER I.

THE JUDGMENT.

§ 532. After a plea or verdict of guilty, or after a verdict against the defendant on a plea of a former conviction or acquittal, if the judgment be not arrested, or a new trial granted, the court must appoint a time for pronouncing judgment.

§ 533. The time appointed must be at least two days after the verdict, if the court intend to remain in session so long, or if not, as remote a time as can reasonably be allowed. But in no case can the judgment be rendered, in less than six hours after the verdict.

It has been the practice, with but few execptions, to pronounce judgment immediately upon conviction. It seems but reasonable, to allow some time either to move for a new trial or in arrest of judgment. In *Liv. Crim. Code*, 540, *art.* 416, three days is allowed for this purpose. Lest judgment should be postponed to another term, the provision contained in this section is introduced.

§ 534. For the purpose of judgment, if the conviction be for a felony, the defendant must be personally present; if it be for a misdemeanor, judgment may be pronounced in his absence.

By the existing practice, the defendant can in no case be sentenced to imprisonment unless he be present. It would seem that this is unnecessary, in cases of misdemeanor, where the imprisonment can in no case exceed a year. Especially is it unnecessary under the provision of the code, authorizing the execution of the judgment upon a certified copy of the sentence. See *sec.* 551.

§ 535. When the defendant is in custody, the court may direct the officer in whose custody he is, to bring him before it for judgment: and the officer must do so accordingly.

§ 536. If the defendant have been discharged on bail, or have deposited money instead thereof, and do not appear for judgment, when his personal attendance is necessary, the court, in addition to the forfeiture of the undertaking of bail or of the money deposited, may direct the clerk to issue a bench warrant for his arrest.

§ 537. The clerk, on the application of the district attorney, may accordingly, at any time after the order, whether the court be sitting or not, issue a bench warrant into one or more counties.

§ 538. The bench warrant must be substantially in the following form:

"County of *Albany*, [or as the case may be.]

"In the name of the people of the state of New-York—

[SEAL.] "To any sheriff, constable, marshal or policeman in this state. A. B. having been on the day of 1850, duly convicted in the *court of sessions of the county of Albany*. (or as the case may be,) of the crime of, [designating it generally.]

"You are therefore commanded, forthwith to arrest the above named A. B., and bring him before that court for judgment; or if the court have adjourned for the term, you are to deliver him into the custody of the sheriff of the county of *Albany*, [or as the case may be, or in the city and county of New-York "to the keeper of the city prison of the city of New-York."]

"City of *Albany*, [or as the case may be] the day of , 1850.

"By order of the court.

"E. F., clerk."

§ 539. The bench warrant may be served in any county, in the same manner as a warrant of arrest; except that when served in another county, it need not be endorsed by a magistrate of that county.

§ 540. Whether the bench warrant be served in the county in which it was issued, or in another county, the officer must arrest the defendant and bring him before the court, or commit him to the officer mentioned in the warrant, according to the command thereof.

§ 541. When the defendant appears for judgment, he must be informed by the court, or by the clerk under its direction, of the nature of the indictment, and of his plea, and the verdict, if any thereon; and must be asked whether he have any legal cause to show, why judgment should not be pronounced against him.

§ 542. He may show for cause, against the judgment,

1. That he is insane; and if, in the opinion of the court, there be reasonable ground for believing him to be insane, the question of his insanity must be tried as provided by sections 722 to 725, both inclusive. If upon the trial of that question, the jury find that he is sane, judgment must be pronounced; but if they find him insane, he must be committed to the state lunatic asylum until he become sane; and when notice is given of that fact, as provided in section 729, he must be brought before the court for judgment:

2. That he has good cause to offer, either in arrest of judgment, or for a new trial; in which case the

court may, in its discretion, order the judgment to be deferred, and proceed to decide upon the motion in arrest of judgment, or for a new trial.

§ 543. If no sufficient cause be alleged, or appear to the court, why judgment should not be pronounced, it must thereupon be rendered.

The last three sections are in conformity with the existing practice.

§ 544. After a plea or verdict of guilty, in a case where a discretion is conferred upon the court as to the extent of the punishment, the court, upon the suggestion of either party, that there are circumstances, which may be properly taken into view, either in aggravation or mitigation of the punishment, may, in its discretion, hear the same summarily at a specified time, and upon such notice to the adverse party as it may direct.

§ 545. The circumstances must be presented, by the testimony of witnesses examined in open court; except, that when a witness is so sick or infirm, as to be unable to attend, his deposition may be taken by a magistrate of the county, out of court, at a specified time and place, upon such notice to the adverse party as the court may direct.

§ 546. No affidavit, or testimony, or representation of any kind, verbal or written, can be offered to, or received by the court, or a member thereof, in aggravation or mitigation of the punishment, except as provided in the last two sections.

§ 547. A violation of the last section is punishable as a misdemeanor, on the part of the person offering or receiving the affidavit or representation; and the person offering it may, in addition, be punished by the court for a contempt.

The practice on the subject embraced in the last four sections is extremely loose, and is wholly unregulated, either by statute or by rule. Where the defendant is convicted, if it be by a plea of guilty, the courts sometimes inform themselves of the circumstances of the case, so as properly to graduate the punishment, by a reference to the depositions on which the defendant was held to answer; and in other cases, by summarily hearing the witnesses or receiving their affidavits. On the other hand, where the defendant pleads, guilty, it is very common to deliver to the court affidavits in mitigation, which are in turn rebutted by the other side. The whole of this practice is extra judicial, and leads to great abuse. The Commissioners think it should be regulated; and for this purpose propose these sections, which, with what has been said, sufficiently explain themselves.

§ 548. If the defendant have been convicted of two or more offences, before judgment on either, the judgment may be, that the imprisonment upon any one may commence at the expiration of the imprisonment upon any other of the offences.

Conformable to the existing practice.

§ 549. A judgment that the defendant pay a fine, may also direct that he be imprisoned until the fine be satisfied, specifying the extent of the imprisonment;

which cannot exceed one day for every two dollars of the fine.

A sentence that the defendant stand committed until a fine be paid, is now virtually a sentence of perpetual imprisonment, unless the fine be either paid or remitted. The Commissioners deem it proper to provide, that the extent of the imprisonment be limited; and they think that the rule prescribed in this section is reasonable

§550. When judgment upon a conviction is rendered, the clerk must enter the same upon the minutes, stating briefly the offence for which the conviction has been had; and must immediately annex together and file the following papers, which constitute the judgment roll:

1. A copy of the minutes of a challenge interposed by the defendant to the panel of the grand jury, or to an individual grand juror, and the proceedings and decision thereon:

2. The indictment, and a copy of the minutes of the plea or demurrer:

3. A copy of the minutes of a challenge, which may have been interposed to the panel of the trial jury, or to an individual juror, and the proceedings and decision thereon:

4. A copy of the minutes of the trial:

5. A copy of the minutes of the judgment:

6. The bill of exceptions, if there be one.

This section abolishes the present technical, and, in many respects, unmeaning form of the judgment roll, and substitutes in its place a plain and accurate history of the case.

CHAPTER II.

THE EXECUTION.

§ 551. When a judgment, except of death, has been pronounced, a certified copy of the entry thereof upon the minutes, must be forthwith furnished to the officer whose duty it is to execute the judgment; and no other warrant or authority is necessary, to justify or require its execution.

§ 552. If the judgment be imprisonment, or a fine and imprisonment until it be paid, the defendant must forthwith be committed to the custody of the proper officer, and by him detained, until the judgment be complied with.

Taken from 2 *R. S.*, *3d ed.*, 824, *sec.* 13, 14; but made applicable to all judgments on conviction, and not merely to a judgment of imprisonment.

§ 553. When the judgment is imprisonment in a county jail, or a fine and that the defendant be imprisoned until he be paid, the judgment must be executed by the sheriff of the county. In all other cases, when the sentence is imprisonment, the sheriff of the county must deliver the defendant to the proper officer, in execution of the judgment.

§ 554. If the judgment be imprisonment, except in a county jail, the sheriff must deliver a copy of the entry of the judgment upon the minutes of the court, together with the body of the defendant, to the keeper of the prison, in which the defendant is to be imprisoned.

§ 555. The sheriff or his deputy, while conveying the defendant to the proper prison, in execution of a judgment of imprisonment, has the same authority to require the assistance of any citizen of this state, in securing the defendant, and in retaking him if he escape, as if the sheriff were in his own county; and every person who refuses or neglects to assist the sheriff, when so required, is punishable, as if the sheriff were in his own county.

The last section is taken from 2 *R. S. 3d ed.*, 824. *sec.* 15.

§ 556. When judgment of death is rendered, the members of the court or the majority of them, of whom the presiding judge must be one, must sign and deliver to the sheriff of the county, a warrant, stating the conviction and judgment, and appointing a day on which the judgment is to be executed, which must not be less than thirty, nor more than sixty days from the time of the judgment.

Taken from 2 *R. S.*, *3d ed.*, 747, *sec.* 11, 12. The only alteration is, in substituting thirty and sixty days, instead of four and eight weeks, as the time within which sentence of death must be executed. This alteration is made to conform the code in this particular, to the uniform mode of prescribing time in statutes, by *days*, and not by *weeks*..

§ 557. The presiding judge of the court at which a conviction requiring judgment of death is had, must, immediately after the conviction, transmit to the governor, by mail, a statement of the conviction and judgment, and of the testimony given at the trial.

§ 558. The governor may thereupon require the opinion of the judges of the court of appeals, and supreme court, and of the attorney-general, or of any of them, upon the statement so furnished.

The last two sections are substantially the same as *Laws of* 1847, *p.* 437, *ch.* 328, *sec* 1, 2.

§ 559. No judge, court or officer, other than the governor, can reprieve or suspend the execution of a judgment of death, except the sheriff, in the cases provided in the next eight sections.

Substantially the same as 2 R. *S.*, *3d ed*, *747*, *sec.* 15.

§ 560. If, after judgment of death, there be good reason to suppose that the defendant has become insane, the sheriff of the county, with the concurrence of a judge of the court by which the judgment was rendered, may summon from the list of grand jurors, a jury of twelve persons to inquire into the supposed insanity, and must give immediate notice thereof to the district attorney of the county.

Taken from *Laws of* 1847, *p.* 437, *sec.* 3; except that the words "a judge of the court by which the judgment was rendered," are substituted in place of the words "a justice of the supreme court, or if he be absent from the county, with the concurrence of the county judge of the county in which the conviction was had;" and except also that the jury is required to be taken from the list of grand jurors.

§ 561. The district attorney must attend the inquisition, and may produce witnesses before the jury; for which purpose, he may issue process in the same manner as for witnesses to attend before the grand jury; and disobedience thereto may be punished at the next court of oyer and terminer of the county, in the same manner as disobedience to process issued by that court.

Taken from 2 *R. S.*, *3d ed.* 747, *sec.* 17.

§ 562. A certificate of the inquisition must be signed by the jurors and the sheriff, and filed with the clerk of the court in which the conviction was had.

§ 563. If it be found by the inquisition, that the defendant is sane, the sheriff must execute the judgment;

but if it be found that he is insane, the sheriff must suspend the execution of the judgment, until he receive a warrant from the governor, or from a majority of the judges of the supreme court elected in the district, directing the execution of the judgment.

The last two sections are taken substantially from 2 *R. S.*, 3*d ed.* 747, 748, *sec.* 18, 19.

§ 564. If the inquisition find that the defendant is insane, the sheriff must immediately transmit it to the governor, who may, when the defendant becomes sane, issue a warrant appointing a day for the execution of the judgment.

New, but necessary to carry out the spirit of the last two sections.

§ 565. When there is good reason to suppose, that a female, against whom judgment of death is rendered, is pregnant, the sheriff of the county, with the concurrence of a judge of the court by which the judgment was rendered, may summon a jury of six physicians of the county, to inquire into the supposed pregnancy. Immediate notice thereof, must be given to the district attorney of the county. The provisions of sections 561 and 562, apply to the proceedings upon the inquisition.

Substantially the same as 2 *R. S.* 3*d ed.* 748, *sec.* 20.

§ 566. If it be found by the inquisition, that the female is not pregnant, the sheriff must execute the judgment. If, however, it be found that she is pregnant, the sheriff must suspend the execution of the judgment, and transmit the inquisition to the governor.

§ 567. When the governor is satisfied that the female is no longer pregnant, he may issue his warrant appointing a day for the execution of the judgment.

The last two sections are in substantial conformity with 2 *R. S., 3d ed.* 748, *sec.* 21, 22.

§ 568. If, for any reason, a judgment of death have not been executed, and it remain in force, the supreme court, at a general term in the district, on the application of the district attorney of the county where the conviction was had, must order the defendant to be brought before it; or, if he be at large, a warrant for his apprehension may be issued by that court, or by a judge thereof.

Substantially the same as 2 *R. S., 3d ed.* 748, *sec* 23; except, that an order to bring up the defendant, is substituted instead of a *habeas corpus*, which seems unnecessary.

§ 569. Upon the defendant being brought before the court, it must inquire into the facts, and if no legal reason exist against the execution of the judgment, must make an order that the sheriff of the proper county execute the judgment at a specified time. The sheriff must execute the judgment accordingly.

Same as 2 *R. S., 3d ed.* 748, *sec.* 24.

§ 570. The punishment of death must be inflicted, by hanging the defendant by the neck until he be dead.

Same as 2 *R. S.*, *3d ed.* 748, *sec.* 25.

§ 571. A judgment of death must, (except in the city and county of New York,) be executed within the walls of the jail of the county in which the conviction was had, or within a yard or enclosure adjoining the jail. In the city and county of New-York, it must be executed within the walls of the city-prison of the city of New-York, or within a yard or enclosure adjoining the same. If there be no such jail or prison in the county in which the conviction was had, or if it become unfit or unsafe for the confinement of prisoners, or be destroyed by fire or otherwise, and the jail of another county have been legally designated, for the confinement of the prisoners of the county in which the conviction was had, the judgment must be executed within the walls of the prison so designated, or within a yard or enclosure adjoining the same.

This section is taken from 2 *R. S.* *3d ed.* 748, *sec.* 26. It is deemed advisable, however, to make it more explicit in reference to the distinction between the city-prison of the city of New-York, and the jails in the other counties. The last sentence, as above, is inserted, in conformity with *Laws of* 1846, *p.* 131, *ch.* 118.

§ 572. The sheriff or under-sheriff of the county must be present at the execution, and must invite the presence, (by at least three days notice,) of the judge, district attorney, clerk and surrogate of the county, together with two physicians and twelve reputable citizens, to be selected by him. He must also, at the request of the defendant, permit any minister of the gospel whom the defendant may name, and any of his relatives, to attend the execution; and also such peace officers, as the sheriff or under-sheriff may deem proper. But no other persons than those mentioned in this section, can be present at the execution; nor can any person under age be allowed to witness the same.

§ 573. The sheriff or under-sheriff, and the judges attending the execution, must prepare and sign, with their names of office, a certificate, setting forth the time and place of the execution, and that the judgment was executed upon the defendant, according to the provisions of the last three sections: and must cause the certificate to be signed by the public officers, and by at least twelve persons, not relatives of the defendant, who witnessed the execution.

§ 574. The sheriff or under-sheriff must cause the certificate to be filed in the office of the clerk of the county, and a copy thereof to be published in the state paper, and in one newspaper, if any, printed in the county.

The last three sections are substantially the same as 2 *R. S, 3d. ed.*, 748, 749, *sec.* 27, 28.

Whether the punishment of death should ever be inflicted for crime, is a question into which the Commissioners did not feel authorized to enter. It was their province to provide for the mode of enforcing the penalties declared by the existing law. How far the penal code needs revision, and whether the severity of criminal punishment should be lessened in any case, and if so, in which of them, it belongs to others to decide.

TITLE X.

OF APPEALS.

CHAPTER I.

APPEALS, WHEN ALLOWED, AND HOW TAKEN.

§ 575. Writs of error and of certiorari, in criminal actions, as they have heretofore existed, are abolished; and hereafter, the only mode of reviewing a judgment or order, in a criminal action, is that prescribed by this chapter.

§ 576. The party aggrieved, whether the people or the defendant, may appeal, from a judgment in a criminal action, in the cases prescribed in this chapter.

§ 577. The party appealing is known as the appellant, and the adverse party as the respondent. But the title of the action is not changed, in consequence of the appeal.

§ 578. An appeal to the supreme court may be taken by the defendant, from a judgment on a conviction; and upon the appeal, any actual decision of the court in an intermediate order or proceeding forming a part of the judgment roll, as prescribed by section 550, may be reviewed.

§ 579. An appeal to the supreme court may be taken by the people, in the following cases, and no other:

1. Upon a judgment for the defendant, on a demurrer to the indictment:

2. Upon an order of the court, arresting the judgment.

§ 580. An appeal may be taken from the judgment of the supreme court to the court of appeals, in the following cases, and no other:

1. From a judgment affirming a judgment of conviction:

2. From a judgment affirming or reversing a judgment for the defendant, on a demurrer to the indictment, or on an order of the court arresting the judgment.

§ 581. An appeal may be taken, as provided in the last three sections, as a matter of right.

Section 575 abolishes all existing modes of reviewing judgments or orders in criminal cases, and substitutes an appeal, in the cases provided in the sections which follow. The form of this section is substantially the same as that of the corresponding one in the amended Code of civil Procedure. (*sec.* 323.)

There are, by the existing practice, two modes of appeal in criminal cases ; *first*, before judgment upon a bill of exceptions, and *second*, upon a judgment.

The first of these modes of appeal, before judgment upon a bill of exceptions, was unknown to the common law, and was created for the first time by the Revised Statutes. Indeed, before that time, there was no bill of exceptions in a criminal case ; the only mode of correcting an error occurring on the trial, being by the reservation of the question by the court in which the trial was had, for the advice of the supreme court. The Revised Statutes gave the right to the defendant, to take exceptions to any decision of the court, in the same cases and manner provided by law in civil cases; and provided that a bill thereof should be settled, signed and sealed, and should be filed with the clerk of the court, and returned upon a writ of error after judgment, or upon a *certiorari* before judgment. 2 *R. S.* 3*d, ed.* 820, *sec.* 21.

The bill of exceptions being settled and signed, judgment upon the conviction is stayed, provided the presiding judge or a judge of the supreme court certify on the bill of exceptions, that in his opinion there is probable cause for the same, or so much doubt as to render it expedient to take the judgment of the supreme court thereon; but this certificate cannot be granted by a judge of the supreme court, unless application therefor be first made to the judge who presided at the trial, and his reasons for refusing it be attached to the bill of exceptions. 2 *R. S.* 3*d. ed.* 821, *sec.* 22—25.

After making provision for admitting the defendant to bail, *Ibid. sec.* 26. it is further provided that when judgment is thus stayed, the district attorney shall immediately sue out a writ of *certiorari*, to remove the indictment, with the bill of exceptions and other proceedings thereon, into the supreme court. *Ibid. sec.* 27. If the supreme court decide against the exceptions, it is authorised either to render judgment and pronounce sentence, or to remit the case for that purpose to the court in which the trial was had. 2 *R. S.* 3*d ed.* 826, *sec.* 27. If a new trial be ordered, it must be in the court in which the first trial was had. *Ibid. sec.* 28.

The second mode of appeal, now in use, is by writ of error upon a judgment; upon which, as has been already seen, the bill of exceptions may be brought up for review. A writ of error may be brought either by the people or by the defendant; except that when brought by the people, it must be founded upon some matter apparent upon the face of the judgment record, the people not being entitled to take a bill of exceptions. It is a writ of right in all except capital cases, in which a special allowance is necessary; but in no case does it operate as a stay of execution, unless a special direction to that effect be inserted in the writ by the officer by whom it is allowed. *2 R. S. 3d ed.* 825, *sec.* 16—18.

The sections under consideration propose to give but one mode of appeal, namely, after judgment; and to make the writ of error a writ of right in all cases, but with the restriction hereafter referred to, that it shall not be a stay of proceedings, unless upon a special order to that effect. In all other respects, the appeal provided by the code is in conformity with the spirit of the existing practice. The only essential change is in substituting an appeal, after judgment, for the double system now allowed. By the present practice, the defendant may appeal upon a bill of exceptions before judgment, as well as in that or any other case after judgment. The inconvenience of this double right to appeal, has forced itself strongly upon the Commissioners. It can only be defended, upon the ground that the defendant should not be sentenced upon a conviction, where there is reasonable ground to suppose that fatal errors have occurred upon the trial. But its continuance leads to this practical inconsistency,—that he must notwithstanding, be sentenced, before his case can be carried beyond the supreme court. This is founded upon the technical rule, that a writ of error cannot be brought except upon final judgment.

The consequence has been, and it has actually occurred in practice, that after a new trial has been denied by the supreme court, the defendant must be sentenced by the court below; and their judgment with a bill of exceptions annexed, must be brought before the supreme court, that their former decision may be re-declared and embodied in the form of a judgment, to the end that it may be reviewed on error by the court of appeals. In one case,—a case of murder,—this useless formality delayed the final decision of the cause for more than a year; and it is apparent, that in all cases, it must be productive of great delay.

The Commissioners see no reason why the substantial rights of the defendant cannot be fully protected, by permitting the judgment to be pronounced upon the verdict in the first instance, by the court in which the defendant is convicted, with a stay of execution, and suitable provisions for admitting him to bail, in cases where it is proper. In this manner, the course of the appeal, through all the courts to which it is allowed, is easy and simple,—the whole record, including the bill of exceptions, is passed upon,— and no real prejudice is suffered by the defendant.

§ 582. An appeal must be taken, within one year after the judgment was rendered.

The chapter of the revised statutes relating to writs of error in criminal cases, contains no limitation of the time within which a writ of error in such case must be brought. 2 *R. S.*, 3*d. ed.*, 825–827. In civil cases, the limitation is two years. 2 *R. S.*, 3*d. ed.*, 687, *sec.* 21.

The Commissioners deem one year a proper allowance in criminal cases, for the reason that, if not brought within that time, the party may be fairly presumed to have acquiesced in the judgment.

§ 583. An appeal must be taken, by the service of a notice in writing on the clerk with whom the judgment roll is filed, stating that the appellant appeals from the judgment.

§ 584. If the appeal be taken by the defendant, a similar notice must be served on the district attorney of the county in which the original judgment was rendered.

§ 585. If it be taken by the people, a similar notice must be served on the defendant, if he be a resident of or imprisoned in the city or county; or if not, on the counsel, if any, who appeared for him on the trial, if he reside or transact his business in the county. If the service cannot, after due diligence, be made, the appellate court, upon proof thereof, may make an order for the publication of the notice, in such newspaper, and for such time as it deems proper.

§ 586. At the expiration of the time appointed for the publication, on filing an affidavit of the publication, the appeal becomes perfected.

The last four sections conform in principle, to the practice prescribed by section 327, of the amended Code of Procedure.

§ 587. An appeal taken by the people, in no case stays or affects the operation of a judgment in favor of the defendant, until the judgment is reversed.

Conformable to the existing practice.

§ 588. An appeal to the supreme court, from a judgment of conviction, stays the execution of the judgment, upon filing, with the notice of appeal, a certificate of the presiding judge of the court in which the conviction was had, or of a judge of the supreme court, that in his opinion there is probable cause for the appeal, but not otherwise.

§ 589. An appeal to the court of appeals, from a judgment of the supreme court, affirming a judgment of conviction, stays the execution of the judgment appealed from, upon filing, with the notice of appeal, a certificate of a judge of the court of appeals, or of the supreme court, that, in his opinion, there is probable cause for the appeal, but not otherwise.

The last two sections are conformable, in their general spirit, to 2 *R. S.*, *3d ed.*, 825, *sec.* 20.

§ 590. The certificate mentioned in the last two sections, cannot, however, be granted upon an appeal on a conviction of felony, until such notice as the judge may prescribe, has been given to the district attorney of the county where the conviction was had, of the application for the certificate. But the judge may stay the execution of the judgment, in the mean time.

This provision is new but seems proper to prevent the hasty or ill-considered allowance of a stay of proceedings.

§ 591. If the certificate, provided in sections 588 and 589, be given, the sheriff must, if the defendant be in his custody, upon being served with a copy of the order, keep the defendant in his custody, without executing the judgment, and detain him to abide the judgment upon the appeal.

Taken from 2 *R. S.*, *3d ed.*, 825, *sec.* 20.

§ 592. If, before the granting of the certificate, the execution of the judgment have commenced, the further execution thereof is suspended, and the defendant must be restored by the officer in whose custody he is, to his original custody.

This section is new, but of its justice and propriety the Commissioners entertain no doubt. Cases are of frequent occurrence, where the judgment is reversed after the defendant has suffered a great portion of the imprisonment imposed by his sentence. By the present practice, unless a stay of proceedings be obtained before the commencement of the execution of the sentence, the defendant must continue to suffer the punishment, though the conviction be clearly wrong. This rests upon the old notion, applicable alike to civil and criminal cases, that an execution once begun to be executed cannot be interrupted. The Revised Statutes have provided for staying proceedings upon an execution in a civil case, at any time before it is fully executed; *2 R. S. 3d ed.*, 689, *sec.* 29, 30; and the reason is, if anything, stronger, for the application of this principle to criminal cases.

§ 593. Upon the appeal being taken, the clerk, with whom the notice of appeal is filed, must, within ten days thereafter, without charge, transmit a copy of the notice of appeal and of the judgment roll, as follows:

1. If the appeal be to the supreme court, to the clerk of that court, where the next general term in the district is to he held.

2. If it be to the court of appeals, to the clerk of that court.

CHAPTER II.

DISMISSING AN APPEAL, FOR IRREGULARITY.

§ 594. If the appeal be irregular in a substantial particular, but not otherwise, the court may, on any day in term, on motion of the respondent, upon five days notice, with copies of the papers on which the motion is founded, order it to be dismissed.

Appeals are frequently dismissed for a departure from some formal requirement of the practice. Nothing but a substantial irregularity should deprive the party of his rights.

§ 595. The court may also, upon like motion, dismiss the appeal, if the return be not made, as provided in section 593; unless, for good cause, they enlarge the time for that purpose.

This section does away with the present practice of a rule to return a writ of error, and places upon the appellant the necessity of having his appeal returned in time; while, upon sufficient cause shown it relieves him from any substantial prejudice from his failure to have it returned.

CHAPTER III.

ARGUMENT OF THE APPEAL.

§ 596. An appeal to the supreme court may be brought to argument by either party, on ten days notice, on any day, at a general term held in the district in which the original judgment was given.

§ 597. An appeal to the court of appeals may, in the same manner, be brought to argument by either party, on any day in term.

§ 598. If a counsel, within five days after the appeal, have given notice to the district attorney, that he appears for the defendant, notice of argument must be served on him, instead of the defendant; otherwise, notice must be served as the court may direct.

§ 599. When the appeal is called for argument, the appellant must furnish the court with copies of the notice of appeal and judgment roll. If he fail to do so, the appeal must be dismissed, unless the court otherwise direct.

§ 600. Judgment of affirmance may be given, without argument, if the appellant fail to appear. But judgment of reversal can only be given upon argument, though the respondent fail to appear.

This section is conformable to the former practice of the court of appeals, as regulated by *Rule* 18, *of* 1847, which provided in substance that the court would not hear an *ex parte* argument in favor of the affirmance of a decree or judgment; but that if the cause were regularly noticed for argument, and placed on the calendar of causes by the respondent or the defendant in error, and the appellant or plaintiff in error did not appear to argue on his part, or did not furnish the printed cases as required by the rules, the decree or judgment should be affirmed. The same practice also prevailed in the court for the correction of errors. It has been changed, however, by *Rnle* 11, *of* 1849, of the court of appeals, which provides that "the party who has noticed and placed the cause on the calendar for argument, may take judgment of affirmance or reversal, as the case may be, if the other party shall neglect to appear and argue the cause, or shall neglect to furnish and deliver cases or points, as required by the ninth and tenth rules."

While the Commissioners readily defer to the superior wisdom of that high tribunal, they are constrained to believe that the practice, as it formerly existed, in criminal cases at least, is better adapted to promote the ends of justice, than that which, under the rule just cited, prevails in the court of appeals. Appeals, as they are proposed by the Commissioners, in both civil and criminal actions, are restricted in all cases, as they always were in the court of errors and court of appeals, to the review of supposed errors, not technically appearing upon the record, but actually occurring in the determination or decision appealed from. It is very proper, therefore, in favor of the decision of the court below, to presume its correctness until the contrary be shown, and as a consequence to provide, that, if the appellant fail to appear to show the errors of which he complains, the judgment should be affirmed. But it does not seem just, on the other hand, if, by reason of accident or neglect which may be the subject of reasonable excuse, the successful party in the court below should fail to appear in the appellate court, he should be deprived of the benefit of a judgment not technically but actually rendered in his favor. It was doubtless upon this view of the subject, that the former practice of the court of errors and court of appeals was founded; and aside from the intrinsic justice of the practice itself, the Commissioners are not aware that it was ever deemed productive of such a degree of inconvenience, either to the court or a party, as to require that it should be changed. At all events, if the change be proper in any case, it should not be made applicable to appeals in criminal cases. With all the safeguards which are thrown around the rights of the prosecution, by retaining the record for a number of days after the judgment, to enable the party against whom it is given, to apply to open the default; cases may arise where a party legally convicted in the court below, might, by such a reversal, escape the consequences of his crime. It is better, therefore, that the court should be subjected to the necessity of examining the case, before reversing, perhaps, a just conviction, than that public justice should be defeated, even though that defeat be occasioned by the neglect of a public officer.

§ 601. Upon the argument of the appeal, if the offence be punishable with death, two counsel on each side must be heard, if they require it. In any other case, the court may, in its discretion, restrict the argument to one counsel on each side. The counsel for the defendant is entitled to the closing argument.

The court of appeals has adopted a rule restricting the argument of a cause to one counsel on each side. In capital cases, it seems but reasonable to extend the privilege to two counsel on each side; and for the reasons stated in the *note to sec.* 440, *p.* 206—209 it is proposed to allow the defendant's counsel to conclude the argument.

§ 602. The defendant need not personally appear, in the appellate court.

This section is designed to remove a doubt, which has sometimes been suggested, as to whether the defendant in a criminal case should not be personally present at the argument. In practice, his presence is not usually required, nor is it for any purpose necessary.

CHAPTER IV.

JUDGMENT, UPON APPEAL.

§ 603. After hearing the appeal, the court must give judgment, without regard to technical errors or defects, or to exceptions which do not affect the substantial rights of the parties.

§ 604. The appellate court may reverse, affirm, or modify the judgment appealed from, and may, if necessary or proper, order a new trial.

This section is taken from the *amended Code of Civil Procedure, sec.* 330, and conformable to 2 *R. S., 3d ed.*, 826, *sec.* 26.

§ 605. When a new trial is ordered, it may be directed to be had, either in the court below, or in the court of oyer and terminer of such county as the appellate court shall deem proper.

Same as 2 *R. S., 3d ed.*, 826, *sec.* 28; except in giving the appellate court power to order the new trial in the court of oyer and terminer of another county, instead of confining it to the court in which the first trial was had.

§ 606. If a judgment against the defendant be reversed, without ordering a new trial, the appellate court must direct, if he be in custody, that he be discharged therefrom, or if he be admitted to bail, that his bail be exonerated, or if money be deposited instead of bail, that it be refunded to the defendant.

Taken from 2 *R. S. 3d ed.* 826, *sec.* 26.

§ 607. On a judgment of affirmance against the defendant, the original judgment must be carried into execution, as the appellate court may direct.

§ 608. When the judgment of the appellate court is given, it must be entered in the judgment book, and a certified copy of the entry forthwith remitted to the clerk with whom the original judgment roll is filed, or if a new trial be ordered in another county, to the clerk of that county, unless the judgment be rendered in the absence of the adverse party, in which case, the court may direct it to be retained, not exceeding ten days.

§ 609. The papers returned to the appellate court, must there remain of record, and are not to be remitted to the court below.

§ 610. After the certificate of the judgment has been remitted as provided in section 608, the appellate court has no further jurisdiction of the appeal, or of the proceedings thereon; and all orders which may be necessary to carry the judgment into effect, must be made by the court to which the certificate is remitted.

The mode of entering the judgment, provided in the last three sections is in conformity with *sections* 279 *and* 280 *of the amended Code of Procedure.* As to the mode of remitting the judgment, it is recommended that a certified copy of the entry alone be remitted to the court below, leaving in the appellate court, as part of its records, the papers returned to it upon the appeal. This seems preferable to the practice adopted by the court of appeals, *Rule* 16, of remitting to the court below the papers returned as well as a copy of the judgment of the court of appeals.

TITLE XI.

OF MISCELLANEOUS PROCEEDINGS.

CHAPTER I.

BAIL.

ARTICLE I.

IN WHAT CASES THE DEFENDANT MAY BE ADMITTED TO BAIL.

There are few subjects which have attracted so much public attention, or called more loudly for searching and thorough reform, than that of *bail in criminal cases.* Whether it be owing to the looseness of the existing law upon the subject, or to the careless exercise of this high discretionary power, the Commissioners will not stop to inquire; but it is nevertheless the fact, that the system of bail, as it now exists in practice, has in a very great number of cases, and those too of the most heinous character, led to the entire defeat of public justice. Between the embarrassments which present themselves in determining in what cases bail may be taken, and the greater difficulty of prescribing in each case, an adequate mode of ascertaining the sufficiency of the bail, both of which result from the fact that there is no other rule than that of discretion,—the defeat of criminal justice has become a work of too easy accomplishment. In the former case, courts and judges have been perplexed by the danger of too indulgent a spirit on the one hand, and of too rigorous a standard of discretion on the other; while in the latter, the responsibility has been cast unon them, without affording them either the means of fully meeting it, or adequate protection in its exercise. It is not then, so much to be wondered at, that by the machinery of what is called straw bail, the vilest criminals have been enabled to elude justice. To provide an effectual remedy for this enormous abuse, has been regarded by the Commissioners as one of their highest duties, and by this and the following chapters of this title, they have endeavored to accomplish their design.

The chapter immediately under consideration defines bail, and prescribes the cases in which it may be taken.

After providing in section 611, a concise definition of bail, section 612 declares that it must be given, by an undertaking, which is uniform in its character with bail in civil actions, as provided in the code of civil procedure.

It may be remarked here, that in every instance where this undertaking is required, its form is given, and that it is more concise and intelligible than the present forms of bonds and recognizances.

In considering the provisions contained in sections 613 to 617, defining the cases which are bailable, the Commissioners propose very briefly to refer to the existing statutes and common law, and to submit the reasons which have led them to recommend the sections under review.

The following are the provisions of the revised statutes, relating to bail before conviction.

"If the offence with which the prisoner be charged, be bailable by a justice of the peace, or an alderman of a city, and the prisoner offer sufficient bail, such bail may be taken, and the prisoner discharged; if no bail be offered, or the offence be not bailable by a justice or alderman, the prisoner shall be committed to prison, except in cases in which a court of special sessons shall be authorized to try the prisoner, as provided by this chapter." 2 *R. S. 3d. ed,* 795, *sec.* 27.

"Officers before whom persons charged with crime shall be brought, shall have power to let to bail as follows:—1. The chancellor, a justice of the supreme court, a circuit judge, or a supreme court commissioner, in all cases: 2. A judge of the county courts, in all cases triable in a court of general sessions: 3. A justice of the peace or alderman of a city, and in the city of New York, a special justice or an assistant justice, in all cases of misdemeanor, and in all cases of felony where the imprisonment in the state prison cannot exceed five years." 2 *R. S. 3d. ed,* 796, *sec.* 31.

"The special justices for preserving the peace in the city of New-York, shall respectively have power to let to bail, in all cases where a judge of the court of general sessions in the said city is authorized by law to let to bail." *Ibid. sec.* 32.

"The court of oyer and terminer held in any county, shall have power to let to bail, any person committed, before indictment found upon any criminal charge whatever." *Ibid. sec.* 33.

"The court of general sessions of any county, shall have power to let to bail persons committed to the prison of the county, before indictment found, for any offence triable in that court." *Ibid. sec.* 34.

"Whenever any prisoner shall be let to bail by any officer out of court, the officer shall immediately cause the recognizance taken by him, to be filed with the clerk of the county, in which the party bailed was imprisoned." *Ibid. sec.* 35.

"Whenever any person shall be let to bail by any court, other than that in which the offence is triable, it shall be the duty of the clerk of the court by which the prisoner was bailed, immediately to transmit the recognizance taken by the court, to the clerk of the county in which the party bailed was imprisoned." *Ibid. sec.* 36.

From these provisions, it is apparent that the *power* to admit to bail before conviction, exists in all criminal cases, without restriction as to the degree or character of the offence. Indeed, before they were adopted, this power was expressly declared by Chief Justice *Savage*, in the case of *The People v. Tayloe*, 5 Cowen, 50, to be unquestionable. "The power of this court, (says he,) to bail in all cases of crime punishable by our laws, is not questioned. And whether the prisoner is to be bailed or remanded, rests in the discretion of the court. That discretion is to be guided by the circumstances of the case, and a consideration of the authorities applicable to those circumstances." And since the passage of the revised statutes, Chief Justice *Spencer*, in a letter appended to Judge *Tallmadge's* review of the *M'Leod* case, 26 *Wend.* 700, referring to the power of bailing upon *habeas corpus*, regards the statute on that subject, as proving "that the fact of an indictment found, even for murder, raises no objection to a discharge or bailing."

The existing rule, therefore, is, that a defendant may in all cases, as a matter of discretion, be admitted to bail. In this respect, all cases,—whether they be of the highest degree of felony, or the lowest degree of misdemeanor,—stand upon the same footing. As to the propriety, however, of exercising this power in a given case, many rules have been established, which now have the force of law. For example, it is said, that if the commitment be on the accusation of a mere misdemeanor, the prisoner may, in general, be let to bail; and this, whether brought up before or after indictment. 3 *Hill*, 667, *note* 42. But in case the commitment be for a felony, it is never a matter of course to let the prisoner to bail, much less to discharge him. *Ibid. note* 43. The right to bail in murder, has been also much discussed; and the practice appears to be well settled, that after indictment, at least, if not before also, bail will not be taken. See 3 *Hill*, 668-670, *note* 44. In other felonies, also, the practice has been settled by the supreme court in *Ex parte Tayloe*, 5 Cowen, 39, to be, that, whether before or after indictment, it is not of course to allow bail, but that if the guilt or innocence of the defendant appear to be indifferent, he may be bailed. See *the cases cited in that case, and in* 3 *Hill*, 672--674, *note* 45.

In regard to bail after conviction, the rule of the common law is, that a prisoner may be let to bail for the purpose of an appeal, if it appear that there is doubt on the law of the case; and especially where the law is against the prosecution. *Bac. Abr.* 353, *Bail in Criminal Cases, D.*; 3 *Hill*, 674, *note* 46. It is provided also by the Revised Statutes, in reference to cases where a bill of exceptions is taken, and a stay of sentence granted, that the court in which the trial was had, or any justice of the supreme court or circuit judge, may let the defendant to bail, upon a recognizance with sufficient sureties, conditioned that he shall appear in the court where the trial was had, at such time as the supreme court shall direct, and that he will obey any order or judgment the supreme court shall make in the premises. 2 *R. S. 3d. ed.* 821, *sec.* 26. Where a writ of error is brought after judgment, it is also provided, that if the offence charged in the indictment, for the removal of which the writ of error shall be allowed, be punishable by imprisonment in a state prison or in a county jail, any officer herein authorised to allow the writ of error, may allow a writ of *habeas corpus*, to bring before him the defendant in the indictment; and may thereupon let him to bail, upon a recognizance with sufficient sureties, conditioned that the defendant shall appear in the supreme court to receive judgment on the writ of error, or in the court in which the trial on the indictment shall have been had, at such time and place as the supreme court shall direct, and that he will obey every order and judgment which the supreme court shall make in the premises. 2 *R. S. 3d ed.* 825, *sec.* 21.

In the case of admission to bail after conviction, it will be perceived that the power is entirely discretionary, except that it does not exist in cases punishable with death. Nor have any well defined limits been set to the exercise of this discretion, except that bail will not be taken unless the case be very doubtful on the merits. See *The State v. Ward*, 2 Hawks, 443; *The People v. Lohman*, 2 Barb. Sup. Ct. Rep. 450.

In the sections under consideration, the Commissioners have proposed to depart in some respects from the existing statutes, and in others to declare or modify the practice under them. For example, it is provided by section 613, that bail shall not be taken in capital cases, or in cases where the defendant is charged with the infliction of a personal injury upon another, likely to produce death, and under such circumstances as that, if death ensue, the offence would be murder. The latter of these cases is included in this section, not merely as falling within the principle applicable to capital cases, but in accordance with the recommendation of a similar provision, in *Liv. Crim. Code*, 510, *art.* 197. The ground upon which the defendant is admitted to bail in any case, or, where he is admitted to bail, the test by which the amount of bail is fixed, is the inquiry whether, in all probability, he will consult his safety by omitting to appear and take his trial at the expense of a forfeiture of his bail. In capital cases, and in cases like those provided for in the last branch of this section, this inquiry is readily answered. It is true that there have been exceptions; but as an almost invariable rule, the defendant in such a case would forfeit any amount of bail, rather than encounter the peril of his life. It is for this reason, that in cases of this nature, the practice in this state has been uniform to refuse to admit the defendant to bail. The Commissioners see no good reason, why this practice should not have the express sanction of law.

Section 614 provides that if the charge be for any other offence than those just referred to, bail may be taken as a matter of right in cases of misdemeanor, and as a matter of discretion in all other cases. As to the propriety of the provision, that the defendant shall be entitled to bail as a matter of right, in cases of misdemeanor, there would seem to be no doubt. Leaving to the magistrate or court to whom the power is confided, a discretion commensurate with the character of each particular case, as to the amount of bail, it will be readily admitted, that a case cannot be conceived, drawing after it the mild punishment incident to a misdedemeanor, in which,—before conviction at least,—adequate bail would not enforce the attendance of the defendant. And it is believed that in practice, no case can be found in which bail under such circumstances has been refused. In cases of felony, it is proposed to adhere to the present practice of making the admission to bail a matter of discretion; protecting the community, however, against the defeat of justice, by requiring, as is done, in subsequent provisions, that this discretion shall be exercised by the court in which the offence is triable, or by a higher class of magistrates than are authorized to determine the question of bail in cases of misdemeanor. See *sections* 618, 619.

The right to bail after conviction is regulated by section 615, which authorises the admission of the defendant to bail upon an appeal, where there is a stay of proceedings, as a matter of right, where the judgment imposes a fine only, and as a matter of discretion, in all other cases except those punishable with death. The propriety of this provision, the Commissioners think is apparent. Where a fine only is imposed, a pecuniary responsibility will of course be sufficient to secure the final enforcement of the judgment. But where the judgment is imprisonment, even though the case be one of misdemeanor only, it may fail of that effect. Hence the right should be absolute in the one case, while in the other, it should be the subject of discretion. The other sections under consideration sufficiently explain themselves, and require no other remark, than in respect to the provision in section 616, that instead of bail for the appearance of the party before the magistrate on the examination, money must be deposited. The subsequent provisions of the code require a thorough scrutiny, in all cases, in regard to the sufficiency of bail. For this purpose, time and opportunity for full inquiry in that respect are proposed to be afforded. It having been already provided, that the examination of the case, upon the defendant being brought before the magistrate, must be completed at one session, unless adjourned for good cause, and that the adjournment cannot be for more than two days, at each time, nor more than six days in all, unless by consent or on motion of the defendant, *sec.* 190, *p.* 87, it necessarily follows, that the process of taking bail would in most cases occupy more time than is required for the examination. By the present practice, bail cannot be taken until after the committal of the defendant. The reason of this rule probably is, that which has just been suggested. Cases have arisen, and may again arise, where its operation is hard and unjust to the defendant. This hardship should be obviated, if it can be done consistently with the claims of public justice; and the Commissioners, after much reflection, are satisfied that it cannot be better done than by the course provided in this section.

§ 611. Admission to bail is the order of a competent court or magistrate, that the defendant be discharged from actual custody, upon bail.

§ 612. The taking of bail consists in the acceptance, by a competent court or magistrate, of the undertaking of sufficient bail for the appearance of the defendant according to the terms of the undertaking, or that the bail will pay to the people of this state a specified sum.

§ 613. The defendant cannot be admitted to bail, where he is charged,

1. With an offence punishable with death: or,

2. With the infliction of a personal injury upon another, likely to produce death, and under such circumstances, as that, if death ensue, the offence would be murder.

§ 614. If the charge be for any other offence, he may be admitted to bail, before conviction, as follows:

1. As a matter of right, in cases of misdemeanor:

2. As a matter of discretion, in all other cases:

§ 615. After the conviction of an offence not punishable with death, a defendant who has appealed, and when there is a stay of proceed'ngs, but not otherwise, may be admitted to bail:

1. As a matter of right, when the appeal is from a judgment imposing a fine only:

2. As a matter of discretion, in all other cases.

§ 616. Before conviction, a defendant may be admitted to bail,

1. For his appearance before the magistrate, on the examination of the charge, before being held to answer.

But in this case, instead of an undertaking, money must be deposited, as provided in section 648.

2. To appear at the court to which the magistrate is required, by section 220, to return the depositions and statement, upon the defendant being held to answer, after examination:

3. After indictment, either upon the bench warrant issued for his arrest, or upon an order of the court committing him, or enlarging the amount of bail, or upon his being surrendered by his bail,—to answer the indictment in the court in which it is found, or to which it may be sent or removed for trial.

§ 617. After conviction and upon an appeal, the defendant may be admitted to bail, as follows:

1. If the appeal be from a judgment imposing a fine only, on the undertaking of bail, that he will pay the same, or such part of it as the appellate court may direct, if the judgment be affirmed or modified or the appeal be dismissed:

2. If judgment of imprisonment have been given, that he will surrender himself in execution of the judgment, upon its being affirmed or modified, or upon the appeal being dismissed.

ARTICLE II.

BAIL, UPON BEING HELD TO ANSWER, BEFORE INDICTMENT.

§ 618. When the defendant has been held to answer. as provided in section 208, the admission to bail may be by the magistrate by whom he is so held, as follows:

1. By any of the magistrates mentioned in section 147, when the offence charged is a misdemeanor, or a felony punishable with imprisonment, not exceeding five years:

2. By a judge of the supreme court, a county judge, the mayor or recorder of a city, a city judge, or a judge of the supeior court or court of common pleas of

the city of New-York, in all cases where bail may be taken, before conviction, as provided in section 616.

§ 619. When, by reason of the degree of the offence, the committing magistrate has not authority to admit to bail, the defendant may be admitted to bail by one of the officers having authority to admit to bail in the case, as provided in the second subdivision of the last section, or by the court to which the depositions and statements are returned by the committing magistrate, as provided in section 220, if the case be triable therein, or if not, by the court to which, after indictment, it may be sent or removed for trial.

The provisions of the Revised Statutes, on the subject of the courts or officers by whom a person charged with a public offence may be admitted to bail, are as follows:

"Officers before whom persons charged with crimes shall be brought, shall have power to let to bail, as follows:

"1. The chancellor, a justice of the supreme court, a circuit judge, or a supreme court commissioner, in all cases:

"2. A judge of the county courts, in all cases triable in a court of general sessions:

"3. A justice of the peace, or alderman of a city, and in the city of New-York, a special justice or an assistant justice, in all cases of misdemeanor, and in all cases of felony where the imprisonment in a state prison cannot exceed five years." 2 *R. S.* 3*d. ed.* 796, *sec.* 31.

"The special justices for preserving the peace in the city of New-York shall respectively have power to let to bail, in all cases where a judge of the court of general sessions in the said city is authorized by law to let to bail." *Ibid. sec.* 32.

"The court of oyer and terminer held in any county, shall have power to let to bail, any person committed, before indictment found, upon any criminal charge whatever." *Ibid. sec.* 33.

"The court of general sessions of any county, shall have power to let to bail persons committed to the prison of such county, before indictment found, for any offence triable in such court." *Ibid. sec.* 34.

In addition to these provisions, a special statute, applicable to the city of New-York only, prescribes that the amount of bail ordered by the committing magistrate, shall be altered only by a court having jurisdiction of the offence for which the prisoner was committed, and renders an officer, who violates that provision, guilty of a misdemeanor. *2 R. S., 3d. ed.*, 670, *sec.* 102.

The last two sections are substituted for the provisions just quoted, so far as relates to the courts, or officers by whom the defendant may be admitted to bail. They preserve the discrimination contained in those provisions, as to the degrees of crime for which each class of courts or officers may admit to bail; and while they substitute in place of officers who are no longer continued, those of the same degree, created under the new constitution, they provide, it is believed, in a less complex manner, as to the courts and officers by whom this power may be exercised.

§ 620. The defendant may be admitted to bail by a magistrate, as provided in the last two sections, upon being held to answer, or at any time before the return of the depositions and statement, to the court. After that time he can be admitted to bail, only by the court in which the offence is triable, if it be sitting, or if not, by one of the magistrates mentioned in the second subdivision of section 618.

It seems proper, that after the jurisdiction of the committing magistrate has ceased over the subject of the complaint, the power to bail should, with all the other proceedings in the case, be vested in the court. In order, however, to prevent the injustice of keeping the defendant in prison, when in the exercise of a sound discretion, he is entitled to be bailed, the power to admit him to bail during the recess of the court, is conferred upon the higher class of magistrates.

§ 621. In the several cities of this state, if the offence charged be a felony, the application for admission to bail must be upon notice of at least two days, to the district attorney of the county; and the committing magistrate, upon the like notice, in writing, requiring him to do so, must transmit the depositions and statement, or a copy thereof, to the court or magistrate to whom the application for bail is to be made.

This section, it will be observed, makes an important discrimination between the cities and other parts of the state, in respect to the mode of applying for admission to bail. In the latter, no notice of the application is made necessary, while in the former, it is required. No one who is conversant with the history of criminal proceedings, need be informed that in cities, and especially in the city of New-York, the most glaring frauds have been perpetrated upon criminal justice, in every stage of the proceedings respecting bail. Either from the looseness with which the magistrates have acted, or the impossibility, under the present practice, of preventing this injustice, the system of bail has become but a legalized mode of effecting the escape of a person charged with crime, and the Commissioners have felt it to be their duty, to provide in every stage of the proceeding, as applicable to these portions of the state, the most stringent regulations, to prevent its continuance. It is there, that the most heinous crimes are ordinarily perpetrated, and as a necessary consequence, that the severest restrictions upon the abuses in this branch of the practice are necessary. Limiting the requirement of a notice to cases of felony, as this section proposes to do, the Commissioners can perceive no injustice in rendering it necessary. That it may operate harshly in some cases, may be admitted. So does every proceeding, which has for its object the investigation of a criminal charge. But when it is taken into view, in how few cases, compared with the number of arrests on charges of high public offences, the presumption of innocence is more than a mere presumption, and that without some degree of severity in the earlier stages of the proceeding, the facilities for defeating public justice may be too greatly multiplied, the conclusion seems inevitable, that they should be obviated by provisions better adapted to the protection of society, than those which are found in the existing law.

§ 622. If the application be to the court, an order must be made, granting or denying it, and if it be granted, stating the sum in which bail may be taken.

§ 623. If the application be to a magistrate, he must certify, in writing, his decision granting or denying the same; and if he grant the application, must state in the certificate the sum in which bail may be taken; which certificate he must cause to be forthwith filed with the clerk of the court to which the depositions and statement are required to be sent.

§ 624. If an application for admission to bail, made to a magistrate, be denied, no subsequent application therefor can be made to another magistrate.

§ 625. A violation of the last section is punishable as a misdemeanor, and the admission of the defendant to bail contrary thereto, may be revoked by the magistrate who made it, or vacated by the court to which the depositions and statement are or must be sent, as provided in section 220, or to which, after indictment, the action must be sent for trial.

§ 626. If the application, when made to a magistrate, be denied, the defendant may appeal from his decision to the court to which the depositions and statements are or must be sent, as provided in section 220, if the case be triable therein, or if not, to the court to which, after indictment, it must be sent for trial.

§ 627. The appeal is, by a notice in writing, to the district attorney, that the defendant appeals from the decision, and that he will apply to the court to be admitted to bail, at a time to be specified, not less than two days from the service of the notice.

§ 628. The decision of the court, granting or denying bail, either upon an original application, or upon an appeal, is final.

§ 629. If the defendant be admitted to bail by a magistrate, the bail must be taken by the magistrate granting the order, or by any other magistrate of the same class, (according to the classification in section 618,) in the same county, city or village. If by the court, it may be taken either by the court, or by any magistrate whom it may designate, in the county in which the defendant is committed.

The object of the last eight sections is so apparent, as scarcely to require explanation. When an application for admission to bail, is made to a magistrate and refused, it seems proper to apply the rule prescribed in the code of civil procedure, prohibiting, under the penalty of a misdemeanor, an application to another magistrate. But while this is done, care has been taken to ensure perfect protection to the rights of the defendant, by giving him a prompt and speedy appeal to the court.

§ 630. Bail is put in, by a written undertaking, executed by two sufficient sureties, (with or without the defendant, in the discretion of the court or magistrate,) and acknowledged before the court or magistrate, in substantially the following form:

"An order having been made on the   day of   , 1850, by A. B., *a justice of the peace of the town of*   , (or as the case may be,) that C. D., be held to answer upon a charge of, (stating briefly the nature of the offence,) upon which he has been duly admitted to bail, in the sum of   dollars:

"We, E. F., of (stating his place of residence and occupation,) and G. H., of (stating his place of residence and occupation,) hereby undertake, that the above named C. D. shall appear and answer the charge above mentioned, in whatever court it may be prosecuted; and shall at all times render himself amenable to the orders and process of the court; and if convicted, shall appear for judgment, and render himself in execution thereof; or if he fail to perform either of these conditions, that we will pay to the people of the state of New-York, the sum of   dollars," (inserting the sum in which the defendant is admitted to bail.)

§ 631. The qualifications of bail are as follows:

1. Each of them must be a resident, and a householder or freeholder within the state:

2. They must each be worth the amount specified in the undertaking, exclusive of property exempt from execution; but the court or magistrate, on taking bail, may allow more than two bail to justify severally in amounts less than that expressed in the undertaking, if the whole justification be equivalent to that of two sufficient bail.

Same as *amended code, sec.* 169.

§ 632. Except as prescribed in the next section, the bail may, in the exercise of a just discretion, be taken, and may justify, without notice to the district attorney, or reasonable notice may be required by the court or magistrate, to be given to the district attorney of the intention to give bail. When given, the notice shall be as prescribed in the next section.

§ 633. In the several cities of this state, if the offence charged be a felony, a previous notice of at least two days, of the time and place of giving the bail, must be served upon the district attorney of the county, stating,

1. The names, places of residence and occupations of the proposed bail:

2. A general description of the real or personal property of the bail, in respect to which they propose to justify as to their sufficiency, with the incumbrances thereon, by mortgage, judgment or otherwise, if any.

The last two sections make the same discrimination between the cities and other parts of the state, which are made in section 621. The reasons for this difference, as stated in the note to that section, *p.* 296, are more strongly applicable to the taking of bail. Whatever objection may possibly be raised, to the requirement of notice of the application for admission to bail, it would seem that no just question can be made as to a provision having for its object, an opportunity on the part of the public prosecutor, to inquire into the sufficiency of the proposed bail. In some portions of the state, what is known as straw-bail has been the ready and successful resort of the most hardened public offenders; and the very name of criminal justice has been rendered an object of ridicule and reproach, by the successful operation of this nefarious system. The most worthless in the community, have been found ready to relieve their associates in crime, by a ready resort to perjury; and the records of our courts are filled with evidence of the fact that it has escaped the scrutiny or eluded the detection of the public officers.

§ 634. The bail must in all cases justify by affidavit, taken before the court or magistrate, as the case may be. The affidavit must state that they each possess the qualifications provided in section 631.

§ 635. The district attorney, or the court or magistrate, may thereupon further examine the bail upon oath, concerning their sufficiency, in such manner as the court or magistrate may deem proper. The questions put to the bail, and their answers must be reduced to writing, and must be subscribed by them.

§ 636. The court or magistrate may also receive other testimony, either for or against the sufficiency of the bail, and may from time to time adjourn the taking of bail, to afford an opportunity of proving or disproving their sufficiency.

§ 637. When the examination is closed, the court or magistrate must make an order, either allowing or disallowing the bail, and must forthwith cause the same, with the affidavits of justification, and the undertaking of bail, to be filed with the clerk of the court to which the depositions and statement must be sent, as prescribed in section 220.

> The mode of justification now pursued, is, merely to take the affidavit required by section 634, except that in the city of New-York, by a special statute, the bail are required to state in their affidavit, the property in respect to which they justify. Even there, however, no power is given to examine them further upon oath, or to take from them an affidavit upon other matters, tending to test their sufficiency, which if false, could be the subject of an indictment for perjury, or to take other testimony. The sections under consideration propose a course of practice in this respect, which, with proper vigilance on the part of the public officers, can hardly fail to secure the sufficiency of the bail.

§ 638. Upon the allowance of the bail and the execution of the undertaking, the court or magistrate must make an order, signed by him, with his name of office, for the discharge of the defendant, to the following effect:

"To the sheriff of the county of , [or, in the city and county of New-York, "to the keeper of the city prison of the city of New-York:"] "A. B., who is detained by you on a commitment to answer a charge for the offence of, [designating it generally,] having given sufficient bail to answer the same, you are commanded forthwith to discharge him from your custody."

§ 639. If the bail be disallowed, the defendant must be detained in custody until other bail be put in and justify.

ARTICLE III.

BAIL, UPON AN INDICTMENT BEFORE CONVICTION.

The provisions of this chapter need no other explanation than what is furnished by the sections themselves. They are in harmony with the last two chapters, so far as the principles contained in them are concerned, and in their details afford, it is believed, an ample guarantee, with proper vigilance on the part of the public officers, for the obtaining of sufficient bail, without imposing any undue hardship on the defendant.

§ 640. When the offence charged in the indictment is a misdemeanor, the officer serving the bench-warrant, must, if required, take the defendant before a magistrate in the county in which it is issued, or in which he is arrested, for the purpose of giving bail as prescribed in sections 319 and 322.

§ 641. If the offence charged in the indictment be a felony, the officer arresting the defendant must deliver him into custody, according to the command of the bench-warrant, as prescribed in section 318.

§ 642. When the defendant is so delivered into custody, if the felony charged be bailable, and the amount of bail have been fixed by the court, as provided in section 320, bail may be taken by the court in which the indictment was found, or to which it is sent or removed, or by any magistrate in the county having authority to admit a defendant to bail, upon being held to answer before indictment, as provided in sections 618 and 619.

§ 643. The bail must be put in, by a written undertaking, executed by two sufficient sureties, with or without the defendant, in the discretion of the court or magistrate,) and acknowledged before the court or magistrate, in substantially the following form:

"An indictment having been found on the day of , 1850, in the *court of sessions of the county of Albany*, [or as the case may be,] charging A. B. with the crime of, [designating it generally,] and he having been duly admitted to bail in the sum of dollars:

"We, C. D., of [stating his place of residence and occupation,] and E. F., of [stating his place of residence and occupation,] hereby undertake, that the above named A. B. shall appear and answer the indictment above mentioned, in whatever court it may be prosecuted, and shall at all times render himself amenable to the orders and process of the court: and if convicted, shall appear for judgment, and render himself in execution thereof; or if he fail to perform either of these conditions, that we will pay to the people of the state of New-York, the sum of dollars," [inserting the sum in which the defendant is admitted to bail.]

§ 644. The provisions contained in sections 631 to 639, both inclusive, apply to the qualifications of the bail, and to all the proceedings respecting the putting in and justifying of bail, and incidental thereto.

ARTICLE IV.

BAIL UPON AN APPEAL.

§ 645. In the cases in which the defendant may be admitted to bail upon an appeal, as provided in section 617, the order admitting him to bail may be made, either by the court from which the appeal is taken, or the presiding judge thereof, or by the appellate court, or a judge thereof, or by a judge of the supreme court.

§ 646. When the admission to bail is a matter of discretion, the court or officer by whom it may be ordered, may require such notice of the application therefor, as he deems reasonable, to be given to the district attorney of the county in which the verdict or judgment was originally rendered.

§ 647. The bail must possess the qualifications, and must be put in in all respects, in the manner prescribed by sections 631 to 639, both inclusive; except that the undertaking of the bail must be to the effect that the defendant will, in all respects, abide the orders and judgment of the appellate court upon the appeal.

ARTICLE V.

DEPOSITE INSTEAD OF BAIL.

The permission to deposit money, instead of giving bail, was introduced by the Commissioners into the civil practice, because, while it afforded the best security, it relieved the defendant from great embarrassment in procuring bail. If he were a stranger, he must necessarily remain in prison, or indemnify, or, what was more frequently the case, hire a private party to become his bail. He was thus, in order to escape imprisonment, subjected on the one hand to the hazard of losing his money, and on the other to the extortion of those who might be disposed to take an undue advantage of his situation. If it was just, therefore, to relieve him from this embarrassment in a civil case, it is more just to do so in a criminal one where the difficulties of his position can otherwise be less easily avoided.

In carrying out this principle, the provisions of this chapter have been substantially taken from the *Amended Code*, *sec.* 197–200.

§ 648. The defendant, at any time after an order admitting him to bail, instead of giving bail, may deposit with the clerk of the county in which he is held to answer, the sum mentioned in the order; and upon delivering to the officer in whose custody he is, a certificate of the deposite, he must be discharged from custody.

§ 649. If the defendant have given bail, he may, at any time before the forfeiture of their undertaking, in like manner deposit the sum mentioned in the undertaking; and upon the deposite being made, the bail is exonerated.

§ 650. If money be deposited, as provided in the last section, bail may be given, in the same manner as if it had been originally given upon the order for admission to bail, at any time before the forfeiture of the deposite. The court or magistrate before whom the bail is taken, must thereupon direct, in the order of allowance, that the money deposited be refunded by the county clerk to the defendant; and it must be refunded accordingly.

§ 651. When money has been deposited, if it remain on deposite at the time of a judgment for the payment of a fine, the county treasurer must, under direction of the court, apply the money in satisfaction thereof, and after satisfying the fine, must refund the surplus, if any, to the defendant.

ARTICLE VI.

SURRENDER OF THE DEFENDANT.

The provisions of this chapter sufficiently explain themselves. They are substantially taken from the *Amended Code sec.* 188, 189.

§ 652. At any time before the forfeiture of their undertaking, the bail may surrender the defendant in their exoneration, or he may surrender himself, to the officer to whose custody he was committed at the time of giving bail, in the following manner:

1. A certified copy of the undertaking of the bail must be delivered to the officer, who must detain the defendant in his custody thereon, as upon a commitment, and by a certificate in writing, acknowledge the surrender:

2. Upon the undertaking and the certificate of the officer, the court in which the indictment or the appeal, as the case may be, is pending, may, upon a notice of five days to the district attorney of the county, with a copy of the undertaking and certificate, order that the bail be exonerated; and on filing the order and the papers used on the application, they are exonerated accordingly.

§ 653. For the purpose of surrendering the defendant, the bail, at any time before they are finally charged, and at any place within the state, may themselves arrest him, or by a written authority endorsed on a certified copy of the undertaking, may empower any person of suitable age and discretion to do so.

§ 654. If money have been deposited instead of bail, and the defendant at any time before the forfeiture thereof, surrender himself to the officer to whom the commitment was directed, in the manner provided in the last two sections, the court must order a return of the deposite to the defendant, upon producing the certificate of the officer showing the surrender, and upon a notice of five days to the district attorney, with a copy of the certificate.

ARTICLE VII.

FORFEITURE OF THE UNDERTAKING OF BAIL, OR OF THE DEPOSITE OF MONEY.

As the practice now stands, there is no rule whatever, as to the time or circumstances under which the forfeiture of bail may be declared. The condition of the recognizance is, in substance, that the defendant will appear in court on a specified day, and that he will abide the order of the court on the indictment, and not depart therefrom without its leave. The result in practice is, that unless he can make an arrangement with the district attorney, as to the time when his appearance will be necessary, he may be compelled to remain in court continually, until the indictment is finally disposed of. There is nothing to prevent the forfeiture of his bail, at any moment during the term, at the option of the district attorney, whether his appearance be then necessary or not. This should not be so. The provisions of this code, in other respects, distinctly inform the defendant when his attendance in court is necessary, and the sections which follow, restrict the right of forfeiture to the failure of the defendant to appear at those times, and then only. *Sec.* 655. And even then, power is given to the court, where a sufficient excuse for his default is shown, to discharge the forfeiture upon equitable terms. *Sec.* 656.

The remedy to enforce the forfeiture is also restricted to an action. *Sec.* 657. This is now the practice, except in the city of New York, in which, by a special statute, a judgment may be summarily, and without any previous notice to the parties, entered upon the recognizance on its being declared forfeited. *Laws of* 1844, *p.* 475, *sec.* 8.

This exception to the general rule probably arose from the

fact, that in view of the kind of bail too often taken in that city, the least delay in enforcing the forfeiture rendered the chances of its ultimate enforcement utterly desperate. By such a course of proceeding, however, the bail are deprived of every opportunity of making a defence; and though they could show that the bond was a forgery, or that its condition had been performed, they are subjected to a final and irreversible judgment. With the safeguards which have been thrown arround the taking of bail, as regulated by this code, it is hoped, that in at least a majority of cases, the necessity for a resort to a proceeding so summary and unjust, will be obviated. But whether it is or not, no good reason is perceived for a difference between the mode of enforcing the liability of bail in a criminal, from that adopted in a civil case.

The provisions in respect to a remission of a forfeiture, *sec.* 659, 660, are taken from the statutes formerly applicable to the courts of common pleas. 2 *R. S.*, 3*d. ed.*, 580, 581, *sec.* 37 – 41.

§ 655. If, without sufficient excuse, the defendant neglect to appear for arraignment, or for trial or judgment, or upon any other occasion where his presence in court may be lawfully required, or to surrender himself in execution of the judgment, the court must direct the fact to be entered upon its minutes; and the undertaking of his bail, or the money deposited, instead of bail, as the case may be, is thereupon forfeited.

§ 656. If, at any time before the final adjournment of the court, the defendant appear and satisfactorily excuse his neglect, the court may direct the forfeiture of the undertaking or deposite to be discharged, upon such terms as are just.

§ 657. If the forfeiture be not discharged, as provided in the last section, the district attorney may, at any time after the adjournment of the court, proceed, by action only, against the bail upon their undertaking.

§ 658. If, by reason of the neglect of the defendant to appear, as provided in section 655, money deposited instead of bail is forfeited, and the forfeiture be not discharged or remitted, as provided in sections, 656 and 659, the county treasurer with whom it is deposited, may at any time after the final adjournment of the court, apply the money deposited to the use of the county.

§ 659. After the forfeiture of the undertaking or deposite, as provided in this chapter, the county court of the county, or in the city of New-York, the court of common pleas of that city, may, upon good cause shown, remit the forfeiture or any part thereof, upon such terms as are just.

§ 660. The application must be upon at least five days notice to the district attorney of the county, with copies of the affidavits and papers on which it is founded; and can be granted, only upon payment of the costs and expenses incurred in the proceedings for the enforcement of the forfeiture.

ARTICLE VIII.

RE-COMMITMENT OF THE DEFENDANT, AFTER HAVING GIVEN BAIL, OR DEPOSITED MONEY INSTEAD OF BAIL.

The principle feature of this chapter, which is new, is the provision contained in section 661, authorising the re-commitment of the defendant, when it appears that his bail or either of them are dead, or insufficient, or have removed from the state. It is more than doubtful whether this power now exists. In a recent case in the city of New-York, where an application for a re-commitment was made, upon a ground similar in principle, the objection was taken, that the court could not make the order, having exhausted its jurisdiction in this respect by taking bail; and *Rex v. Salter*, 2 Chit. Rep. 109, was cited as sustaining the objection. The necessity of such a power is apparent. It would be a reproach to the administration of criminal justice, that where a fraud had been practiced upon the court in the matter of bail, or where, without the power to re-commit, the defendant might elude the consequences of crime, the court should be left without authority to prevent the wrong.

The other provisions of this chapter sufficiently explain themselves.

§ 661. The court to which the committing magistrate returns the depositions and statement, or in which an indictment or an appeal is pending, or to which a judgment on appeal is remitted to be carried into effect, may, by an order entered upon its minutes, direct the arrest of the defendant, and his commitment to the officer to whose custody he was committed at the time he was admitted to bail, and his detention, until legally discharged, in the following cases:

1. When, by reason of his failure to appear, he has incurred a forfeiture of his bail, or of money deposited instead thereof, as provided in section 655:

2. When it satisfactorily appears to the court that, his bail, or either of them, are dead, or insufficient, or have removed from the state:

3. Upon an indictment being found, in the cases provided in section 323.

§ 662. The order for the re-commitment of the defendant must recite, generally, the facts upon which it is founded, and direct that the defendant be arrested by any sheriff, constable, marshal or policeman in this state, and committed to the officer to whose custody he was committed, at the time he was admitted to bail, to be detained until legally discharged.

§ 663. The defendant may be arrested pursuant to the order, upon a certified copy thereof, in any county, in the same manner as upon a warrant of arrest; except, that when arrested in another county, the order need not be endorsed by a magistrate of that county.

§ 664. If the order recite, as the ground upon which it is made, the failure of the defendant to appear for judgment upon conviction, the defendant must be committed, according to the requirement of the order.

§ 665. If the order be made for any other cause, and the offence be bailable, the court may fix the amount of bail, and may direct in the order, that the defendant be admitted to bail in the sum fixed, which must be specified in the order.

§ 666. When the defendant is admitted to bail, the bail may be taken by any magistrate in the county, having authority, in a similar case, to admit to bail upon the holding of the defendant to answer before indictment, as prescribed in sections 618 and 619, or by any other magistrate to be designated by the court.

§ 667. When bail is taken upon the re-commitment of the defendant, the undertaking of bail must be in substantially the following form:

"An order having been made on the day of 1850, by the court of (naming the court,) that A. B., be admitted to bail in the sum of dollars, in an action pending in that court against him in behalf of the people of the state of New-York, upon an [information presentment, indictment, or appeal, as the case may be,]

"We, C. D., of [stating his place of residence and occupation,] and E. F., of [stating his place of residence and occupation,] hereby undertake, that the above named A. B., shall appear in that or any other court, in which his appearance may be lawfully required, upon that [information, presentment, indictment or appeal, as the case may be,] and shall at all times render himself amenable to its orders and process, and appear for judgment, and surrender himself in execution thereof; or if he fail to perform either of these conditions, that we will pay to the people of the state of New-York the sum of dollars," [inserting the sum in which the defendant is admitted to bail.]

§ 668. The bail must possess the qualifications, and must be put in, in all respects, in the manner prescribed by sections 631 to 639, both inclusive.

CHAPTER II.

COMPELLING THE ATTENDANCE OF WITNESSES.

§ 669. The process by which the attendance of a witness, before a court or magistrate is required, is a subpœna.

§ 670. A magistrate, before whom an information is laid, or to whom a presentment of a grand jury is sent, may issue subpœnas, subscribed by him, for witnesses within the state, either on behalf of the people or of the defendant.

The power contained in this section, is not now expressly conferred, but is indispensably necessary.

§ 671. The district attorney of the county may issue subpœnas, subscribed by him, for witnesses within the state, in support of the prosecution or for such other witnesses as the grand jury may direct, to appear before the grand jury, upon an investigation pending before them.

§ 672. The district attorney may, in like manner, issue subpœnas subscribed by him, for witnesses within the state, in support of an indictment, to appear before the court at which it is to be tried.

The power of the district attorney, as it now exists, to issue subpœnas, is conferred by the section of the revised statutes, which provides, that "the district attorney of every county, shall have power to issue subpœnas for witnesses in support of any prosecution, to appear at any court, without the seal of such court; and every such subpœna, subscribed by the district attorney issuing the same, shall be as valid and effectual, as if the seal of the court, at which any witness named therein, is required to appear, had been affixed thereto." 2 *R. S. 3d. ed.* 815, *sec* 64.

The last two sections extend this power, to the case of witnesses before the grand jury, as well as before the court; and in the former case, make it the duty of the district attorney to issue subpœnas to witnesses, not merely on the part of the people, but to such other witnesses as the grand jury may direct. This provision is in accordance with *sec.* 261, *p.* 130.

§ 673. The clerk of the court at which an indictment is to be tried, must, at all times, upon the application of the defendant, and without charge, issue as many blank subpœnas, under the seal of the court and subscribed by him as clerk, for witnesses within the state, as may be required by the defendant.

In substantial conformity with 2 *R. S., 3d ed.* 814, 815, *sec.* 60–63.

§ 674. A subpœna, authorised by the last four sections must be substantially in the following form:

"In the name of the people of the state of New-York: To A. B.

"You are commanded to appear before *C. D. a justice of the peace of the town of* , [or "the grand jury of the county of ," or "the court of sessions of the county of ," or as the case may be,] at [naming the place,] on [stating the day and hour,] as a witness in a criminal action prosecuted by the people of the state of New-York, against E. F.

"Dated at the town of , [as the case may be,] the day of , 1850.

"G. H., justice of the peace," [or "I. K., district attorney," or "By order of the court, L. M., clerk," as the case may be.]

§ 675. If books, papers or documents be required, a direction to the following effect must be contained in the subpœna: "And you are required also, to bring with you the following," [describing intelligibly the books, papers or documents required.]

§ 676. A peace officer must serve, in his county, city, town or village, as the case may be, any subpœna deliverered to him for service, either on the part of the people or of the defendant; and must make a written return of the service, subscribed by him, stating the time and place of service, without delay. A subpœna may, however, be served by any other person.

While this section preserves the right of any one to serve a subpœna, it makes it the duty of a peace officer to do so. The only statutory provision now in force on this subject, is that which authorises the district attorney to send subpœnas into a foreign county for witnesses on criminal process, to the sheriff of the county in which the witnesses reside, and makes it the duty of the sheriff to serve the subpœnas, and make his return without delay to the district attorney. 2 *R. S.*, 3*d ed.* 815, *sec.* 65.

The last section extends this duty to every peace officer, within his county, city, town or village. The term *peace officer*, as here used, is defined in *sec.* 154, *p.* 73, to include a sheriff of a county, or a constable, marshal or policeman of a city, town or village.

§ 677. A subpœna is served, by delivering it, or by showing it, and delivering a copy thereof, to the witness personally.

The mode of service here prescribed, is in conformity with the existing practice. In civil cases, the service is not complete, without a tender of the fees allowed by statute to the witness. The revised statutes provide, that " it shall not be necessary to pay or tender any fees whatever, to any witnesses subpœnaed on the part of the people of this state, in support of any prosecution, or to any witness subpœnaed on the part of any defendant, in any indictment; but such witness shall be bound to attend, as if the fees allowed by law to witnesses in civil cases, had been duly paid to him." 2 *R-S.*, 3*d ed.* 815, *sec.* 67.

The section under consideration, having prescribed the

only mode of making the service, it is unnecessary to insert the statutory provision just quoted.

§ 678. When a person attends before a magistrate, grand jury or court, as a witness on behalf of the people, upon a subpœna, or pursuant to an undertaking, and it appears that he has come from a place out of the county, or that he is poor, the court, if the attendance of the witness be upon a trial, by an order entered upon its minutes, or in any other case, the county judge, or in the city of New-York, the recorder or city judge of that city, by a written order, may direct the county treasurer to pay the witness a reasonable sum, to be specified in the order, for his expenses.

This section is in conformity with the spirit of the existing statutes. 2 *R. S.*, 3*d ed,* 841, *sec.* 19; *Laws of* 1846, *p.* 63. *ch.* 59.

§ 679. Upon the production of the order, or a certified copy thereof, the county treasurer must pay the witness the sum specified therein, out of the county treasury.

The same in substance as 2 *R. S.* 3*d. ed.* 841, *sec* 21.

§ 680. No person is obliged to attend as a witness, before a court or magistrate out of the county where the witness resides or is served with the subpœna, unless the judge of the court in which the offence is triable, or a judge of the supreme court, or a county judge, or in the city of New-York, the recorder or city judge of that city, upon an affidavit of the prosecutor or district attorney, or of the defendant or his counsel, stating that he believes that the evidence of the witness is material, and his attendance at the examination or trial necessary, shall endorse on the subpœna an order for the attendance of the witness.

The Commissioners, in their first report, *p.* 250, 251, took occasion to call the attention of the legislature to what they deemed the gross disregard by the law, of the convenience of witnesses; and suggested a remedy for the evil, so far as it was applicable to civil cases As the legislation of this state now stands, a witness may be compelled to attend in any part of the state, remote from his home, upon a subpœna which was furnished to the party in blank, and which, when directed to the witness by the party himself, as caprice or any other motive may dictate, uncontrolled by the supervision of any other power, absolutely requires his attendance, and subjects him to the penalties of a contempt, for disobedience. Their views on this subject, met, at first, with favor on the part of the legislature; but the action of the last session, reversed its former views, and left the practice in civil cases, as it stood before. Whether, or not, the fact that a witness is entitled, in those cases, to what the law has seen fit to term, his fees and expenses for attending, was regarded by the legislature as sufficient to protect the witness against unnecessary vexation, it isnot proper here to inquire. But whether it did or not, this argument is of no force, in a criminal case. There, with the exception of a witness for the people, who is called from another county, or who is poor, and whose expenses are in such case provided for, the witness is obliged to obey, at his own expense, a subpœna, which, although bearing the seal of the court, is in truth, so far as its actual authority is concerned, the act of the party alone.

The object of this section is, to make the subpœna, when designed to enforce the attendance of a witness from another county, in reality; what, by a fiction alone, it now is,—the act of the court or of a judicial officer and to exempt the witness from the necessity of attending, unless under such a sanction. The justice of this provision is confidently submitted to the wisdom of the legislature.

§ 681. Disobedience to a subpœna, or a refusal to be sworn or to testify, may be punished by the court or magistrate, as for a criminal contempt in the manner provided in the code of civil procedure.

§ 682. A witness, disobeying a subpœna issued on the part of the defendant, also forfeit, to the defendants the the sum of fifty dollars, which may be recovered in a civil action.

The last two sections are conformable to 2 *R. S.*, 3*d. ed.*, 497, *sec.* 53.

CHAPTER III.

EXAMINATION OF WITNESSES, CONDITIONALLY.

The mode of proceeding provided in this chapter and in the next, differs materially, as will be perceived, from that prescribed in similar cases by the code of civil procedure. The reason of the difference will be apparent, upon a comparison of the provisions.

This chapter is founded upon the section of the Revised Statutes which provides, that after an indictment shall be found against any defendant, he may have witnesses examined in his behalf, conditionally, on the order of a judge of the court in which the indictment is pending, in the same cases, upon the like notice to the district attorney, and with the like effect, in all respects, as in civil suits. 2 *R. S.* 3*d ed.* 817, *sec.* 77.

§ 683. When a defendant has been held to answer a charge for a public offence, he may, either before or after indictment, have witnesses examined conditionally on his behalf, as prescribed in this chapter, and not otherwise.

> This section goes beyond the provision of the revised statutes just cited, in providing for the examination, at any time after the defendant has been held to answer, whether before or after indictment. The necessity for preserving the testimony of the witness, is equally great in either case. Besides, according to *sec.* 9, *p.* 6, the proceedings before indictment, are just as much a part of a criminal action, as those which take place afterwards.

§ 684. When a material witness for the defendant is about to leave the state, or is so sick or infirm, as to afford reasonable grounds for apprehending that he will be unable to attend the trial, the defendant may apply for an order that the witness be examined conditionally.

§ 685. The application must be made upon affidavit, showing,

1. The nature of the offence charged;

2. The state of the proceedings in the action;

3. The name and residence of the witness, and that his testimony is material to the defence of the action; and,

4. That the witness is about to leave the state, or is so sick or infirm, as to afford reasonable grounds for apprehending that he will be unable to attend the trial.

The last two sections are the same in substance as 2 *R. S., 3d. ed.*, 488, *sec.* 2.

§ 686. The application, if made during the term, must be made to the court.

§ 687. If not made during the term, it may be made as follows:

1. When the indictment is pending in a court of oyer and terminer, or in a court of sessions other than in the city of New-York, to a judge of the supreme court, or to the county judge:

2. When the indictment is pending in the court of sessions of the city of New-York, to the recorder or city judge or one of the judges of the court of common pleas of that city:

3. When the indictment is pending in a city court, to the recorder or city judge of the city in which it is pending.

The provision of the revised statutes, from which the last two sections are taken, but which, in terms, applies to civil actions only, directs the application to be made to a judge. 2 *R. S., 3d. ed.*, 488, *sec.* 2. This should not be allowed in a criminal action, unless the court be not sitting.

§ 688. If the court or officer be satisfied, that the examination of the witness is necessary to the attainment of justice, an order must be made, that the witness be examined conditionally, at a specified time and place, and that a copy of the order, and of the affidavit on which it was granted, be served on the district attorney, within a specified time before that fixed for the examination.

§ 689. If the order be made by the court, it may direct that the examination be taken before a judge thereof, or before a magistrate in the county, to be named in the order. If made by any of the officers mentioned in section 687, it must direct the examination to be taken before him.

§ 690. On proof being furnished to the officer before whom the examination is appointed, of the service upon the district attorney, of a copy of the order, and of the affidavit on which it was granted, if no counsel appear on the part of the people, the examination must proceed.

Taken from 2 *R. S. 3d ed.*, 489, *sec.* 5.

§ 691. If the district attorney or other counsel appear on the part of the people, and it be shown to the satisfaction of the court or officer, by affidavit or other proof, or on the examination of the witness, that he is not about to leave the state, or is not sick or infirm, or that the application was made to avoid the examination of the witness on the trial, the examination cannot take place; otherwise it must proceed.

Taken from 2 *R. S.*, 3*d ed.*, 488, *sec.* 4.

§ 692. The testimony given by the witness must be reduced to writing, and authenticated in the same manner as the testimony of a witness taken in support of an information, as prescribed in section 203.

§ 693. The deposition must be retained by the officer taking it, and filed by him in the office of the clerk of the court without unnecessary delay.

Founded upon 2 *R. S. 3d ed.* 489, *sec.* 6.

§ 694. The deposition, or a certified copy thereof, may be read in evidence by either party on the trial, upon its appearing that the witness is unable to attend, by reason of his death, insanity, sickness or infirmity, or of his continued absence from the state.

Taken from 2 *R. S*, *3d. ed.*, 489, *sec.* 7.

§ 695. The deposition cannot, however, be read, if it appear that the copy of the order and of the affidavit on which it was founded, was not served on the district attorney, as directed, or that the examination was in any respect unfair or not conducted as prescribed in this chapter.

Taken from 2 *R. S.*, *3d. ed.*, 489, *sec.* 8.

§ 696. Upon the reading of the deposition in evidence, the same objections may be taken to a question or answer contained therein, as if the witness had beeen examined orally in court.

Taken from 2 *R. S.*, *3d. ed.*, 489, *sec.* 9.

§ 697. The attendance of the witness may be enforced, by a subpœna subscribed by the officer, or issued under the seal of the court.

Taken from 2 *R. S. 3d. ed.*, 489, *sec.* 10, *p.* 320, 321.

§ 698. Disobedience to the subpœna, or a refusal to be sworn or to testify, may be punished by the court or officer, as for a criminal contempt, in the manner provided in the code of civil procedure; and the witness also forfeits to the defendant, the sum of fifty dollars, which may be recovered in a civil action.

See *sec.* 681, 682, of this code, *p.* 320, 321.

CHAPTER IV.

EXAMINATION OF WITNESSES, ON COMMISSION.

SECTION 699. Witness residing out of the state, to be examined for defendant, as provided in this chapter.
700. In what cases defendant may apply for order to examine witnesses on commission.
701. Commission, defined.
702. Application for commission, on what facts to be founded.
703. If during term, to be made to the court.
704. If not during term, to whom to be made.
705. Notice of application, when required and how given.
706. Order for commission, when granted.
707. Trial to be stayed until execution and return of commission.
708. Interrogatories, and notice of settlement.
709. Cross-interrogatories, and notice of settlement.
710, 711. What may be inserted in interrogatories.
712. Direction as to return of commission.
713. Commission, how executed.
714. Copy of last section to be annexed to commission.
715, 716. Commission, how returned, when delivered to agent for that purpose.
717. When and how filed.
718. Commission returned by mail, how disposed of.
719. Commission and return to be open for inspection, and copies to be furnished.
720. Deposition to be read in evidence. What objections may be taken thereto.

This chapter is founded upon the section of the revised statutes, which provides, that when any issue of fact is joined upon any indictment, the defendant therein may apply to the court, in which such indictment is pending, to examine any material witness residing out of this state; and such court may grant the same, upon the same proof, and in the like cases and on similar terms, as provided by law in civil cases; and the officer prosecuting in behalf of this state, shall be permitted to join in such commission, and to name witnesses on the part of the people. 2 *R. S.*, *3d. ed.*, 816, *sec.* 75. Interrogatories, to be annexed to such commission, shall be settled, and such commission shall be issued, executed and returned, in the manner prescribed by law in respect to commissions in civil cases; and the depositions taken thereon and returned, shall be read in the same cases, and with the like effect, as in civil suits. *Ibid.* 817, *sec.* 76.

§ 699. When an issue of fact is joined upon an indictment, the defendant may have any material witness residing out of the state, examined in his behalf, as prescribed in this chapter, and not otherwise.

§ 700. When a material witness for the defendant, resides out of the state, the defendant may apply for an order that the witness be examined on a commission.

These sections are in conformity with the provisions of the revised statutes just cited.

§ 701. A commission is a process issued under the seal of the court, and the signature of the clerk, directed to one or more persons, designated as commissioners, authorizing them to examine the witness upon oath, on interrogatories annexed thereto, and to take and return the deposition of the witness, according to the directions given, with the commission.

§ 702. The application must be made upon affidavit, showing,

1. The nature of the offence charged:

2. The state of the proceedings in the action, and that issue of fact has been joined therein:

3. The name of the witness, and that his testimony is material to the defence of the action:

4. That the witness resides out of the state.

This provision is new, but is deemed necessary, in order to enable the court, from the facts stated in the affidavit, to judge of the propriety of granting the application.

§ 703. The application, if made during the term, must be made to the court.

§ 704. If not made during the term, the application may be made as follows:

1. When the indictment is pending in a court of oyer and terminer, or in a court of sessions, except in the city and county of New-York, to a judge of the supreme court or to the county judge:

2. When the indictment is pending in the court of sessions of the city of New-York, to the recorder or city judge, or one of the judges of the court of common pleas, of that city:

3. When the indictment is pending in a city court, to the recorder or city judge of the city in which it is pending.

The last two sections are founded on the same principle as sections 686 and 687, respecting the examination of witnesses conditionally. See *the note to those sections, p* 323. They are also in substantial conformity with the provisions applicable to civil cases, in 2 *R. S., 3d. ed.*, 490, *sec.* 12, 13.

§ 705. If the application be made to the court, it may be without notice to the district attorney, unless the court direct notice to be given, in which case it must prescribe the manner of giving the same. If made to one of the officers mentioned in the last section, the application must be upon five days notice to the district attorney, with a copy of the affidavit upon which it is founded.

When the application is made to the court, notice is unnecessary, inasmuch as the district attorney is generally present. If, however, he be absent, the court can, under the provisions of this section, direct notice to be given to him. When made out of court, this section requires a notice.

§ 706. If the court or officer to whom the application is made, be satisfied that the witness resides out of the state, and that his examination is necessary to the attainment of justice, an order must be made that a commission be issued to take his testimony, and that the people be permitted to join in the commission, and to examine witnesses in support of the indictment.

In conformity with 2 *R. S.* 3*d. ed.*, 816, *sec.* 75.

§ 707. If the application for a commission be granted, the court or judge must insert in the order therefor, a direction that the trial of the indictment be stayed for a specified time, reasonably sufficient for the execution and return of the commission.

A commission is sometimes taken out in civil as well as criminal cases, without being made a stay of proceedings, and at the consequent peril, of the party issuing it, of its return in time. In criminal cases, at least, this should not be. The commission should not issue at all, unless, as provided in section 706, *p.* 329, the examination of the witness is necessary for the attainment of justice; and where that is the case, a stay of proceedings for a reasonable time, should follow of course.

§ 708. When the commission is ordered, the defendant must serve upon the district attorney, and the district attorney, if he intend to join in the commission and examine witnesses in support of the indictment, must serve upon the defendant or his counsel, a copy of the interrogatories to be annexed thereto, with a notice of two days of their settlement, before an officer who might have granted the order out of term, as provided in section 704.

§ 709. The district attorney, and the defendant, may, in the same manner serve cross-interrogatories, to be annexed to the commission, with the like notice of the settlement thereof.

The last two sections are in conformity with the practice in civil actions, as established under the provision in 2 *R. S.*, 3*d. ed.*, 490, *sec.* 15, adapting them, however, to the right given to the prosecution, to join in the commission.

§ 710. In the interrogatories, either party may insert any question pertinent to the issue.

§ 711. Upon the settlement of the interrogatories, the judge must expunge every question not pertinent to the issue, and modify the questions, so as to conform them to the rules of evidence, and when settled, must endorse upon them his allowance and annex them to the commission.

§ 712. Unless the parties otherwise consent, by an endorsement upon the commission, the officer must endorse thereon a direction, as to the manner in which it must be returned; and may, in his discretion, direct that it be returned by mail or otherwise, addressed to the clerk of the court in which the indictment is pending, designating his name and the place where his office is kept.

The last three sections are taken from 2 *R. S.*, *3d. ed.*, 490, *sec.* 16, but are more full and explicit, in respect to the power of the judge, upon the settlement of the interrogatories. Much confusion and embarrassment have arisen. from objections being taken and sustained on the trial, to the form of questions, which, if they had been taken before the judge, might have been obviated; and valuable testimony has not unfrequently been lost, which, if that had been done, might have been preserved to the party.

§ 713. The commissioners or any one of them, unless otherwise specially directed, may execute the commission as follows:

1. They must publicly administer an oath to the witness, that his answers given to the interrogatories, shall be the truth, the whole truth, and nothing but the truth:

2. They must cause the examination of the witness to be reduced to writing:

3. They must write the answers of the witness, as nearly as possible in the language in which he gives them, and read to him each answer as it is taken down, and correct or add to it, until it is made conformable to what he declares is the truth:

4. If the witness decline answering a question, that fact, with the reason for which he declines answering it, as he gives it, must be stated:

5. If papers or documents are produced before them, and proved by the witness, they must be annexed to his deposition, and be subscribed by the witness, and certified by the commissioners:

6. The commissioners must subscribe their names to each sheet of the deposition, and annex the deposition, with the papers or documents proved by the witness, to the commission, and must close it up under seal, and address it, as directed thereon.

7. If there be a direction on the commission, to return it by mail, the commissioners must immediately deposit it in the nearest post-office. If any other direction be made, by the written consent of the parties, or by the officer, on the commission, as to its return, they must comply with the direction.

This section is founded upon 2 *R. S.*, *3d ed.* 490, *sec.* 17, but is more full and explicit, and embodies the manner of examination prescribed in section 203 of this code, *p.* 95, in respect to taking the testimony of witnesses by a magistrate, on the examination of the case.

§ 714. A copy of the last section must be annexed to the commission.

Taken from 2 *R. S.*, 3*d ed.* 491, *sec.* 17.

§ 715. If the commission and return be delivered by the commissioners to an agent, he must deliver it to the clerk to whom it is directed, or to a judge of the court in which the indictment is pending, by whom it may be received and opened, upon the affidavit of the agent, that he received it from the hands of one of the commissioners, and that it has not been opened or altered since he received it.

The same in substance, as 2 *R. S.*, 3*d ed.* 491, *sec.* 18.

§ 716. If the agent be dead, or from sickness or other casualty, unable personally to deliver the commission and return, as prescribed in the last section, it may be received by the clerk or judge from any other person, upon his making an affidavit that he received it from the agent, that the agent is dead, or from sickness or other casualty, unable to deliver it, that it has not been opened or altered since the person making the affidavit received it, and that he believes it has not been opened or altered, since it came from the hands of the commissioners.

The same in substance, as 2 *R. S.*, 3*d ed.* 491, *sec.* 19.

§ 717. The clerk or judge receiving and opening the commission and return, must immediately file it, with the affidavit mentioned in the last two sections, in the office of the clerk of the court in which the indictment is pending.

The same in substance, as 2 *R. S.*, *3d ed.* 491, *sec.* 20.

§ 718. If the commission and return be transmitted by mail, the clerk to whom it is addressed, must receive it from the post office, and open and file it in his office, where it must remain, unless the court otherwise direct.

The same in substance, as 2 *R. S.*, *3d ed.* 491, *sec.* 21.

§ 719. The commission and return must at all times be open to the inspection of the parties, who must be furnished by the clerk with copies of the same, or of any part thereof, on payment of his fees, at the rate of five cents for every hundred words.

The same in substance, as 2 *R. S. 3d. ed.* 491, 492, *sec.* 23.

§ 720. The deposition, taken under the commission, may be read in evidence by either party on the trial, and the same objections may be taken to a question in the interrogatories, or to an answer in the deposition, as if the witness had been examined orally in court.

The same in substance, as 2 *R. S. 3d. ed.* 492, *sec.* 24.

CHAPTER. V.

INQUIRY INTO THE INSANITY OF THE DEFENDANT, BEFORE TRIAL, OR AFTER CONVICTION.

§ 721. An act done by a person in a state of insanity, cannot be punished as a public offence; nor can a person be tried, adjudged to punishment, or punished, for a public offence, while he is insane.

Taken from 2 *R. S. 3d ed.* 784, 785, *sec.* 2.

§ 722. When an indictment is called for trial, or, upon conviction, the defendant is brought up for judgment, if a doubt arise as to the sanity of the defendant, the court must order a jury to be impanelled, from the jurors summoned and returned for the term, or who may be summoned by direction of the court, as provided in sections 389 to 394, both inclusive, to inquire into the fact.

§ 723. The trial of the indictment or the pronouncing of the judgment, as the case may be, must be suspended, until the question of insanity is determined by the verdict of the jury.

The last two sections are in conformity to the existing practice.

§ 724. The trial of the question of insanity must proceed, in the following order:

1. The counsel for the defendant must open the case, and offer evidence in support of the allegation of insanity:

2. The counsel for the people may then open their case, and offer evidence in support thereof:

3. The parties may then respectively offer rebutting testimony only, unless the court for good reason, in furtherance of justice, permit them to offer evidence upon their original case.

4. When the evidence is concluded, unless the case is submitted to the jury, on either side or on both sides, without argument, the counsel for the people must commence, and the defendant or his counsel may conclude the argument to the jury.

5. If the indictment be for an offence punishable with death, two counsel on each side may argue the cause to the jury; in which case, they must do so alternately. If it be for any other offence, the court may, in its discretion, restrict the argument to one counsel on each side.

6. The court must then charge the jury.

This section, with the exception of the fifth subdivision, is adapted from section 440. The reasons given in the note to that section, *p.* 206—209, are equally applicable to this. The fifth subdivision is taken from section 442, *p.* 209.

§ 725. The provisions of sections 474 and 476, in respect to the duty of the court upon questions of law, and of the jury upon questions of fact, and the provisions of section 477, in respect to the charge of the court to the jury, upon the trial of an indictment, apply to the trial of the question of insanity.

See the *notes to sec.* 474, 476, 477, *p.* 223, 224.

§ 726. If the jury find the defendant sane, the trial of the indictment must proceed, or judgment may be pronounced, as the case may be.

§ 727. If the jury find the defendant is insane, the trial or judgment must be suspended, until he become sane; and the court, if it deem his discharge dangerous to the public peace or safety, may order that he be, in the mean time, committed by the sheriff to the state lunatic asylum, and that upon his becoming sane, he be re-delivered by the superintendent of the asylum to the sheriff.

Conformable to 1 *R. S. 3d ed.* 813, *sec.* 44.

§ 728. The commitment of the defendant, as mentioned in the last section, exonerates his bail, or entitles a person authorised to receive the property of the defendant, to a return of money he may have deposited instead of bail.

The commitment of the defendaut to the asylum, should have the same effect in discharging the security given for his appearance, as his recommitment for any other cause as prescribed in sec. 661, *p.* 312, 313.

§ 729. If the defendant be received into the asylum, he must be detained there until he become sane. When he becomes sane, the superintendent must give notice of that fact to the sheriff and district attorney of the county. The sheriff must thereupon, without delay, bring the defendant from the asylum, and place him in the proper custody until he be brought to trial or judgment, as the case may be, or be legally discharged.

Conformable to 1 *R S. 3d ed.* 813, *sec.* 45.

§ 730. The expenses of sending the defendant to the asylum, of keeping him there, and of bringing him back, are, in the first instance, chargeable to the county from which he was sent; but the county may recover them from the estate of the defendant, if he have any, or from a relative, town, city, or county, bound to provide for and maintain him elsewhere.

Conformable to 1 *R. S. 3d ed.* 813, *sec.* 44.

CHAPTER VI.

COMPROMISING CERTAIN PUBLIC OFFENCES, BY LEAVE OF THE COURT.

The principle involved in this chapter is not new, in the legislation of this state. It is, that misdemeanors, where a civil remedy is not only given to the party injured but is a more appropriate remedy, may be compromised, upon leave of the court. There are many cases, which are technically public offences, but which are in reality rather of a private than a public nature, and where the public interests are better promoted by checking than by encouraging criminal prosecutions. Of this class are libels, and simple assaults and batteries; or those which according to section 731, are not committed by or upon an officer of justice, while in the execution of the duties of his office, or riotously, or with an intent to commit a felony. With these exceptions, cases of this nature have by the policy of our statutes, always been considered fit subjects of compromise: 2 *R. S. 3d ed.* 815, 816, *sec.* 68—71; 1 *R. L. of* 1813, *p.* 499, *sec.* 19; a policy which has been carried by the courts, still further than the terms of the statute. For while they will not permit a compromise after conviction, *The People v. Bishop*, 5 Wend. 111, nor stay the indictment, because a civil action is pending for the same cause, *The People v. The Judges of Genesee*, 13 Johns. 85, yet, in the case last cited, it was taken as undeniable, that judgment after conviction might be stayed, until after the determination of a civil action for the same matter, to enable the court to award an appropriate sentence, in view of the completeness of the civil remedy.

The chapter in question, however, contains one important, and as the Commissioners think, necessary departure from the existing statutes. By 2 *R. S. 3d ed.* 815, 816, *sec.* 68, 69, the authority to permit this compromise, is given also to the committing magistrate. This should not be. It is too grave a dispensing power, to be confided to any other than the court to which the case must be returned; and it is accordingly confined by section 732, to the court. The reasons for this change, seem too obvious to require illustration. Where an assault and battery, for example, partakes of the character contemplated in the exceptions in section 731, the public has an interest in its prosecution : and to allow a compromise, by the permission of the magistrate, when it is often difficult to determine whether one of those elements enters into the offence or not, and upon his inexperience or mistaken judgment, to withdraw the case from either a public investigation, or at all events from the scrutiny of the court, in no degree comports with either the solemnity or the object of a criminal proceeding.

§ 731. When a defendant is held to answer, on a charge of a misdemeanor, for which the person injured by the act constituting the offence, has a remedy by a civil action, the offence may be compromised, as provided in the next section, except when it was committed,

1. By or upon an officer of justice, while in the execution of the duties of his office;

2. Riotously: or,

3. With an intent to commit a felony.

§ 732. If the party injured appear before the court, to which the depositions and statement are required, by section 220, to be returned, at any time before trial on an indictment for the offence, and acknowledge in writing that he has received satisfaction for the injury, the court may, in its discretion, on payment of the costs incurred, order all proceedings to be stayed upon the prosecution, and the defendant to be discharged therefrom. But in that case, the reasons for the order must be set forth therein and entered upon the minutes.

§ 733. The order authorised by the last section, is a bar to another prosecution for the same offence.

§ 734. No public offence can be compromised, nor can any proceeding for the prosecution or punishment thereof, upon a compromise, be stayed, except as provided in sections 731 and 732.

CHAPTER VII.

DISMISSAL OF THE ACTION, BEFORE OR AFTER INDICTMENT, FOR WANT OF PROSECUTION OR OTHERWISE.

SECTION 735. Dismissal, when a person held to answer is not indicted at the next term thereafter.

736. When a person indicted is not brought to trial at the next term thereafter.

737. Court may order action to be continued, and in the mean time discharge defendant from custody, on his own undertaking, or on bail.

738. If action dismissed, defendant to be discharged from custody, or his bail exonerated, or deposite of money refunded.

739. Court may, of its own motion, or on application of district attorney, order indictment to be dismissed. Order to state reasons.

740. Nolle prosequi abolished. No indictment to be dismissed or abandoned, except according to this chapter.

741. Dismissal, a bar, in misdemeanor; but not in felony.

This chapter is intended to remedy, what the Commissioners deem defects in the existing practice, productive not only of great inconvenience, but of flagrant injustice. When a defendant is held to answer, or is indicted, there is now no mode of his compelling the prosecution to proceed to trial, or of his being relieved from the indictment, in the event of their failure to do so. Until the attorney-general sees fit to exercise his power to enter a *nolle prosequi*, or the district attorney to exert his more limited authority, of applying to the court for permission to do so, the indictment may be kept forever suspended over the head of the defendant. The only remedy he can obtain, after months, or even years, of inexcusable neglect to bring him to trial, is by an order of the court, discharging him either upon bail or upon his own recognizance. The legislature have provided, that in all cases, except upon a charge of murder, an indictment must be found within three years; 2 *R. S. 3d ed.*, 812, *sec.* 37; and in other special cases, within two years; *Laws of* 1848, *p.* 118, *ch.* 105; *Ibid. p.* 148, *ch.* 111; provisions which the Commissioners have substantially incorporated in this code, *sec.* 140—144, *p.* 67, 68. The design of these provisions is to prevent the defendant from being exposed to the hazard of a trial, after so great a lapse of time as to justify the belief, that however innocent, the means of proving his innocence may not be within his reach; and yet, when an indictment is once found, there is no limitation of time, within which it must be brought to trial.

The provisions of the Revised Statutes on this subject, are as follows:

"If any prisoner indicted for any offence triable in the court of general sessions, and committed to prison, whose trial shall not have been postponed at his instance, shall not be brought to trial before the end of the next term of the court of general sessions, which shall be held in the county in which he is imprisoned, after such indictment found, he shall be entitled to be discharged, so far as relates to the offence for which he was committed." 2 *R. S.*, 3*d ed.*, 821, *sec.* 28.

"If any prisoner indicted for any offence not triable in a court of general sessions, but which may be tried in a court of oyer and terminer, and committed to prison, whose trial shall not have been postponed at his instance, shall not be brought to trial before the end of the next court of oyer and terminer which shall be held in the county in which he is imprisoned, after such indictment found, he shall be entitled to be discharged, so far as relates to the offence for which he was committed." 2 *R. S.*, 3*d ed.*, 821, 822, *sec.* 29.

"If satisfactory cause shall be shown by the district attorney, to any court to which application shall be made under either of the two last sections, for detaining such prisoner in custody or upon bail, until the sitting of the next court in which he may be tried, the court shall remand such prisoner, or shall hold him to bail, as the case may require." 2 *R. S.*, 3*d ed.*, 822, *sec.* 30.

To obviate the injustice referred to, and which is not theoretical merely, but of frequent practical occurrence, the Commissioners have introduced sections 735 and 736, authorizing a dismissal of the indictment, in those cases, unless good cause to the contrary be shown; while, where such cause is shown, they leave it, by section 737, discretionary with the court, to continue the action from term to term, and in proper cases to hold the defendant, or to discharge him, as it may now do, upon bail, or upon his own undertaking. By this course, the oppression of the defendant is prevented, and a control over the case is given to the court, by which the defeat of justice is rendered impossible. They define also, by section 738, the effect of the dismissal, to be the discharge of the defendant or his bail, but declare by section 741, that it shall be a bar to another prosecution for the same offence, in cases of misdemeanor only.

They propose, also, by sections 739 and 740, to change the practice in respect to entering a *nolle prosequi*. By the law as it now stands, the attorney general may, by virtue of the prerogative of his office, enter a *nolle prosequi* in any case. In respect to the district attorney, however, who is, except in very few cases, the sole representative of the state in the prosecution of indictments, it is provided by statute, that he cannot enter a *nolle prosequi* upon an indictment, nor in any other way discontinue or abandon it, without the leave of the court having jurisdiction of the offence charged, entered in its minutes. 2 *R S., 3d ed.*, 814, *sec.* 54. Under this provision, it was held by the supreme court, in *The People* v. *M'Leod*, 25 *Wend.*, 483, 1 *Hill*, 377, that the court does not possess the power to order a *nolle prosequi*, unless by consent or on motion of the district attorney. Practically, therefore, the power of the district attorney, in this respect, is greater than that of the court; the latter being unable, no matter how unjust may be the continuance of the indictment against the defendant, to relieve him from that injustice, until the district attorney chooses to consent that it do so.

Section 739 remedies this defect, by authorizing the court, either of its own motion, or upon the application of the district attorney, and in furtherance of justice, to dismiss the indictment; while, as a wholesome restraint upon this discretion, it requires that the reasons of the dismissal be set forth in the order, and entered upon the minutes.

Section 740 abolishes the *nolle prosequi*, and takes away the right of the attorney-general, or any other officer, to dismiss or abandon the indictment, and leaves that power, where it should alone rest, in the hands of the court.

§ 735. When a person has been held to answer for a public offence, if an indictment be not found against him, at the next term of the court at which he is held to answer, the court must order the prosecution to be dismissed, unless good cause to the contrary be shown.

§ 736. If a defendant, indicted for a public offence, whose trial has not been postponed upon his application, be not brought to trial at the next term of the court in which the indictment is triable, after it is found, the court must order the indictment to be dismissed, unless good cause to the contrary be shown.

§ 737. If the defendant be not indicted or tried, as provided in the last two sections, and sufficient reason therefor be shown, the court may order the action to be continued from term to term, and in the mean time may discharge the defendant from custody, on his own undertaking, or on the undertaking of bail for his appearance to answer the charge at the time to which the action is continued.

§ 738. If the court direct the action to be dismissed, the defendant must, if in custody, be discharged therefrom, or if admitted to bail, his bail is exonerated, or money deposited instead of bail must be refunded to him.

§ 739. The court may, either of its own motion, or upon the application of the district attorney, and in furtherance of justice, order an action, after indictment, to be dismissed; but in that case, the reasons of the dismissal must be set forth in the order, which must be entered upon the minutes.

§ 740. The entry of a *nolle prosequi* is abolished; and neither the attorney general, nor the district attorney, can discontinue or abandon a prosecution for a public offence, except as provided in the last section.

§ 741. An order for the dismissal of the action, as provided in this chapter, is a bar to another prosecution for the same offence, if it be a misdemeanor; but it is not a bar, if the offence charged be a felony.

CHAPTER VIII.

REMITTING THE PUNISHMENT, IN CERTAIN CASES.

SECTION 742. Punishment, upon conviction of a master of a vessel from a foreign country, for bringing a foreign convict into this state, may be remitted, on court being satisfied that he has returned the convict, and on payment of the costs of the prosecution.

§ 742. When the master of a vessel arriving from a foreign country, is convicted of having knowingly brought a person convicted therein of a public offence, which, if committed in this state, would be a felony, to a place within the state, the court before which the conviction is had, may, if satisfied that the defendant has reconveyed the convict to the place from which he took him, and on payment of the costs of prosecution, order the punishment upon the conviction to be remitted.

The provision contained in this section, was first enacted in 1833, and is to be found in 2 *R. S.*, 3*d ed.*, 781, *sec.* 40, 41.

CHAPTER IX.

PROCEEDINGS AGAINST CORPORATIONS.

The existing statutes seem to regard an indictment, as the first proceeding against a corporation charged with a public offence. They no where speak of a complaint or information against them, and none of the proceedings which they prescribe in respect to an ordinary criminal case, before indictment, are applicable to corporations. The only sections contained in the revised statutes, which relate to proceedings to bring a corporation before the court, to answer to a criminal charge, are as follows:

" When an indictment shall be found against any corporation, a summons against the defendants may be issued and served in the same manner as provided by any statute in civil cases; and if such corporation do not appear according to the summons, a *distringas* may be issued and levied upon their personal estate and chattels real; and the issues levied thereon may be ordered to be sold, and the money arising therefrom shall be detained until such corporation appear, and plead to the indictment, when it may be paid to them, after deducting such costs and expenses incurred, as shall be allowed by the court." 2 *R. S.*, 3*d ed.* 832, *sec.* 39.

"But if such corporation shall neglect to appear and plead to such indictment, within two terms after the return of the *distringas* against them, the court shall order the money levied thereby, after deducting the costs and expense of the proceedings, to be paid to the county treasurer for the use of the poor of such county." *Ibid. sec.* 40.

This code makes no distinction between natural persons and corporations, in respect to the manner of commencing criminal actions. They must all be commenced, either by an information before a magistrate, or by the presentment of a grand jury.

This chapter, *sec.* 743 – 748, provides for the mode of bringing the case of a corporation defendant before the grand jury, and *sec.* 749, for their appearance and plea. In the proceedings, as thus provided, it is believed a greater degree of simplicity has been attained, than is to be found in the practice as it now exists.

§ 743. Upon an information or presentment against a corporation, the magistrate must issue a summons, signed by him, with his name of office, requiring the corporation to appear before him, at a specified time and place, to answer the charge; the time to be not less than ten days after the issuing of the summons.

§ 744. The summons must be in substantially the following form:

"County of *Albany*, [or as the case may be.]

'In the name of the people of the state of New-York:

"To the [naming the corporation.]

"You are hereby summoned to appear before me, at [naming the place,] on [specifying the day and hour,] to answer a charge made against you, upon *the information of A. B.*, [or "the presentment of the grand jury of the county of *Albany*," or as the case may be,] for [designating the offence, generally.]

"Dated at the *city*, [or "town,"] of , the day of , 1850.

G. H., *Justice of the Peace.*"
[or as the case may be.]

§ 745. The summons must be served at least five days before the day of appearance fixed therein, by delivering a copy thereof and showing the original to the president, or other head of the corporation, or to the secretary, cashier, or managing agent thereof.

The mode of service prescribed in this section, is the same as in the *Amended Code, sec.* 134, *subd.* 1.

§ 746. At the time appointed in the summons, the magistrate must proceed to investigate the charge, in the same manner as in the case of a natural person brought before him, so far as those proceedings are applicable.

§ 747. After hearing the proofs, the magistrate must certify upon the depositions, either that there is or is not sufficient cause to believe the corporation guilty of the offence charged, and must return the depositions and certificate, in the manner prescribed in section 220.

§ 748. If the magistrate return a certificate that there is sufficient cause to believe the corporation guilty of the offence charged, the grand jury may proceed thereon, as in the case of a natural person held to answer.

§ 749. If an indictment be found, the corporation may appear by counsel, to answer the same. If they do not thus appear, a plea of not guilty must be entered, and the same proceedings had thereon as in other cases.

§ 750. When a fine is imposed upon a corporation, on conviction, it may be collected by virtue of the order imposing it, by the sheriff of the county, out of their real and personal property, in the same manner as upon an execution in a civil action.

The last section will be found to provide a more simple mode of procedure, than that now required by the Revised Statutes, which provide that "when a fine shall be imposed upon any corporation, the same may be collected by *distingas* against their personal estate and chattels real." 2 *R. S.*, 3*d ed.*, 832, *sec.* 41.

CHAPTER X.

ENTITLING AFFIDAVITS.

SECTION 751. Affidavits defectively entitled, valid.

§ 751. It is not necessary to entitle an affidavit or deposition, in the action, whether taken before or after indictment, or upon an appeal; but if made without a title, or with an erroneous title, it is as valid and effectual for every purpose, as if it were duly entitled, if it intelligibly refer to the proceeding, indictment or appeal in which it is made.

This section is taken from the *Amended Code, sec.* 406. It was there introduced, to obviate the objection, which is sustained by abundant common law authority, that such an affidavit, whether intelligibly referring to the action or proceeding in which it is taken, or not, is a nullity; inasmuch as, if false, no indictment for perjury can be maintained upon it. *Milliken* v. *Selye*, 3 Denio, 56, and the cases there cited.

CHAPTER XI.

ERRORS AND MISTAKES, IN PLEADINGS AND OTHER PROCEEDINGS.

Section 752. No departure from the forms prescribed by this code, or error or mistake in a pleading or proceeding, material, unless it prejudice or tend to prejudice a substantial right.

§ 752. Neither a departure from the form or mode prescribed by this code, in respect to any pleadings or proceedings, nor an error or mistake therein, renders it invalid, unless it have actually prejudiced the defendant, or tend to his prejudice, in respect to a substantial right.

The preceding provisions of this code, and the remarks which have been made upon them, abundantly show, that its leading object is to remove the many grounds of objection to criminal proceedings, on the ground of their departure from the literal requirements of law. The old rule, that penal statutes are to be strictly construed, which it is in another place proposed to abrogate, has led, in its practical enforcement, to the defeat of justice, upon mere form; a principle totally at variance with that by which the proceedings here prescribed are to be governed.

CHAPTER XII.

DISPOSAL OF PROPERTY, STOLEN OR EMBEZZLED.

§ 753. When property, alleged to have been stolen or embezzled, comes into the custody of a peace officer, he must hold it, subject to the order of the magistrate authorised by the next section to direct the disposal thereof.

Same in substance as 2 *R. S.*, 3*d ed.*, 831, *sec.* 34.

§ 754. On satisfactory proof of the title of the owner of the property, the magistrate before whom the information is laid, or who examines the charge against the person accused of stealing or embezzling the property, may order it to be delivered to the owner, on his paying the reasonable and necessary expenses incurred in its preservation, to be certified by the magistrate. The order entitles the owner to demand and receive the property.

Same in substance as 2 *R. S.*, 3*d ed.*, 831, *sec.* 35.

§ 755. If property stolen or embezzled come into the custody of a magistrate, it must be delivered to the owner, on satisfactory proof of his title, and on his paying the necessary expenses incurred in its preservation, to be certified by the magistrate.

Same in substance as 2 *R. S.*, 3*d ed.*, 832, *sec.* 36.

§ 756. If property stolen or embezzled have not been delivered to the owner, the court before which a trial is had for stealing or embezzling it, may, on proof of his title, order it to be restored to the owner.

Same in substance as 2 *R. S.*, 3*d ed.*, 832, *sec.* 37; except that it authorises the order to be made by the court in which a *trial* for stealing or embezzling the property is had, instead, as there prescribed, of the court in which a *conviction* is had. It does not follow that, because the defendant is acquitted, the prosecutor is not entitled to the property. The acquittal may, and almost invariably does, proceed upon other grounds than a dispute of the title of the person from whom the property is alleged to be taken.

§ 757. If property stolen or embezzled, be not claimed by the owner, before the expiration of six months from the conviction of a person for stealing or embezzling it, the magistrate or other officer having it in his custody, must, on payment of the necessary expenses incurred in its preservation, deliver it to the county superintendents of the poor, or in the city of New-York, to the governors of the alms house, to be applied for the benefit of the poor of the county or city, as the case may be.

Same in substance as 2 *R. S.*, 3*d ed.*, 832, *sec.* 38.

§ 758. When money or other property is taken from a defendant, arrested upon a charge of a public offence, the officer taking it, must, at the time, give duplicate receipts therefor, specifying particularly the amount of money or the kind of property taken; one of which receipts he must deliver to the defendant, and the other of which he must forthwith file with the clerk of the court to which the depositions and statement must be sent, as provided in section 220.

This provision is new, but is deemed necessary, in order to prevent abuses by public officers, in taking property and retaining it, without furnishing to the party from whom it is taken, such evidence as will enable him to assert his right to his possession. When property is taken by a sheriff or other officer, under legal process, the delivery of an inventory is required; and there is, if anything, a stronger reason for imposing this duty, upon an officer who takes property under the circumstances contemplated by this chapter.

§ 759. The clerks in each of the police offices in the city of New-York, must enter in suitable books, a description of every article of property, alleged to be stolen or embezzled, and brought into the office, or taken from the person of a prisoner; and must attach a number to each article, and make a corresponding entry thereof. They must also enter in a suitable book, a statement of all property stolen or embezzled, of which information is given to them, and must daily furnish a copy of that statement, to the chief of police in the city of New-York.

Taken substantially from *Laws of* 1846, *p.* 404, *sec.* 9.

§ 760. The common council of the city of New-York may designate one or more of the police clerks in that city, to take charge of all property alleged to be stolen or embezzled, and which may be brought into the police office or taken from the person of a prisoner, and may prescribe regulations in regard to the duties of the clerk or clerks so designated, and to security for the faithful performance of the duties imposed by this section.

CHAPTER XIII.

REPRIEVES, COMMUTATIONS AND PARDONS.

§ 761. The governor has power to grant reprieves, commutations and pardons, after conviction, for all offences, except treason and cases of impeachment, upon such conditions, and with such restrictions and limitations, as he may think proper, subject to the regulations provided in this chapter.

§ 762. He may also suspend the execution of the sentence, upon a conviction for treason, until the case can be reported to the legislature, at its next meeting, when the legislature must either pardon or commute the sentence, direct the execution thereof, or grant a further reprieve.

§ 763. He must annually communicate to the legislature, each case of reprieve, commutation or pardon; stating the name of the convict, the crime of which he was convicted, the sentence and its date, and the date of the commutation, pardon or reprieve.

The last three sections, are taken from the constitution, *art.* 4, *sec.* 5.

§ 764. When an application is made to the governor for a pardon, he may require the presiding judge of the court, before which the conviction was had, or the district attorney by whom the action was prosecuted, to urnish him without delay, with a statement of the facts proved on the trial, and of any other facts having reference to the propriety of granting or refusing the pardon.

§ 765. At least ten days before the governor acts upon an application for a pardon, written notice of the intention to apply therefor, signed by the person applying, must be served upon the district attorney of the county where the conviction was had, and proof, by affidavit, of the service, must be presented to the governor.

§ 766. Unless dispensed with by the governor, a copy of the notice must also be published, for thirty days from the first publication, in the state paper, and in a paper in the county in which the conviction was had, nearest to the place of conviction; and in the city of New-York, in a paper designated by the governor, with reference to its having the largest circulation.

The last three sections are in substantial conformity with *Laws of* 1849, *p.* 450, 451, *ch.* 310.

§ 767. When the governor grants a reprieve, commutation or pardon, he must, within ten days thereafter, file all the papers presented to him in relation thereto, in the office of the secretary of state, by whom they must be kept as records, open to public inspection.

PART V.

OF PROCEEDINGS IN THE POLICE COURTS.

TITLE I.

OF THE PROCEEDINGS IN POLICE COURTS, IN THE COUNTIES OTHER THAN NEW-YORK.

§ 768. In the cases in which the police courts have jurisdiction, as provided in section 56, when the defendant is brought before the magistrate, the charge against him must be distinctly read to him, and he must be required to plead thereto.

Taken from 2 *R. S.*, 3*d ed.* 799, *sec.* 8.

§ 769. The defendant may plead the same pleas as upon an indictment, as provided in section 351. His plea must be oral, and entered upon the minutes of the magistrate.

§ 770. Upon a plea other than a plea of guilty, if the defendant do not demand a trial by jury, the magistrate must proceed to try the issue.

Taken from 2 *R. S.*, 3*d ed.* 799, *sec.* 9.

§ 771. Before the magistrate hears any testimony upon the trial, the defendant may demand a trial by jury.

Taken from 2 *R. S*, 3*d ed.* 799, *sec.* 10.

§ 772. If a trial by jury be demanded, the magistrate must, in the presence of the defendant, draw from the justice's jury box, twelve ballots, containing the names of persons to form the jury.

The revised statutes provide, that upon the demand of a jury in a court of special sessions, "the court shall issue a *venire*, directed to any constable of the county or marshal of the city, where the offence is to be tried, commanding him to summon twelve good and lawful men, qualified to serve as jurors, and not exempt from such service by law, and who shall be in no wise of kin, either to the complainant or the defendant, to be and appear before such court, at a time not more than three days from the date of the *venire*, and at a place to be named therein, to make a jury for the trial of such offence." 2 *R. S.*, 3*d ed.* 800, *sec.* 10.

The mode of drawing the jury, as prescribed by this section, has reference to the regulation prescribed by the code of civil procedure, for furnishing justices of the peace with lists of jurors, known as justice's jurors, from which ballots are to be prepared and deposited in the justice's jury box.

§ 773. The magistrate must thereupon deliver a list of the jurors drawn, to a peace officer of the town or city, with an endorsement thereon, signed by him, with his name of office, to the following effect:

"The peace officer of the town [or "city"] of to whom this is delivered, is required to summon the persons named in the within list, to appear before me, at [naming the place,] on [naming the day and hour,] to serve as jurors at a police court for the trial of a criminal charge against A. B.

"Dated at the town [or "city"] of , the day of , 1850.

"C. D.,

Justice of the peace of the town [or "city"] of ," [as the case may be.]

§ 774. The officer to whom the list is delivered, must forthwith summon each of the jurors named therein, personally, or by leaving a written notice at his place of residence, with some person of suitable age and discretion. He must also, at or before the time named therein, return the list to the magistrate, specifying the persons summoned, and the manner of service in respect to each of them.

It being left discretionary with the officer, by the present practice, whom he shall summon as jurors, it is provided by the Revised Statutes, that "the officer to whom such *venire* shall be delivered, shall execute the same fairly and impartially, and shall not summon any person whom he shall suspect to be biased or prejudiced for or against the defendant. He shall summon the jurors personally, and shall make a list of the persons summoned, which he shall certify and annex to the *venire*, and return with it to the court." 2 *R. S.*, 3*d. ed.*, 800, *sec.* 11.

Another and a fairer mode of selecting the jury, being prescribed by section 772, the last two sections provide, in conformity with it, for the mode of summoning it by the officer

§ 775. The names of the persons returned as jurors, must be written on separate ballots, folded as nearly alike as possible, and so that the name cannot be seen, and must, under the direction of the magistrate, be deposited in a box, or other convenient thing.

Substantially the same as 2 *R. S.*, 3*d ed.*, 800, *sec.* 12.

§ 776. The magistrate must then draw out six of the ballots, successively; and if any of the persons whose names are drawn do not appear, or are challenged and set aside, such further number must be drawn as will make a jury of six, after all legal challenges have been allowed.

Substantially the same as 2 *R. S.*, 3*d ed.*, 800, *sec.* 13.

§ 777. The same challenges may be taken by either party, to the panel of jurors, or to an individual juror, as on the trial of an indictment for a misdemeanor, so far as applicable; except, that the challenge must, in all cases, be tried by the magistrate.

The Revised Statutes speak of "all legal causes of challenge" being allowed, in trials in courts of special sessions. 2 *R. S.*, 3*d ed.*, 800, *sec.* 13. In this expression, they refer, of course, to challenges, as understood at common law that subject never having been, as yet, regulated by statute. Inasmuch as it is proposed to be regulated by this code, *sec.* 405–439, *p.* 188—203, this section is rendered necessary.

§ 778. If six of the jurors summoned do not attend, or be not obtained, the magistrate may direct the officer to summon any of the bystanders, or others, who may be competent, and against whom there is no sufficient cause of challenge, to act as jurors.

Substantially the same as 2 *R. S.*, *3d ed.*, 800, *sec.* 14.

§ 779. If the officer to whom the order is delivered, do not return it, as required by section 774, he may be punished by the magistrate, as for a contempt; and the magistrate must issue a new order for the summoning of the same jurors, in substantially the same form; upon which the same proceedings must be had, as upon the one first issued.

Substantially the same as 2 *R. S.*, *3d ed.*, 800, *sec.* 15.

§ 780. When six jurors appear and are accepted, they constitute the jury.

§ 781. The magistate must thereupon administer to the jury, the following oath or affirmation: "You do "swear," [or "you do solemnly affirm," as the case may be,] "that you will well and truly try this issue, between the people of the state of New-York and A. B., the defendant, and a true verdict give, according to the evidence."

Taken from 2 *R. S. 3d ed* 800, *sec.* 16.

§ 782 After the jury are sworn, they must sit together and hear the proofs and allegations of the parties, which must be delivered in public, and in the presence of the defendant.

Taken from 2 *R. S.*, *3d ed.*, 800, *sec.* 17.

§ 783. After hearing the proofs and allegations, the jury may either decide in court or may retire for consideration. If they do not immediately agree, an officer must be sworn to the following effect: "You do swear, that you will keep this jury together in some private and convenient place, without food or drink, except bread and water, unless otherwise ordered by the court; that you will not permit any person to speak to or communicate with them, nor do so yourself, unless it be to ask them whether they have agreed upon a verdict; and that you will return them into court when they have so agreed, or when ordered by the court."

This section is founded upon 2 *R. S.*, 3*d ed.*, 800, *sec.* 17, which, however, omits to prescribe the form or substance of the oath of the officer. For the sake of greater convenience, the form of the oath is here given, in conformity with section 478 of this code, p. 225.

§ 784. When the jury have agreed on their verdict, they must deliver it publicly to the magistrate, who must enter it in his minutes.

Taken from 2 *R. S.*, 3*d ed*, 800, *sec.* 19.

§ 785. The jury cannot be discharged, after the cause is submitted to them, until they have agreed upon and rendered their verdict, unless, for good cause, the magistrate sooner discharge them.

§ 786. If the jury be discharged, as provided in the last section, the magistrate may proceed again to the trial, in the same manner as upon the first trial; and so on, until a verdict is rendered.

The existing statutes are silent, on the subject embraced in the last two sections. Its regulation in these courts is just as necessary as in any other court. These provisions are conformable to sections 486, 487, p. 228, 229.

§ 787. When the defendant pleads guilty, or is convicted either by the magistrate or by a jury, the magistrate must render judgment thereon, of fine or imprisonment, or both, as the case may require; but the fine cannot exceed fifty dollars, nor the imprisonment six months.

Substantially the same as 2 *R. S.*, *3d ed.*, 800, *sec.* 20.

§ 788. A judgment that the defendant pay a fine, may also direct that he be imprisoned until the fine be satisfied; specifying the extent of the imprisonment, which cannot exceed one day for every two dollars of the fine.

This section is founded on 2 *R. S.*, *3d ed.*, 801, *sec.* 20; but in respect to the duration of imprisonment for not paying a fine, is the same as section 549 of this code, p. 260, 261.

§ 789. When the defendant is acquitted, either by the magistrate or by a jury, he must be immediately discharged; and if the magistrate certify, upon his minutes, or the jury find that the prosecution was malicious or without probable cause, the magistrate must order the prosecutor to pay the costs of the proceedings, or to give satisfactory security, by a written undertaking, with one or more sureties, to pay the same to the county within thirty days after the trial.

Taken from 2 *R. S.*, *3d ed*, 801, *sec.* 21, 24. See also, *Germond vs. The People*, 1 Hill, 343.

§ 790. If the prosecutor do not pay the costs or give security therefor, the magistrate may enter judgment against him for the amount thereof, which may be enforced, in all respects, in the same manner as a judgment rendered by a justice's court held by a justice of the peace.

Taken from 2 *R. S. 3d ed.*, 801, *sec.* 22.

§ 791. When a conviction is had, upon a plea of guilty or upon a trial, the magistrate must make and sign, with his name of office, a certificate in substantially the following form:

"Police court,

"County of *Albany*. Town of *Bern*, [or as the case may be.]

"The people of the state of New-York
against
A. B.

January 1, 1850.

"The above named A. B, having been brought before me, C. D., a justice of the peace of the town [or city,] of [as the case may be,] charged with [briefly designating the offence,] and having requested to be tried by a police court, [or "having been required by me to give bail for his appearance at the next court of sessions of this county, and having omitted to do so for twenty-four hours after being so required," as the case may be.]

"And the above named A. B. having thereupon pleaded not guilty, [or as the case may be,] and demanded [or "failed to demand," as the case may be,] a jury, and having been thereupon duly tried, and upon such trial, duly convicted,

"I have adjudged,—That he be imprisoned in the jail of this county, days, [or "pay a fine of dollars and be imprisoned until it be paid, not exceeding days," or both, as the case may be.]

"Dated at the *town* [or "city"] of , the day of , 1850.

"C. D.

Justice of the peace of the town [or "city,] of " [as the case may be.]

No subject is more fruitful of difficulties, or gives rise to a greater amount of litigation, than the want of compliance on the part of courts and officers of special jurisdiction, with the statutory requirements as to their records and certificates. The form contained in this section is prescribed, with a view, if possible, to prevent their recurrence.

§ 792. If the defendant have pleaded guilty,—instead of the second paragraph, the certificate must state substantially as follows: "And the above named A. B. having been thereupon duly convicted, upon a plea of guilty."

§ 793. Within twenty days after the conviction, the magistrate must cause the certificate to be filed in the office of the clerk of the county.

Conformable to 2 *R. S*, *3d ed.*, 804, *sec.* 46.

§ 794. The certificate, made and filed as prescribed in the last two sections, or a certified copy thereof, is conclusive evidence of the facts stated therein.

Taken from 2 *R. S.*, *3d ed.*, 804, *sec.* 47.

§ 795. The judgment must be executed by the sheriff of the county, or by a constable, marshal or policeman of the city, village or town in which the conviction is had, upon receiving a copy of the certificate prescribed in section 791, certified by the magistrate or the county clerk.

Taken from 2 *R. S.*, *3d ed.*, 803, *sec.* 38.

§ 796. If a fine imposed be paid before commitment, it must be received by the magistrate, and be applied to the payment of the expenses of the prosecution. The residue, if any, must be paid by the magistrate, within thirty days after its receipt, into the county treasury.

Taken from 2 *R. S.*, *3d ed.*, 803, *sec.* 39.

§ 797. If the defendant be committed for not paying a fine, he may pay it to the sheriff of the county, but to no other person; who must in like manner, within thirty days after the receipt thereof, pay it into the county treasury, as provided in the last section.

Taken from 2 *R. S.*, *3d ed.*, 804, *sec.* 40.

§ 798. If the magistrate or sheriff receiving the fine, fail to pay it or such part of it as is so payable, into the county treasury, the county treasurer must immediately commence an action against him therefor, in the name of the county.

Taken from 2 *R. S., 3d ed.*, 804, *sec.* 41.

§ 799. The magistrate may issue subpœnas for witnesses, as provided in section 670, and punish disobedience thereof, as provided in section 681.

The provision of the Revised Statutes, from which this section is taken, is as follows :—" In case any person summoned to appear before any court of special sessions, as a juror or witness, shall fail to appear, he shall be liable to the like penalties, and may be proceeded against in the like manner, as provided by law in respect to jurors and witnesses, in justices' courts." 2 *R. S., 3d ed.*, 804, *sec.* 43.

In the section under consideration, the power to issue subpœnas and to punish witnesses for disobedience, is confined, as it should be, to the magistrate holding the court. The authority to administer oaths to witnesses is omitted as unnecessary, it being an incidental power of all courts.

§ 800. If a person summoned as a juror fail to appear, he may be punished by a fine not exceeding five dollars, imposed by the magistrate, by an order entered in his minutes. The order is deemed a judgment, in all respects, in favor of the poor of the town or city.

Conformable to 2 *R. S., 3d ed.*, 804, *sec.* 43, and to the provisions of the Revised Statutes respecting justices' courts, which are there referred to.

§ 801. No fees are payable to a juror or witness, for his service or attendance in a police court.

Taken from 2 *R S*, *3d ed.*, 804, *sec.* 44.

§ 802. When the defendant, upon being brought before the magistrate, requests a trial by a police court, the preliminary examination of the case is dispensed with.

Substantially the same as 2 *R. S.*, *3d ed.*, 801, *sec.* 25.

§ 803. During the twenty-four hours allowed to the defendant to give bail, as provided in the second subdivision of section 56, and until judgment is given, he may be continued in the custody of the officer, or committed to the jail of the county to answer the charge, as the magistrate may direct.

§ 804. The commitment must be signed by the magistrate, by his name of office, and must be in substantially the following form:

"The sheriff of the county of , is required to receive and detain A. B., who stands charged before me for [designating the offence, generally,] to answer the charge before a police court in the town [or city] of , as the case may be.]

"Dated at the town [or city] of , the day of , 1850.

"C. D., Justice of the peace of the town [or city] of , [as the case may be.]

§ 805. When committed, the defendant must be delivered to the custody of the proper officer, by any peace officer in the county to whom the magistrate may deliver the commitment.

§ 806. Either before or after his committal, or upon being committed, the defendant must, if he require it, be admitted to bail.

§ 807. The bail must be taken by the magistrate, by a written undertaking, executed by the defendant, with one or more sufficient sureties approved by the magistrate, in a sum not exceeding two hundred dollars.

§ 808. The undertaking must be in substantially the following form:

"A. B. having been duly charged before C. D., a justice of the peace in the town [or city] of , [as the case may be,] with the offence of, [designating the offence generally.]

"We undertake that he shall appear thereon, from time to time, until judgment, at a police court in the town [or city] of , [as the case may be,] held by the justice above named, or that we will pay to the county of , [naming the county in which the court is held,] the sum of dollars," [inserting the sum fixed by the magistrate.]

"Dated at the town [or city] of ," [as the case may be.]

§ 809. If the defendant fail to appear according to the undertaking, the magistrate, unless a sufficient excuse be shown, must declare the undertaking of bail forfeited, and the county treasurer must immediately commence an action, for the recovery of the sum mentioned therein, in the name of the county.

§ 810. The county court of the county, or in the city of New York, the court of common pleas of that city, may remit the forfeiture or any part thereof, in the cases and in the manner provided in the code of civil procedure.

TITLE II.

OF THE PROCEEDINGS IN THE POLICE COURTS, IN THE CITY AND COUNTY OF NEW-YORK.

In all the counties of the state, except New-York, the courts of special sessions have heretofore had the authority, which is continued by the last title, to try the case by a jury, when demanded by the defendant. In the city of New-York, however, that power has not existed, and the court alone has tried and determined the case, subject, however, to the right of the defendant, to annul the conviction, by appealing to the court of general sessions. It is provided in this respect, by the revised statutes, that in hearing and determining an accusation cognizable by it, the court of special sessions in New-York shall proceed in the same manner as the other courts of special sessions in the state, except as to the summoning of a jury, and shall sentence the offender upon conviction; that any person, however, so sentenced, without having demanded a trial by jury, may appeal from the sentence to the court of general sessions; that the appeal must be made at the time sentence is pronounced, and that thereupon the conviction shall be void; that the court of special sessions shall enter the appeal upon its minutes, and shall proceed, in the same manner as if no such trial had been had, to take a recognizance from the accused, with sufficient sureties, to appear at the general sessions, or in default of giving the recognizance, shall commit him to prison, and shall take the same measures to insure the attendance of the witnesses in behalf of the prosecution, at the court of general sessions, as in other cases; and that the court of general sessions shall proceed, in every such case, by indictment and other proceedings, in the same manner as if no such trial or conviction had been had. 2 *R. S.*, 3*d ed.*, 802, 803, *sec.* 29—33.

This incongruous proceeding, by which the defendant, after having taken his chance af an acquittal by the court of special sessions, may, by his own act, vacate a conviction, was introduced for the purpose of obviating the constitutional objection to the trial of the case without a jury. It seems to the Commissioners, that this can be better as well as less awkwardly effected, by providing for the demand of a jury in the first instance, and that if it be demanded, the jurisdiction of the court shall cease, and the same proceedings be had in respect to an examination, and holding the defendant to answer or discharging him, as in ordinary cases triable at the sessions. This is done by sections 812 and 813; the former of which provides, in addition, that the defendant may be tried by the police court, when he requests to be so tried, as well as when he does not demand a jury.

The other provisions of this title are sufficiently explained in the note to each section.

§ 811. The police courts, in the city and county of New-York, must proceed upon a charge for a public offence, in the manner prescribed in the last title, except as provided in the next seven sections.

§ 812. When a police court, in the city and county of New-York, has jurisdiction of the offence, as provided in section 56, it must proceed to the trial, in the following cases:

1. When the defendant has requested to be tried by a police court:

2. When, (not having made such request, and after having been required by the magistrate before whom he was brought, to give bail for his appearance at the next court of sessions, he has omitted to do so for twenty-four hours after being so required,) a jury is not demanded by him, on being brought before the court for trial.

§813. If, in the case mentioned in the second subdivision of the last section, a jury be demanded, the magistrate before whom the defendant was originally brought, must proceed to the examination of the charge, and hold the defendant to answer, or discharge him, as provided in sections 187 to 220, both inclusive.

§ 814. The trial must, in all cases, be before the court without a jury.

Substantially the same as 2 *R. S. 3d ed.* 802, *sec.* 29.

§ 815. Subpœnas for witnesses, and the certificate of the judgment, must be signed by the clerk of the court, who must also enter all the proceedings of the court, and the sentences upon convictions, in a book of minutes, and when necessary, certify the proceedings of the court.

Conformable to 2 *R. S. 3d ed.* 803, *sec.* 34, 35.

§ 816. Fines, imposed by the court, must be received by the clerk, if paid before committal in execution of the judgment. He must every thirty days, render to the comptroller of the city, accounts of the fines imposed and received by him, and of the expenses attending the court.

Taken from 2 *R. S. 3d ed.* 803, *sec.* 39.

§ 817. All fines, not paid to the clerk, as provided in the last section, must be received by the sheriff of the city and county of New-York; who must, within thirty days thereafter, pay them to the comptroller of the city, in the same manner as he is required to pay fines imposed by the court of sessions, and received by him.

Founded upon, but slightly varied from 2 *R. S. 3d ed.* 803, *sec.* 36.

§ 818. No transcript of a conviction, had in a police court in the city and county of New-York, need be certified or filed; but a copy of the minutes of the conviction, certified by the clerk, is conclusive evidence of the facts coutained therein.

Conformable, in its general spirit, to 2 *R. S.* 3*d ed.* 804, *sec.* 47.

TITLE III.

OF APPEALS FROM THE POLICE COURTS.

This title entirely changes the mode of appeal from a judgment of conviction in a court of special sessions, as well as the proceedings upon it and its effect. The judgment must now be reviewed by the supreme court, upon *certiorari*, which must be applied for to a judge of that court, or an officer authorized to perform the duties of a judge in vacation, within ten days after the conviction, upon an affidavit specifying the supposed errors in the proceedings or judgment complained of. If the officer be satisfied that there is error, he must allow the writ; but where there has been a jury trial, it cannot be allowed on the ground that the verdict was against evidence. The writ and affidavit must be delivered to the magistrate, within ten days after the allowance, and within twenty days after that time, the magistrate must make and file his return to the matters stated in the affidavit. He may be compelled by *mandamus*, to make this return, or to amend and perfect it. The certified copy of the *certiorari*, affidavit and return, must be served by the defendant upon the attorney general, with at least four days' notice of argument; and the supreme court must then proceed to hear the parties, and give judgment upon the return.

If, at the time of the conviction, the defendant notify the magistrate that he intends to remove the conviction by *certiorari*, the magistrate must take security from him, if offered, to appear at the next court of general sessions, and abide its judgment, and must thereupon suspend the execution of the sentence; which, however, he is required to pronounce and enter upon his minutes. The court of sessions then has power to continue the recognizance, or take a new one, until the decision of the supreme court. If the conviction be reversed, the supreme court must award a writ of *supersedeas* for the discharge of the defendant; but whether reversed or affirmed, if the defendant have given security for his appearance at the court of sessions, the judgment must be remitted to that court; which, upon reversal, must discharge the defendant, and upon affirmance, must proceed to execute the judgment of the court of special sessions, or to sentence the defendant, if it have not already been done. If the prosecution of the *certiorari* be unreasonably delayed, the supreme court may quash it, and remit the proceedings to the court of sessions, which is required to proceed as upon a judgment of affirmance.

This is a brief summary of the practice, as it now exists, in relation to appeals from the courts of special sessions, as taken from 2 *R. S. 3d ed.*, 805, 806.

In place of this cumbrous and inconvenient practice, the Commissioners propose, by this title, to substitute one which they deem much more simple and practical in its character.

Its outline is analogous to that which they proposed to the legislature in their first report, *p.* 223—230, in respect to appeals from justices' and other inferior courts, and which was adopted in the code of 1848, *sec.* 301—320. Referring the legislature to the sections themselves, for a more full explanation of the change, and to the notes to some of them in which a portion of the existing practice is preserved, they will state concisely its principles and its leading details.

A judgment of conviction in a police court may be reviewed by the court of sessions of the county, upon appeal, and not otherwise. This appeal is not allowable, except for an error of the court, in the course of the proceedings or in the determination of the cause, and cannot be had in any case, upon the ground that the verdict of the jury was against evidence. For the purpose of appealing, an affidavit must be made within ten days after the judgment, stating the facts showing the alleged errors, and be presented to the county judge or a judge of the supreme court, or in New York to the recorder or city judge, who, if he think the question should be decided by the court of sessions, must allow the appeal, and upon the allowance, must admit the defendant to bail. The affidavit and allowance of the appeal must, within five days be delivered to the police court, which must, within ten days thereafter, make and file a return to the matters stated in the affidavit. The return may be compelled, or a further or amended return ordered, as by the present practice. When the return is made, the defendant may bring the appeal to argument, on at least five days' notice to the district attorney, instead of the attorney general, as required by the present practice. If he omit to do so, or to serve a copy of the return upon the district attorney, the appeal must be dismissed, unless, for good cause, the court otherwise direct. If the appeal be brought to a hearing, it must be argued, though no one appear to oppose; but if brought on by the district attorney, he may take judgment of affirmance, unless the defendant appear. [The reasons for this latter provision, are stated in the note to *sec.* 600, *p.* 279, which contains a similar provision, in respect to appeals in criminal actions prosecuted by indictment.] The appeal must be heard upon the original return.

After hearing the appeal, the court must give judgment, without regard to technical errors or defects, which have not prejudiced the substantial rights of the defendant, and may render such judgment as the court below should have rendered, or may, according to the justice of the case, affirm or reverse the judgment, in whole or in part, as to all or any of the defendants, if there be more than one, or order a new trial. On affirmance, the court must direct the execution of the judgment, and on reversal, it must direct the defendant to be discharged. If a new trial be ordered, it must be had in the court of sessions, as upon an indictment, and that court may, in like manner, proceed to judgment and execution, or take any other proceedings necessary to carry the judgment on appeal into effect.

If the judgment on the appeal be against the defendant, he may appeal to the supreme court, whose judgment is final, and is to be carried into effect in the same manner as if the appeal had been taken from a judgment upon an indictment.

By this system, the defendant has, as in civil cases, (according to the practice as established by the code of civil procedure,) two appeals; the same rule being applied as in respect to civil cases, that no appeal to the court of appeals can be had in a case originating before a court held by a justice. This was a portion of the original plan of the Commissioners, as presented in their first report, *p.* 21, 22, and sanctioned by the legislature in the adoption of the original as well as of the amended code, but which it remained for the provisions of this title to render perfect and complete.

§ 819. A judgment upon conviction, rendered by a police court, may be reviewed by the court of sessions of the county, upon an appeal, as prescribed by this title, and not otherwise.

§ 820. An appeal cannot be allowed, for any other cause than the erroneous decision of the court, in the course of the proceedings before it, or in the determination of the cause: and it can in no case be allowed, upon the grouud that the verdict was against evidence, when the action was tried by a jury.

§ 821. For the purpose of appealing, the defendant, or some one on his behalf, must, within ten days after the judgment, make an affidavit, stating the facts showing the alleged errors in the proceedings or conviction complained of, and must, within that time, present it to the county judge or a judge of the supreme court, or in the city and county of New-York, to the recorder or city judge of that city, and may apply thereon for the allowance of the appeal.

§ 822. If, in the opinion of the judge, it is proper that the question arising on the appeal should be decided by the court of sessions, he must endorse on the affidavit an allowance of the appeal to that court.

§ 823. Upon allowing the appeal, the judge may take from the defendant, a written undertaking, with such sureties as he may approve, that the defendant will abide the judgment of the court of sessions upon the appeal; and may thereupon order that he be discharged from imprisonment, on service of the order upon the officer having him in custody, or if he be not in custody, that all proceedings on the judgment be stayed.

§ 824. The undertaking upon the appeal, must be immediately filed with the clerk of the court of sessions.

§ 825. The affidavit and the allowance of the appeal must be delivered to the magistrate who tried the case, or, if in the city and county of New-York, to the clerk of the police court, within five days after the allowance of the appeal; and when so delivered, the appeal is deemed taken.

§ 826. The magistrate or court rendering the judgment, must make a return to all the matters stated in the affidavit, and must cause the affidavit and return to be filed in the office of the clerk of the court of sessions, within ten days after the service of the affidavit and allowance of the appeal.

§ 827. If the return be not made within the time prescribed in the last section, the court of sessions or the presiding judge thereof, may order that a return be made within a specified time which may be deemed reasonable; and the court may, by attachment, compel a compliance with the order.

§ 828. If the return be defective, a further or amended return may be ordered, and the order may be enforced in the manner provided in the last section.

§ 829. When the return is made, the appeal may be brought to argument by the defendant, on any day in term, upon a notice of not less than five days before the term, to the district attorney of the county.

§ 830. If the defendant omit to bring the appeal to argument, as provided in the last section, the court must dismiss it, unless it continue the same, by special order, for cause shown.

§ 831. The defendant must serve upon the district attorney, a copy of the return, with or before the notice of argument. If he fail to do so, the appeal must be dismissed, upon proof of the failure, unless the court otherwise direct.

§ 832. If the appeal be brought to hearing by the defendant, it must be argued, though no one appear to oppose; but if brought on by the district attorney, he may take judgment of affirmance, unless the defendant appear to argue the appeal.

§ 833. The appeal must be heard upon the original return; and no copy thereof need be furnished for the use of the court.

§ 834. After hearing the appeal, the court must give judgment, without regard to technical errors or defects, which have not prejudiced the substantial rights of the defendant; and may render the judgment which the court below should have rendered, or may, according to the justice of the case, affirm or reverse the judgment, in whole or in part, as to all or any of the defendants, if there be more than one, or may order a new trial.

§ 835. When judgment is given upon the appeal, it must be entered upon the minutes.

§ 836. If the judgment be affirmed, the court must direct its execution, and if the defendant have been discharged on bail, after the commencement of the execution of a judgment of imprisonment, as provided in section 823, must commit him to the proper custody for the remainder of his term of imprisonment.

§ 837. If the judgment be reversed, and the defendant be imprisoned in pursuance of the judgment of the police court, the court of sessions must order him to be discharged.

§ 838. If a new trial be ordered, it must be had in the court of sessions, in the same manner as upon an issue of fact on an indictment; and that court may proceed to judgment and execution, as in an action prosecuted by indictment.

§ 839. If any proceedings be necessary to carry the judgment upon the appeal into effect, they must be had in the court of sessions.

§ 840. If the judgment on the appeal be against the defendant, he may appeal therefrom to the supreme court, in the same manner as from a judgment in an action prosecuted by indictment, and may be admitted to bail upon the appeal, in like manner.

§ 841. The judgment of the supreme court upon the appeal, is final.

§ 842. The same proceedings mnst be had, to carry into effect the judgment of the supreme court upon the appeal, as if it had been taken upon a judgment in an action prosecuted by indictment.

PART VI.

OF SPECIAL PROCEEDINGS OF A CRIMINAL NATURE.

TITLE I.

OF CORONERS' INQUESTS, AND THE DUTIES OF CORONERS.

§ 843. When a coroner is informed, that a person has been killed or dangerously wounded by another, or has suddenly died, under such circumstances as to afford a reasonable ground to suspect that his death has been occasioned by the act of another, by criminal means, or has committed suicide, he must go to the place where the person is, and forthwith summon not less than nine, nor more than fifteen persons, qualified by law to serve as jurors, to appear before him forthwith, at a specified place, to inquire into the cause of the death or wound.

The revised statutes provide, that "whenever any coroner shall receive notice that any person has been slain, or has suddenly died, or has been dangerously wounded, it shall be the duty of such coroner to go to the place where such person shall be, and forthwith to summon not less than sixteen, nor more than twenty-three persons, qualified by law to serve as jurors, and not exempt from such service, to appear before such coroner forthwith, at such place as he shall appoint, to make inquisition concerning such death or wounding." 2 *R. S., 3d ed.*, 827, *sec.* 1.

This section varies from these requirements in two respects. In the first place, it restricts the cases in which the coroner is required to summon a jury, to the case of a person "who has been killed or dangerously wounded by another, or has suddenly died, under such circumstances as to afford a reasonable ground to suspect that his death has been occasioned by the act of another, by criminal means, or has committed suicide." There seems to be no good reason for requiring an inquest, in any other case than those here mentioned. It is a proceeding of a criminal nature, and so far as the public have an interest in its being held, it may be, with great propriety confined to these cases. A sudden death by any other means, like a death from ordinary disease, does not seem to require the interposition of a public officer.

The other branch of the section, that providing for the summoning of not less than nine nor more than fifteen jurors, is in conformity with *Laws of* 1847, *p.* 112, *ch.* 118, *sec.* 1.

§ 844. When six or more of the jurors appear, they must be sworn by the coroner to inquire who the person was, and when, where and by what means he came to his death or was wounded, as the case may be, and into the circumstances attending the death or wounding, and to render a true verdict thereon, according to the evidence offered to them, or arising from the inspection of the body.

Same as 2 *R. S.*, 3*d ed.*, 827, *sec.* 2, as altered by *Laws of* 1847, *p.* 112, *ch.* 118, *sec.* 2.

§ 845 The coroner may issue subpœnas for witnesses, returnable forthwith, or at such time and place as he may appoint. He must summon and examine as witnesses, every person who, in his opinion, or that of any of the jury, has any knowledge of the facts; and he must summon as a witness a surgeon or physician, who must, in the presence of the jury, inspect the body, and give a professional opinion as to the cause of the death or wounding.

Substantially the same as 2 *R. S.*, 3*d ed.*, 827, *sec.* 3.

§ 846. A witness served with a subpœna may be compelled to attend and testify, or punished by the coroner for disobedience, as upon a subpœna issued by a magistrate, as provided in sections 670 and 681.

Substantially the same as 2 *R. S.*, 3*d ed.*, 827, *sec.* 4.

§ 847. After inspecting the body, and hearing the testimony, the jury must render their verdict, and certify it by an inquisition in writing, signed by them, and setting forth who the person killed or wounded is, and when, where, and by what means he came to his death or was wounded; and if he were killed or wounded, or his death were occasioned by the act of another, by criminal means, who is guilty thereof.

Substantially the same as 2 *R. S.*, 3*d ed.*, 827, *sec.* 5.

§ 848. The testimony of the witnesses examined before the coroner's jury, must be reduced to writing by the coroner, or under his direction, and must be forthwith filed by him, with the inquisition, in the office of the clerk of the court of sessions of the county, or of a city court, having power to inquire into the offence by the intervention of a grand jury.

The same in substance as 2 *R. S.*, 3*d ed.* 828, *sec.* 6; except, that the provision, that if the party charged be not in custody, the coroner shall have power to issue pr.cess for his apprehension, in the same manner as justices of the peace, is omitted. Section 851 provides for the warrant of the coroner, but varies it from that which may be at present issued by that officer, in the manner explained in the note to that section.

§ 849. If, however, the defendant be arrested before the inquisition can be filed, the coroner must deliver it with the testimony, to the magistrate before whom the defendant is brought, as provided in section 851, who must return it, with the depositions and statement taken before him, in the manner prescribed in section 220.

See *note to sec.* 851, p. 388

§ 850. If the jury find that the person was killed or wounded by another, under circumstances not excusable or justifiable, by law, or that his death was occasioned by the act of another, by criminal means, and the party committing the act be ascertained by the inquisition, and be not in custody, the coroner must issue a warrant, signed by him with his name of office, into one or more counties, as may be necessary, for the arrest of the person charged.

§ 851. The coroner's warrant must be in substantially the following form:

"County of *Albany*, [or as the case may be.]

"In the name of the people of the state of the New-York: To any sheriff, constable, marshal, or policeman in this state:

"An inquisition having been this day found by a coroner's jury, before me, stating that *A. B. has come to his death, by the act of C. D., by criminal means,* [or as the case may be, as found by the inquisition :]

"You are therefore commanded, forthwith to arrest the above named C. D.., and take him before the nearest and most accessible magistrate in this county."

"Dated at the *city of Albany,* [or as the case may be,] the day of , 1850.

"E. F.,

Coroner of the county of *Albany.*"

[or as the case may be.]

It is provided by the Revised Statutes, that a coroner issuing a warrant of arrest, shall have the same power to examine the defendant, as is possessed by a justice of the peace, and shall in all respects proceed in the like manner. 2 *R. S., 3d ed.,* 828, *sec.* 7. The more appropriate duty of the coroner seems to be, to ascertain the cause of the death; and although, to prevent any prejudice arising from delay, the Commissioners have retained the provision authorising the coroner to issue a warrant, they think that his jurisdiction over the case should there terminate, and that it should then be delivered over to a magistrate for examination. The form of the warrant, as prescribed in this section, is in conformity with this idea.

§ 852. The coroner's warrant may be served in any county; and the officer serving it must proceed thereon, in all respects, as upon a warrant of arrest on an information; except, that when served in another county, it need not be endorsed by a magistrate of that county.

§ 853. The magistrate, when the defendant is brought before him, must proceed to examine the charge contained in the inquisition, and hold the defendant to answer, or discharge him therefrom, in the same manner, in all respects, as upon a warrant of arrest on an information.

See *sections* 187–220, *p.* 83–103.

§ 854. Upon the arrest of the defendant, the clerk with whom the inquisition is filed, must, without delay, furnish to the magistrate a certified copy of it, and of the testimony returned therewith.

§ 855. The coroner must, within thirty days after an inquest upon a dead body, deliver to the county treasurer, any money or other property which may be found upon the body, unless claimed in the meantime by the legal representatives of the deceased. If he fail to do so, the treasurer may proceed against him for its recovery, by a civil action in the name of the county.

Taken from 2 *R. S.*, *3d ed.*, 828, *sec.* 10.

§ 856. Upon the delivery of money to the treasurer, he must place it to the credit of the county. If it be other property, he must, within thirty days, sell it at public auction, upon reasonable public notice; and must, in like manner, place the proceeds to the credit of the county.

Taken from 2 *R. S.*, *3d ed.*, 828, *sec.* 11.

§ 857. If the money in the treasury be demanded within six years, by the legal representatives of the deceased, the treasurer must pay it to them, after deducting the fees and expenses of the coroner and of the county, in relation to the matter, or it may be so paid at any time thereafter, upon the order of the board of supervisors.

Taken from 2 *R. S.*, 3*d ed.*, 828, *sec.* 11.

§ 858. Before auditing and allowing the account of the coroner, the board of supervisors must require from him a statement in writing, of any money or other property found upon persons on whom inquests have been held by him, verified by his oath, to the effect that the statement is true, and that the money or property mentioned in it has been delivered to the legal representatives of the deceased, or to the county treasurer.

Taken from 2 *R. S.*, 3*d ed.*, 828, *sec.* 12.

§ 859. In the city of New-York, if the coroner be absent or be unable, for any cause, to attend, the duties imposed by this title may be performed by a police justice, but by no other officer, with the same authority, and subject to the same obligations and penalties as apply to the coroner.

Taken from 2 *R. S.*, 3*d ed.*, 828, *sec.* 9.

§ 860. The coroner is entitled, for his services, in holding inquests and performing any other duty incidental thereto, to such compensation as may be fixed by the board of supervisors, and can receive for those services, no other compensation or fees whatever. In the city of New-York, the compensation so fixed must be an annual salary.

Substantially the same as 2 *R. S.*, *3d. ed.*, 829, *sec.* 13, except that it is deemed proper to make the office of coroner, in the city of New-York, a salaried office.

TITLE II.

OF SEARCH WARRANTS.

§ 861. A search warrant is an order in writing, in the name of the people, signed by a magistrate, directed to a peace officer, commanding him to search for personal property, and bring it before the magistrate.

§ 862. It may be issued, upon either of the following grounds:

1. When the property was stolen or embezzled; in which case, it may be taken, on the warrant, from any house or other place in which it is concealed, or from the possession of the person by whom it was stolen or embezzled, or of any other person in whose possession it may be:

2. When it was used as the means of committing a felony; in which case, it may be taken, on the warrant, from any house or other place in which it is concealed, or from the possession of the person by whom it was used in the commission of the offence, or of any other person in whose possession it may be:

3. When it is in the possession of any person, with the intent to use it as the means of committing a public offence, or in the possession of another, to whom he may have delivered it for the purpose of concealing it, or preventing its being discovered; in which case, it may be taken, on the warrant, from such person, or from a house or other place occupied by him, or under his control, or from the possession of the person to whom he may have so delivered it.

The Revised Statutes limit the right to a search warrant, to cases where personal property has been stolen or embezzled. 2 *R. S.*, 3*d ed*, 831, *sec.* 29. The Commissioners think that it should be extended to other cases; and accordingly propose, in the second and third subdivisions of the last section, that it may be issued to search for and take property, where it was used as the means of committing a felony, or where it is in the possession of any person, with the intent to use it as the means of committing a public offence, or in the possession of another to whom he may have delivered it for the purpose of concealing it or preventing its being discovered.

In the higher class of crimes, the testimony is almost invariably circumstantial; and no class of circumstances is more important, in cases of that description, in detecting and punishing guilt, than tracing to the possession of the defendant, property either used as the means of committing the offence, or intended to be used for that purpose. It is now usually obtained by the officers of justice, by the assumption of a responsibility on their part, which has no express sanction of law; and though they are rarely prosecuted for assuming this responsibility, it is rather owing to the fact, that the accused party seldom escapes punishment, than to the legality of the act. The propriety of legalizing the search for and seizure of property under these circumstances, cannot admit of doubt. Mr. Livingston, in his criminal code, in accordance with this idea, provided that search warrants may be issued, to seize forged instruments in writing, or counterfeited coin intended to be passed, or the instruments or materials prepared for making them; arms or munitions, prepared for the purpose of insurrection or riot; and weapons, implements or other articles, necessary to be produced on the trial of one accused of a crime. *Liv. Crim. Code,* 481, *art.* 43, *Rules* 1, 6.

§ 863. A search warrant cannot be issued, but upon probable cause, supported by affidavit, naming or describing the person, and particularly describing the property, and the place to be searched.

This section is taken from article 4, of the amendments to the constitution of the United States, which provides that "the right of the people to be secure in their persons, houses, papers and effects, against unreasonable searches and seizures, shall not be violated; and no warrants shall issue, but upon probable cause, supported by oath or affirmation, and particularly describing the place to be searched, and the persons or things to be seized."

§ 864. The magistrate must, before issuing the warrant, examine, on oath, the complainant and any witnesses he may produce, and take their depositions in writing, and cause them to be subscribed by the parties making them.

§ 865. The depositions must set forth the facts tending to establish the grounds of the application, or probable cause for believing that they exist.

The last two sections are introduced, to supply what the Commissioners deem a defect in the existing statutes, which merely provide, that "upon complaint being made on oath to any officer or magistrate specified in the second title of this chapter, as authorised to issue warrants for the apprehension of offenders, that any personal property has been stolen or embezzled, and that the complainant suspects that such property is concealed in any particular house or place, if such magistrate be satisfied that there is reasonable ground for s ch suspicion, he shall issue a warrant to search for such property." 2 *R. S. 3d ed.*, 831, *sec.* 29.

In practice, the affidavit on which a search warrant is obtained, is usually very loosely drawn. It is proper that great care should be exercised in the proceedings leading to the issuing of a search warrant, especially in view of its extension to the cases mentioned in section 862, and the policy suggested in the note to that section, *p.* 392. These sections are similar to sections 148 and 149; and the reasons given in the note to those sections. *p.* 71, are equally applicable here.

§ 866. If the magistrate be thereupon satisfied of the existence of the grounds of the application, or that there is probable cause to believe their existence, he must issue a search warrant, signed by him with his name of office, to a peace officer in his county, commanding him forthwith to search the person or place named, for the property specified, and to bring it before the magistrate.

Taken substantially from 2 *R. S.*, *3d ed.*, 831, *sec.* 29.

§ 867. The warrant must be in substantially the following form:

"County of *Albany*, [or as the case may be.]

"In the name of the people of the state of New-York: To any sheriff, constable, marshal or policeman in the county of *Albany*, [or as the case may be:]

"Proof, by affidavit, having been this day made before me, by [naming every person whose affidavit has been taken,] that [stating the particular grounds of the application, according to section 862; or if the affidavits be not positive, "that there is probable cause for believing that,"—stating the ground of the application in the same manner;]

"You are therefore commanded, in the day time, [or "at any time of the day or night," as the case may be, according to section 871,] to make immediate search *on the person of C. D.*, [or "in the house, situated"—describing it or any other place to be searched with reasonable particularity, as the case may be,] for the following property: [describing it with reasonable particularity;] and if you find the same or any part thereof, to bring it forthwith before me, at [stating the place.]

"Dated at the city of *Albany*, [or as the case may be] the day of , 1850.

"E. F.,

Justice of the peace of the *city* [or town] of [or as the case may be.]

§ 868. A search warrant may, in all cases, be served by any of the officers mentioned in its direction, but by no other person, except in aid of the officer, on his requiring it, he being present and acting in its execution.

The revised statutes provide, that a search warrant shall be executed by a public officer, and not by a private citizen. 2 *R. S.*, 3*d ed* 831, *sec.* 32. The last section embodies the same principle, but is more explicit, in declaring in what cases a private citizen may aid in the execution of the warrant, according to the weil established principles of the common law.

§ 869. The officer may break open an outer or inner door or window of a house, or any part of the house, or any thing therein, to execute the warrant, if, after notice of his authority and purpose, he be refused admittance.

Declaratory of the common law rule. *See sec.* 173, *p.* 79.

§ 870. He may break open any onter or inner door or window of a house, for the purpose of liberating a person, who, having entered to aid him in the execution of the warrant, is detained therein, or when necessary for his own liberation.

Same as *sec.* 174, *p.* 80.

§ 871. The magistrate must insert a direction in the warrant, that it be served in the day time, unless the affidavits be positive that the property is on the person, or in the place to be searched; in which case, he may insert a direction, that it be served at any time of the day or night.

This section is substantially the same as 2 *R. S.* 3*d ed.* 831, *sec.* 31. In *Liv. Crim. Code,* 483, *Rule* 5, it is provided that a search warrant can only be issued in the day time. Exceptions to this rule may well exist, and they are provided for in this section.

§ 872. A search warrant must be executed, and returned to the magistrate by whom it was issued, if issued in the city and county of New-York, within five days after its date, and if in any other county, within ten days. After the expiration of those times respectively, the warrant, unless executed, is void.

A search warrant is always called for by some sudden exigency. This section seems proper, to prevent its execution at a time when the neeessity for it does not exist.

§ 873. When the officer takes property under the warrant, he must give a receipt for the property taken, (specifying it in detail,) to the person from whom it was taken by him, or in whose possession it was found, or, in the absence of any person, he must leave it in the place where he found the property.

Taken substantially from *Liv. Crim. Code*, 483, *Rule* 10.

§ 874. When the property is delivered to the magistrate, he must, if it was stolen or embezzled, dispose of it as provided in sections 755 to 757, both inclusive. If it were taken on a warrant issued on the grounds stated in the second and third subdivisions of section 862, he must retain it in his possession, subject to the order of the court to which he is required to return the proceedings before him, or of any other court in which the offence, in respect to which the property was taken, is triable.

§ 875. The officer must forthwith return the warrant to the magistrate, and deliver to him a written inventory of the property taken, made publicly, or in the presence of the person from whose possession it was taken and of the applicant for the warrant, if they be present; verified by the affidavit of the officer, and taken before the magistrate, to the following effect: "I, A. B., the officer by whom this warrant was executed, do swear that the above inventory contains a true and detailed account of all the property taken by me on the warrant."

§ 876. The magistrate must thereupon, if required, deliver a copy of the inventory to the person from whose possession the property was taken, and to the applicant for the warrant.

The last three sections are in conformity with *Liv. Crim. Code*, 482, *Rule* 9.

§ 877. If the grounds on which the warrant was issued be controverted, the magistrate must proceed to take testimony in relation thereto.

§ 878. The testimony given by each witness must be reduced to writing and authenticated in the manner prescribed in section 203.

The examination provided in the last two sections, is designed to enable the magistrate to determine the proper disposition of the property. It is but right, therefore, that it should be taken in such a form as to protect the rights of the parties. For the manner of taking the testimony prescribed in this section, see *sec.* 203, *p.* 95.

§ 879. If it appear that the property taken is not the same as that described in the warrant, or that there is no probable cause for believing the existence of the grounds on which the warrant was issued, the magistrate must cause it to be restored to the person from whom it was taken.

§ 880. The magistrate must annex together the depositions, the search warrant and return, and the inventory, and return them to the next court of sessions of the county, or city court, having power to inquire into the offence in respect to which the search warrant was issued, by the intervention of a grand jury, at or before its opening on the first day.

§ 881. A person, who, maliciously and without probable cause, procures a search warrant to be issued and executed, is guilty of a misdemeanor.

§ 882. A peace officer, who, in executing a search warrant, wilfully exceeds his authority, or exercises it with unnecessary severity, is guilty of a misdemeanor.

No greater invasion of the rights of the citizen can be conceived, than the malicious procurement or oppressive execution of a search warrant. The only remedy provided by the law, in this case, is a civil action. The Commissioners deem it just and proper to protect the rights of the citizen, by making the invasion of them in either of these respects a criminal offence.

§ 883. When a person charged with a felony, is supposed by the magistrate before whom he is brought, to have upon his person a dangerous weapon, or anv thing which may be used as evidence of the commission of the offence, the magistrate may direct him to be searched in his presence, and the weapon or other thing to be retained, subject to his order or the order of the court in which the defendant may be tried.

The principle of this section has been already explained in the note to *section* 862, *p.* 392, 393.

TITLE III.

OF THE OUTLAWRY OF PERSONS CONVICTED OF TREASON.

§ 884. When, upon a bench warrant issued for the apprehension of a person who has pleaded guilty, or against whom a verdict has been rendered, upon an indictment for treason, it is duly returned that the defendant cannot be found, the district attorney of the county may apply to the court in which the conviction was had, for judgment of outlawry.

Substantially the same as 2 *R. S.*, 3*d ed.*, 829, *sec.* 14.

§ 885. The application must be founded upon the return of the bench warrant, and upon proof, by affidavit, that the defendant has escaped, and on diligent search cannot be found within the county.

Substantially the same as 2 *R. S. 3d ed.* 829, *sec.* 15.

§ 886. The court, upon being satisfied that the defendant has escaped, and cannot, upon diligent search, be found in the county, must make an order that he appear on the first day of the next term, to receive judgment upon the conviction or be outlawed.

Substantially the same as 2 *R. S.*, *3d ed.*, 829, *sec.* 16.

§ 887. The order must be immediately published, once a week for six successive weeks, in a newspaper published in the county, and in the state paper. The expense of the publication is a county charge.

Substantially the same as 2 *R. S. 3d ed.* 829, *sec.* 17.

§ 888. If the defendant appear, judgment must be rendered against him upon the conviction. If he do not appear, the court upon proof of the due publication of the order, must render judgment that the defendant be outlawed, and that all his civil rights be forfeited.

Taken from 2 *R. S. 3d ed.* 829, *sec.* 15, 16.

§ 889. The defendant is thereupon deemed civilly dead, and forfeits to the people of this state during his lifetime, and no longer, all freehold estate in real property, of which he was seised in his own right, at the time of committing the treason, or at any time thereafter, and all his personal property.

Conformable to 2 *R. S.*, *3d ed.*, 829, *sec.* 20 ; and to 2 *R. S.*, *3d ed.*, 746, *sec.* 3.

§ 890. Upon a judgment of outlawry, the judgment roll must be made up, and filed with the clerk of the county in which the conviction was had, and docketed with the same effect as in a civil action. A transcript thereof may also be filed and docketed, with the like effect, in any other county.

Taken from 2 *R.* S. 3*d ed.* 829, *sec.* 21.

§ 891. The judgment roll consists of the several matters prescribed in section 550, except the fifth subdivision; to which must be annexed a certified copy of the order to appear for judgment, the affidavits proving its publication, and a certified copy of the judgment of outlawry.

§ 892. An appeal may be taken by the defendant, at any time, from a judgment of outlawry.

The last section is taken from 2 *R. S.* 3*d ed.* 830, *sec.* 22.

§ 893. The appeal may be taken in person or by counsel, in the same manner, and the proceedings thereon are the same, as upon an appeal from a judgment of conviction on an indictment.

§ 894. If the judgment be reversed, on appeal, the defendant is restored to his civil rights.

The last section is the same as 2 *R. S.* 3*d ed.* 830, *sec.* 23.

§ 895. Notwithstanding judgment of outlawry against the defendant, he may be arrested at any time thereafter, to receive judgment upon the conviction.

Same as 2 *R. S.* 3*d ed.* 830, *sec.* 22.

§ 896. No other proceeding for the outlawry of the defendant in a criminal action, can be had, than that provided in this title.

Taken from 2 *R. S. 3d ed.* 830, *sec.* 24.

TITLE IV.

OF PROCEEDINGS AGAINST FUGITIVES FROM JUSTICE.

CHAPTER I.

FUGITIVES FROM ANOTHER STATE OR TERRITORY, INTO THIS STATE.

§ 897. A person charged in any state or territory of the United States, with treason, felony, or other crime, who shall flee from justice and be found in this state, must on demand of the executive authority of the state or territory from which he fled, be delivered up by the governor of this state, to be removed to the state or territory having jurisdiction of the crime.

Declaratory of the duty imposed upon the governor, by *art.* 4, *sec.* 2, *subd.* 2, of the constitution of the United States.

§ 898. A magistrate may issue a warrant for the apprehension of a person so charged, who shall flee from justice and be found within this state.

Taken from 2 *R. S., 3d ed.*, 797, *sec.* 37.

§ 899. The proceedings for the arrest and commitment of the person charged, are in all respects similar to those provided in this code, for the arrest and commitment of a person charged with a public offence committed in this state; except, that an exemplified copy of an indictment found, or other judicial proceeding had against him, in the state or territory in which he is charged to have committed the offence, may be received as evidence before the magistrate.

Conformable to 2 *R. S., 3d ed*, 797, *sec.* 38.

§ 900. If, from the examination, it appear, that the person charged has committed the crime alleged, the magistrate, by warrant reciting the accusation, must commit him to the proper custody in his county, for a time specified in the warrant, which the magistrate deems reasonable, to enable the arrest of the fugitive under the warrant of the executive of this state, on the requisition of the executive authority of the state or territory in which he committed the offence, unless he give bail, as provided in the next section, or until he be legally discharged.

Conformable to 2 *R. S., 3d ed.*, 797, *sec.* 39.

§ 901. The magistrate may admit the person arrested, to bail, by an undertaking, with sufficient sureties and in such sum as he deems proper, for his appearance before him at a time specified in the undertaking, and for his surrender to be arrested upon the warrant of the governor of this state.

Taken from 2 *R. S.*, *3d ed.*, 797, *sec.* 40.

§ 902. Immediately upon the arrest of the person charged, the magistrate must give notice to the district attorney of the county, of the name of the person and the cause of his arrest.

Taken from 2 *R. S.*, *3d ed.*, 797, *sec.* 41.

§ 903. The district attorney must immediately thereafter, give notice to the executive authority of the state or territory, or to the prosecuting attorney or presiding judge of the criminal court of the city or county therein, having jurisdiction of the offence, to the end that a demand may be made for the arrest and surrender of the person charged.

Taken from 2 *R. S.*, *3d ed.*, 797, *sec* 41.

§ 904. The person arrested must be discharged from custody or bail, unless before the expiration of the time designated in the warrant or undertaking, he be arrested under the warrant of the governor of this state.

Taken from 2 *R. S.*, *3d ed.*, 797, *sec.* 42.

§ 905. The magistrate must return his proceedings to the next court of sessions of the county, which must thereupon inquire into the cause of the arrest and detention of the person charged; and if he be in custody, or the time for his arrest have not elapsed, it may discharge him from detention, or may order his undertaking of bail to be cancelled, or continue his detention for a longer time, or re-admit him to bail, to appear and surrender himself within a time specified in the undertaking.

Taken from 2 *R. S.*, 3*d ed.* 797, 798, *Sec.* 43.

CHAPTER II.

FUGITIVES FROM THIS STATE, INTO ANOTHER STATE OR TERRITORY.

This chapter is designed to regulate a very important branch of criminal practice. The power to demand a fugitive from justice, is one of the most delicate acts of sovereign authority, and should only be exercised in cases where the public welfare demands it. The cases in which its exercise is most frequently called for, though falling within the legal definition of public offences, are rather of a private than a public character; and it is well known, that the executive has always been in the habit of scrutinizing them with great jealousy. The Commissioners refer to cases of false pretences, to which, in a former part of this report, they have already alluded, as requiring greater vigilance on the part of the grand jury in their investigation, than is sometimes extended to them; see *p.* 116, 117; and a higher degree of evidence to sustain them, than that which is now required. See *sec.* 455, *and note, p.* 216. In cases of this description, the Commissioners believe that a large portion, if not a majority of the applications, for the exercise of this high prerogative on the part of the governor, are made, not directly by the public authorities, but by the private party on whose complaint the prosecution is instituted. They are informed, moreover, that it has been the practice of those who have filled the executive chair, in some, if not in all instances, of prosecutions for this offence, to require that the party, on whose application the requisition is granted, bear the expense of its execution. This practice has no doubt proceeded upon the principle, that these prosecutions are so far of a private character, as to justify the executive in imposing this condition, with a view to save the public treasury from an unnecessary burden.

Whatever may be the reason for it, the Commissioners are constrained to believe that it should not exist. Its tendency is, to convert the officer with whom the requisition is intrusted, rather into a private than a public agent; and cases are within the knowledge of the Commissioners, which fully justify them in recommending a system of regulation by which this practice shall be discontinued. It has frequently happened, that the person to whom the requisition has been delivered has gone with it to a remote state, and on the strength of its possession, has negociated for a settlement of the debt, out of the fraudulent contraction of which it arose, and holding it as a rod over the party, has wrung from his fears a compromise of the prosecution. Nor is this to be wondered at. Prosecutions of this nature seldom spring from the mere love of justice, but ordinarily are rather prompted by a spirit of revenge, or what is perhaps more frequently the case, of cupidity. The officer, therefore, who takes the requisition, at the expense of a private party, will naturally act for the promotion of the interests of his employer, rather than from the mere desire to enforce, in his public relation, the process of the law. He will do this, from no motive corrupt in itself perhaps, but because his own interests are equally involved in the success of a compromise, with those of his employer.

The Commissioners do not propose to restrict in any degree, the discretion of the executive or the manner of its exercise, in this or any other criminal case. But, believing as they do, that the highest considerations of policy require the exclusion of every motive of private interest, in the execution of this, more than in that of any other legal process, they propose by this chapter, that where a requisition is granted, it shall be executed, as it is presumed to be issued, for the public good alone, and that the public treasury shall therefore answer for its execution; and that the officer to whom it is intrusted, shall be prohibited, under the penalty of a misdemeanor, from receiving any compensation, fee or reward, for any act or service in respect to it.

§ 906. When the governor shall demand from the executive authority of a state or territory of the United States, or of a foreign government, the surrender to the authorities of this state, of a fugitive from justice, the accounts of the persons employed by him for that purpose, must be paid out of the state treasury.

§ 907. No compensation, fee, or reward of any kind, can be paid to, or received by a public officer of this state, for a service rendered or expense incurred, in procuring from the governor the demand mentioned in the last section, or the surrender of the fugitive, or for conveying him to this state, or detaining him therein.

§ 908. A violation of the last section is a misdemeanor.

TITLE V.

OF PROCEEDINGS RESPECTING PERSONS HELD TO LABOR OR SERVICE, IN A STATE OR TERRITORY OF THE UNITED STATES, AND ESCAPING INTO THIS STATE.

The remark which has been made, p. 269, 270, in respect to the infliction of capital punishment, is equally applicable to the subject embraced in this chapter. The plan of this code embraces the whole system of procedure in special proceedings of a criminal nature, as well as in criminal actions. This subject falls within the former class, and must therefore be embraced in the code, in order to render it complete. In presenting the sections which follow, the Commissioners have n.t intended to express any opinion of their own, as to whether the existing statutes should be carried as far or farther than they now extend. The policy of this state in respect to this subject, has been settled by the legislature; and with the exception of the alteration of a few immaterial details, which are explained in the notes to the sections themselves, and of the provisions in respect to jury trial, and the writ of *homine replegiando*, (which, according to the decision of the supreme court of the United States, in *Prigg v. The Commonwealth of Pennsylvania*, 16 Peters, 539—674, are unconstitutional,) they have pursued the existing statutes.

§ 909. When a person, legally held to labor or service in a state or territory of the United States, escapes into this state, the person entitled to his services, or his agent duly authorised, may apply for a warrant to arrest the fugitive,

1. To the supreme court at a special term:

2. To a judge of the supreme court:

3. To a judge of the superior court, or court of common pleas of the city of New York:

4. To a county judge:

5. To the recorder of a city: or

6. To a city judge.

This section differs in two respects from the corresponding provision of 2 *R. S.*, 3*d ed.*, 653, 654, *sec.* 6.

First:—That provision requires the application to be made to a court or officer authorized to issue writs of *habeas corpus*, as prescribed by 2 *R. S.*, 3*d ed.*, 660, *sec.* 37. In accordance with the general plan of the code, the enumeration of the court and officers to whom the application may be made, is deemed more convenient. This enumeration contains the same courts and class of officers, as in the revised statutes, except in conforming them to the constitution and the provisions of the code.

Second:—The provision of the revised statutes above referred to, requires the issuing of a *habeas corpus*. The section under consideration substitutes a warrant, as being in accordance with the other provisions of the code on similar subjects, but invests it with the same authority and incidents as now attach, in this respect, to a *habeas corpus*.

§ 910. No other officer of this state, than those mentioned in the last section, can issue the warrant: and any other officer who does so, is guilty of a misdemeamor, and forfeits five hundred dollars to the party aggrieved, recoverable in a civil action.

This section is taken from 2 *R. S., 3d ed.*, 658, *sec.* 29. The reasons for it cannot be better expressed, than by quoting the language of the revisers, in introducing the corresponding provision in the revised statutes. *Revisers' Notes*, 3 *R. S., 2d ed.*, 783. "No subject," say they, "has given rise to so much irritation in our neighboring states, or is so likely to occasion difficulty in our own, as the arrest and carrying away of fugitives from service. The act of congress vests the very delicate power of determining upon the right of a human being to personal liberty, in any magistrate of a county, city or town corporate, wherein a seizure shall be made." That congress have no right to compel the state courts or magistrates to execute the laws of the Union, is sufficienly established. (See, on this subject, the case of *Prigg v. the Commonwealth of Pennsylvania*, 16 Peters, 539-674.)

"The case presented in the foregoing sections, is one where the legal knowledge, firmness and independence of our highest judicial officers, seem required, as well to protect the defenceless, as to insure confidence in the decision, and give effect to the claim. The provisions here offered, conform substantially to the act of congress referred to, but vary the details, so as to afford the utmost opportunity for a fair investigation, and to check any abuse of such a claim."

§ 911. The person alleged to be entitled to the service of the person claimed as a fugitive, is designated in this title as the claimant, and the alleged fugitive as the defendant.

§ 912. The application must be founded on proof, by affidavit, setting forth, minutely and particularly, the grounds of the claim to the services of the fugitive, the time of his escape, and where he then is.

Taken from 2 *R. S. 3d ed.* 654, *sec.* 7.

§ 913. If the court or magistrate be thereupon satisfied of the existence of the alleged facts, he must issue a warrant to the sheriff of the county where the defendant is, commanding him to take the defendant, and bring him before the court or magistrate issuing the warrant, at a specified time, to answer the claim.

Taken from 2 *R. S. 3d ed.* 653, 654, *sec.* 6.

§ 914. The sheriff must thereupon execute the warrant, by arresting the defendant and taking him according to its command, before the court or magistrate by whom it was issued.

Taken from 2 *R. S. 3d ed.* 654, *sec.* 8.

§ 915. The court or magistrate must proceed to hear the allegations and proofs of the parties; and must, if required, allow a reasonable time to either party, to produce further necessary proof.

Taken from 2 *R. S. 3d ed.* 654, *sec.* 9.

§ 916. If time be allowed, as provided in the last section, the court or magistrate must commit the defendant to the custody of the sheriff of the county, for safe keeping, or may discharge him from actual custody, upon his giving a written undertaking, executed by sufficient sureties, to the effect that the defendant will appear before the court or magistrate, at a specified time and place, to abide the decision of the claim, or that the sureties will pay to the claimant, the sum specified in the undertaking, and which must be an amount deemed sufficient by the court or magistrate.

Taken from 2 *R. S. 3d ed.* 654, *sec.* 9.

§ 917. If, upon the hearing of the parties, the court or magistrate be satisfied that the claim is not sustained, the defendant must be discharged; and the claimant thereupon forfeits to the defendant one hundred dollars, recoverable in a civil action. The defendant may also recover in the same action, his costs and expenses in resisting the claim, and the damages he may have sustained.

§ 918. If the claim be sustained, the court or magistrate must grant to the claimant a certificate, stating that it satisfactorily appears that the defendant, (describing him by his name, age, size, and personal appearance,) owes service or labor to the claimant, (stating his name and place of residence,) and allowing the claimant, or his agent named in the certificate, to take the defendant, and convey him to the place of residence of the claimant.

§ 919. The defendant must thereupon be delivered to the claimant, or to his agent named in the certificate, who may remove him through and out of this state, on the ordinary route, to the place of residence of the claimant.

The last three sections are taken substantially from the original revised statutes, 2 *R. S.*, *1st ed.* 560, 561, *sec.* 10–

12. They were repealed by an act passed in 1840, giving the defendant the right to a trial by jury; 2 *R. S.* 3*d ed.* 654—657, *sec.* 10—27; but which, according to the case of *Prigg v. The Commonwealth of Pennsylvania,* 16 Peters, 539—674, is unconstitutional, See also, *Jack v. Martin,* 12 Wend. 314; *S. C., in the court of errors,* 14 Wend. 507.

§ 920. No person, claiming that he or another is entitled to the services of a person alleged to be held to labor or service in a state or territory of the United States, can take or remove, or do any act towards removing, from this state, the person whose service or labor is soclaimed, except as authorized by this title.

T.ken from 2 *R. S.,* 3*d ed.* 658, *sec.* 32.

§ 921. A violation of the last section is a felony, and subjects the person guilty thereof, to imprisonment in the state prison, not exceeding ten years, and to a penalty of five hundred dollars, recoverable in a civil action, by the party aggrieved.

Taken from 2 *R. S.,* 3*d ed.* 657, *sec.* 26.

§ 922. No judge or other officer of this state can grant or issue a certificate, or other process, for the removal from this state, of a person claimed, as held to labor or service in a state or territory of the United States, otherwise than in pursuance of the provisions of this title.

Taken from 2 *R. S.,* 3*d ed.* 657, *sec.* 25.

§ 923. A violation of the last section is a misdemeanor.

Taken from 2 *R. S.*, 3*d ed.* 657, *sec.* 25.

TITLE VI.

OF PROCEEDINGS RESPECTING BASTARDS.

CHAPTER I. Proceedings before magistrates.
II. Appeals from the orders of magistrates.
III. Enforcement of the undertaking for the support of the bastard or its mother, or for appearance on appeal.

The provisions of this title, contained in the three chapters above enumerated, are in substantial conformity with the corresponding provisions of the Revised Statutes, referred to in the notes to the several sections. While those provisions are much condensed, their spirit has been preserved. The Commissioners have, however, omitted the portions of the Revised Statutes, relating to the duties of superintendents and overseers of the poor, and alms-house officers, as belonging rather to the political than the judicial regulations on the subject. In this respect, as in every other embraced in this code, they have confined themselves to matters strictly of a judicial nature.

CHAPTER I.

PROCEEDINGS BEFORE MAGISTRATES, RESPECTING BASTARDS.

SECTION 924. Definition of a bastard.
925. Who are liable for its support.
926. When bastard, chargeable to the public, is born or likely to be born, application to be made to a justice of the peace or police justice, to inquire into the facts.
927. Examination by the magistrate, and warrant against the father.
928. Justice designated as a magistrate, and person proceeded against as defendant.
929. Warrant, when to be served in another county.
930. Magistrate in another county, may take undertaking for support of bastard and mother, or for appearance of defendant at the sessions.
931. On giving undertaking, defendant to be discharged.

§ 924. A bastard is a child who is begotten and born,

1. Out of lawful matrimony:

2. While the husband of its mother was separate from her, for a whole year previous to its birth: or

3. During the separation of its mother from her husband, pursuant to a judgment of a competent court.

The same in substance as 1 *R. S.*, *3d ed.* 822, *sec.* 1.

§ 925. The father and mother of a bastard are liable for its support. In case of their neglect or inability, it must be supported by the county, city or town in which it is born, as provided by special statutes.

The same in substance as 1 *R. S.*, *3d ed.* 822, *sec.* 2.

§ 926. If a woman be delivered of a bastard, or be pregnant of a child likely to be born such, and which is chargeable to a county, city or town, a superintendent of the poor of the county, or an overseer of the poor or other officer of the almshouse of the town or city where the woman is, must apply to a justice of the peace or police justice in the county, to inquire into the facts of the case.

The same in substance as 1 *R. S.*, *3d ed.* 823, *sec.* 5.

§ 927. The magistrate must, by the examination of the woman on oath, and any other testimony which may be offered, ascertain the father of the bastard, and must issue his warrant, directed to a peace officer of the county, commanding him, without delay, to apprehend the father and bring him before the justice, for the purpose of having an adjudication as to the filiation of the bastard.

The same in substance as 1 *R. S.*, *3d ed.* 823, *sec.* 6.

§ 928. An officer issuing a warrant or making an examination, as provided in this title, is designated as a magistrate, and the person against whom the warrant is issued, as the defendant.

§ 929. If the defendant reside in another county than that in which the warrant issued, the magistrate must, by an endorsement thereon, direct the sum in which the defendant shall give security, and the officer must deliver the warrant to a justice of the peace or police justice in the city or town in which the defendant resides or is found. The magistrate to whom it is presented, on proof, under oath, of the signature of the magistrate who issued the warrant, must then endorse a direction thereon, that it be served in the county in which he resides, and the defendant may be arrested in that county accordingly. Upon this proof, the magistrate endorsing the warrant is exempted from liability to a civil or criminal action, though it afterwards appear that the warrant was illegally or improperly issued.

The first sentence of this section is the same in substance as 1 *R. S.*, 3*d ed.* 823, *sec.* 7; the second is taken from 2 *R. S.*, 3*d ed.*, 835, *sec*, 73, and is conformable in its language to *sec.* 157, of this code, *p.* 73, 74.

§ 930. When the defendant is arrested in another county, he must be taken before the magistrate who endorsed the warrant, or before another magistrate of the same city or county, who may take from the defendant an undertaking, with sufficient sureties, to the effect:

1. That he will indemnify the county, and town or city, where the bastard was or is likely to be born, and every other county, town or city, against any expense for the support of the bastard, or of its mother during her confinement and recovery, and to pay the costs of arresting the defendant, and of any order of filiation that may be made, or that the sureties will pay the sum endorsed on the warrant; or,

2. That the defendant will appear and answer the charge, at the next court of sessions of the county where the warrant was issued, and obey its order thereon.

The same in substance as 1 *R. S., 3d ed.*, 823, *sec.* 8.

§ 931. When either of the undertakings mentioned in the last section is given, the magistrate must discharge the defendant, and must endorse a certificate of the discharge upon the warrant. He must also deliver the warrant, with the undertaking, to the officer, who must return it to the magistrate granting the warrant, by whom the same proceedings must be had, as if he had taken the undertaking.

The same in substance as 1 *R. S., 3d ed.*, 824, *sec.* 9.

§ 932. If the defendant do not give security, as provided in section 930, the officer must take him before the magistrate who issued the warrant.

The same in substance as 1 *R. S., 3d ed.* 824, *sec.* 10.

§ 933. If, however, the magistrate who issued the warrant, be absent or unable to act, the defendant must be taken before the nearest or most accessible magistrate in the same county. The officer must, at the same time, deliver to the magistrate, the warrant with his return endorsed and subscribed by him.

Taken from 2 *R. S., 3d ed.* 835, *sec.* 74; and conformable in its language, to *sec.* 162, of this code, *p.* 75.

§ 934. The magistrate before whom the defendant is brought, as provided in the last two sections, must immediately associate with himself, another justice of the peace or police justice in the same county or city; and the two magistrates thus associated, must inquire into the charge, and must examine on oath, the woman who is the mother of or pregnant with the bastard in the presence of the defendant, in respect to the charge, and hear any testimony which may be offered in relation thereto.

Taken from 1 *R. S.*, 3*d ed.* 824, *sec.* 11.

§ 935. The magistrates may, on the application of the defendant, for good cause, adjourn the examination, not exceeding thirty days, upon the defendant giving an undertaking, with two sufficient sureties, to the effect that he will appear before the magistrates at the time appointed, or that the sureties will pay the sum mentioned therein, which must be fixed by the magistrates, and which must be a full indemnity for the expense of supporting the bastard and its mother, as provided in section 937.

Taken from 1 *R. S.*, 3*d ed.* 824, *sec.* 12.

§ 936. Upon the hearing, the magistrates must determine who is the father of the bastard, and must proceed as follows:

1. If they determine that the defendant is not the father of the bastard, he must be forthwith discharged:

2. If they determine that he is the father, they must make an order of filiation, specifying therein the sum to be paid weekly or otherwise, by the defendant, for the support of the bastard: and if the mother be indigent, the sum to be paid by the defendant for her support, during her confinement and recovery:

3. They must certify the reasonable costs of arresting the defendant, and of the order of filiation:

4. They must reduce their proceedings to writing, and subscribe them.

Taken from 1 *R. S.*, 3*d ed.*, 824, 825, *sec.* 13.

§ 937. If the defendant be adjudged to be the father, he must immediately pay the amount certified for the costs of the arrest and of the order of filiation, and enter into an undertaking, with sufficient sureties approved by the magistrates, to the effect,

1. That he will pay weekly or otherwise, as may have been ordered, the sum directed for the support of the child, and of the mother during her confinement and recovery, or which may be ordered by the court of sessions of the county; and that he will indemnify the county, and town or city, where the bastard was or may be born, (as the case may be,) and every other county, town or city, which may have been or may be

put to expense for the support of the bastard, or of its mother during her confinement and recovery, against those expenses, or that the sureties will do so, not exceeding the sum mentioned in the undertaking, and which must be fixed by the magistrates: or,

2. That he will appear at the next court of sessions of the county, to answer the charge and obey its order thereon, or that the sureties will pay a sum equal to a full indemnity for supporting the bastard and its mother, as provided in the first subdivision of section 930.

Taken from 1 *R S.*, 3*d ed.* 825, *sec.* 14

§ 938. Upon a compliance with the provisions of the last section, the magistrates must discharge the defendant; but otherwise, they or either of them must, by warrant, commit him to the county jail, or in the city of New-York, to the city prison of that city, until he be discharged by the court of sessions of the county, or deliver an undertaking, as prescribed by the last section.

Taken from 1 *R. S.*, 3*d ed.*, 825, *sec.* 15.

§ 939. During the examination, and until the defendant is discharged by the magistrates, he must remain in custody of the officer who arrested him, unless an undertaking have been given for his appearance, as provided in sections 930 and 937; and when committed to prison, he must be actually confined therein.

Taken from 1 *R. S.*, 3*d ed.*, 825, *sec.* 17.

§ 940. When security taken out of the county, for the appearance of the defendant at the court of sessions, as provided in section 930, is returned to the magistrate who issued the warrant, he must associate with himself another magistrate of the same county, and the magistrates thus associated must proceed as provided in sections 934 and 936, both inclusive.

Taken from 1 *R. S.*, *3d ed.*, 826, *sec.* 18.

§ 941. The examination may be had, and the order of filiation made, in the absence of the defendant, unless, before the order is made, he require of the magistrate issuing the warrant, that the examination be had in his presence, in which case the examination must be had, as if the defendant had originally appeared.

Taken from 1 *R. S.*, *3d ed.*, 826, *sec.* 19.

§ 942. In making an examination authorised by this chapter, the magistrate issuing the warrant, or the magistrates making the examination, may compel the mother of a bastard, chargeable to a county, city or town, or a woman pregnant of a child likely to be born such, to disclose the name of the father of the bastard; or if she refuse to do so, may, by a warrant setting forth the cause thereof, at the expiration of one month from her delivery, if sufficiently recovered, commit her to the county jail, or in the city of New-York, to the city prison of that city, until she disclose the name of the father.

Taken from 1 *R. S.*, *3d ed.*, 826, *sec.* 20.

§ 943. If the mother of a bastard, chargeable or likely to become chargeable, as provided in section 926, be possessed of property in her own right, any two magistrates of the county or city where she is, on the application of any of the officers mentioned in that section, must examine into the matter, and may make an order charging the mother with the payment of money weekly, or otherwise, for the support of the bastard.

Taken from 1 *R. S.*, *3d ed.*, 826, *sec.* 21.

§ 944. If, after service of the order upon the mother, she do not comply therewith, she must be committed to the county jail, or in the city of New-York, to the city prison of that city, until she comply, or enter into an undertaking, with sufficient sureties approved by the magistrates, to the effect that she will appear at the next court of sessions of the county, to answer the matters stated in the order, and obey its order thereon, or that the sureties will pay the sum mentioned in the undertaking, and which must be fixed by the magistrates.

Taken from 1 *R. S.*, *3d ed.*, 826, *sec.* 22.

§ 945. The magistrates, who may have made an order against the father or mother of a bastard, as provided in sections 936 and 943, may, from time to time, for good cause, reduce the amount therein directed to be paid, and upon the application of any of the officers mentioned in section 926, the court of sessions of the county, upon ten days notice to those officers, or to the father and mother of the bastard, may reduce or increase the amount so directed to be paid.

Taken from 1 *R. S.*, *3d ed.*, 826, *sec.* 23.

§ 946. If the father or mother of a bastard, or of a child likely to be born such, abscond from their place of residence, leaving the bastard chargeable or likely to become chargeable to the public, a superintendent of the poor of the county, or an overseer of the poor, or other officer of the alms-house of the town or city where the bastard was born, or is likely to be born, may apply to any two magistrates of the city or county where any property, real or personal, of the father or mother may be, for authority to take the same. Upon due proof of the facts on oath, to the satisfaction of the magistrates, they must issue their warrant, and proceed thereon, in the manner provided in title 9, of this part, in relation to persons absconding and leaving their children chargeable to the public.

Taken from 1 *R. S.*, *3d ed*, 831, 832, *sec.* 52.

CHAPTER II.

APPEALS FROM THE ORDERS OF MAGISTRATES, RESPECTING BASTARDS.

§ 947. A person deeming himself aggrieved by the order of two magistrates, made pursuant to the last chapter, may appeal therefrom to the next court of sessions of the county; except that a person who has executed an undertaking to obey an order of filiation, and indemnify the public, as provided in section 937, cannot appeal from any other part of the order mentioned in section 936, than that which fixes the weekly or other allowance to be paid.

Taken from 1 *R. S.*, *3d ed.*, 827, *sec.* 24.

§ 948. When the father or mother of the bastard has entered into an undertaking for appearance at the next court of sessions of the county, as provided in sections 937 and 944, it is an appeal from the order of filiation or maintenance; and no other notice thereof is necessary. In any other case, the appeal is taken, by a written notice of at least ten days before the court, to the magistrates who made the order, and to the party affected thereby, or to the officer at whose instance it was obtained.

Taken from 1 *R. S.*, *3d ed.* 827, *sec.* 24.

The next section in the revised statutes, *Ibid.* sec. 25, is omitted. It is as follows: " No justice of the peace, who shall have assisted in any judgment, or in making any order appealed from, shall sit in the court of general sessions, upon the hearing of any appeal made from such judgment or order." This provision is inserted in the part of the code of civil procedure, which relates to the courts and judicial officers, and need not be repeated here.

§ 949. The magistrates receiving an undertaking for appearance at the court of sessions, must transmit it to the court, before its opening, with a certified copy of the order appealed from.

Taken from 1 *R. S.*, *3d. ed.*, 827, *sec.* 26.

§ 950. The court must immediately, or at any other time it may appoint, proceed to hear the allegations and proofs of the parties; and the party in whose favor the order was made, must support it by evidence. If the mother of the bastard be dead or insane, her testimony on the examination before the magistrates, is receivable in evidence:

Taken from 1 *R. S.*, *3d ed.*, 827, *sec.* 28.

§ 951. The court may affirm or vacate an order of filiation or maintenance, or may reduce or increase the sum ordered to be paid for the support of the bastard or its mother; and, disregarding defects in form in the order, must amend it according to the fact. If, when the appeal is heard, the bastard be not born, the court may adjourn the hearing, until it be born, and in that case, must take an undertaking from the party appealing, for his appearance, in such sum and with such sureties as the court may deem sufficient.

Taken from 1 *R. S.*, *3d ed.*, 827, 828, *sec.* 29.

§ 952. If the woman alleged to be pregnant, be not so, or be married before her delivery, or the child be not born alive, the defendant must be discharged from custody, or from the obligation of his undertaking, either by the court or magistrates, upon that fact being made to appear.

Taken from 1 *R. S.*, *3d ed.*, 828, *sec.* 30.

§ 953. If, upon the hearing of the appeal, the court of sessions affirm an order of filiation or maintenance, it must require the defendant to enter into an undertaking, with sufficient sureties, approved by the court, to the effect that he will pay, weekly or otherwise, according to the order as made by the magistrate or modified by the court, the sum directed for the support of the bastard, and of the mother during her confinement and recovery; and that he will indemnify the county, and town or city where the bastard was or may be born, (as the case may be,) and every other county, town or city, which may have been put to expense for the support of the child, or of its mother during her confinement and recovery, against those expenses, or that the sureties will do so, not exceeding the sum mentioned in the undertaking, and which must be fixed by the court.

Taken from 2 *R. S.*, *3d. ed.*, 828, *sec.* 31.

§ 954. If, on judgment of affirmance, the defendant do not enter into an undertaking, as provided in the last section, he must be committed to the county jail, or in the city of New-York, to the city prison of that city, until he do so, or be discharged by the court.

Taken from 1 *R S.*, *3d ed.*, 828, *sec.* 32.

§ 955. The undertaking for the appearance of the defendant, at the court of sessions, upon an appeal, is forfeited, by his neglect to appear, or to give the undertaking mentioned in the last two sections unless he be discharged by the court.

Taken from 1 *R. S.* *3d. ed.* 828, *sec.* 33.

§ 956. When the mother of a bastard is bound to appear at the court of sessions, or is committed as provided in section 944, the court must proceed in respect to the matter, in the same manner as upon an appeal.

Taken from 1 *R, S. 3d ed.*, 828, 829, *sec.* 34.

§ 957. If the court be satisfied that the mother has property in her own right, sufficient to enable her to support the bastard or contribute to its support, it must confirm the order mentioned in section 943, or may vary the sum ordered to be paid weekly or otherwise; or if not, it must discharge her from custody or from the obligation of her undertaking.

Taken from 1 *R. S., 3d ed.*, 829, *sec.* 35.

§ 958. If the court affirm or modify the order, as provided in the last section, it must require the defendant to enter into an undertaking, with sufficient sureties approved by the court, to the effect that she will pay, weekly or otherwise, according to the order, as made by the magistrates or modified by the court, the sum directed for the support of the bastard, or that the sureties will do so, not exceeding the sum mentioned in the undertaking, and which must be fixed by the court. If the undertaking be not given, she must be committed in the manner provided in section 954.

Taken from 1 *R. S., 3d ed.*, 829, *sec.* 36.

§ 959. The court must award costs to the party in whose favor an appeal is determined. When awarded against county superintendents, or overseers of the poor of a town, not liable for the support of its own poor, they must be paid by the county treasurer, on delivering to him a certified copy of the order and of the taxed costs, and must be charged by him to the town in the same county, liable to support the bastard, or if there be none, to the county. In the city of New-York, when costs are awarded upon an appeal, to the person charged as the father or mother of the bastard, they must, upon the production of similar vouchers, be paid by the comptroller of that city, and charged to the appropriation made to the governors of the alms-house thereof.

Taken from 1 *R. S.*, *3d ed.*, 829, *sec.* 37.

§ 960. In other cases, the payment of the costs may be enforced by the court, as in a civil action. If the party against whom they are awarded, reside out of the jurisdiction of the court, an action may be brought on the order, by the party entitled to the costs, in which the production of a certified copy of the order and of the taxed costs, is conclusive evidence.

Taken from 1 *R. S.*, *3d ed.*, 829, *sec.* 38.

§ 961. If the court vacate an order of filiation, for any other cause than upon the merits, it must proceed, and may make an original order of filiation, in the manner prescribed in the second subdivision of section 936, or bind the person charged, in an undertaking, in a sum and with sureties approved by the court, to appear at the next court of sessions.

Taken from 1 *R. S., 3d ed.*, 829, *sec.* 39.

§ 962. If the order be vacated for any other cause than on the merits, and the person charged be bound as provided in the last section, the same proceedings may be had by the magistrate, for the apprehension of the defendant, and for making an order of filiation, and for the commitment of the defendant for not giving an undertaking, as are authorised in the first instance. And the same proceedings must be subsequently had, in all respects.

Taken from 1 *R. S., 3d ed.*, 829, *sec.* 40.

§ 963. When a person is committed to prison, charged as the father of a bastard, or of a child likely to be born a bastard, and when the mother of a bastard is so committed, for not giving an undertaking to support the bastard, or to indemnify the public, the court must inquire, from time to time, into the circumstances and ability of the father or mother, to support the bastard and to procure security therefor.

Taken from 1 *R. S., 3d ed.*, 830, *sec.* 41.

§ 964. If the court be at any time satisfied, that the father or mother is wholly unable to support the bastard, or to contribute to its support, or to procure security therefor, it may, in its discretion, order the father or mother to be discharged from imprisonment.

Taken from 1 *R. S.*, 3*d ed.* 830, *sec.* 42.

§ 965. Before granting the order, the court must be satisfied, that reasonable notice has been given to the overseers of the poor, or to the county superintendents, or chief officers of the almshouse, at whose instance the party was committed, of the intention to apply for a discharge, and must hear the allegations and proofs of the superintendents, overseers or officers, and may examine the party applying on oath respecting the subject of the application.

Taken from 1 *R. S.*, 3*d ed.* 830, *sec* 43.

§ 966. A person committed, as provided in the last section, cannot be discharged from imprisonment, except by the court of sessions of the county.

Taken from 1 *R. S.* 3*d ed.* 830, *sec.* 44.

CHAPTER III.

ENFORCEMENT OF THE UNDERTAKING FOR THE SUPPORT OF THE BASTARD OR ITS MOTHER, OR FOR APPEARANCE ON APPEAL.

§ 967. If an undertaking for the appearance at the court of sessions, of a person charged as the father or mother of a bastard, be forfeited, the court may order it to be prosecuted; and the sum mentioned therein may be recovered, and when collected, must, except in the city of New-York, be paid to the county treasurer, and by him credited to the town in the same county, liable to the support of the bastard, or if there be none, to the county. In the city of New-York, the court must order the undertaking to be prosecuted by the governors of the almshouse, and when collected, it must be paid into the city treasury. In every other county, it must be prosecuted by the district attorney.

Taken from 1 *R. S.*, *3d. ed.*, 830, *sec.* 46; except the provision as to the city of New-York, which is new.

§ 968. When an undertaking to obey an order, in relation to the support of a bastard, or of a child likely to be born a bastard, or of its mother, is forfeited, it may be prosecuted in the name of the county superintendents of the county, or the overseers of the poor of the town, which was liable for the support of the bastard, or which may have incurred any expense in the support of the bastard, or of its mother, during her confinement and recovery; or in the city of New-York, in the name of the corporation of that city.

Taken from 1 *R. S.*, 3*d ed.* 830, *sec.* 47.

§ 969. In the action mentioned in the last section, it is not necessary to prove the actual payment of money by a county superintendent, overseer of the poor, officer of an almshouse, or other person; but the neglect to pay a sum ordered to be paid by competent authority, for the support of the bastard, or of its mother, is a breach of the undertaking, and the measure of the damages is the sum ordered to be paid, and which was withheld at the time of the commencement of the action, with interest thereon.

Taken from 1 *R. S.*, 3*d ed.* 831, *sec.* 48.

§ 970. For a breach of the undertaking, after the recovery of damages or the commencement of an action, another action may, in the same manner, be brought. The money collected upon the undertaking, must be paid, and credited, in the manner provided in section 967.

Taken from 1 *R. S.*, 3*d ed.* 831, *sec.* 49.

§ 971. If, in the action, costs be awarded against the plaintiffs, they may be recovered, as follows:

1. If against the corporation of the city of New-York, in the same manner as in any other action:

2. If against county superintendents or overseers of the poor, they must, upon the delivery of a transcript of the judgment, be paid by the county treasurer, and by him charged to the town in the same county, liable for the support of the bastard, or if there be none, to the county.

This section is substituted for 1 *R. S.*, *3d ed.* 831, *sec.* 50; but does not depart from the spirit of the provision there contained.

§ 972. An action may be maintained by the parties authorized by section 968, upon an order made by two magistrates, or by a court of sessions, for the payment of a sum weekly or otherwise, for the support of the bastard or its mother, notwithstanding an undertaking may have been given to comply with the order; and in case of the death of the person against whom the order was made, an action may be maintained thereon against his executors or administrators. But when an undertaking is given to appear at the next court of sessions, no action can be brought on the order until it is affirmed by the court.

Taken from 1 *R. S.*, *3d. ed.* 831, *sec.* 51.

TITLE VII.

OF PROCEEDINGS RESPECTING VAGRANTS.

§ 973. The following persons are vagrants:

1. A person who, not having visible means to maintain himself, lives without employment:

2. A person who, being an habitual drunkard, abandons, neglects, or refuses to aid in the support of his family:

3. A person who has contracted an infectious or other disease, in the practice of drunkenness or debauchery, requiring charitable aid to restore him to health:

4. A common prostitute, who has no lawful employment, whereby to maintain herself:

5. A person wandering abroad and begging, or who goes about from door to door, or places himself in the streets, highways, passages, or other public places, to beg or receive alms:

6. A person wandering abroad and lodging in taverns, groceries, ale-houses, watch or station-houses, out-houses, market-places, sheds, stables, barns or uninhabited buildings, or in the open air, and not giving a good account of himself:

7. A person, who, having his face painted, discolored, covered or concealed, or being otherwise disguised, in a manner calculated to prevent his being identified, appears in a road or public highway, or in a field, lot, wood or enclosure.

This section is taken substantially, with the exception of the seventh subdivision, from 1 *R. S. 3d ed.*, 802, *sec.* 1, and from the act specially applicable to the city of New-York, *Laws of* 1833, *p* 9, *ch.* 11, *sec.* 1. Upon a comparison of the latter act with the Revised Statutes, it will be found to be more full, but not materially variant in principle. They have been blended, in the section under consideration, because there is no good reason why a definition applicable to one part of the state, should not equally extend to all.

The seventh subdivision is taken from the act to prevent persons from appearing disguised and armed, passed in 1845, and which is transcribed in 1 *R. S.*, 3*d ed.*, 803, *sec.* 5.

§ 974. A peace officer must, when required by any person, carry a vagrant before a justice of the peace or police justice of the same city, village or town, or before the mayor, recorder, or city judge of the same city, for the purpose of examination.

Taken from 1 *R. S.* 3*d ed.*, 802, *sec.* 2; and *Laws of* 1833, *p.* 9, *ch.* 11, *sec.* 2.

§ 975. If the magistrate be satisfied, from the confession of the person so brought before him, or by competent testimony, that he is a vagrant, he must convict him, and must make and sign, with his name of office, a certificate in substantially the following form:

"I certify that A. B., having been brought before me, charged with being a vagrant, I have duly examined the charge, and that upon his own confession in my presence, [or 'upon the testimony of C. D.,' &c., naming the witnesses,] by which it appears that he is a person [pursuing the description contained in the subdivision of section 973, which is appropriate to the case,] I have adjudged that he is a vagrant.

"Dated at the *town* [or city] of , the day of , 1850.

"E. F.,

"Justice of the peace of the town of ," [or as the case may be.]

The form of convictions in cases of vagrancy, has given rise to more discussion, and has led to greater embarrassments than almost any other proceeding of a criminal nature. Being summarily reviewable on *habeas corpus*, and it being well established, that every fact necessary to give the magistrate jurisdiction, as well as to show that it has been exercised in due form, and that nothing can be intended in its support, it is of daily occurrence, that discharges are granted for this cause. The cases in which a sufficient compliance with the requirements of the statute is had, are very rare; and its scarcely going too far, to say, that they constitute a small proportion of the cases in which there is a conviction. A convenient form is therefore given, embodying all that is necessary, and an adherence to which will save great confusion and difficulty.

§ 976. The magistrate must immediately cause the certificate, which constitutes the record of conviction, to be filed in the office of the clerk of the county, and must by a warrant, signed by him with his name of office, commit the vagrant, if not a notorious offender, and a proper object for such relief, to the county poor-house if there be one, or to the alms-house or poor-house of the city, village or town, for not exceeding six months, at hard labor, or if the vagrant be an improper person to be so committed, he must be committed for a like term, to the county jail, or in the city of New-York, to the city prison or penitentiary of that city.

Taken substantially from 1 *R. S.*, *3d ed.*, 802, *sec.* 3, and *Laws of* 1833, *p.* 9, 10, *sec.* 3.

§ 977. If a child be found begging for alms, or soliciting charity from door to door, or in a street, highway, or public place in a city, village or town, a justice of the peace or police justice, on complaint and proof thereof, must commit the child to the county poor-house or other place provided for the support of the poor, to be kept, employed and instructed in useful labor, until discharged by the county superintendents of the poor, or in the city of New-York, by the governors of the alms-house, or bound out as an apprentice by them, as prescribed by special statutes.

Taken substantially from 1 *R. S.*, *3d ed.* 802, 803, *sec.* 4.

§ 978. It is the duty of every peace officer of the county, city, village or town, where a person described in the seventh subdivision of section 973, is found, to arrest and take him before a magistrate mentioned in section 974, to be proceeded against as a vagrant; and when the peace officer is credibly informed, that the vagrant is within the county, city, village or town, he must pursue him, and in like manner arrest him and convey him before the magistrate.

§ 979. A private citizen of the county, may also, without warrant, exercise the powers conferred upon a peace officer by the last section.

The last two sections are substantially the same as in the act of 1845, transcribed in 1 *R. S. 3d ed.* 803, *sec.* 6.

§ 980. In the execution of the duties imposed by section 978, the peace officer may command the aid of as many male inhabitants of his county, city, village or town, as he may think proper; and a citizen so commanded, may provide himself or be provided with, such means and weapons as the officer giving the command may designate.

Same as in the act of 1845, 1 *R. S.*, 3*d ed.* 803, 804, *sec.* 7. See also, *sec* 84, *of this code, p.* 45.

§ 981. A person commanded to aid the officer, as prescribed in the last section, and who without lawful cause refuses or neglects to do so, is guilty of a misdemeanor, and is punishable by a fine not exceeding two hundred and fifty dollars, or by imprisonment not exceeding one year, or both.

Same as in act of 1845, 1 *R. S.*, 3*d ed.* 804, *sec.* 8. See also, *sec.* 86, *of this code, p.* 45.

§ 982. A magistrate to whom complaint is made against a person charged as a vagrant, as described in the seventh subdivision of section 973, may, by a warrant, signed by him with his name of office, depute an elector of the county to arrest and bring the vagrant before him, to answer the complaint: and if the name of the person complained of be not known, he may be described in the warrant and in all subsequent proceedings thereon, by a fictitious name.

Same in substance as in act of 1845, 1 *R. S.*, 3*d ed.* 804, *sec.* 9.

TITLE VIII.

OF PROCEEDINGS RESPECTING DISORDERLY PERSONS.

SECTION 983. Who are disorderly persons.
984. On complaint, warrant to be issued.
985. On confession or proof that he is a disorderly person, security to be required.
986. If security given, defendant to be discharged. If not, to be convicted. Form of certificate.
987. Certificate, to constitute record of conviction, and to be filed. Commitment thereon.
988. Undertaking, when forfeited.
989. How prosecuted, and proceeds how applied,
990. When new security may be required, or defendant committed after recovery on undertaking.
991. Defendant committed for not giving security, how discharged.
992. Keeper of prison, to return list of disorderly persons committed to court of sessions.
993. Examination of the case by the court.
994. Court may discharge, or authorise the binding out of disorderly person.
995. Court may also commit him to prison. Nature and duration of imprisonment.
996. Order to procure materials and implements, and to compel him to work.
997. Expense of materials or implements, how paid for, and proceeds of labor, how disposed of.

§ 983. The following are disorderly persons:

1. Persons who actually abandon their wives or children, without adequate support, or leave them in danger of becoming a burden upon the public, or who neglect to provide for them according to their means:

2. Persons who threaten to run away, and leave their wives or children a burden upon the public:

3. Persons pretending to tell fortunes, or where lost or stolen goods may be found:

4. Keepers of bawdy houses or houses for the resort of prostitutes, drunkards, tipplers, gamesters, or other disorderly persons:

5. Persons who have no visible profession or calling, by which to maintain themselves, but who do so, for the most part, by gaming:

6. Jugglers, common showmen and mountebanks, who exhibit or perform for profit puppet shows, wire or rope dancers, or other idle shows, acts or feats:

7. Persons who keep, in a public highway or place, an apparatus or device for the purpose of gaming, or who go about exhibiting tricks or gaming, therewith:

8. Persons who play, in a public highway or place, with cards, dice or any other apparatus or device for gaming.

This section, with the exception of the first sub-division, is taken, without substantial alteration, from 1 *R. S. 3d ed.* 819, *sec.* 1. That subdivision is taken from an act passed in 1833, specially applicable to the city of New-York. *Laws of* 1833, *p.* 11, *sec.* 7.

§ 984. Upon complaint on oath, to a justice of the peace or police justice of a city, village or town, or to the mayor, recorder or city judge of a city, against a person, as being disorderly, the magistrate must issue a warrant, signed by him with his name of office, requiring a peace officer to arrest the defendant, and bring him before the magistrate for examination.

Taken from 1 *R. S.*, *3d ed.*, 820, *sec.* 2.

§ 985. If the magistrate be satisfied, from the confession of the defendant, or by competent testimony, that he is a disorderly person, he may require that the person charged give security, by a written undertaking, with one or more sureties approved by the magistrate, to the following effect:

1. If he be a person described in the first or second subdivision of section 983, that he will support his wife and children, and will indemnify the county, city, village or town, against their becoming, within one year, chargeable upon the public:

2. In all other cases, that he will be of good behavior for the space of one year;

Or that the sureties will pay the sum mentioned in the undertaking, and which must be fixed by the magistrate.

This section, except the first subdivision, is in accordance with 1 *R. S*, *3d ed.*, 820, *sec.* 2. The first subdivision is more explicit, and is designed to meet the distinct case which constitutes the defendant a disorderly person.

§ 986. If the undertaking be given, the defendant must be discharged. But if not, the magistrate must convict him as a disorderly person, and must make and sign with his name of officc, a certificate in substantially the following form:

"I certify, that A. B., having been brought before me, charged with being a disorderly person, I have duly examined the charge, and that upon his own confession in my presence, [or 'upon the testimony of C. D.,' &c., naming the witnesses,] by which it appears that he is a [pursuing the description contained in the subdivision of section 983, which is appropriate to the case,] I have adjudged that he is a disorderly person.

"Dated at the *town* [cr 'city' of ——, the day of , 1850.

"E. F.,
Justice of the peace of the town of ," [or as the case may be.]

The note to *sec.* 975, *p.* 439, 440, is applicable to this section.

§ 987. The magistrate must immediately cause the certificate, which constitutes the record of conviction, to be filed in the office of the clerk of the county, and must, by a warrant signed by him, with his name of office, commit the defendant to the county jail, or, in the city of New-York, to the city prison or penitentiary of that city, for not exceeding six months at hard labor, or until he give the security prescribed in section 985.

Taken from 1 *R. S.*, 3*d ed.*, 820, *sec.* 2.

§ 988. The undertaking mentioned in section 985, is forfeited, by the commission of any of the acts which constitute the person by whom it was given a disorderly person, and in the case of a person described in the seventh and eighth subdivision of section 983, by his playing or betting, at one time or sitting, for money or property exceeding the value of two dollars and fifty cents.

Taken from 1 *R. S.*, *3d ed.*, 820, *sec.* 3.

§ 989. When an undertaking is forfeited, it may be prosecuted in the name of the county superintendents of the county, or the overseers of the poor of the town, or, in the city of New-York, in the name of the corporation of that city, and the sum collected in the action must be paid into the county or city treasury, as the case may be, for the benefit of the poor.

Taken from 1 *R. S.*, *3d ed.*, 820, *sec.* 4.

§ 990. Upon a recovery on the undertaking, the court in which it is had, may require from the defendant new security, in the manner provided in section 985, or if he fail to give it, may commit him in the manner provided in section 987.

Taken from 1 *R. S.*, *3d ed*, 820, *sec.* 5.

§ 991. A person committed as a disorderly person, on failure to give security, may be discharged by any two justices of the peace or police justices, in the county, upon giving security, as originally required, pursuant to section 985.

Taken from 1 *R. S.*, *3d ed.* 820, *sec.* 6.

§ 992. The keeper of every prison to which disorderly persons may be committed, must return to the court of sessions of the county, on the first day of its next term, a list of the persons so committed and then in his custody, with the nature of the offence of each, the name of the magistrate by whom he was committed, and the term of his imprisonment.

Taken from 1 *R. S.*, *3d ed.* 820, *sec.* 7.

§ 993. The court of sessions must thereupon inquire into the circumstances of each case, and hear any proof that may be offered, and must examine the record of conviction, which is evidence of the facts contained in it, until disproved.

The same as 1 *R. S.*, *3d ed.* 820, *see.* 8.

§ 994. The court may discharge a person so committed, from imprisonment, either absolutely or upon his giving security as provided in section 985, or if he be a minor, may authorise the county superintendents of the poor, or the overseers of the poor of the town, or in the city of New York, the governors of the alms house, to bind him out in some lawful calling as a servant, apprentice, mariner or otherwise, until he be of age; or if he be of age, to contract for his service with any person, as a laborer, servant, apprentice, mariner or otherwise, for not exceeding one year. The binding out or contract, pursuant to this section, has the same effect as the indenture of an apprentice, with his own consent and that of his parents, and subjects the person bound out or contracted, to the same control of his master and of the court of sessions of the county, as if he were bound as an apprentice.

Taken from 1 *R. S.*, 3*d ed.*, 820, 821, *sec.* 9.

§ 995. The court may also, in its discretion, order a person convicted as a disorderly person, to be kept in the county jail, or, in the city of New-York, in the city prison or penitentiary of that city, for a term not exceeding six months at hard labor.

Taken from 1 *R. S.*, 3*d ed.* 821, *sec.* 10.

§ 996. If there be no means provided in the prison, for employing the offender at hard labor, the court may direct the keeper to furnish him such employment as it may specify, and for that purpose, to purchase materials and implements, not exceeding a prescribed value, and to compel the offender to perform the work allotted to him. The expenses incurred in carrying the order in effect, must be paid to the keeper by the county treasurer, upon the delivery to him of the order of the court, and an account under the oath of the keeper, of the materials and implements furnished.

Taken from 1 *R. S., 3d ed.* 821, *sec.* 11, 12.

§ 997. The keeper must sell the produce of the labor of the offender, and must account for the cost of the materials or implements purchased, and for one half of the surplus, to the board of supervisors, and pay it into the county treasury, and pay the other half of the surplus to the person by whom it was earned, on his discharge from imprisonment. He must also account to the court, when required, for the materials or implements purchased, and for the disposition of the proceeds of the labor of the offender.

Taken from 1 *R. S., 3d ed.*, 821, *sec.* 13.

TITLE IX.

OF PROCEEDINGS RESPECTING THE SUPPORT OF POOR PERSONS.

§ 998. The father, mother and children, of sufficient ability, of a poor person who is insane, blind, old, lame, impotent or decrepid, so as to enable by work to maintain himself, must at their own charge, relieve and maintain him in a manner to be approved by the overseers of the town where he is, or in the city of New-York, by the governors of the alms-house.

Substantially the same as 1 *R. S. 3d ed.*, 782, *sec.* 1.

§ 999. If a relative of a poor person fail to relieve and maintain him, as provided in the last section, the overseers of the poor of the town where he is, or in the city of New-York, the governors of the alms-house may apply to the court of sessions of the county where the relative dwells, for an order to compel such relief, upon at least ten days written notice, served personally, or by leaving it at the last place of residence of the person to whom it is directed, in case of his absence, with a person of suitable age and discretion.

Substantially the same as 1 *R. S. 3d ed.*, 782, *sec.* 2.

§ 1000. At the time appointed in the notice, the court must proceed summarily to hear the allegations and proofs of the parties, and must order such of the relatives of the poor person, mentioned in section 998, as were served with the notice and are of sufficient ability, to relieve and maintain him, specifying in the order the sum to be paid weekly for his support, and requiring it to be paid by the father, or if there be none, or if he be not of sufficient ability, then by the children, or if there be none, or if they be not of sufficient ability, then by the mother.

Substantially the same as 1 *R. S. 3d ed.*, 782, *sec.* 3.

§ 1001. If it appear that any such relative is unable wholly to maintain the poor person, but is able to contribute towards his support, the court may direct two or more relatives, of different degrees, to maintain him, prescribing the proportion which each must contribute for that purpose; and if it appear that the relatives are not of sufficient ability wholly to maintain him, but are able to contribute something, the court must direct the sum, in proportion to their ability, which they shall pay weekly for that purpose.

Substantially the same as 1 *R. S.*, *3d ed.*, 782, *sec.* 4.

§ 1002. The order may specify the time during which the relatives must maintain the poor person, or during which any of the sums directed by the court are to be paid, or it may be indefinite, or until the further order of the court. The court may from time to time, vary the order, as circumstances may require, on the application either of any relative affected by it, or of an officer on whose application the order was made, upon ten days written notice.

Substantially the same as 1 *R. S.*, *3d ed.*, 783, *sec.* 5.

§ 1003. The costs and expenses of the application must be ascertained by the court, and paid by the relatives against whom the order is made; and the payment thereof, and obedience to the order of maintenance, and to any order for the payment of money, may be enforced by attachment.

Substantially the same as 1 *R. S.*, *3d ed.*, 783, *sec.* 6.

§ 1004. If a relative, required by an order of the court, to relieve or maintain a poor person, neglect to do so in the manner approved by the officers mentioned in section 998, and neglect to pay to them weekly the sum prescribed by the court, the officers may maintain an action against the relative, and recover therein the sum prescribed by the court, for every week the order has been disobeyed, to the time of the recovery, with costs, for the use of the poor. In the city of New-York, the action must be in the name of the corporation of that city.

Substantially the same as 1 *R. S.*, 3*d* *ed.*, 783, *sec.* 7.

§ 1005. When the father, or the mother being a widow or living separate from her husband, absconds from their children, or a husband from his wife, leaving any of them chargeable or likely to become chargeable upon the public, the officers mentioned in section 998, may apply to any two justices of the peace or police justices in the county in which any real or personal property of the father, mother or husband is situated, for a warrant to seize the same. Upon due proof of the facts, the magistrates must issue their warrant, authorising the officers so applying to take and seize the property of the person so absconding.

Substantially the same as 1 *R. S.*, 3*d* *ed.*, 783, *sec.* 8.

§ 1006. The officers so applying may seize and take the property, wherever it may be found in the same county; and are vested with all the right and title thereto, which the person absconding then had. The sale or transfer of any personal property, left in the county from which he absconded, made after the issuing of the warrant, whether in payment of an antecedent debt or for a new consideration, is absolutely void. The officers must immediately make an inventory of the property seized by them, and return it, together with their proceedings, to the next court of sessions of the county where they reside, there to be filed.

Substantially the same as 1 *R. S.*, 3*d* *ed.*, 783, *sec.* 9.

§ 1007. The court, upon inquiring into the circumstan-stances of the case, may confirm or discharge the warrant and seizure; and if it be confirmed, must, from time to time, direct what part of the personal property must be sold, and how much of the proceeds of the sale, and of the rents and profits of the real property, if any, are to be applied towards the maintenance of the children or wife of the person absconding.

Substantially the same as 1 *R. S. 3d ed.* 783, 784, *sec.* 10.

§ 1008. If the party against whom the warrant issued, return and support the wife or children so abandoned, or give security satisfactory to any two justices of the peace, or police justices in the city, village or town, to the overseers of the poor of the town, or in the city of New-York, to the governors of the alms house, that the wife or children so abandoned shall not be charge-to the town or county, then the warrant must be discharged by an order of the magistrates, and the property taken by virtue thereof restored to the party.

Substantially the same as 1 *R. S. 3d ed.* 784, *sec.* 11.

§ 1009. The officers must sell at public auction the property ordered to be sold, and receive the rents and profits of the real property of the person absconding, and in those cities, villages or towns which are required to support their own poor, the officers charged therewith must apply the same to the support of the wife or children so abandoned; and for that purpose must draw on the county treasurer, or in the city of New-York, upon the comptroller, for the proceeds, as directed by special statutes. They must also account to the court of sessions of the county, for all money so received by them, and for the application thereof, from time to time, and may be compelled by that court to render that account at any time.

Substantially the same as 1 *R. S.*, *3d ed.* 784, *sec.* 12.

§ 1010. In those counties where all the poor are a charge upon the county, the superintendents of the poor are vested with the same powers, as are given by this title to the overseers of the poor of a town, in respect to compelling relatives to maintain poor persons, and in respect to the seizure of the property of a parent absconding and abandoning his family: and are entitled to the same remedies in their names, and must perform the duties required by this title, of overseers, and are subject to the same obligations and control.

Substantially the same as 1 *R. S.*, *3d ed.* 784, *sec.* 13.

TITLE X.

OF PROCEEDINGS RESPECTING MASTERS, APPRENTICES AND SERVANTS.

§ 1011. If an apprentice or servant, lawfully bound to service as prescribed by special statutes, wilfully absent himself therefrom, without the leave of his master, or refuse to serve according to his duty, or be guilty of any misdemeanor or ill behavior, his master may take him before a justice of the peace or police justice in the county, or before the mayor, recorder or city judge of the city where he resides, and make complaint of the facts under oath, or may, without taking him before the magistrate, make the like complaint.

§ 1012. If the complaint be made in the absence of the defendant, and the facts be proved to the satisfaction of the magistrate, he must issue a warrant, signed by him, with his name of office, to a peace officer of the county or city, commanding him to arrest the defendant and bring him before the magistrate forthwith, or at a specified time and place, to answer the complaint.

§ 1013. The peace officer must accordingly execute the warrant, by arresting the defendant and taking him before the magistrate.

The last three sections are more full and explicit than the corresponding provisions of the Revised Statutes, though similar in their general spirit. Those provisions are as follows:

"If any such person shall refuse to serve according to the provisions of this title, or the terms of his contract or indentures, his master may apply to any justice of the peace of the county, or to the mayor, recorder or any alderman of the city, where he shall reside, who shall be authorised by warrant or otherwise, to send for the person so refusing, and if such refusal be persisted in, to commit such person, by warrant, to the bridewell, house of correction, or common jail of the city or county, there to remain until such person will consent to serve according to law." 2 *R. S. 3d ed.* 219, *sec.* 29.

"On complaint being made on oath, by any master, touching any misdemeanor or ill behavior of any such person, to any two justices of the peace of the county, or to the mayor, recorder and alderman of any city, or any two of them, it shall be their duty to cause the person complained of, to be brought before them, and to hear, examine and determine the complaint." 2 *R. S. 3d ed.* 219, *sec.* 30.

§ 1014. The magistrate must immediately, or at a time to which he may, for good cause, adjourn the matter, proceed to hear the allegations and proofs of the parties, and if the complaint appear to be well founded, must commit the defendant to the county jail, or in the city of New-York, to the city prison of that city, for not exceeding one month, at hard labor, where he must be confined in a room with no other person; or may, by a certificate, signed by him with his name of office, discharge the defendant from the service of his master, and the master from all obligations to the defendant.

Substantially the same as 2 *R. S. 3d ed.* 219, *sec.* 31.

§ 1015. If a master be guilty of cruelty, misusage, refusal of necessary provisions or clothing, or any other violation of duty towards his apprentice or servant, as prescribed by special statutes, or by the indenture or contract of service, the apprentice or servant may make complaint on oath, to any two of the magistrates mentioned in section 1011, who must summon the defendant before them, at a specified time and place.

§ 1016. The magistrates must immediately, or at a time to which they may, for good cause, adjourn the matter, proceed to hear the allegations and proofs of the parties, and if the complaint be well founded, must, by a certificate under their hands, with their name of office, discharge the apprentice or servant from the service of his master; or if not, they must, by a similar certificate, dismiss the complaint.

The last two sections are substituted for the following provision of the Revised Statutes: "If any master shall be guilty of any cruelty, misusage, refusal of necessary provisions or clothing, or any other violation of the provisions of this Title, or of the terms of the indenture or contract, towards any such person so bound to service, such person may make complaint to any two of the officers specified in the preceding thirtieth section, who shall summon the parties before them, and examine into, hear and determine the complaint, and by certificate under their hands, discharge such person from his obligation of service." 2 *R S. 3d ed.* 219, *sec.* 32.

§ 1017. The preceding sections of this title do not extend to an apprentice, whose master has received, or is entitled to receive, a sum of money with him, as a compensation for his instruction.

Same as 2 *R. S., 3d ed.* 219, *sec.* 33.

§ 1018. Where money is paid or agreed to be paid, on binding out a clerk or apprentice, he may make the complaint mentioned in section 1015, and the magistrates to whom it is made, must examine it, as provided in section 1016, and on such examination, may make such order and direction between the parties, as the justice of the case may require.

Same as 2 *R. S. 3d ed.* 219, *sec.* 34.

§ 1019. If, in the case mentioned in the last section, the complaint cannot be compromised, the magistrates must take a written undertaking from the master, for his appearance at the next court of sessions of the county, in a sum, and with sureties approved by them.

Same as 2 *R. S. 3d ed.* 219, *sec.* 35.

§ 1020. Upon hearing the parties, the court may, by an order entered upon the minutes, direct that the clerk or apprentice be discharged from service, and that the money paid or agreed for in binding him out, be refunded, if paid, to the person who advanced it, or his personal representatives, or if not paid, that it be discharged, and that any security given therefor be delivered up or cancelled.

Same as 2 *R. S.* 3*d ed.*, 219, 220, *sec.* 36.

§ 1021. The master of a clerk or apprentice, where money is paid or agreed for on binding him out, may make the complaint mentioned in section 1011, and the magistrate to whom it is made, must proceed thereupon, as provided in sections 1012 to 1014, both inclusive, and may discharge the complaint, or if in his opinion it be well founded, may take a written undertaking, in a sum and with sureties to be approved by him, for the appearance of the clerk or apprentice at the next court of sessions of the county.

Same as 2 *R. S.*, 3*d ed.*, 220, *sec.* 37.

§ 1022. Upon hearing the parties, the court may proceed as provided in section 1020, and may punish the clerk or apprentice, by fine or imprisonment, or both, as for a misdemeanor.

Same as 2 *R. S.*, 3*d ed.*, 220, *sec.* 38

§ 1023. Upon the death of a master to whom a person has been bound to service, as clerk, apprentice or servant, by the county superintendents of the poor, or by the overseers of the poor, or in the city of New-York, by the governors of the alms-house, the personal representatives of the master may, with the written consent of the clerk, apprentice or servant, acknowledged before a justice of the peace or police justice, assign the indenture or contract of service to another, who thereby becomes vested with all the rights of the master.

Same as 2 *R. S.*, 3*d ed.* 220, *sec.* 41.

§ 1024. If, in the case mentioned in the last section, the written consent of the clerk, apprentice or servant be refused, the assignment may be made with the same effect, under an order of the court of sessions of the county, upon fourteen days notice of the application therefor, to the apprentice, or to his parent or guardian, if there be any in the county.

Same as 2 *R. S*, 3*d ed.* 220, *sec.* 42.

TITLE XI.

OF CRIMINAL STATISTICS.

In a note to a corresponding portion of the code of civil procedure, the Commissioners have given the reasons which have influenced them, in proposing a plan for collecting the statistics of litigation. The same reasons apply to the provisions of this title. There are other reasons also, of great weight. The increase or diminution of crime, affords the best means of determining the effect of particular laws, as well as the general tendency of the public morals. Without this knowledge, legislators must grope their way in the dark.

The provisions of this title are taken from, and are in substantial conformity with, 2 *R. S.*, 3*d ed.*, 833—835, *sec.* 52—58.

§ 1025. Within ten days after the adjournment of a court of oyer and terminer or of sessions, or of a city court, the clerk must transmit to the secretary of state, by mail, a certified statement of the number of indictments tried thereat, specifying the number for each offence, the number on which convictions were had, the number on which the defendant was acquitted, and the number of indictments against persons discharged without trial, specifying the number for each offence.

§ 1026. Within ten days after the adjournment of each of the courts mentioned in the last section, the sheriff of the county where it was held, must report by mail to the secretary of state, the name, occupation, age, sex, and native country of every person convicted at that court, of a public offence, with the degree of instruction which each person convicted has received, and such other information in relation to the persons so convicted, and their offences, as the secretary of state may require.

§ 1027. A report must be made, in like manner, by the sheriff of every county in which there is a city, in respect to persons convicted at a city or police court, held within that city. The report, in respect to city courts, must be made within thirty days after the adjournment of each of those courts; and in respect to the police courts, on the first days of January and July in each year.

§ 1028. The report required by the last three sections, must be made in the form prescribed by the secretary of state.

§ 1029. To enable the sheriff to make his report, he may, either before or after conviction, by himself or his deputies, make all necessary inquiries of the persons convicted, and of the keeper of a jail, penitentiary, or other prison where the persons convicted are confined, as well as of all other persons.

§ 1030. The sheriff is entitled for his services, to a reasonable sum, to be audited and allowed by the board of supervisors of his county, and to be paid from the county treasury.

§ 1031. Every magistrate holding a police court at which a person is convicted of a public offence, must, on being so required, furnish to the sheriff of the county, all the information he can obtain, to enable the sheriff to make the report required by section 1027, and must make such inquiries of the persons convicted before them, and of others, as the secretary of state may direct.

§ 1032. When a county clerk transmits to the secretary of state, transcripts of convictions had in courts of oyer and terminer or of sessions, or in a city court, he must transmit therewith, copies of all certificates of convictions in police courts, filed with him.

§ 1033. The clerk of each police court in the city and county of New-York, must, on the first day of every month, transmit by mail, to the secretary of state, a transcript of the entry of every conviction had in that court, during the preceding month, containing the name of the offender, a description of the offence, and the judgment upon the conviction.

§ 1034. For every neglect of a magistrate, clerk, or sheriff, to comply with the requirements of this title, he forfeits the sum of fifty dollars, to be recovered in a civil action, in the name of the people of this state.

§ 1035. The secretary of state must cause this title to be published, with forms and instructions for the execution of the duties therein prescribed, and to be distributed among the officers therein mentiontioned; the expense of which must be paid by the treasurer, on the warrant of the comptroller. He must also annually report to the legislature, the results of the information obtained in pursuance of this title.

TITLE XII.

MISCELLANEOUS PROVISIONS, RESPECTING SPECIAL PROCEEDINGS OF A CRIMINAL NATURE.

§ 1036. The party prosecuting a special proceeding of a criminal nature, is designated in this code as the complainant, and the adverse party as the defendant.

§ 1037. The provisions of section 751, in respect to entitling affidavits in a criminal action, are applicable to special proceedings of a criminal nature.

See *sec.* 751, *p.* 319.

§ 1038. The courts and magistrates before whom a special proceeding is prosecuted, may issue subpœnas for witnesses, and punish their disobedience in the same manner as in a criminal action.

See *sec.* 670, 674, 675, 681, *p.* 315—320.

PART VII.

Of the costs in criminal actions and proceedings.

The rate of fees in this part, instead of being regulated in reference to each particular service rendered, is, in conformity with the fee bill in the code of civil procedure, based upon a fair equivalent in each consecutive stage of the proceedings. The inducement which the present fee bill in criminal cases, 2 *R. S.*, 3*d ed.* 835 - 841, *sec.* 1 – 23, holds out, to swell the costs, by crowding into the case as many services as possible, whether necessary or not, is thus taken away. The particular allowances proposed in this part, have been carefully considered, and are deemed just.

§ 1039. All statutes, establishing or regulating the costs or fees of public officers, in criminal actions or proceedings, are repealed; and hereafter, the only costs or fees allowed in a criminal action or proceeding, are those provided by this code.

§ 1040. The magistrate, if he be a justice of the peace, or a police justice, appointed or elected in a city, village or town, may receive,

For all the proceedings before him, to and including the commitment or discharge of the defendant or holding him to answer, two dollars.

For all proceedings (including the trial, judgment, and commitment,) had before him, while holding a police court, two dollars, or conducting a special proceeding.

For taking bail, after a commitment by another magistrate, one dollar.

§ 1041. The clerk may receive,

On the trial of an issue, one dollar.

On entering judgment, fifty cents.

He can receive no other fee, for any service whatever, in a criminal action or proceeding, except for copies of papers delivered to a person at his request, at the rate of five cents for every hundred words.

§ 1042. The peace-officer may receive,

For making an arrest fifty cents, together with five cents for every mile necessarily travelled by him, in rendering the service, and in taking the defendant before a court or magistrate, or carrying him to prison.

For serving a subpœna, fifteen cents, together with five cents for every mile necessarily travelled by him, in rendering the service.

The board of supervisors may allow any further compensation, for the service of process, and for other services in criminal cases, which they may think reasonable.

§ 1043. The sheriff may receive,

For summoning a grand jury, ten dollars.

For summoning a trial jury, ten dollars.

For carrying a single convict to the state prison, for every mile necessarily travelled from the county prison, forty cents; two convicts, sixty-five cents; more than two and not exceeding four convicts, seventy cents; five convicts, seventy-five cents; for every additional convict, such reasonable allowance as the comptroller may think just. He may also receive, for the maintenance of the convict on his way to the state prison, such sum as he may actually expend for it, not exceeding one dollar for every thirty miles travelled.

§ 1044. The fees allowed by the last four sections, are county charges, and must be audited and paid by the board of supervisors of the county in which the services were rendered; except, that the fees of the sheriff for conveying convicts to the state prison, must be paid by the agent of the prison to which the convicts are carried, and by him charged in his accounts with the state.

GENERAL PROVISIONS AND DEFINITIONS APPLICABLE TO THIS CODE.

§ 1045. The rule of the common law, that penal statutes are to be strictly construed, has no application to this code. This code establishes the law of this state, respecting the subjects to which it relates; and its provisions, and all proceedings under it are to be liberally construed, with a view to promote its objects, and in furtherance of justice.

This section declares the same principle in reference to penal statutes, as is declared in the code of civil procedure respecting statutes in derogation of, or variant from, the common law.

The rule applicable to penal statutes, is well settled to be, that they are to be strictly construed; *Sprague v. Birdsall*, 2 Cowen, 419; that they, as well as statutes in derogation of the common law, are not to be extended beyond their express words, or their clear import; *Sharp v. Speir*, 4 Hill, 76; *Sharp v. Johnson*, 4 Hill, 92; *Bennett v. Ward*, 3 Caines, 259; *Hallett v. Novion*, 14 Johns., 273; and that it is not open to an equitable construction. *Myers v. Foster*, 6 Cowen, 567. This rule differs from that applicable to ordinary statutes, which is, that they are to be so construed as to give effect to the will of the legislature, as either expressed in the language of the statute itself, or as deducible from the fair and reasonable import of its terms, its object, the evil to be remedied, and the circumstances under which it was passed.

If any reason were wanting, to show the inutility, not to say absurdity of this distinction, it is to be found in the refinements and subtleties to which it has led, and of which some idea may be formed, from the specimens already given, in the remarks of the Commissioners on the existing rules of pleading. See *p.* 144, 145.

This section is proposed, for the purpose of abrogating a distinction which has in it no principle of substantial justice, and whose highest aim, practically considered, seems to be, to render the law inconsistent with its spirit, and as a consequence, absurd and ridiculous.

§ 1046. No part of this code is retroactive, unless expressly so declared.

§ 1047. Unless when otherwise provided, words used in this code in the present tense, include the future as well as the present. Words used in the masculine gender comprehend as well the feminine and neuter. The singular number includes the plural, and the plural the singular. And the word person includes a corporation, as well as a natural person.

§ 1048. The term "writing" includes printing.

§ 1049. The term "oath," includes an affirmation.

§ 1050. The term "signature," includes a mark, when the person cannot write; his name being written near it, and the mark being witnessed by a person who writes his own name as a witness, except to an affidavit or deposition, or a paper executed before a judicial officer; in which case the attestation of the officer is sufficient.

§ 1051. Unless when otherwise provided, the term "magistrate" signifies any one of the magistrates mentioned in section 147.

See *p.* 69, 70.

§ 1052. Unless when otherwise provided, the term "peace officer," signifies any one of the officers mentioned in section 154.

See *p.* 73.

§ 1053. This code applies to criminal actions, and to all other proceedings in criminal cases which are herein provided for, from the time when it takes effect; and all such actions and proceedings, theretofore commenced, must be conducted in the same manner as if this code had not been passed; except, that sections 16 to 59, both inclusive; 84 to 87, both inclusive; 97 to 99, both inclusive; 145 to 842 both inclusive; 884 to 896, both inclusive; and 1039 to 1052, both inclusive, apply thereto, so far as they are applicable; without prejudice however to any proceeding already had therein.

§ 1054. This code shall take effect, on the first day of July, 1850.

APPENDIX:

REFERRED TO IN SECTION 293, OF THIS CODE, AND CONTAINING THE MANNER OF STATING THE ACT CONSTITUTING THE OFFENCE.

The forms given in this Appendix, embrace a few only of the indictments for public offences. The Commissioners have selected them promiscuously, from a large number which they had prepared and considered. Believing, however, that the forms here presented will sufficiently illustrate the principles upon which indictments should be drawn, they have deemed it unnecessary to swell their report, by the addition of a larger number.

The prefatory matter is stated in section 292, *p.* 150, 151. The forms given, follow that statement.

No. 1.

IN AN INDICTMENT FOR MURDER.

Without the authority of law, and with malice aforethought, killed C. D., by [shooting him with a gun or pistol, or, by administering to him poison, or, by pushing him into the river, whereby he was drowned, or, by throwing him from the window of a building, or, by means unknown to the grand jury, or as the case may be.]

In this form, the words "with malice aforethought," are used in the same sense in which they are understood in the existing forms of indictment for murder; and are intended to comprehend the several divisions of that offence, as it is defined by statute. 2 *R. S.*, 3*d ed.* 746, *sec.* 5.

IN AN INDICTMENT FOR ARSON.

No. 2.

Arson, in the first degree.

Wilfully set fire to, [or burned,]. in the night time, a dwelling house, in which there was at the time, a human being, namely, C. D., [or whose name is unknown to the grand jury.]

2 *R. S.*, 3*d ed*, 747, *sec.* 9.

No. 3.

Arson, in the second degree.

Wilfully set fire to, [or burned,] an inhabited dwelling house in the day time, in which there was at the time, a human being namely C. D., [or whose name is unknown to the grand jury.]

2 *R. S.* 3*d ed.* 755, *sec.* 1.

No. 4.

or,

Wilfully set fire to, [or burned,] in the night time a shop, [or warehouse, or building,] (not being a dwelling house, in which there was at the time a human being,) and which shop, [or warehouse or building,] was adjoining to, [or within the curtilage of] an inhabited dwelling house, so that such house was endangered by such firing.

2 *R. S.*, 3*d ed.* 755, *sec.* 2.

No. 5.

Arson, in the third degree.

Wilfully set fire to, [or burned,] in the day time, a shop, [or warehouse or building,] (not being a dwelling house in which there was at the time a human being,) and which shop, [or warehouse or building] was adjoining to, [or within the curtilage of] an inhabited dwelling house, so that such house was endangered by such firing.

2 *R. S.*, 3*d ed.*, 755, *sec.* 3.

No. 6.

or,

Wilfully set fire to [or burned] in the night time, the house of C. D., (not being a dwelling-house in which there was at the time a human being, nor a shop, or warehouse, or building) adjoining to, [or within the curtilage of,] an inhabited dwelling-house which was endangered by such firing.)

2 *R. S.*, 3*d ed.* 755, *sec.* 4.

No. 7.

or,

Wilfully burned the ship named the , which was at the time insured by the Insurance company of the city of New-York, against loss or damage by fire, with intent to prejudice such insurers.

2 *R. S*, 3*d ed.*, 755, *sec.* 6.

No. 8.

Arson, in the fourth degree.

In the day time, wilfully set fire to [or burned] the house [or building] of C. D., (not being, &c., [as in No. 5, to the end.]

2 *R. S.*, 3*d ed.*, 755, *sec.* 6.

No. 9.

or,

Wilfully set fire to [or burned] a saw-mill [or carding machine, or a building containing a carding machine, or a stack of grain, or a stack of hay,] not belonging to the said A. B.

2 *R. S.*, 3*d ed.*, 755, *sec.* 7.

IN AN INDICTMENT FOR MANSLAUGHTER.

No. 10.

Manslaughter, in the first degree.

Was engaged in the perpetration of the following misdemeanor: [stating it, as in an indictment therefor.]

And the said A. B., while engaged in the perpetration of such misdemeanor, without a design to effect death, by his act, [or procurement, or culpable negligence,] killed C. D., by [striking him with a club, or by other means, to be stated as in No. 1.]

2 *R. S.*, 3*d ed.*, 750, *sec.* 6, *subd.* 1.

No. 11.

or,

Deliberately assisted one C. D. in the commission of self murder, which crime the said C. D. then and there committed, by hanging himself by the neck until he was dead, [or as the case may be.]

2 *R. S.*, 3*d ed.*, 750, *sec.* 7.

No. 12.

Manslaughter, in the second degree.

Killed C. D., in the heat of passion, but in a cruel and unusual manner, and not under such circumstances as to constitute excusable or justifiable homicide, by striking him with a club, [or stating the means according to the fact.]

2 *R. S.*, 3*d ed.*, 750, *sec.* 10.

No. 13.

Manslaughter, in the third degree.

Unnecessarily killed one C. D. by striking him with a club, [or stating the means, according to the fact,] while resisting an attempt by the said C. D. to commit an assault and battery upon him, [describing the offence or unlawful act attempted, according to the fact.]

2 *R. S.*, 3*d ed.*, 750, *sec.* 11.

or,

No. 14.

Was the owner of a bull, [or other mischievous animal, describing it,] and knowing its propensities, wilfully suffered such bull to run at large, [or kept it without ordinary care,] and the said bull, while so at large, [or not confined,] killed one C. D., who took all the precautions which the circumstances would permit, to avoid such bull.

2 *R. S.*, 3*d ed.*, 751, *sec.* 14.

or,

No. 15.

Was managing a steamboat called the
for gain, and wilfully [or negligently] received on board so many passengers [or such a quantity of lading] that the said boat sunk, [or was overset,] whereby C. D., who was on the said boat, was drowned, [or otherwise killed, according to the fact.]

2 *R. S*, 3*d ed.*, 751, *sec.* 16.

IN AN INDICTMENT FOR RAPE.

No. 16.

Forcibly ravished E. F., a woman of the age of ten years or upwards.

2 *R. S.*, 3*d ed.* 752, *sec.* 22, *subd.* 2.

or,

No. 17.

Carnally and unlawfully knew G. H., a female child under the age of ten years.

2 *R. S.*, 3*d ed.*, 752, *sec.* 22, *subd.* 1.

IN AN INDICTMENT FOR ROBBERY.

No. 18.

Robbery, in the first degree.

Feloniously took a gold watch, [or as the case may be,] the property of C. D., from his person and against his will, by violence to his person, [or by putting him in fear of some immediate injury to his person]

2 *R. S.*, 3*d ed.*, 764, *sec.* 55.

or,

No. 19.

Feloniously took a gold watch, [or as the case may be,] the property of C. D., in his presence and against his will, by violence to his person, [or by putting him in fear of some immediate injury to his person.]

2 *R. S.*, 3*d ed.*, 764, *sec.* 55.

No. 20.

Robbery, in the second degree.

Feloniously took a gold watch, [or as the case may be,] the property of C. D,, in his presence [or from his person,] which was delivered [or suffered to be taken] through fear of some injury to his person [or property, or to the person of a relative or member of his family,] threatened to be inflicted at a different time, which fear was produced by the threats of the said A. B.

2 *R. S.*, 3*d ed.*, 764, *sec.* 56.

IN AN INDICTMENT FOR GRAND LARCENY.

No. 21.

Feloniously took and carried away a gold watch, [or as the case may be,] the personal property of C. D., [or of a person whose name is unknown to the grand jury,] of the value of more than twenty-five dollars.

2 *R. S.*, 3*d ed.*, 765, *sec.* 63.

No. 22.

or,

Feloniously took and carried away, in a dwelling-house, [or ship, or vessel,] a gold watch, [or as the case may be,] the personal property, &c., as in No. 21, to the end.

2 *R. S.*, 3*d ed.*, 765, *sec.* 64.

No. 23.

or,

Feloniously took and carried away, in the night time, from the person of C. D., a gold watch, [or as the case may be,] the personal property of the said C. D., [or of a person whose name is unknown to the grand jury,] of the value of more than twenty-five dollars.

2 *R. S.*, 3*d ed.*, 765, *sec.* 65.

IN AN INDICTMENT FOR PETIT LARCENY.

No. 24.

Stole, took and carried away a silver watch, [or as the case may be,] the personal property of C. D., [or of some person unknown to the grand jury,] of the value of twenty-five dollars or under.

2 *R. S.*, 3*d ed.*, 776, *sec.* 1.

IN AN INDICTMENT FOR BURGLARY.

No. 25.

Burglary, in the first degree.

Broke into and entered in the night time, the dwelling-house of C. D., in which there was at the time a human being, namely, the said C. D., [or, whose name is unknown to the grand jury,] with intent to commit larceny, [or other public offence, describing it generally] therein, by forcibly bursting or breaking the wall [or, an outer door, or, a window, or, a shutter of a window,] of such house, [or as the case may be.]

2 *R. S.*, 3*d ed.* 756, *sec.* 10, *subd.* 1.

No. 26.

or,

Broke into and entered, in the night time, the dwelling house of C. D., in which there was at the time a human being, namely, the said C. D., [or, whose name is unknown to the grand jury,] with intent to commit larceny, [or any other public offence, describing it generally,] therein, by unlocking an outer door by means of false keys, [or by picking the lock of an outer door.]

2 *R. S.*, 3*d ed.* 756, *sec.* 10, *subd.* 1.

No. 27.

Burglary, in the second degree.

Broke into and entered, in the day time, the dwelling house &c., [as in Nos. 25, and 26, to the end.]

2 *R. S.*, 3*d ed.* 756, *sec.* 11.

No. 28.

Burglary, in the third degree.

Broke and entered, in the day [or night] time, a building within the curtilage of the dwelling-house of C. D., but not forming a part thereof, with intent to steal therein, [or if to commit any other public offence, describing it generally.]

2 *R. S.* 3*d ed.*, 757, *sec.* 17, *subd*. 1.

IN AN INDICTMENT FOR FORGERY.

No. 29.

Forgery, in the first degree.

Forged [or counterfeited, or falsely altered, by erasing a material part thereof, or as the case may be,] an instrument purporting to be [or being] the last will and testament of C. D., devising certain real and personal property, with intent to defraud.

2 *R. S.*, 3d *ed.*, 758, *sec.* 22, *subd.* 1.

No. 30.

Or,

Forged a certificate, purporting to have been issued by J. C., an officer duly authorized to make such certificate, of the acknowledgment of C. D., of the execution by him, of a conveyance to E. F., of certain real property in the town of   , with intent to defraud the said C. D.

2 *R. S.*, 3d *ed.*, 758, *sec.* 22, *subd.* 2.

No. 31.

Forgery, in the second degree.

Counterfeited the great seal of this state, with intent to defraud.

2 *R. S.*, 3d *ed.*, 758, *sec.* 24.

No. 32.

Or,

Falsely made an impression, purporting to be the impression of the great seal of this state, on an instrument in writing, being [or purporting to be] a , [stating generally the purport of the instrument,] with the intent to defraud.

2 *R. S.*, 3*d ed.*, 758, *sec.* 24.

No. 33.

Or,

Counterfeited a gold [or silver] coin of the republic of Mexico, called a dollar, which was at that time current, by custom or usage, with this state.

2 *R. S.*, 3*d ed.*, 759, *sec.* 28.

No. 34.

Forgery, in the third degree.

Counterfeited a gold [or silver] coin of the republic of France, called a franc, with the intent of exporting the same, to injure or defraud the citizens of that republic.

2 *R. S.*, 3*d ed.*, 759, *sec.* 29.

No. 35.

Forgery, in the fourth degree.

Had in his possession, a counterfeit of a gold [or silver] coin of the republic of Mexico, called a dollar, which was at that time current in this state, knowing the same to be counterfeited, with intent to defraud, or injure] by uttering the same as true, [or false]

2 *R. S.*, 3*d ed.*, 761, *sec.* 38.

IN AN INDICTMENT FOR PERJURY.

No. 36.

On his examination as a witness, duly sworn to testify the truth, on the trial of a civil action in the court of , between C. D., plaintiff, and E. F., defendant, which court had authority to administer such oath, he testified falsely, that [stating the facts alleged to be false,] the matters so testified being material, and the testimony being wilfully and corruptly false.

2 *R. S.*, 3*d ed.*, 767, *sec.* 1, *subd.* 1. See also, *sec.* 308 *of this code*, *p.* 155.

IN AN INDICTMENT FOR BIGAMY.

No. 37.

Having a wife then living, unlawfully married one G. A.

2 *R. S.*, 3*d ed.*, 772, *sec.* 8.

IN AN INDICTMENT FOR VIOLATING THE GRAVE.

No. 38.

Removed the dead body of O. P., [or, a human being, whose name is unknown to the grand jury,] from the grave, for the purpose of selling the same.

2 *R. S.*, *3d ed.*, 774, *sec.* 13.

IN AN INDICTMENT FOR LIBEL.

No. 39.

Published in a newspaper called the   , the following libel, concerning C. D.

See sec. 306, *p.* 154, 155.

IN AN INDICTMENT FOR AN ASSAULT AND BATTERY.

No 40.

Assaulted and beat C. D.

www.ingramcontent.com/pod-product-compliance
Lightning Source LLC
La Vergne TN
LVHW101452200926
848483LV00001B/111
* 9 7 8 1 8 8 6 3 6 3 3 5 9 *